WOMANHOOD
IN AMERICA

WOMANHOOD

IN AMERICA

FROM COLONIAL TIMES

TO THE PRESENT

THIRD EDITION

MARY P. RYAN
University of California, Irvine

FRANKLIN WATTS
New York   London   Toronto   Sydney

Photographs courtesy of: New York State
Historical Association (Abigail Adams) and
UPI (Eleanor Roosevelt), p. 185; Museum of
History and Technology, Smithsonian
Institution (The Senate Chamber) and Sophia
Smith Collection, Smith College (Woman
and Political Peers), p. 186; Architect of
the U.S. Capitol, p. 187; Library of Congress,
p. 188; University of Chicago Press, p. 189;
Smith College Archives, p. 190; Eastman
House, p. 191; Newsweek Books, p. 192.

Library of Congress Cataloging in Publication Data

Ryan, Mary P.
Womanhood in America.

Includes bibliographical references and index.
1. Women—United States—History. 2. Women—
United States—Social conditions. 3. Sex role.
4. Sex discrimination—United States. I. Title.
HQ1410.R9   1983   305.4'0973   82–23892
ISBN 0-531-09894-X
ISBN 0-531-05648-1 (pbk.)

Franklin Watts, Inc.
387 Park Avenue South
New York, New York 10016

C O N T E N T S

WOMANHOOD
IN   AMERICA

INTRODUCTION TO
THE THIRD EDITION

Since the early 1970s when this book was first conceived, women's history has developed from an outburst of eager feminist inquiries into a mature field of scholarship, with all the accoutrements of any academic discipline, including its own conferences, professional organizations, journals, and reference tools. The sheer volume of information about women's past has multiplied incredibly: the population encompassed by the historical record has expanded beyond a few notable women to take in ordinary wives and workers, and the impact of women on historical development has been traced past a small circle of suffragists and politicians' wives to include the everyday activities of the mass of womankind.

The accumulation of knowledge about women in twentieth-century America has been especially prodigious over the last four years and made possible substantial revisions in the last three chapters of this edition of *Womanhood in America*. The simple collection of facts is the least of the recent accomplishments in the field of women's history. The study of women's past has been guided by advances in theory, new concepts, and novel hypotheses, often drawn from the diverse bodies of thought that compose the interdisciplinary field of women's studies. Thus the second, and now the third edition of this book not only add new details to the picture of women's past but also attempt to frame them in greater conceptual clarity. In 1982 it is possible to define the object and the subject matter of women's history with more precision.

1

When this intellectual enterprise began, as part of the reawak-
ened feminist consciousness of the 1960s, the subject of women's
history seemed obvious. *Homo sapiens*, sex female—whatever she
said, did, and experienced in the past was the topic of women's
history. Our subject matter, in other words, was identified by sexual
biology. Modern science tells us with its customary certitude that
the female of the human species is distinguishable from the male
by but a single chromosome within a complex genetic structure.
This **XX** pattern in but one particle of the human genetic code
decrees that the human fetus develops a uterus, ovaries, and a vagina
and will be equipped in adulthood to bear young. The male fetus,
the geneticist tells us, develops just as the female for the first six
weeks of its existence, after which its distinctive pattern of chromosomes, **XY**, will signal the atrophy of an embryonic uterus and
trigger hormones that produce the male sex organs. Although this
delicate process is subject to malfunction, it does assure that almost
every child enters the world with a relatively unambiguous sexual
identity, either male or female.

At the time of birth, culture takes over from biology, announcing the sex of the infant with gender names, appropriate pronouns,
and such quaint sexual labels as the familiar pink and blue ribbons.
It may be several years, however, before boys and girls come to
recognize the gender classifications that will mark them for life.
When examined by cognitive psychologists, young children are
often confused about sex differences for the first three years of life
and fail to internalize an unequivocal gender identity until the age
of five or six. Experiments conducted during the 1960s indicated
that the awakening of gender identity was not an entirely equan-
imous experience for little girls. While the little boy quickly achieved
an egotistical delight in his maleness, the girl child hesitated and
often failed to accept her sexual identity with unequivocal pleasure.
The girl might be ignorant of the precise anatomical differences
between males and females and, of course, was unaware of the
permutations of chromosomes. Yet by this tender age she had become conscious of the sexual dichotomy in the human race, and
upon comparison of adult males and females, she had concluded
that her own sex had been sentenced to inferiority. In the person
of the adult female, whom they have clearly identified as their
model, these six-year-old girls spied some ominous signs of their
womanhood to come.

Behind the little girl's troubled sexual identity lay elaborate cultural patterns and social structures that predate her own birth and extend far back into the history and experience of her fore-mothers. Much of women's history, particularly when inspired by feminism, seeks to understand the process whereby female biology is translated into this disconcerting experience of womanhood. Recent feminist scholars have given this process a variety of names. One of the clearest, most comprehensive, and useful concepts is the "gender system," whose initial architect, anthropologist Gayle Rubin, defined as follows: "Every society has a sex/gender system — a set of arrangements by which the biological raw material of human sex and procreation is shaped by human, social intervention." The gender system is as pervasive as social distinctions based on age and race and more universal than class divisions. It concerns far more than the physical relations of the sexes. Gender operates, according to sociologist Harriet Hölter, as a kind of "master status system" which parcels out all society's duties, rewards, functions, and values according to sex. In this book, everything which the operation of the gender system determines to be female will be called woman-hood, and is the subject of this survey of American history.

Recent scholarship, especially anthropological literature, has isolated various components of the gender system as they recur in all known human cultures. Scholars working from a Marxist-fem-inist perspective, for example, find it useful to distinguish between production and social reproduction, that is, to separate the status of woman within the primarily economic structures of society from her role in procreation, the family order, and the general mainte-nance and propagation of everyday social and cultural life. Sexual differentiation permeates both these spheres, however, and women often play a central part in mediating between productive and reproductive activities, between the demands of the economy and the needs of families. Certainly female experience is rarely confined to family relations and excluded entirely from the productive sphere. It is useful, then, to also acknowledge a broad and intricate division of labor and function in which sex operates as a major organizing principle.

In one society men may be hunters and women gatherers; in another men will make tools, while women fashion baskets; in another men can be doctors, women only nurses; in yet another men will be the priests and women the healers. This is not to say that women have been universally excluded from hunting, tool making, medical practice, and religious leadership. The process, if not the pattern, is universal; every society to one degree or another allocates human labor by sex. Moreover, one essential social task is almost universally assigned to females, the care of infants and children. Child care is the most entrenched and well-fortified female position in most gender systems.

In practice, the sexual division of labor also tends to carve up physical territory according to sex. The pattern of inhabiting distinct social spaces, in other words, is another central component of the gender system. While men frequent fields and taverns and factories, women may congregate around the hearth, the village well, or their kitchen tables. In some cultures, the sex-segregated places are surrounded by exact and formidable boundaries and males and females are rarely permitted to tread into one another's territory. The sexes may come together only for sexual congress and common meals. In other times and places great stock is put on association and companionship between males and females. Nonetheless, womanhood has always had a geography of its own. To some degree or another there have been limits placed on where, when, and with whom women congregate. Woman's role as child bearer occupies the center of her segregated sphere and tends to confine her to a social space that is more domestic than social, more sedentary than nomadic, more private than public.

The gender system is not concerned solely with such material aspects of life as economics and geography. It leaves its imprint even on the mind and personality. With a few notable exceptions, most cultures approve one set of personal characteristics for men and another for women. This component of the gender system conforms to one predominant pattern, taking shape around the poles of male forcefulness and female nurturing. No less than 85 percent of the cultures examined in one anthropological survey consciously trained males to be aggressive and females to be supportive. These normative personality types neatly mesh with the prescribed behavior proper to each sex; they cultivate mental and emotional capacities conducive to worldly success in the male and suppress the female urge to desert her more domestic role and more private sphere. The sexual arrangement of desirable character traits is not merely random and benign; females are not just different, but equal. At times, woman's character is an object of scorn, suspicion, even

contempt. Some cultures decree menstrual taboos and rites of pur-
gation to protect men from contamination by the female sex. In
other cultures femininity is more honorable. Woman is, in fact,
placed upon a pedestal and celebrated for her sexual and social
purity. In either case, whether venerated for her chastity or condemned as unclean, woman is treated as a species apart from those
males who generate the dominant religion or ideology of most
societies. Woman has been so persistently regarded as a passive
object rather than a participant in cosmological systems, that Simone
de Beauvoir has labeled her sex the universal "other."

In fact, on almost all planes of the gender system, women are
relegated to marginal or secondary positions. The economic rewards
for fulfilling female roles in the division of labor are universally less
than what males are accustomed to receive. Even honorific recompense is measured out inequitably to women. In one African
tribe, for example, men and women perform almost identical productive functions; one sex cultivates sweet potatoes, the other yams.
Yet it is the male produce, the yam, which is considered the superior
crop and given the place of honor in community rituals. It should
be clear, then, that gender also operates as a system of stratification,
one which despite all its cross-cultural variations consistently confers
some measure of inequality on the female sex.

This inequity suggests that the gender system also deals in
matters of power, and grants to men superior ability to control
others, particularly females. In most all societies legitimate official
power of authority is primarily a male prerogative. The uppermost
pinnacles of political power are usually male clubs. Men alone are
chiefs, sheiks, and presidents. Still, females are by no means im-
potent. They have multiple and sometimes nefarious means of influencing others, especially in their families and their neighborhoods.
Women can seldom be found, however, in official and lofty positions, from which they can directly and overtly control social and
political life. Nor are women well represented among cultural leaders, priests, publishers, and TV executives. In economic, political,
and cultural matters, then, the gender system has almost always
operated as a system of superior male power. Feminists often call
this characteristic of the gender system patriarchy, and invest it
with a causal role in shaping womanhood across time. Because this
term connotes the supremacy which men exercise through their
position as fathers, however, it is most appropriate to one particular

historical incidence of male dominance. It will be used in this study only to designate those situations in which male-dominated kinship systems form the basis of overall social organization.

Men have retained, even enhanced their power outside of the tribal organization, where all authority was based in family, clan, and kinship networks. They exercise authority in courts, congresses, and corporate offices as well as families. Moreover, the superior status of males is not maintained in the simple personalized fashion that the term patriarchy implies. Thus the broader term, male dominance, designates a multiplicity of social processes which, for all their variety and intricacy, repeatedly deal to women an unequal share of wealth, honor, and authority.

Although the most obvious effect of gender is to distinguish, separate, and stratify the female from the male, this should not obscure the fact that all societies also insist that women and men maintain regular, enduring, and orderly connections with one another. This final component of the gender system, which has been called the social relations of the sexes, is just beginning to be subjected to historical study. It calls on students of gender to be attentive to all those points where male and female experience intersect in formalized and repeated ways, for example, in the rules of kinship and marriage, in the institution of the family, in sexual intimacy, and, more rarely, in larger social or public forums. This component of the gender system, like all the others, tends to operate to the relative disadvantage of women. The relations of the sexes are generally organized so that the female parties to cross-gender associations have less power and less autonomy. Marriage, for example, has usually placed wives in a position of greater dependency if not subordination.

How and why, then, do gender systems guarantee the inequality of women, the domination of males? This is a central concern of feminist scholarship and a driving motivation for the investigation of woman's past.

The persistent social inequality and cultural differentiation between the sexes has prompted countless intellectual excursions in search of a single biological explanation for the "eternal feminine." In the last century, scientists fastened on anything from a cubic centimeter difference in brain size to a slight curvature of the skeleton as the natural explanation of sexual inequality. Contemporary researchers look to a microscopic bit of protein, the chromosome,

as the biological first cause of womanhood. Contemporary geneti-
cists confess that beyond ensuring that females will be capable of
bearing and nursing children, the XX pattern has "no known direct
influence on subsequent sexual or psychosexual development." The
determination of the effect of prenatal hormones on the brain pathways of animals also yields an indecisive verdict for human beings,
in whom these neural pathways "have not been anatomically identified." Furthermore, "the higher primates and man especially are
more subject to the influence of postnatal biographical history."
The examination of human subjects whose hormones are out of
balance or whose sex identity is ambiguous has also led to only
minimal and tentative conclusions about the biological sources of
behavioral differences between normal men and women.

The only indisputable and unambiguous natural differences between the sexes are patently obvious: their different genital construction and reproductive systems. Beyond the roles of men and
women in the acts of sexual intercourse and procreation there are
no incontrovertible biological determinants of the functions of the
sexes. Neither does the physiology of sex decree personality differences that are essential to reproduction. Nature supplies only those
sexual differences essential to reproduction. In so doing, however, it
creates a highly visible division of the human race. This separation
of the human species into blatantly dichotomous sexes provides a
symbol and rubric, not a direct instrumental cause, for a long series
of artificial distinctions. The ancient and obvious categories of male
and female provide a convenient beginning for dividing and organizing aspects of social life, including the distribution of economic
tasks, public responsibilities, and position in the community hierarchy. When these divisions are made, woman's biology has operated as a stigma, signaling inferiority in a social network designed
by human beings, not decreed by nature.

Still, a perplexing question remains: Why have human cultures,
unchained by the dictates of nature, recurrently interpreted fe-
maleness as a justification for social inferiority? Anthropological
literature is replete with conjectured solutions to this problem,
among them, the assertion of male domination through superior
size and strength, the greater efficiency of assigning secondary domestic roles to the necessarily more sedentary child bearer, or the
hypothesis that the female's reproductive function is associated with
the mysterious and often hostile forces of nature, and therefore causes

her to appear as man's opponent rather than his ally in conquering the material world. These theories — the biological, functional, and symbolic, respectively — have considerable credibility when applied to technologically primitive societies, where the maximum use of human energy is imperative to survival and sustains a sexual division of labor that delegates hunting and defense to men while women tend children and the home fires. Yet each of these propositions falls short of explaining womanhood in its entirety and its pervasive inequality. Each loses its cogency in advanced societies where muscular force has lost much of its usefulness and when so much of nature, including reproduction, has been brought within human control.

Neither biology, anthropology, nor existent feminist theory can fully explain how much various social orders, ranging from polyandrous tribes to Victorian households, all culminate in sexual inequality. The gender system takes on myriad different shapes according to time and place. To accommodate such great complexity, theories of gender must be flexible and multifaceted enough to scrutinize a whole web of social relationships: between women's status and production, reproduction, ideology, and political organization. Despite the increasing sophistication of feminist theory on all these levels of analysis, the understanding of womanhood in its fullest detail and intricacy requires historical study.

Womanhood is always manufactured at a precise point in time and under specific circumstances. Historical methods of investigation can offer a close-up view of how biological females are installed in the ever-changing matrix of roles, characteristics, and rewards that is womanhood. At the historical level of analysis, the origins of female inequality become more concrete and specific. At discrete moments in time, woman's relative powerlessness, regardless of its cause, is clearly apparent; her vulnerability to an unequal share in the division of labor, power, and honor becomes obvious. The causes of sexual inequality, then, can be understood within the context of the options granted to men and to women by their times and their history. In reality, womanhood has never been created, and thus cannot be explained, outside of history.

This particular historical investigation begins on the North American continent in the seventeenth century, and will commence with an examination of a gender system that derived from the European mores of the first settlers. It is useful, however, to consider at least one example of the many native American tribes, which had built up a great diversity of gender systems in the Western Hemisphere long before the era of colonization. One Indian nation is particularly useful to consider, for the gender system of the Iroquois, as described by French missionaries in the eighteenth century, seemed to have been remarkably generous to women. Although by no means a matriarchy, the Iroquois social system came perhaps as close as any known civilization to the standard of sexual equality. Iroquois matrons chose the chieftains and delegates to tribal councils, where they also had a vote on issues of war and peace. Women were even more influential in the everyday activities of their villages. They were responsible for distributing surplus produce and supervised the selection of marriage partners for their children. Half the positions of religious authority were held by women who also participated in organizing the major festivals and rituals of the tribe. Iroquois culture, its myths and rituals, treated women with relative dignity and respect. This was not a case of female domination; males alone, for example, were invested with the direct political authority of chiefs. Yet this native American tribe granted women a degree of political, economic, and cultural power that impresses anthropologists and historians alike.

The case of the Iroquois, furthermore, prompts some queries about just what social conditions facilitate this degree of equality. The distinctive economic system of the Iroquois warrants consideration on this score, for simple agrarian economies like theirs have often been associated with a measure of equity between males and females. Iroquois women, like the females of many relatively egalitarian African societies, participated fully in agricultural production. While men cleared the land and helped in the harvest, women were solely responsible for planting and cultivating grain, the tribe's staple. This central role in production was associated with further economic rights and responsibilities. Women directed whatever limited exchange of goods occurred within the tribe. They also may have held special rights to the land, although this vital resource was most likely owned by neither male nor female, but communally. Iroquois egalitarianism, in sum, coexisted with a simple agricultural economy, limited market activity, a weak sense of private property, and the integration of women in the productive system.

Another correlate of women's status within the tribe commands special attention. The spatial arrangement of everyday life among the Iroquois was such that women had relatively easy access to the forums of collective decision making. A female's domestic and reproductive roles did not isolate her from politics and society. Rather, these functions gave women a special vantage point for participating in community activities, for the residential unit was the hub of Iroquois society. The families that composed the tribe resided, worked, and deliberated about their common fate in large collective shelters called longhouses. The co-residents, furthermore, were bound together by their ties to the female line. This matrilocal pattern of residence determined that while women lived with their sisters and mothers, men moved in with their wives' kin upon marriage. The central social space of the society, then, was a sphere of special familiarity and comfort for women and one that reinforced bonds between members of the female sex. Female bonds also laced through economic life. Women tilled the fields together and often elected one of their number as the head of the work crew. Only intertribal affairs—chiefly the defense alliances of the Five Iroquois Nations— were distanced from this female center of power. This distinctive territorial arrangement, one characterized by a very rudimentary development of either purely domestic units or remote political institutions, has been found to be associated with relative sexual equality in such diverse portions of the globe as the Philippines and Western Africa. Thus the degree to which any society distinguishes between public and private sectors seems to be another important indication of woman's status within the gender system.

These relationships between modes of production, the private/public dichotomy, and the degree of sexual stratification are still largely hypothetical; social scientists have not established any immutable laws about the patterning of gender systems. Yet both these aspects of social organization provide useful guiding hypotheses when analyzing sex differentiation over time.

On the eve of European settlement, however, Western civilization seems to have advanced beyond the point when either the mode of production or the arrangement of social space would offer much hope of relatively elevated power and status for women. By the seventeenth century the English economy had developed into a complex market system, which enshrined private property in the rural farms as well as the artisan shops and merchant houses of its towns and cities. Concomitantly, married women had been denied the right to hold property in their own right and females had been excluded from guilds, banks, and merchant exchanges, and were granted only the meager wages of servants. They were spatially removed from centers of political as well as economic power. The rise of the nation-state created a new center of power which, with the exception of an occasional monarch like Elizabeth, was largely dominated by males. Thus European colonization of the Western Hemisphere seemed likely to propagate a gender system that severely subordinated and circumscribed females.

The Atlantic passage, however, temporarily routed the evolution of womanhood around such a historical path. For the first several generations of settlement, roughly between the mid-seventeenth and the mid-eighteenth century, the American gender system took a very distinctive shape that will be outlined in the first chapter. First of all, the exigencies of surviving in the wilderness placed a premium on woman's participation in production, accorded her a central position in economic life, and discouraged any refined notions about her distinctive or feminine temperament.

At the same time, women of the seventeenth century found political influence relatively accessible; the citadel of public power in London was far too remote to intervene in local affairs, and even the provincial government had little control over the collective life of the small isolated villages where colonial population concentrated. Thus, politics was effectively contained within small and familiar institutions, like the town meeting, the local courthouse, or a circle of households, where women had a good chance of exerting influence if not direct political authority. Still, the colonists carried across the Atlantic some contrary notions, especially a strong commitment to private property as controlled by the fathers of households. But this ideal of patriarchy, which decreed subordination of women in families and their total exclusion from formal institutions of political power, was often undermined in practice, particularly in the South where fathers and husbands seldom survived long enough to consolidate their power. This practical equality, which existed side by side with the ideal of patriarchal authority, is fittingly symbolized by a favorite title of womanhood in the seventeenth century, "Adam's Rib."

This gender system was necessarily ephemeral. By the mid-eighteenth century Western history had caught up with the American frontier. The simple subsistence division of labor dissolved with the effervescent growth of commercial capitalism. Production and distribution for profit, be it on the farm or in a bustling seaport, eroded the material base of Adam's Rib. Women could now be removed to the margins of production, some to the fashionable drawing rooms of the rich, others to the almshouses, still others to peripheral duties on commercial farms specializing in single-crop production for the market. Patriarchy was undermined by the same forces, as fathers lost their ability to ordain the status of their sons and their daughters in the more mobile individualistic circumstances of the commercial age. Logically, the ethic of independence that blossomed in the era of the American Revolution could have had a liberating impact on women as well as men. In fact, women were not welcomed into the ranks of republican citizenship. To the contrary, the formation of a federated United States and the centralization of politics in the national capital marked a substantial expansion of the official public sector, and placed women at a greater distance from the citadels of political power in America.

In its social and economic aspects, meanwhile, the gender system remained in a state of disarray. No universally recognized emblem of womanhood replaced the symbol of Adam's Rib. Furthermore, beginning in the late seventeenth century (detailed in Chapter 2), the experience of women diverged fundamentally according to the different ranks of the emerging class structure.

Not until the mid-nineteenth century, when American capitalism was well along on the path to industrial hegemony, could American culture agree upon a new standard of womanhood, one that best suited those native-born American women who were a part of an emerging middle class. The new order dictated that economic production be removed from the household unit. Whether the women of industrial society remained ever-secluded in the home or spent a few years in the lowest ranks of the work force, their sex was identified primarily with specialized domestic functions, supplying the immediate physical and emotional needs of husbands and children. The quintessential standard of femininity became nurturance, first of individual families and through them of all America. Nineteenth-century industrial society for the first time deemed "work" as a male prerogative and in turn glorified woman for her domestic and maternal functions. The construction of this ideal-type of womanhood entailed major revisions in the American system of sexual distribution: the stark spatial separation of male and female into public and private spheres, a schizoid division of human personality into the feminine and the masculine, and the unrelenting bombardment of popular culture with sex stereotypes.

The nineteenth century, in other words, saw a clear segregation of the sexes that seemed, on the surface, to remove women to the periphery of society and economics. In actuality, whether in the home or as short-term workers in the nation's first factories, women played a pivotal role in the coming of industrial capitalism, as will be documented in Chapter 3.

The maturation of industrial capitalism in the late nineteenth century coincided with the development of sophisticated social organization within woman's sphere itself. The most dramatic remodeling of woman's sphere was accomplished by the female social reformers of the Progressive Era, who capitalized on the presumed moral superiority and purity of their sex to justify an active female campaign to clean up society and politics. By the turn of the century these social housekeepers had formed a tightly organized and extensive national corps of reformers, with their own internal hierarchy and power networks. The Progressive women took particular concern for the welfare of lower-class, chiefly immigrant women, who themselves had assumed vital places in industrial society.

Working-class women had also advanced beyond the home. They regularly enrolled in the female sector of the economy in their youth, chiefly in domestic service and small industries such as garment making. The income of working daughters was simply one aspect in a complicated system whereby women brought money into immigrant homes and provided essential supplements to the working-class standard of living. However active socially and economically, these women of the late nineteenth century still retained the characteristics of occupants of woman's sphere. Both social housekeepers and working-class women eschewed the individualistic ethic and personal sense of achievement that identified a masculine breadwinner, preferring the altruistic, nurturing image of the "breadgiver," the title of the fourth chapter. The crowning moment in the history of this gender system was the passage of the Nineteenth Amendment in 1920. The successful conclusion of the suffrage campaign testified to the sophistication of a movement that was built around woman's sphere and often rhetorically exploited women's Victorian attributes of purity and selflessness.

At the same time, however, the winning of the vote omened the corrosion of woman's sphere, for now, at least in political terms, women were to be officially integrated with men, entitled at last to full participation in the public sphere. Popular culture in the twentieth century was also obsessed with bringing males and females together, not so much in politics as in sexual intimacy. Accordingly, it was the erotic rather than the chaste connotations of femininity that became the central imagery of twentieth-century womanhood. This image appeared most prominently in the advertising copy that began to proliferate after 1920, signaling the increasing importance of the consumer sector of the American economy. Women were deeply implicated in this advanced stage of capitalist development. Not only was their image used as enticement to consumers, but women themselves acquired an expanded role as the preeminent American shoppers. Beneath the glossy image of the sexy saleslady were the most fundamental structural shifts in the gender system. The most crucial of all was the steady advance of women and increasingly large numbers of wives and mothers into the paid labor force. In other words, those women born into the twentieth century were destined to play a variety of roles, spanning the public and the private sectors as they skipped quickly through their duties as sex partners, shoppers, wives, mothers, and workers. Yet, whether measured in wage ratios or the proportion of women in positions of power, womanhood still incurred inequality as of the mid-twentieth century.

This most recent epoch of woman's history had a particularly difficult chronology, spanning alternate decades of war and peace, depression and prosperity. Yet this fractured pattern itself can be seen as a defining characteristic of twentieth-century womanhood, repeatedly jarred like the fragments of a kaleidoscope from one configuration of roles and images into another. One thing was clear, however: the gender system no longer clearly compartmentalized womanhood into a private, a domestic, or a reproductive world.

This progression toward a more heterosocial and symmetrical gender system has been dissected into three different stages, and is presented in three different chapters of this book. The first stage, depicted in Chapter 5, recounts how the generation of women who came of age early in this century inhaled the liberating vapors of emancipation from Victorian restrictions, greater independence of parental families, promises of sexual fulfillment, and the freedom of more streamlined homes. Chapter 6 will follow this generation and their daughters into the 1940s and '50s, when they encountered two apparently antithetical models of femininity, first of the wartime production workers glorified during World War II, and then of the housewife who reigned over the suburbs during the 1950s. In actuality both these two decades participated in the same trend toward sexual symmetry, most especially through the integration of more and more women, and even wives and mothers, into the paid labor force. The last chapter will follow the women of the twentieth century as they challenged the asymmetry of the gender system on a variety of fronts, through the women's liberation movement, by a massive influx into the labor force and a drastic decline in their fertility, marriage rate, and the stability of their families.

In sum, then, this book will describe the creation and transformation of womanhood in America, isolating these three distinct patterns in the gender system: first, the integral position of women in the patriarchal household economy of the seventeenth century; second, the segregated woman's sphere under industrial capitalism; and finally, the more integrated and balanced, but still unequal relations of the sexes during the twentieth century. The bold outlines of these gender systems have been deciphered from a variety of historical sources. The shifting models of womanhood are constructed primarily from the prevailing images or norms of femininity on the one hand, and woman's actual societal roles as revealed by a variety of social statistics on the other.

The common denominator of popular ideas and an array of social and economic data can serve to adumbrate the history of womanhood, to outline, that is, the general pattern of the gender system as it set limits and channeled experience for masses of women. The history and concept of womanhood should also be flexible enough to account for multiplicity as well, especially variation by class, race, ethnic group, and geographical region. No single typology of womanhood, however, can adequately depict actual female experience, the millions of unique lives that participate in the creation, the maintenance, and the transformation of any gender system. From the perspective of the individual female, womanhood is not a rigid external pattern but the plastic creation of her own acts. Despite the causal power of themes like the mode of production, the boundaries of private and public life, and the power of ideology, in explaining variations in women's status, none of these concepts act as deterministic agents forcing women to conform to their dictates.

The actual position of women in any gender system is too complex and variable to justify mechanical theories of causation and is more contingent upon female cooperation, participation, and even invention than such models imply. By virtue of her low social status, woman confronts a web of constrictions upon individual autonomy slightly more formidable, but not fundamentally different, from the way men make history. Woman is only placed at a slightly greater disadvantage in the test of history as described by Karl Marx: "Men make their own history, but they do not make it just as they please; they do not make it under circumstances chosen by themselves, but under circumstances directly encountered, given, and transmitted from the past."

Within these constrictions, which are the bedrock of human history, women have always maneuvered to maximize their power, comfort, and freedom. The pioneer women's historian, Mary Beard, used the phrase "Woman as a Force in History" to denote this active, social-historical role of the second sex. Hardly anyone would be so foolish as to suggest that females, who have labored unremittingly to support and sustain themselves, their families, and their communities, have left no imprint on the course of history. More recent work by women historians has carried this argument one step further, to the point where we can observe women in the concrete acts of influencing social change and shaping womanhood itself. This vision of women making their own history is particularly acute among historians of the early nineteenth century, the initial stages of American industrialization. This important turning point in the history of America and of womanhood is the subject of a chapter, completely revised in the second edition, which tried among other things to demonstrate how women, acting through benevolent and reform associations, put their own stamp on industrial society and helped build woman's sphere as they saw fit.

The early nineteenth century was a particularly crucial moment in the history of womanhood, marking the transition from one gender system to another. The 1960s and '70s, the subject of the last chapter, may well turn out to be an equally momentous time in the history of women. The year 1978 brought a crucial watershed for women; for the first time the majority of all adult females were enrolled in the paid public labor force, including the majority of married women and large numbers of the mothers of schoolchildren and even infants. In other words, the sexual division of labor, perhaps the most fundamental component of the gender system, has become extremely muted and confused, as females become as integral as men to the public operation of the economy and the financial maintenance of their families. Not even this sharply diminished role differentiation, however, promises immediate equality to women.

Woman's status in the labor force, her rank and her wages, are still markedly inferior. Yet the advance of women into the male sphere coexists with a vocal and widespread demand for sexual equality. The revival of feminism in the late 1960s demonstrates that more American women than ever before are intent on making their own history. In the process they are assaulting the whole gender system as they reject both the segregation and the inequality of the sexes.

The writing and the reading of this book are a part of this auspicious moment in the history of women. This volume is offered as an appeal for continued investigation of women's history, whose still tentative outlines are presented here. It is also hoped that it will be of some assistance in the continuing feminist struggle.

ONE

ADAM'S RIB:
THE FIRST CENTURY
OF AMERICAN WOMANHOOD

uropean colonists in North America in the seventeenth century re-created womanhood from a complex array of discordant historical materials. The Europe from which the first settlers emigrated was quaking with the most basic and far-reaching social change: the transformation from feudalism to capitalism. The social structure of seventeenth-century England was complex enough to accommodate several varieties of womanhood: the diverse female roles appropriate to peasants, ladies, shopkeepers, merchants, artisans, yeoman farmers, servants, and laborers. The Protestant Reformation had splintered the religious unity of the Old World as well, and English dissenters, especially Puritans and Quakers, had some novel ideas about gender.

Seventeenth-century England also harbored a complicated array of domestic patterns and thus provided many different contexts for the development of women's family roles. One recent historian has found traces of feudal lineages, patriarchal nuclear families, and affectionate domestic circles, all cohabiting in the same volatile century.[1] Only selected elements among these disparate classes and cultures would migrate across the Atlantic. Upon arrival in the New World they would be metamorphosed once again. London sophisticates, for example, might be forced to revert to medieval farming techniques in order to survive in the wilderness. Finally, American womanhood would take different shapes within the varying nationalities, climes, and regions that composed the British

19

colonies in the seventeenth century. Accordingly, there were several
modes of early American womanhood bearing the distinctive mark-
ings of New England Puritans, southern planters, Pennsylvania
Quakers, and the Dutch traders of New Amsterdam.

Historians have only begun to explore the variety of women's
experiences which composed this intricate colonial mosaic. New
England's Puritans were the most literate of all the colonists and
thus have left the fullest description of colonial ideals of womanhood. Our picture of early American womanhood, and hence this
chapter, is still marred by these regional limits of the historical
record. One image of women reverberated through Puritan sermons,
that of the "helpmeet," an industrious partner in the colonial family
economy. The helpmeet was often dressed in an appropriately homely
metaphor, the title "Adam's Rib." A sermon occasioned by a Puritan
wedding and published in Boston in 1750 spelled out the social
status of the ideal helpmeet. "Our ribs were not ordained to be our
rulers," proclaimed the Reverend William Secker. "They are not
made of the head to claim superiority, but out of the side to be
content with equality."[2] The twentieth-century mind has some difficulty deciphering this lesson in the anatomy of male-female relations. Surely this Puritan preacher could not be expounding the
radical modern notion of sexual equality. His imagery belies such
an intention; the lowly and dependent portion of Adam's skeleton
hardly symbolizes either equality or autonomy.

Still, the phrase "out of the side to be content with equality"
does convey something of the essence of the seventeenth-century
gender system. Men and women were on equal terms in at least
one essential: the value and degree of their participation in the social
economic development of the American colonies. This "equality"
of woman was not conferred by pastoral decree but necessitated by
the arduous task that faced American settlers, that of planting a
society in the wilderness. No man, no woman, could be exempted
from this toilsome undertaking. Woman's central place alongside
man in economic production and social organization granted her a
basic and integral role in the community not altogether unlike the
function of the ribs in the human skeleton. Although women performed functions equal and similar to those of men, their status
still ensued "out of the side" of males, the husbands and fathers
who alone held independent and powerful positions in colonial
society. Adam's Rib might claim a crude functional equality, but

Adam himself could assume command of the operations of the household. Only the patriarch of the family, furthermore, could rise to leadership in political, cultural, and religious affairs. The tension built into this gender symbolism, the contradiction between equality of function and dependency of status, marked every aspect of early American womanhood. This contradiction is resolved somewhat by the fact that most social and economic life transpired within the colonial household, a busy work space, where, of necessity, the patriarch and his helpmeet cooperated extensively and thus shared a casual equality.

The concept of Adam's Rib as propounded in 1750 had evolved out of the many different models of ordering of the sexes that accompanied the first settlers into the New World. First of all, no simple sex labels were affixed to the remnants of feudalism that were transported to the proprietary colonies such as Maryland. Here the female scions of important English families, most notably Margaret and Mary Brent, were granted manorial rights over thousands of acres. Likewise, the bustling commercial centers of Holland sent women like the Widow Margaret Hardenbrook Philipse to New Amsterdam where she converted her land resources into a merchant fortune and organized the first regular ship passages across the Atlantic. The Pilgrims added some egalitarian religious ideas to these multifarious notions about womanhood. John Robinson asserted, for example, that any man "yea, or any woman either, may as truly, and effectively loose and bind, both in heaven and earth, as all ministers in the world."[3] Similar sentiments impelled the likes of Mistress Anne Hutchinson to become the center of religious controversy in Massachusetts Bay. Seventeenth-century Europe, ripped apart by social change, opened many avenues for women, including removal to the open spaces of America.

Few of those who found their way to the colonies shared the lofty status and expectations of Margaret Brent, Widow Philipse, and Mistress Hutchinson. Three-quarters of the English population from which America's first settlers were recruited were simple farmers, tied for generations to small plots of land or common fields, which were tended by men and women alike. The early years of the Old World peasant woman's life of toil might be spent in servitude before she entered her own rugged home upon her marriage in her mid to late twenties. The female side of her later life derived primarily from her reproductive function, recurrent childbearing with its incumbent risks of death and infant mortality.[4] As the seventeenth century advanced, however, this timeless pattern of survival was fractured by the enclosure of peasant fields and the advance of a more complicated cash economy. Faced with the possibility of landlessness, or awakened by ambition for economic betterment, uprooted English farmers might venture as far afield as the shores of North America.

The ships that made the Atlantic passage carried principally these classes of English men and women: propertyless husbandmen, yeoman farmers, artisans, and common laborers. One in three of the passengers disembarking in Virginia were women, usually in their early twenties, and the majority of them were indentured servants who had pledged years of labor for the hope of later assuming positions of material comfort in families of their own. Single Dutch women often hired themselves out to merchants and planters in New Netherlands to pay their passage to the New World. New England immigrants came more often in family units, two of every three members of which were likely to be women. Passenger lists on New England vessels consisted of groups such as John Carver's entourage, including "Katharine, his wife; Desire Minter; two men servants . . . , a boy; a maidservant and a child that was put to him."[5]

WOMEN IN THE AGRARIAN HOUSEHOLD ECONOMY

Whether they came indentured to Virginia planters, in the hire of New Amsterdam merchants, or sheltered in New England families, women were eagerly awaited in the colonies. A petition put before the Virginia House of Burgesses in 1619 surmised that "in a newe plantation it is not known whether man or woman be most necessary."[6] The petitioners made this assertion in order to induce the Assembly to grant land in the name of wives as well as male settlers. In Virginia and throughout the colonies the fate of women would hinge upon the distribution of this basic commodity of the seventeenth-century economy, the land. For a fleeting historical moment the inhabitants of the New World considered holding this life source of the community in common.

The Pilgrims set down in Plymouth with the radical intention

of laboring in one communal field and sharing its fruits, each according to his or her need. Yet William Bradford recounts the swift demise of this experiment. "For the young men, that were the most able and fit for labor and service, did repine that they should spend their time and strength to work for other men's wives and children without any recompense . . . and for men's wives to be commanded to do service to other men . . . they deemed it a kind of slavery, neither could many husbands well brook with it."[7] Thus   •
private property based in the family quietly embedded its tenacious roots in American soil, and soon that plant would bear fruit in sexual inequity.

Occasionally a village or colony would allocate land to women. The town of Salem set out small maid-lots, and Pennsylvania generously offered 75 acres to all women above the age of fourteen.[8] Within a few short years, however, each village and every colony had eliminated these tenuously-held rights of women to acquire land independently. The women who were given any consideration in matters of land distribution fell into the category of wives or dependents of patriarchal households. For example, Lord Baltimore calculated the family allowances of Maryland in the following manner: 100 acres for an adult male, 100 acres for his wife, 50 acres for his child, 100 acres for a manservant, and 60 acres for a womanservant.[9] All this acreage was the legal possession of the male household head; neither wives nor maidservants held independent title to land in Maryland. The town meeting of Sudbury, Massachusetts, contemplated distributing its land in a similar manner (in fact, setting aside a half acre more for wives than for husbands), but decided instead to determine the size of land grants by the social status of the male head of the household.[10] Most early American communities founded their economic structure on the latter principles.

When the settlers of Jamaica, New York, set down the economic order of the town in 1656, for example, they promised a plot of land "to all who troubled to settle." Yet not a single woman appeared on the lists of allocations that followed.[11] Neither did communities founded late in the seventeenth century, like Worcester, Massachusetts, leave any trace of land titles allotted to women. The first, most crucial act of colonial settlement, the division of the land, simply denied the independent economic existence of women.

The subsequent day-to-day exchanges of landed property also

tended to exclude women, in accordance with the provision of English common law that regarded marriage as the civil death of the wife. Married or single, the colonial woman would pass most of her life under the family system of private property, which allowed only heads of households, and thus predominantly males, the privileges of owning and exchanging land. Colonial statutes recognized women not as owners but as a species of property themselves; the Massachusetts Body of Liberties lumped women with goods and estates in proclaiming that "no man shall be deprived of his wife or children." The Massachusetts legal code did include a section entitled "the liberties of women," which granted wives the right to be provided for in their husbands' wills.[12] In both New England and the South a colonial widow was assured of receiving at least one-third of her deceased husband's estate. It was primarily through widowhood that women received an economic identity of their own. By the late seventeenth century a widowed woman was listed among the top three landowners of Dedham, Massachusetts; more than a dozen women appeared in the top tax bracket of Jamaica, New York, at the turn of the century; and as the first generation of settlers grew to maturity, the female heirs assumed the direction of sizable estates in towns throughout the colonies.[13]

The special status of the widow was, however, perfectly consistent with the concept of Adam's Rib: "It is between a man and his wife in the House as it is between the Sun and the Moon in the heavens when the great light goes down, the lesser light gets up. When the one ends in setting, the other begins in shining. The wife may be sovereign in her husband's absence, but she must be subject in his presence." The status of wife included the role of "deputy husband," as historian Laurel Thatcher Ulrich has called it, and permitted women to enlarge their range of action and power during their husbands' absence and after the death of the patriarch.[14] The rise of the widow to the direction and command of her late husband's estate did not elevate the female sex per se, but registered the colonists' determination to keep private property in family units, in order that it might descend intact from fathers to sons. According to English common law, as well as legal practice in the American colonies, a widow was entitled to the use of her legacy only during her widowhood or natural life. Thereafter, it would revert to her husband's chosen heirs, usually his sons. A typical bequest would read like this one dated 1707 and probated in Virginia: "My wife

Alice, to have and enjoy the Land I live on for her widowhood. After her death or remarriage the land is to return to my son William."[15]

The discrimination against daughters was equally direct and explicit. The Massachusetts statute granted property to female descendants only when parents had "no male heirs of their body." In practice, daughters rarely inherited landed property, while the value of the personal property they were willed (cows and feather beds being favorite items) was well below the value of bequests to their brothers. One Massachusetts will, for example, simply stipulated that "each daughter have half so much as each son." Wills probated in the Southern colonies conformed to similar standards of gender inequity.[16]

The fact that women could obtain property primarily through death or default did not diminish the energy and efficiency with which they entered into land dealings and other economic activities. The loopholes of inheritance freed some women to engage wholeheartedly in the exchange of land and other property. One Virginia widow, Elizabeth Caursley, not only sold a piece of land, but with her capital purchased two menservants. Another good wife of Ipswich, Massachusetts, managed to accumulate enough income from the sale of poultry to extend a loan to her husband.[17] Westward in New Amsterdam, married women broke all the rules of propriety by bombarding the court with suits involving every possible economic matter. Occasionally a local magistrate would order an aggressive woman to "exhibit authority from her husband and then institute her action in writing." But this caveat did not deter countless numbers of bold women from undertaking suits in their own names or even in behalf of their spouses. The economic consequence of the New Amsterdam wife was acknowledged by many men in the community who called women to court to account for the debts incurred by their husbands. When one Aaltje Albers was held to account for the debt of her husband, Jacob Hay, she retorted that she "had no knowledge of her husband's affairs, and he may speak to her husband."[18]

Seventeenth-century probate records reveal that women encroached further into the property sphere than the limits of the law recognized. First of all, daughters were seldom entirely forgotten and unprotected in their fathers' wills. If the family had prospered, sizable goods and estates could be bequeathed to females. One New

England father could afford to make a special grant to his daughter's daughters "because Mary and Susanna theyr husbands have lands to Give theyr Sons." Others, such as William Carpenter of Providence, made provision for married daughters in clear contravention of the postulates of common law. Carpenter's legacy to his daughter was written as follows: ". . . both for herself and who so ever shee shall make her heirs, executors and administrators to assign to have and to hold as her proper lawful right and inheritance forever without any condition." This father went to exorbitant lengths of verbiage to guarantee his daughter's ownership independent of her husband. Widows also found a means of maintaining their own property upon remarriage. The procedure was a legally binding premarital contract, such as a Plymouth document dated 1667, guaranteeing the bride's right to "enjoy all her house and lands, goods and cattle that she is now possessed of, to her own proper use to dispose of them at her own free will from time to time and at any time as she shall see cause."[19]

The routine legal practices of the colonies granted other concessions to women. Numerous deeds were not only signed by wives as well as husbands but were studded with such clauses as "with the full and free consent of my wife," or the "free and voluntary consent of my wife." Married women also retained control of the dowries with which they entered their husbands' households, and courts were careful to investigate any transaction made by husbands that might abrogate this right. In some colonies women were "privately examined" to ensure that they had not been coerced into surrendering dower. Finally, in Virginia and New York, as well as Massachusetts Bay, women were routinely made the executrices of their husbands' estates, indicating widespread confidence in the colonial woman's aptitude for economic management. These generous concessions and bequests to women cannot be dismissed simply as the gestures of southern gentlemen or loving Puritan fathers. Rather, they were the self-interested acts of farm managers who were cognizant of the economic prowess of their wives and daughters. As we shall see, every farmer knew full well that he would not prosper without the ready cooperation of the females in his household. These little rewards and acts of recognition were necessary to ensure the continuous assistance of the female helpmeet.

Any immigrant to the New World (whatever his foreseeable occupation) was wisely advised to acquire a working female partner.

An advertisement for hired employment on a southern plantation, for example, was addressed to "a right good Overseer, having a wife."[20] In the first days and months of settlement, woman's contribution was even more elementary than this. As soon as the Pilgrims landed, by William Bradford's account, "The women now went willingly into the fields and took their little ones with them to set corn." In this respect the settlers followed an old tradition of the Western Hemisphere, where Indian women performed the bulk of the agricultural labor. At the initial stage of settlement, when the home existed only as a primitive hut or cavern dug from earth, no woman's work could be confined to the niceties of housekeeping. Once the first crop had been harvested, however, women were exempted from most field labor and employed around the newly-built cabin. Then custom decreed that only "those wenches that are not fit to be so employed were put into the ground."[21] These "wenches" included female immigrants from Africa whose exile to the fields signaled their swift descent from servitude to slavery.

Confinement to the household, on the other hand, was no mere courtesy to white womanhood. This demarcation of the separate spheres of the two sexes constituted a utilitarian division of labor into equal parcels of essential duties and responsibilities. The economic places of men and women were contiguous; one largely out of doors and in the fields, the other in the home plot and the house. These two imprecise divisions converged in one economic unit, the agrarian household where male and female labor commingled in the integral productive enterprise that ensured survival. It might be said that the male's duty was to procure the family's sustenance, while the female's charge was to prepare these supplies for household use, yet neither sex could be excluded from the process of "work," "providing," or "support." The household economy of the seventeenth century, at a time when 90 percent of the colonial population was employed in agricultural pursuits, would have been crippled without the labor of women. It was this basic economic law of preindustrial America that conferred a woman's tenuous property rights as well as her title Adam's Rib.

The woman's side of the economic partnership included but also transcended the obligation to maintain the home. The single task of feeding the family entailed not only cooking, but also the cultivation, processing, and manufacture of food products. It was the wife's duty, with the assistance of daughters, womenservants, and neighbors, to plant the vegetable garden, breed the poultry, and care for the dairy cattle. She transformed milk into butter and cheese and butchered livestock in addition to presiding over the kitchen. Along with these daily chores, husbandwomen salted, pickled, preserved, and manufactured enough beer and cider to see the village through the winter.

Still, the woman's work was hardly done. To clothe the colonial population, women not only plied the needle, but operated wool carders and spinning wheels and participated in the manufacture of thread, yarn, and cloth as well as apparel. Her handwrought candles lit the house; medicines of her own manufacture restored her family to health; her homemade soap cleansed her home and family. Wives of artisans and small merchants assumed these same responsibilities in the homes, garden plots, and dairies of towns and villages. Rare was the woman who could disengage herself from these productive enterprises. Even Mrs. Philip Schuyler, mistress of a New Netherlands manor, could be found working in her dairy and poultry house, or sewing garments for her extensive family and many servants.[22] Wives of Southern planters were not ladies of leisure but the administrators and suppliers of the slave household. Prospective female settlers in the American colonies could contemplate the active life described in a Pennsylvania advertisement of the eighteenth century: "raising small stock, dairying, marketing, combing, carding, spinning, knitting, sewing, pickling, preserving, etc."[23] The women on seventeenth-century farms not only kept house but practiced a score of trades in a household economy.

These economic responsibilities constituted more than a sum of menial chores. Rather, they created the office of female household manager. The mistress of the household organized and supervised an economic system, allocating labor to children and servants, overseeing the home production that supplied the basic needs of the colonial population. On occasion women could receive reimbursement for social services performed within the home, among them, the housing of boarders or caring for the sick, orphaned, and poor of the town.

No unit of economic production, however, can be perfectly self-sufficient. The early American home economy was not an ironclad fortress, for there were times when every farm family was forced to procure a few necessities from outsiders. When, for example, the home factory produced an excess of soap and was undersupplied with eggs, an exchange with another household was in order. In such situations the colonial woman would routinely barter the products of her labor on the neighborhood market. These simple exchanges find illustration even in the letters written to Margaret Winthrop, a governor's wife: "By Mrs. Pestor I beged garlick and sage and to borrow a gander, I have three gooses and not a husband for them, which lost me at least 40 eggs last year." Few colonial families possessed all the tools and equipment—spinning wheels, churns, candle molds, etc.—or had a large enough labor force, to enable them to complete all the productive tasks traditionally assigned to women. Accordingly, the process of domestic production spanned households and linked women together in a larger network of exchanging goods, services and labor.[24]

These commonplace domestic details suggest the female roles of manager, producer, and trader, which regularly took women outside the home into the sphere of economic distribution. The women traders of New Amsterdam bartered at a frenzied pace, exchanging a seemingly inexhaustible supply of commodities— pens, tubs, brandy, garments, cows—incurring debts, and producing conflicts at almost every turn. Without the walls of the household, women peddled their skills as well as their products. An active colonial economist named Susan Helline is found suing for lack of payment for twelve hens as well as "her paynes and tyme in looking to John Major's wife tyme she did lay in child birth." The Virginia court swiftly awarded the midwife a settlement.[25] The colonial woman's role in economic distribution was second nature to Mrs. Mary Rowlandson. Not even Indian captivity could suppress her trading instinct, as she bartered well-knit stockings and her supply of tobacco for religious privileges and domestic amenities. Mrs. Rowlandson saw her release from captivity as a beneficent act of God. "As he wounded me with one hand so he healed me with the other." The irreverent modern observer, nonetheless, cannot help but attribute her survival in part to the acumen of the trading woman of the seventeenth century.[26]

Not all the female enterprises of the era transpired under the supervision of husbands and fathers. Many New England girls served an economic apprenticeship as indentured servants, bound out until the age of eighteen when their labors were then rewarded with a few acres, some clothes, or a few coins. Some women acquired a trade in the course of servitude as well. Susan Warner of Providence, for one, was promised such training in "the art and mistery of a tailor whereby she might attain to the knowledge of that trade so as to do and perform it."[27] Although colonial practice frowned upon the unmarried, and commonly placed bachelors and spinsters within a patriarchal household, it did not restrain single women from gainful employment. The Massachusetts law regulating single persons stipulated that "This act shall not be construed to the extent to hinder any single woman of good repute from the exercise of any lawful trade, employment for a livelihood hereunto and it shall have the allowance and approbation of the selectmen . . . any law, usage or custom to the contrary not withstanding." The selectmen of Massachusetts had many occasions to make this clause operative. In 1690, for example, town officers of Boston consented to the request of more than thirty women, married and single, to saw lumber and manufacture potash. Elsewhere in New England women collectively removed such labors as slaughtering and flour processing from the household.[28]

At least one New England woman fled the Puritan commonwealth entirely in pursuit of economic independence. Called before the court of New Amsterdam and asked "has she a husband and where?" Elizabeth Kay replied "Yes She has a husband at Boston being a Barber and she left him because it was more economic to do so. Her husband's hand shakes so he cannot follow his trade."[29] The economic independence that resonated in Elizabeth Kay's speech before the court testifies to the capacity of colonial women to separate themselves from husbands and fathers and stand alone, detached from Adam.

Still, such women were exceptional. The infrequent appearances of female names in the records of colonial economic transactions were only minor blemishes on the overall pattern of male dominance. Even the raucous female traders of New Amsterdam performed in the shadow of more extensive and lucrative male enterprises. The women who intruded into the probate courts were predominantly widows, heiresses of great estates, exceptional spinsters, or eccentric troublemakers. Such rare women, nonetheless, demonstrated the potentiality of countless numbers of nameless women, whose economic power remained obscured by the patriarchal dominance of husbands and fathers. Most women would live out their lives as silent partners in the household economy, productively active, essential to the family's survival, and free to barter their surplus goods, but denied ultimate control of the basic commodity of preindustrial society—the land—and unfamiliar with the institutions of ultimate economic authority—the courthouse, the land office, the public markets. Yet colonial daughters, mothers, and wives were unlikely to feel useless or alienated from their labors. The subsistence economy did not eviscerate the female personality by inhibiting women from dealing directly with the material world and battling with nature to serve human needs.

This basic practical value of female labor served as the economic foundation for the seventeenth-century image of woman. It was acknowledged in every major treatise on womanhood in early America. Benjamin Wadsworth's advice for the "Well-Ordered Family" plotted this sexual division of labor: "The husband should endeavor that his wife may have food and raiment suitable for her. He should contrive prudently and work diligently that his family and his wife particularly may be well provided for. The wife also in her place should do what she can that the man has a comfortable support." Cotton Mather scolded all Puritans with the reminder that "sloth and idleness in husband or wife are sinful and shameful." When Mather's theology veered dangerously close to the capitalist ethic, his doctrine embraced women as well as men. He described the virtuous woman as one "who takes a most laudable course for her own temporal prosperity. She is to be praised as a woman that effectively layes up for herself a competent and convenient portion of worldly comfort."

In the sphere of economics, these colonial spokesmen defined sex roles that often blurred the distinction between men and women. Wadsworth foisted the role of helpmeet on both wife and husband, and William Secker went so far as to inform his male parishioners that "the woman is a parallel Line drawn equal with him." The few early Americans who had the time and capacity to make cultural pronouncements on the relations of the sexes simply articulated economic roles already rooted in the primitive economic organization of the New World.[30]

THE SOCIAL DIMENSIONS OF EARLY AMERICAN WOMANHOOD

This is not to say that American colonists were merely pawns of economic necessity nor intent upon the crass and single-minded pursuit of material gain. The economic activities of colonial Americans transpired within a dense social network and were constantly mediated by the values of the community. Economic behavior was scrutinized by both the church and town meeting, and production was contained within the social institution of the family. In the seventeenth-century scheme of social organization, church, town, and colony were no more than congregants of households. The colonial population collected in scattered family nuclei to practice religion, implement political decisions, and maintain social order. It was within these "Little Commonwealths," as John Demos has maintained, that colonial society took form. Without the participation of the female sex, needless to say, the construction of this all-important social and economic unit was impossible.

Colonial leaders had these social imperatives in mind as they hectically recruited female immigrants. Lord Baltimore of His Majesty's Council for Virginia requested a supply of women to be sent to the New World for "when the plantation grows to strength, then it is time to plant with women as well as with men; that the plantation may spread into generations, and not ever be pierced from without." Sir Edwin Sandys implemented this policy in Virginia when in 1619 he ordered one hundred women from England and offered them to prospective husbands along with the additional matrimonial incentive of 120 pounds of the best leaf tobacco. Sandys reasoned that the presence of women in Virginia "would make the men more settled and less moveable, who by defect thereof as it is credibly reported, stay there but to get something and then return to England."[31] The calculations of Lord Baltimore and Governor Sandys rested on more than the procreative powers of women or simple clichés about the conservative essence of femininity. They recruited women in order to foster the family organization that alone would firmly attach settlers to the colony and provide the social stability in which colonial civilization could take root.

Their goals were not, however, swiftly achieved. Throughout the seventeenth century, male immigrants to the Chesapeake colonies outnumbered women three to one. This unbalanced sex ratio combined with an exceedingly high death rate to further reduce the number of settlers who would marry and rear families. Through most of the seventeenth century, therefore, the population of Virginia and Maryland consisted largely of single men. Southerners did not even mate enough to reproduce themselves until the first decade of the eighteenth century. Immigrants from Africa were even slower to form families, because the slave merchants of the seventeenth century captured males in great excess of females. The female immigrants to the South, despite their rarity and presumed high value as wives, were also late to wed. Most arrived in the colonies at a relatively late age for single women and then were prohibited from marrying until they had completed their indenture. The servant women of the South lived in highly precarious social circumstances. American folklore harbors their songs of weary protest, and court records abound with reports of their masters' abuse. One in five of them was apt to bear a bastard and suffer the consequences of her sexual transgressions at the whipping post and in an extension of her term of service. A similar proportion of the women pioneers of the South would die before they reached the age of thirty. Those who survived and married were likely to witness the death of a husband and several children. In the South, then, a very unstable and truncated family system formed an amorphous social context of womanhood.[32]

Women in the other colonies were far more likely to work out their roles and status within the relations of the family. The Dutch General Court and Council of New Netherlands took pains to escort its population into legitimate families, ruling that "no male and female shall be allowed to keep house together like man and wife before they have legally been married, under a fine of 100 florins or as much or more or less than their position admits."[33] New England bachelors and spinsters were swiftly placed within an established household by order of the local court, and Massachusetts Bay colony went so far as to organize unmarried arrivals into makeshift family units. Demographic conditions were also conducive to the formation of stable families in the North. The typical woman in the northern colonies probably lived well into her fifties, having spent more than thirty years married and rearing children. In New England especially, men and women alike were promptly and securely placed in the nexus of colonial social life, the family.[34]

Once situated at the center of local society, women were delegated a whole panoply of social functions, which were far more extensive than the private family services connoted by the term "housework." Women's parental duties, first of all, extended to servants and apprentices in perhaps one-third of all colonial families. Husbands and wives were advised "always remember, that my servants are in some sort my children. In a care, that they may want nothing that be good for them, I would make them as my children.

And, as for the methods of instilling piety which I use with my children, may be properly and prudently used with them."[35] The mistress of the household was thereby employed in an extensive task of socialization, conducting the training, disciplining, education, and acculturation of the next generation, her servants as well as her own offspring. Should the marital partnership be broken by the death of her husband, the colonial woman would be solely responsible for the servants and children and would be held to account for her performance of a master's duties. Widows were often brought to court for breach of indenture contracts, for failing to instill morality and religion in their charges, or to pay fines for the antisocial acts of their servants.

Within the microcosmic society of the colonial household, women did service as welfare workers as well as socializers. Town officers, vestrymen, and justices of the peace sent widows, orphans, the poor, and even criminals into respectable homes for care and rehabilitation, thereby conferring on many colonial dames the roles of custodian, caretaker, and jailor. The town records of Worcester, Massachusetts, are replete with examples of these female functions. In 1779, for example, Catharine Segar was acknowledged to have nursed "a mulatto child, one of the poor of the town"; Lydia Taylor nursed and boarded an entire family. Another woman of Worcester named Martha Wiley cared for a poor sick woman for a period of years and received more than 100 pounds from the town purse for her efforts.[36]

Not even the generous spaces of the colonial household set limits on the social range of Adam's Rib. Anne Bradstreet's poetic eulogy to her mother, for example, did not stop with an accounting of household roles—"The Worthy Matron," "loving mother," "instructor of her family"—but went on to praise her as "A friendly neighbor" who "The public meeting ever did frequent." In northern New England during the first century of settlement, the circuit of women's sociability extended not just to the church but through a regular round of neighborly visits, a village trade route, and frequent opportunities for shared work such as quilting bees. In New England the dense pattern of settlement around the village meetinghouse and commons put women in easy reach of one another. While the scattered settlement patterns and scarce churches in other regions may have created isolation for farmers' wives, women in all the colonies were spared the injunction to retreat demurely behind domestic curtains.[37]

The far-reaching social obligations of a colonial woman undoubtedly left an imprint on her personality. Although women's position at the center of the little commonwealth rendered privacy and the luxury of solitude almost impossible, it also banished loneliness, claustrophobia, and insulation from the essential operations of society. In the social sphere, as well as in matters of economics, the women of the seventeenth century enjoyed integral participation in community life.

Despite her basic role and functions, however, the social status of woman, her power and prestige in the community, derived from and was inferior to that of the patriarchal head of her household. Woman's vow to obey her spouse was repeatedly underscored by colonial writers and preachers. She owed her mate "reverent subjection" and was obliged to submit to his superior judgment in all things. New England clergymen referred to male authority as a "government" that the female must accept as "law," while Southern husbands, such as William Byrd of Virginia, charged assertive wives with "impertinence." Not only were women obliged to scrupulously abide by the lawful commands of patriarchs, but they were "still subject even to those who are sinful and unkind."[38]

These norms should not be construed as a simple license for male tyranny or as a categorical endorsement of patriarchal domination. They cannot be detached from the larger ideological context, which viewed the whole of society as an intricate series of ranks, a profusion of finely graded positions of authority and subordination, which neither male nor female could circumvent. No individual, of either sex, could presume to be one among equals in the seventeenth-century community. The enforcement of inequality extended even to stipulating the appropriate apparel for members of different social strata. At best, colonial Americans, male as well as female, could hope for occasional opportunities to excel as well as defer, to dictate as well as submit.

Within the church, all parishioners were subservient to the minister and found their destined place somewhere within the hierarchy of elders, deacons, and the general congregation, whose pews were in turn assigned according to their relative wealth and godliness. Outside the church this hierarchy was dismantled, only to be replaced by yet another clearly defined scale of authority and subordination. In the New England town meeting or southern courthouse the minister might be reduced to submission before magistrates and justices, while all the members of the community were again arranged into precise ranks according to their property and prestige. This complex status system prompted seventeenth-century Americans to speak not of equality but of relative inequality. The word "relative" was used by the American colonist to designate these multiple scales of authority of which the family order was but one example. Within the household, the ranks descended from the patriarchal father to his wife (the mistress of the household), and on to the children and then to servants and any other non-kinsmen who resided in the home.

Thus woman's social place varied with her position in the family. Should she be the mistress of the household, her relative inequality would dictate submission to her husband and authority over her offspring and servants. Were she a widow, she took possession of ultimate power within the little commonwealth. Within this hierarchical *Weltanschauung* of the seventeenth century, inequality was not the peculiar stigma of womanhood, but rather a social expectation for both sexes. A Boston publication dated 1726 spelled out the logic of inequality in no uncertain terms: "Of all the orders of which are unequal [husbands and wives are] nearest to Equality and in several respects they stand on equal ground. These two make a pair which infers so far a parity."[39]

These lines of authority were deemed essential to the efficient operation of the colonial household, a hub of crucial social and economic activities that sheltered a large number of individuals. The submission of wife to husband was designed to ward off internecine household conflict. It was said that in the home "differences will arise and be seen so the one must give way and apply to the other; this God and nature layeth upon the women rather than upon the men."[40] Yet seventeenth-century commentators eschewed the tyrannical exercise of patriarchal authority. Every treatise on household organization cautioned against dictatorial male rule. While Benjamin Wadsworth acknowledged the husband was "the Head on whom chief respect and honor is to be put," he quickly added, "and as wives should honor and reverence their Husbands; so husbands should put respect upon their Wives too. Though the wife is the weaker vessel, yet honor is to be put upon her in her station."

Cotton Mather explained the expedience of this deference to inferiors: "For husbands owe mutual duties to their wives and parents to their children. Now if husbands and parents violate their obligations, if parents conduct themselves with discouraging severity and fastidious moroseness toward their children whom they are forbidden to provoke to wrath, if husbands vex and despise their wives, whom they are commanded to love and to spare as the weaker vessels; does it not follow, children shall be less obedient to their parents and wives will rebel against their husbands?" The majority of American fathers and husbands, including those far beyond the hearing of Cotton Mather, were most likely shrewd enough to mitigate their authority in their daily dealings with those female partners whose cooperation was so essential to the well-being of the household.

Should the colonial man be so foolhardy as to deal brutally with his wife, daughters, or female servants, colonial courts would intervene in woman's behalf. Massachusetts law stipulated that "evere marreyed woman shall be free from bodily correction or stripes by her husband unless it is his own defense upon her assault. If there be any just cause of correction, complaint shall be made to authorities assembled in some court from which only she shall receive it." Throughout the colonies women took frequent advantage of this recourse, appearing before the court to complain of their husbands' abuses. The repeated mistreatment of a New Amsterdam woman prompted the court to bar her husband from the home entirely. The judges summarily announced that this disreputable spouse was to "deliver the hay to his wife's house and not to presume to come molest her in any way."[41]

Female children were also allowed access to the court to escape the abuses of their fathers. Such a case in Virginia read as follows: "Elizabeth Campbell complains of her father William Campbell, that he does not provide for her and the other children — to be summoned."[42] Womenservants made use of this same privilege, appearing before the courts to ask remedy for the misconduct of their masters or demand fulfillment of the codicils of their indenture contracts. In Virginia orphaned women, some as young as fourteen, were granted the right to select their own guardians, that is, to choose for themselves a congenial patriarch.[43] In Virginia the exercise of patriarchal authority was especially weak. The family itself was so unstable and ephemeral an institution, given the peculiar demography of the South, that fathers had a very shaky base from which to exercise their prerogatives.

In New England, on the other hand, Puritan theology worked to mitigate the domestic despotism of patriarchy. Puritan divines sternly admonished the New England wife never to make an idol of her male superior: "While she looks upon [her husband] as her guide by the constitution of God, she will not scrupple with Sarah to call him the Lord, and though she does not fear his blows she does fear his frowns, being loathe in anything to grieve him."[44] Furthermore, since woman's obligation to honor and comfort her husband was clearly designed to ensure order in the social unit of the family, it emanated more from practical social necessity than from a belief in the innate inferiority of women per se. For example, Benjamin Wadsworth could write as follows: "Yea, 'tho possibly thou hast greater abilities of mind than he has, art of some high birth, and he of a more mean extract, or didst bring more Estate at Marriage than he did; yet since he is thy Husband God had made him thy head and set him above thee and made it thy duty to love and reverence him."[45] Any male or female in Wadsworth's congregation was instructed to accept such orders of an arbitrary God with little question and without detriment to his or her individual self-esteem. At any rate, a woman's sense of self-worth found solid confirmation day in and day out as her labors contributed to the prosperity of her family and the good order of society.

THE PRIVATE LIVES
OF COLONIAL WOMEN

It is difficult to disentangle an exclusively female side of colonial life from this wide and dense web of social and economic relations. The roles of wife, mother, daughter, were not confined within a feminine sanctum during the first century of settlement and illuminated by a spotlight of acute gender consciousness. The domestic experience of colonial women is almost inaccessible to the historian and leaves a trace primarily in the prescriptive literature penned by a few spokesmen for colonial culture, almost all of them Puritan ministers. As these men were responsible for the few formal postulates on the order of the sexes that colonial men and women would chance to hear, they are worth analyzing. Furthermore, the tenets circulated by New England ministers were designed to suit the everyday social and economic roles of colonial women, and hence they reflect, however obliquely, the actual practice of the mistresses of well-ordered families.

Literature written in early America rarely singled out female or domestic themes for special attention. Therefore, the account of the female life cycle that follows is necessarily sketchy. Cotton Mather directed his Puritan flock to rejoice in the birth of a child of either sex, dissociating New Englanders from the invidious distinctions between boys and girls found in English folklore. Colonial parents did not resort to pink or blue ribbons to announce the sex of the newborn. Indeed, it was not until children reached the age of five or six that they discarded infant gowns to don the pantaloons and skirts that differentiated boys from girls. At this tender age the female child would take her place alongside her mother and sisters as an apprentice in home economy. According to Cotton Mather, the girl's training would include, in addition to the practice of housewifery, needlework, and cooking, such accomplishments relating to household business as arithmetic and bookkeeping. This education would often occur outside the parental home.

In Puritan England as many as three of four women were put out to service in their early teens. The rate of servitude could not have been much lower in New England where, according to a census dated 1689, one in three households contained servants, a ratio that would accommodate a large proportion of the women in those youthful age groups when service was common.[46] Thus women's ties to their immediate kin, including their own mothers, were often broken early in the life cycle, quickly introducing females to a larger, more social than domestic, world.

While a girl was trained for the economic specialties of the household, she was not necessarily socialized to femininity. The colonial library was not stocked with books exclusively for women. The rare treatise on women and for women, such as Cotton Mather's *Ornaments of the Daughters of Zion*, held in disrepute those traits of character that are often characterized as feminine. At the outset, Mather announced that "Favor is deceitful and Beauty is Vain." He went on to describe the physical attributes of the beautiful woman in the most rudimentary terms, "proportion and symmetry of the parts, skin well varnished . . . Harmoniousness of Countenance." This meager catalogue of female attractions did not offer the colonial woman much opportunity for the scrutiny and cultivation of her appearance. Puritan culture forbade any artificial embellishment of her features and colonial sumptuary laws denied most women even such simple adornments as a wedding band and a bit of lace on their Sunday dresses. Furthermore, any attire that encumbered the operations of the home economy was patently offensive: "For a woman to put herself into a Fashion that shall prejudice either her Health or her Work is to break all the commandments."[47]

Those segments of the colonial population that succumbed to the corrupting influence of English fashion were not composed exclusively of women. Ministers in thriving seaboard towns lamented "the manifest pride openly appearing among us in that long hair like women's hair is worn by some, or even their own hair made into periwigs, and by some women wearing bodies of hair and then the cutting, curling and laying on of hair."[48] Both sexes should beware of the vanities of beauty and fashion and women in particular were enjoined to refrain from using such wiles to captivate the gullible male. The Daughters of Zion were cautioned against deceiving "unwary men into those amours which beguiling looks and smiles do often betray the children of men."[49]

Colonial culture granted little expression of the "feminine" preoccupations of beauty, fashion, and flirtation, as might be expected in a social system where such frivolities had no functional purpose and at a time when looking glasses were luxuries possessed by only a tiny minority of families. A woman, even with a well-stocked arsenal of endearing looks and manners, could not single-handedly capture a husband. The New England girl was repeatedly discouraged from musing about her marital future. Cotton Mather advised the American girl that if God ordained her to be a spinster, "she makes the *Single State* a *Blessed One* by improving her leisures from the Encumbrances of a family in caring for the things of the Lord."[50] Although such an eventuality was to be lamented ("For a Woman to be Praised is for her to be Married"), young women were not to presume to take the selection of a spouse into their own hands. Their marriages were subject not only to the approval of parents but also to the vicissitudes of the colonial economy. Only when the local pool of land resources could provide sustenance for a new family could a young man turn his attention to courtship. Even then, the woman's parents would conduct the economic negotiations pursuant to matrimony, and the amount of dower they could offer a prospective bridegroom would weigh heavily in the outcome. Parents tended to time marriages according to the ages rather than the personal predilections of their daughters, arranging the wedding of their eldest first, followed by her siblings in a precise age sequence.[51]

Young men and women would, of course, have some freedom to conduct informal courtships. (Walking home from church services was an opportune occasion to explore their attraction to one another.) Young men were advised to "choose by Ears, as well as Eyes," paying particular attention to a woman's potential for practical household service.[52] Her orderliness, sobriety, manufacturing skills, should overshadow the soft graces of feminine appearance and decorum. The proper emotional tie between the affianced was described as a tendency to affection and sympathy, which was likely to blossom into conjugal love after their marriage. Accordingly, the young women of New England were not encouraged to cultivate the general sentiment of heterosexual love. Even after the colonial woman had soberly maneuvered through the complicated procedures of courtship, she might have her choice of a marriage partner overruled by the court. Such was the fate of Abigail Silbey of Providence, barred from marrying one Thomas Cooper who, according to the town fathers, had already "forsaken a sober wife, and may do the same to this one."[53]

The thoughts of the women who traversed the maze of courtship are by and large irretrievable from the colonial past. We do get a brief look at one woman's reaction to her suitor, however, in the diary of Samuel Sewell. Sewell plied a widow named Winthrop with such sweet talk as the declaration that her kisses were "better than the best canary." When she remained opposed to the match he tried another tack, telling her, "I loved her and was fond to think that she loved me and she might do some good to help support me." Still Mrs. Winthrop preferred her independence and refused to "leave her house, children, neighbors and business."[54] The prosperous widow proved a very difficult catch indeed. A New York woman was similarly insensitive to the nuances of courtship: "I am sick of all this choosing. If a man is healthy and does not drink and had a good little handful of stock and a good temper and is a good Christian, what difference can it make to a woman which man she takes. There is not so much difference between one man and another." The New York *Post* observed a less calculating attitude toward marriage among the lower classes of the city, who "couple from a hearty good liking and oftenest with a mutual good disposition in all things."[55] Even this is a relatively dispassionate attachment between a bride and groom. It would suggest that the young women of the colonial era devoted little of their psychic energies to falling in love. Certainly they had neither the time, the incentive, nor the socialization to cultivate the extravagant sentiments of romance.

Young women could not, at the same time, elude confronting questions of sexuality. No daughter lodged in the crowded quarters of the colonial household, where every available space became a collective bedroom, could remain ignorant of the facts of life. Female servants were in an especially vulnerable position. Many a young woman came to court suing her master for support of her bastard child, or accusing a fellow servant of seduction. The illegitimacy rate was particularly high among the servants of the Chesapeake colonies. For the northern colonies, the most reliable evidence of premarital sexual relations is found in church records, which recorded births that occurred within eight months of marriage. In the seventeenth century less than 10 percent of the first births to New England couples were of this nature. Even then, these children were conceived after their parents had announced their marriage banns and after many years of rigid sexual control. Women in simple agricultural communities similar to seventeenth-century American settlements checked their sexual impulses more out of economic expedience and fear of social reprisals than out of prudishness. Many of those women who bore children out of wedlock, for example, demanded that their sex partners promise to support any child that might result from their union.[56]

Despite such sexual prudence, nearly every town held within it at least one woman who displayed a more defiant and irrepressible sex drive. One New Amsterdam woman allegedly "ran along the road with a can of wine one evening" and took a strange man as her sexual prey.[57] A Virginia woman seduced her partner in an open field with such delightful consequences that she pledged she "would give him as much cloth as would make him a sheet." (Here we have yet another use made of a woman's skill at manufacture and barter.)[58] Yet women also appear, and probably more frequently, as the victims of predatory males. Elizabeth Dickerman of Middlesex, Massachusetts, suffered such abuse by her master, John

Harris. "After forcing her to be naught with him," Harris told Elizabeth Dickerman that "if she told her dame what carriage he did show to her shee had as good be hanged." Another resident of Middlesex County displayed the crassest form of male sexuality: "He flung the mayd downe in the street and got atop her." Not even the godly commonwealth of Massachusetts Bay could eradicate the crime of rape. Another servant woman reported that her master "caught me by the wrist and pulled me on side of my bed," resulting in the birth of a bastard child. While the charges of rape were quite rare in New England courts, they were treated seriously, leading to executions in at least six cases.[59]

Women would pay the greater price for illicit sex, pregnancy, and childbirth. Colonial society redoubled her burden by heaping shame and punishment upon the unwed mother. For simple fornication, male and female commonly were awarded equal fines and an equivalent number of lashes. Occasionally a local court would take into consideration special factors in its distribution of punishment. Such an example is the case of John Littell, made to "lay neck and hyels close for three hours" and fined five shillings for fornication with Ellen Muce, who "not approvinge the same," was only whipped.[60] Fornication itself was equally offensive in male and female, but when biology fated the woman to bear a bastard child the scales of justice lost their balance. In Worcester, where both parties to the act of fornication were fined fifty shillings, the charge of giving birth to a bastard child brought a five-pound fine and ten stripes.[61] Although the father of the child was obliged to support his offspring and share in the mother's punishment, he often escaped the court's notice. Even the gruesome custom of browbeating a woman in labor to reveal the name of her child's father often failed to establish the bastard's lineage. Thus women often stood alone before colonial courts, suffering the lash in solitude, carrying a child without the aid of an economic partner. Under threat of such dire consequences, most colonial women deferred sexual gratification until after marriage.

The typical age at marriage varied somewhat over time and in the different colonies. In New England through most of the seventeenth century, women tended to marry in their early to mid-twenties. In the Chesapeake colonies during the first years of settlement, marriage occurred a few years later, largely due to the relatively advanced ages of the migrants and their extended indenture contracts, which prohibited marriage. Only in the South after 1680 did women wed at the young age so often ascribed to early America. When the daughters of southern migrants grew up in the late seventeenth century, they were not inhibited by indenture and were still surrounded by large numbers of recently arrived and eligible males. In some Maryland counties they became brides at the median age of seventeen.[62] For most of the seventeenth century, however, and especially in the North, women would not begin their marital and sexual lives until they were quite mature and well-prepared to assume the responsibilities of the mistress of a household.

Marriage would occasion only a brief celebration and then, without benefit of a honeymoon, the bride would assume the direction of her own household economy. The exclusively private and domestic function of the colonial wife cannot be easily separated from the more wide-ranging economic and social duties performed within her household. Still, the rudiments of bourgeois ideology had crossed the Atlantic with the colonists and thus transmitted to the New World the Puritan's heightened respect not only for private property, but also for the conjugal relationship that enclosed it. Colonial culture paid special regard to the bonds of matrimony and their incumbent responsibilities, the first of which was to dwell together as husband and wife and to exclude all others from their sexual union. Puritans readily acknowledged the sexual needs of women, whose "intemperate longings" the husband was duty-bound to gratify. When a husband failed to meet his wife's sexual needs, be it because of impotence or willful denial, a marriage could be dissolved. When one resident of Middlesex County refused to engage in intercourse with his wife for a period of two years, he was excommunicated from the church.[63]

The husbands and wives of the colonial era did not recod for posterity the details of their sex lives. Voyeurs and family historians can get only a glimpse of the sexual behavior of past times as it was occasionally reflected in public records and literary accounts. These sources do indicate that seventeenth-century colonists, and even the Puritans, cannot be summarily dismissed as prudes and must not be confused with Victorians. The first European settlers in the New World were more likely to recall the robust and playful sexuality of the Elizabethan Age. According to Elizabethan folklore, moreover, women were the more lustful sex, endowed, some thought, with nearly insatiable sexual appetites. Experienced widowed women were considered particularly ardent (one proverb recommended, "He who wooeth a widow must go stiff before"). These notions found their way to the New World, carried there by the likes of Thomas Morton, renowned for cavorting with Indian maidens around the Maypole of Marymount. Morton hoped to make an international business of such hedonism. He wrote to London advertising the use of beaver skins as an aphrodisiac. The pelts were "of such masculine virtue," Morton promised, "that if some of our ladies knew the benefit thereof, they would desire to have ships sent of purpose to trade for the tail alone."[64]

Although the New England Puritans were considerably more straitlaced than this, and indeed banished Thomas Morton from their colony, they did allow for restrained and even joyous sensuality within matrimony. As Benjamin Wadsworth put it in a treatise on the "Well-Ordered Family," a Puritan could guiltlessly "rejoice with the wife of thy youth. Let her breast satisfy thee at all times. And be always ravished with her love." The wife's own title to sexual pleasure remained somewhat ambiguous. Adultery and fornication trials, which often contain explicit descriptions of the sex act, suggest that the sexual behavior of the American male was not calculated to give women the maximum pleasure. Intercourse took place in an abrupt, perfunctory fashion: the male either lying atop the female or pressing against her as she leaned on a gate or wall. At the same time there is some indication, especially among the Puritans, with their special reverence of conjugal relations, that women's sensual needs were treated with greater sensitivity within marriage. Benjamin Wadsworth presented the ideal marital relation this way: "The wife hath not power of her body, but the husband. And likewise also the husband hath not power of his body but the wife; Defraud not the other that Satan tempt you to inconstancy." These reciprocal clauses, addressed one to the man and one to the woman, imply a sense of mutuality rather than male dominance in matters sexual.[65]

Wadsworth and all his peers, however, had no tolerance for "inconstancy" or any sexuality outside of marriage. Adultery was punishable by death, a penalty that was exacted perhaps a half-dozen times in the history of the American colonies. More commonly, the offending couple was subjected merely to fines, lashes, or the pillory. Whatever the sanction employed, extramarital sex was in practice deemed more offensive in women than in men. Adultery was defined as sexual congress with a married woman. The married man who committed indiscretions with single women was charged with the lesser offense of fornication. This legal sophistry is understandable if allowance is made for the extensive disruption that would ensue from the birth of another man's child within that all-important institution, the colonial family. Still, the onus of marital infidelity clearly fell on the female sex.

Women fared better in other domestic exchanges, particularly in the understanding that husbands and wives "have a very quiet and tender love and affection to another."[66] The Puritans, in their veneration of the family, elevated conjugal love to a lofty status and assigned it as a duty to husbands and wives alike. Benjamin Wadsworth told the marital couple that "the duty of love is mutual, it should be performed by each to each of them." This sexually balanced conception of love never tilted in the direction of the woman. Love was never accounted one of the peculiar virtues or characteristics of the female sex. If anything, the more loving nature was attributed to colonial men. According to one Puritan divine, "Man is an affectionate creature. Now the woman should be such towards the man as to require his affections by increasing his delectation. That the new blosomed love may not be blasted as soon as it blosomed, a spouse should carry herself to her husband as not to disturb his love by her contention nor to destroy his love by her alienation."[67]

Whatever degrees of emotional attachment husband or wife felt for one another, the duty of love served to undercut the hierarchical structure of the colonial household. Benjamin Wadsworth articulated this phenomenon in this description of the ideal love of a man for his wife: "Though he governs her, he must not treat her as a servant, but as his own flesh, he must love her as himself." Cotton Mather employed such phrases as "One Mind in Two Bodies" to describe the temperamental unity between husband and wife, while William Secker resorted to such glowing images as "two Flowers in one nosegay" and "two candels burning together which makes the house more lightsome."[68] These mystical metaphors of love actually served a very practical social function, for in the absence of loving intercourse between husbands and wives, the household might erupt in "civil war" or become the "most miserable [relation] of any in the world."[69] Maintenance of the little commonwealth required the constant and wholehearted cooperation of husband and wife, for without it, the prosperity and stability of colonial society were jeopardized. The Puritan writers designed the loving communion of husband and wife for this prosaic purpose. A woman's love for her husband, and his in return, became, as a consequence, a "duty," a "performance," not a rarefied emotion. In Wadsworth's "Well-Ordered Family," love took the form of a routine of kindnesses; "delight in each other's company," "be helpful to each other," "bear one anothers burdens," "Unite prudent consuls," "be patient one towards another."[70]

In summary, when early Americans spoke of love they were not withdrawing into a female byway of human experience. Domestic affection, like sex and economics, was not segregated into male and female spheres. Woman's love was expressed in active interchange with her marital partner. It did not precede marriage but grew out of the day-to-day cooperation, sharing, and closeness of the diversified home economy. The reciprocal ideal of conjugal love thrived in the common social and economic sphere where men and women were integrally associated. Conjugal affection was intertwined with the persistent obligations of the household partnership.

One segment of colonial domestic life, however, was reserved purely and exclusively for women—the bearing of children. The reproductive powers of women were cause for boasting in the New World: "Our land free, our men honest and our women fruitful."[71] The Atlantic passage did seem to fructify the wombs of seventeenth-century women, whose fertility far surpassed that of Englishwomen. In the course of her married life, the New England wife bore an average of eight children, and thereby doubled the colonial population every twenty years. Once the demographic conditions of the South stabilized in the first decade of the eighteenth century, the women of the Chesapeake colonies became just as fertile as New England wives.[72]

The experience of Sarah Stearns, wed to Peter Place of Providence in December 1685, illustrates the rigors of colonial reproduction. Sarah Place gave birth to her first child on November 12, 1686; in 1706 she was still engaged in reproduction, bearing an eighth child in June of that year.[73] Like many a colonial wife, Mrs. Place suffered the pains of childbirth eight times and carried a child within her body for six years all told. A child probably suckled at her breast for another eight years, in the prime of her life. As the doctrines of Puritanism were minutely debated, colonies formed, charters suspended, rebellions suppressed, and wars fought, America's women gave their time and stamina to populate the New World. In the first trying century of settlement, when human laborers were desperately needed, the reproductive energies of women assured the survival of the colonies and generated American history.

The prospect of childbirth engendered considerable anxiety in settlements like Plymouth Colony, where it was likely to end the mother's life in one in every thirty cases, thus causing one-fifth of all maternal deaths.[74] Early Americans could not ignore the threatening implications of maternity, which they called a "sentence," a "curse," the "travail of woman." Cotton Mather felt called upon to exhort the colonial woman to submit to the dangers of childbirth: "It will be a very blameable Indecency and Indiscretion in you to be dissatisfied at your state of Pregnancy. . . . It will indeed look too unnatural in you to complain of a state whereunto the Laws of Nature, established by God had brought you." Mather did not see fit to camouflage the dangers of pregnancy by celebrations of the joys of maternity: "The griefs which you are now suffering in your Body are the Fruits of Sin"; "For ought you to know your Death has entered into you."[75] Colonial ministers, in full cognizance of the temptations to abort, recurrently reminded their parishioners that "to purposefully destroy the fruit of the womb is murder."[76] Still, women continued to devise primitive abortion techniques.

As childbirth was one of the few absolutely exclusive female functions in an agrarian society, it also became the occasion for a close female bonding and mutual support. Men were banned from the birth chamber and criminally prosecuted for witnessing parturition or acting as midwives. Thus childbirth became an interlude of female friendship and support in the otherwise sexually mixed social networks that surrounded and penetrated the little commonwealths. Before the husband politely vacated the scene of birth he might summon a score of friends and kinswomen to his wife's side. "Sister Hicks, old Mrs. Knowlton, Mrs. Whipple, Mrs. Hepzibah Maynard, Mrs. Byles and Mrs. Rogers were call'd and brought, and stay'd all Day and Night." Friends such as these would provide physical and emotional support during labor, sometimes holding the pregnant woman upright between them, or allowing her to sit on their laps to ease the birth process. Often they stayed on to celebrate; sometimes "an elegant supper" would be served. Female neighbors, friends, and kin returned often to visit the female sanctum during the new mother's brief respite from household chores.[77]

The conscientious mother would suckle her newborn child, for to employ a wet nurse was judged "very criminal and blameworthy" as well as extravagant when she held a "bottle in her breasts." Carrying the fetus, enduring parturition, and suckling the infant commanded women's attention for large portions of their life span. Statistics available for the eighteenth century indicate that the typical colonial woman could expect to spend some twenty years with an infant under her charge, almost forty years rearing children. These functions decreed by woman's anatomy did not, however, confer upon her a peculiarly feminine nature and temperament. An elaborate mystique of motherhood did not grow up around the time-consuming and oft-repeated physical ordeal of childbearing. The biological intimacy of mother and child did not ordain an instinctive emotional attachment between the two. The first act of a devout mother symbolized detachment from the fruit of her womb: "Give up your New-born Child unto the Lord."[78] A woman of Puritan upbringing could not vainly presume that a child was her private creation and personal possession. Neither was any colonial woman likely to merge her identity with a child torn from her by the pain of parturition and in great danger of infant mortality. Cotton Mather spoke to these uncertainties of motherhood when he asserted that "Children are mere Loans from God which He may call for when he pleases; and [the mother] quietly submits."[79] Puritan preaching and woman's experience united to inhibit the growth of excessive maternal affection.

After infancy, in what was termed the second stage of childhood, defined by Isaac Ambrose as the period "from the time [the child] begins to be of any direction, till it be fit to be placed forth,"[80] a woman relinquished her special ties and exclusive obligations to her progeny. Thereafter, directives regarding childbearing were addressed to parents, not to mothers. Parents were called to the cooperative enterprises of catechizing, training, and laying up property for their offspring. Together they were to "nourish and bring them up," "carefully provide for their outward supply and comfort."[81] The physical care and supervision of a young child might also be placed in the custody of his or her older siblings, servants, or neighbors, rather than the mother, while vocational training would be directed by the parent of the child's own sex or take place outside the family entirely. A child might be judged "fit to be placed forth" as early as six years of age. The father, as legal guardian, could decide the time and conditions of his children's apprenticeship, but most often mothers were parties to these negotiations as well. In the service of the master, the child was removed entirely from any detrimental maternal or paternal indulgence.

Furthermore, mothers as well as fathers could be called before the courts if their child care fell short of community standards. A Virginia widow, Martha Ryan, was summoned for "not bringing up her children in a Christian-like manner."[82] On occasion the court would decide to take a child away from a disreputable mother and place him or her in a more respectable home. Colonial husbands might also specify such a procedure in their wills. Samuel Taylor, for example, bequeathed his land to his wife but stipulated that "my children be put out to learn trades with people who will take care of them." Customarily, however, colonial patriarchs strove to bind their households together after their deaths, as did John Smith of Providence. He willed his land and mill in equal shares to his wife and his eldest son. John Junior's legacy was granted on the condition that "he fayle not to be helpe full to his mother to bring up the rest of his brothers and sisters, some of them being very young." Here an elder son was charged with parental duties, again illustrating the tight-knit social fabric of the colonial household of which motherhood was one integral part, not a single strand.[83] Even the responsibility of parenting extended outside the female role, past the individual household and beyond domesticity.

Most colonial women lived out their lives in a hub of busy household activity with children nearly always underfoot.[84] The death of a worthy matron brought forth community recognition of her life of service. Thomas Sheffield eulogized his wife as follows: "She was a woman of incomparable meekness of spirit, toward myself especially, and very loving, of great prudence to take care for and order my family affairs, being neither too lavish nor sordid in anything, so that I knew not what was under her hand. She had an excellency to reprove for sin, and discern the evil of me. She loved God's people dearly and was studious to profit by their fellowship and therefore loved their company." The eulogies that followed the deaths of the wives of other prominent colonists, such as Margaret Winthrop, echoed these same themes; "she was a woman of singular virtue, modesty and piety, and specially loved and honored in the country."[85] Such testimonials were remarkably free from sentimentality and largely incognizant of the delicate virtues of femininity. While women were praised for meekness, they were acclaimed as well for discerning the weaknesses of their spouses and reproving them for their failures. Although woman's worth encompassed modesty and piety, it rested primarily on the capacity to manage a household economy. She was praised for her love of family but equally honored for loving her neighbors. The accolades of colonial men were placed at the feet of an industrious, productive partner, an efficient mistress of the household, a responsible member of the community.

As the colonial woman functioned alongside the more authoritative male at the heart of the colonial social and economic order, she had little need or opportunity for acquiring and exhibiting a peculiarly feminine personality. Consequently, colonial culture did not take great pains to parcel out a whole series of temperamental attributes according to sex. Women were not endowed with such now-familiar traits as maternal instincts, sexual purity, passivity, tranquillity, or sensitivity. Surely, colonial writers took note of characteristics common to women and observed differences between the sexes, but these were too sparse, muted, and peripheral to the cultural priorities to give shape to a feminine mystique. American folk culture often described women as loose-tongued and of lusty manner, and regarded females with the deep-seated suspicion that could lead even to accusations of witchcraft. Yet the British colonies in North America do not seem to have produced the extreme misogyny whereby English peasants valued their horses more highly than their wives, and parsons compared women to "The dregs of the devil's dunghill."[86] While women were regarded as the "weaker vessels," of lesser mental and physical endowment than men, every seventeenth-century commentator granted women the intellectual capacity to judge and advise the patriarch of the household.

Puritan writers were particularly deferential to women. Cotton Mather openly defended the sex against assaults upon their intelligence. "If any men are so wicked (and some sects of men have been so) as to deny your being rational creatures, the best means to confute them will be proving yourselves religious ones." Mather offered as evidence several models of female genius, leadership, and piety: Hebrew prophets, ancient queens, and contemporary writers. Elsewhere Mather dramatized the fact that women could also be stronger vessels than men in the physical sense, citing as evidence the case of a woman who carried a wounded husband on her back for three hundred miles, and made a heroine of one Hannah Dusten, a frontier wife who held ten Indian scalps to her credit. A casual observer of the colonial household could attest to the strength of women as they routinely lifted heavy caldrons from the fireplace. Accordingly, colonial culture did not delight in calling attention to the delicate frame and petite stature of its women.

Womanly meekness and modesty held larger sway in the colonial image of woman. These retiring qualities had religious origins in the virtue of fear of the Lord: "Favor is deceitful and Beauty is Vain, but a woman that Fears the Lord, she is that shall be praised." The injunction to humbly prostrate oneself before the Almighty and His earthly emissaries in the church, state, and family was basic to social order. Timidity and squeamishness, on the other hand, were inappropriate to the temporal concerns of frontier women, who braved the Atlantic, Indian raids, and hostile forests.[87]

All these ascribed sexual distinctions regarding character, furthermore, were differences of degree, not kind. Meekness was but a species of the general virtue of humility prescribed for both sexes; craving for a fashionable dress was but a female symptom of the vice vanity in personal appearance; the seductiveness of Eve was a sinful weakness that she shared with the lustful Adam. The strengths and failings of women were treated simply as virtues or vices, not as instincts or innate characteristics which God, nature, or hormones had distributed unevenly among the sexes. Colonial men and women were held to a single standard of good behavior and equipped with a will free to perfect the temporal manifestations of their character. In sum, the concepts of masculinity and femininity remained ill-defined in agrarian America. The Christian theology that flourished there celebrated a contrary tenet of scripture: "There is neither Jew nor Greek, Bond nor Free, Male nor Female, for ye all are one in Christ Jesus."[88] Colonial Americans inherited a social and economic structure that was uniquely hospitable to certain aspects of the sexual equality implied by this Christian concept. The agrarian frontier economy kept the sexual division of labor simple and primitive, while the household system of social organization precluded the isolation of women in a private and undervalued sphere. These factors in turn inhibited the cultural gestation of extreme sexual stereotypes. By latter-day standards the differences in personality attributed to males and females were relatively few, a matter of degree rather than kind, and seldom ascribed to sexual biology per se.

WOMEN AND THE PUBLIC SPHERE

It would be an historical error, however, to conclude that the overall status of women during the colonial period was somehow superior to the position of the sex subsequently. Despite the primitive development of gender stereotypes, sexual balance and equity was very rare outside the unit of the household. Benjamin Wadsworth interpreted the phrase "All are one in Christ Jesus" to the effect that "it does not dissolve the Relations between Husbands and Wives, Parents and Children, Masters and Servants, Rulers and Subjects."[89] Within the family, women might on occasion usurp or share the superior relationship, but all the positions of power outside it were open only to males. In the public centers of power—the ministry, the colonial assemblies, the town meetings—men alone could take up the role of "Rulers."

The informal politics of small villages, especially during the early years of settlement, however, may have granted women a significant measure of power in the community. There is at least one report of women voting in an early New England town meeting, while in the frontier South a woman named Mary Musgrove became a kind of general and diplomat. Mistress Margaret Brent assumed the responsibilities, if not the title, of governor during Lord Baltimore's absence from Maryland. Yet once the emergencies of early settlement had subsided, the colonies acted quickly to bar women from formal political activities. The case of Margaret Brent illustrates the carefully drawn boundaries of legitimate female power. After informally acting as agent of the proprietor of the colony and attorney in her own right, Mistress Brent demanded admission to the Maryland Assembly in 1647, denying the legitimacy of "all precedings in the present assembly unless she may be present and have a vote." She came armed with sizable property holdings, lofty social status, connections with the proprietor, and a widely acknowledged administrative ability. Still her petition was denied as simply "beyond her sex." Even as colonial towns became progressively more lenient in granting the vote to men of little property, they adamantly refused citizenship to women with large holdings of taxable land and a major stake in the ordering of society. In Jamaica, New York, at a time when more and more widowed women appeared on the tax lists, town orders were issued with the flagrantly patriarchal salutation "Know all men."[90]

It might be argued that this practice worked to the benefit of colonial women, freeing them from the time-consuming and burdensome duties that colonial citizenship entailed. Yet woman's political losses clearly outweighed her gains. Nearly every New England man who took the time to appear regularly at town meetings was granted some office, be it selectman, constable, or the humble fence viewer. Only by diligently performing in this position could a colonist achieve the community prestige that might lead to a higher office and a larger portion during the next distribution of town land. When women as apolitical beings were freed from the obligation to work periodically on the town road or to assist in the construction of the meetinghouse, they also lost the wholesome opportunity to engage in socially recognized collective labor. Once denied access to the political arena, women not only lost opportunities for social mobility and cooperative social action, but also for education in the procedures of public debate and the orderly resolution of conflict. Women made no direct, forthright contribution to the political consensus so basic to the good order of the agrarian community.

The political deliberations of the townsmen could, however, have a profound impact on women themselves. Town officers ruled on their most private concerns and basic well-being—their land, their taxes, their family affairs. Women appeared regularly before the local courts as plaintiffs and defendants but never sat as judges or jurors or indisputable witnesses. When a woman was brought to trial for murder in Virginia, female witnesses were accompanied by their sons and husbands who "recognized that they appear in court."[91] Women summoned to court for domestic and sexual offenses would confront a body composed of husbands, fathers, and sons. The precarious position of female family heads caused them to make more than their share of appearances before magistrates. Many came begging the court's advice and assistance.

Mary Walling is a good example of the women whose families' futures rested in the hands of the town court. Her husband, Thomas, had "departed the town," leaving her to address the city fathers, humbly desiring them "to take charge of a boy put out to her, the said Mary being unable any longer to take care of him." The judges took this occasion not only to grant her specific request but also to assign one of their number as Mary Walling's guardian, dismantle her property, and lay claim to her livestock.[92] Such were the hazards to which women were liable when they placed their fate in the hands of an all-male political structure.

Single women, especially those with children, were particularly vulnerable to summonses from the courts, for without male partners they were presumed to be in precarious economic circumstances and prone to becoming "chargeable to the town." One Johanna Harrad was called before the deputies of Providence "to see what securitye may be put to clear the Town of what Charges may arise from her. And if none will be put in sufficient Securitye. Then to send her back again to Boston." Johanna Harrad was one of many strangers—men, women, and families—who were asked to post bond before they were granted the right to settle in a town. Local courts were particularly suspicious of strange women and doubly so if they entered the town with children but unaccompanied by a husband. Such women would have great difficulty disputing the magistrates' prejudgment of their indigency or immorality.

Mrs. Hannah Hayman bore the full brunt of such prejudice and was thereby sentenced to the ranks of New England's "strolling poor." She confessed to the Providence deputies that her husband had gone off to sea six months earlier, leaving her to wander from Boston to Dorchester, Dedham, Reston, and finally to Providence. The last town proved no more hospitable than the others. The decision of the court read as follows: "We are willing for our securetye and for ye safety of the woman to take the way as the law directs that shee may be sent from constable to constable to the place of her abode."[93]

The cruel practice of community ostracism was designed to maintain the order and uniformity of the close-knit agrarian community, not to punish the female sex. Yet women were more likely to suffer the consequences of this and many other procedures of the town, further exacerbating their political alienation. Although never a barrister, a selectman, or even a swinekeeper, a woman could expect to become the supplicant, ward, or outcast of the town. At best she was the passive beneficiary of town benevolence, sharing perhaps in a legacy like the one bequeathed to the town of Jamaica to be distributed to the "poor, viz., poor widows and children, persons blind or male or aged that are unable to get their living."[94] Lumped together with the lame, the aged, and children as a town charge, or carefully scrutinized and controlled by the court and town meeting, the political condition of poor, husbandless, and fatherless women was not altogether unlike that of the cows and pigs that strayed through the village. Certainly women and livestock received about equal notice in the records of public discourse in colonial America.

Set apart from the political center of authority, but an equally important public arena in the American colonies, was the church. Here too women were excluded from full participation and high office. Many American colonists shared in the religious heritage of English dissenting sects, from which had sprung such radical dogmas as the religious equality of the sexes. The English Levellers, for example, pronounced that women "by birth have as much natural freedom as any other, and therefore ought not to loose their liberty without their consent."[95] Quaker immigrants to America imbibed this heritage to the extent that they invited women to participate fully in the practices of their congregations. The Quakers' women's meeting carried on a full agenda of church business.

New England Puritans accorded women a moral status equivalent to men and an equal opportunity for salvation, but little more. In Puritan meetinghouses and Anglican churches the hierarchy of the sexes remained intact. Even the offertory procession filed by in a precisely ranked order of the sexes: "The magistrates, and chiefe gentlemen first, and the Elders and all the congregation of men, and most of them that are not of the church, all single persons, widows and women in the absence of their husbands, came up one after another." If not granted a higher status by association with a venerable spouse, women were relegated to the last place in the religious hierarchy, this despite the fact that by the late seventeenth century females constituted the majority of members in most churches.[96]

The ritual of an offertory procession might be dismissed as merely an archaic custom, but the systematic exclusion of women from positions of clerical authority had far-reaching consequences. The colonial ministry was the seat of cultural power as well as religious influence. Clerics were responsible for most of the reading materials penned and published in the American colonies. They alone had the privilege of rising before the public in Sunday sermons and weekly lectures to bespeak, inculcate, and propagate community values. There was no female input into this colonial cultural network. Women had no direct say in the attitudes toward their sex that pastors circulated throughout the colonies, no opportunity to publicly rebut the accusations of a Cotton Mather or Benjamin Wadsworth, nor of John Winthrop. Denied admission to the training grounds of the colonial ministry—Harvard, Yale, Oxford, and Cambridge—women were seldom equipped to argue the fine points of theology with their pastors. They were customarily taught only to read the Bible and passively accept its tenets as interpreted by the male clerical elite.

The secular education of women was also meager. The New England colonies took considerable pains to educate American youth, but their enthusiasm flagged when it came to women. Females were banned from institutions of higher learning and were commonly admitted to the public schoolhouse only during those hours and seasons when boys were occupied with other affairs or were needed in the fields. The burden of educating colonial children was not placed upon the school, however, but on the household. Parents and masters were charged with teaching the basic skills of reading and writing to girls and boys alike. Despite the fact that woman's right to read and write was often written into indenture contracts and colonial laws, the vast majority of females signed colonial documents with a crude mark, indicating a rate of literacy substantially lower than that of men.

It is not surprising, therefore, that few colonial women won acclaim for their intellectual acumen. Those determined women who did succeed in wresting an education from a hostile culture were severely castigated. One woman who dared to write a theological treatise was rudely rebuffed by her brother: "Your printing of a book is beyond your sex and doth rankly smell." John Winthrop maintained that such intellectual exertion could even rot the female mind. He attributed the madness of Ann Hopkins, wife of the Connecticut governor, to her intellectual curiosity. "If she had attended her household affairs and such things as belong to women and not gone out of her way to meddle in the affairs of men whose minds are stronger she'd have kept her wits and might have improved them usefully."[97] Ann Bradstreet, the first major American poet, responded to such arrogant insults to her sex with these ironic

lines: "Let Greeks be Greeks, and women what they are / Men have
precedency and still excell / it is but vain unjustly to wage war? /
Men can do best and women know it well / pre-eminence in all
and each is yours / Yet grant some small acknowledgement of
ours."[98]

A few colonial women objected to the limitations placed upon
them with stronger protests than Ann Bradstreet's mild-mannered
verse. These rugged and resourceful dames could not politely turn
away as the doors of meetinghouses, rectories, colleges, and libraries
were slammed in their faces. While Margaret Brent fought on the
political front with her challenge to the Maryland Assembly, Anne
Hutchinson did battle with the chief magistrates and ministers of
Massachusetts Bay. Mistress Hutchinson was fully versed in Puritan
theology, including those tenets that promised an elevated status
for women. She found in the covenant of grace confirmation of the
special powers of individuals predestined for salvation, including
women, to divine the will of God. Assured of her sanctification,
she deemed it proper to articulate her own antinomian theology
and, by inference, to criticize the patriarchal ministers and magistrates who held it to be heresy. She also dared to conduct religious
conversations with the women of Boston, a practice for which she
also had a theological justification: "I conceive there lyes a clear
rule in Titus, that the elder women should instruct the younger."
Mistress Anne Hutchinson had touched upon a basic contradiction
in the Puritan doctrine of woman's place. Yet the Winthrops and
the Mathers held to their perilous ground and exiled her not only
as a heretic but for "acting the part" rather of "a husband than a
wife," and for conducting herself in a manner "not fitting for your
sex." Still, Anne Hutchinson exacted a price from the Massachusetts
fathers for their arbitrary treatment of women, a controversy that
wreaked havoc in Boston, rocked the colony, and embarrassed its
governor. At the very outset of the colonial experiment, the cost
of repressing women was made clear.[99]

Other religious women proved nearly as troublesome as Anne
Hutchinson, particularly those well versed in the liberating doctrines of the Society of Friends. The next thorn to be lodged in
John Winthrop's side was Mary Dyer, banished three times from
the Puritan colony and thrice returned. Only a hanging could silence
this bold Quaker. But before she died, Mary Dyer stood before the
authorities of Massachusetts Bay to demand religious tolerance. "I

say I am a living testimony for [the Quakers] and the Lord, that
he hath blest them and sent them unto you: therefore be not found
fighting against God, but let my council and request be accepted
with you to repeal all such laws that the Truth and Servants of the
Lord may have free passage among you." Mary Dyer, inspired by
the Quaker belief in the inner light of godly wisdom that resided
in all men and women, presumed to judge and dramatize the errors
of male leaders. Yet, rather than challenging the legitimacy of male
leadership, she closed her protest "In Love and in the Spirit of
Meekness."[100] Anne Hutchinson also accepted the legitimacy of a
political and religious elite composed entirely of men. She submitted
to the magistrates' decisions with the compliant utterance "I will
freely let you for I am subject to your authority."[101] Neither of these
women were self-conscious feminists. Almost by accident they stumbled upon the sexual contradictions of colonial America. Encouraged
by the half-promises of sexual equality made by certain religious
sects, they tested the outermost barriers to female freedom in their
own time but never assaulted the fortress of sexual inequality itself.

The fact remains that discontented women caused their share
of trouble in the American colonies. Not all the rebellious women
were of the stature of Hutchinson and Dyer. Their protests, although
most often oblique and half-conscious, nevertheless underscored the
sexual contradictions of colonial society. In the first half-century of
the history of the town of Salem, for example, five of the nine
religious dissenters were females, women like Mary Oliver, an An-
abaptist, petty thief, and runaway wife, whose retort to her male
superiors was recited in less elegant tones than those of Anne Hutchinson. Of the Salem judge, Mary Oliver said "I hope to live and
tear his flesh to pieces." In the New England colonies as a whole,
heresy was one of the major reasons women were brought to trial
during the seventeenth century, and in this measure of independence
they surpassed men.[102]

Many another minor social conflict was sparked by the contradictions in woman's economic role. Woman's functions as manufacturer and trader, first of all, proved the source of controversy as
well as economic utility. The economic conflicts in which men were
likely to get embroiled largely stemmed from dealings in landed
property, the value and ownership of which could be legally determined by reference to deeds, contracts, and wills. If need be,
men could debate and resolve their differences before the public in

the town meeting. Women's economic exchanges, on the other hand, were conducted in private in an unsystematized and unpredictable fashion.

In New Amsterdam, women's economic enterprises created pandemonium. The many appearances of one Geertje Teunis before the Council of New Amsterdam illustrate the special pitfalls of female business. On one occasion the court was asked to rule upon the equity of a single transaction in which the following items were exchanged: a stocking, six sleeves, some seaware, several quarters of brandy, a tub, and assorted coins. Such complicated exchanges, and the quibbling that arose from them, led women like Geertje Teunis into vitriolic personal quarrels. One of her creditors charged that this epitome of the women of trade called him a "drunken rogue and a knave." Geertje countercharged that the plaintiff "abused her first for a whore and beast whereto she said I hold you for a rogue and a knave, till you have proved that I am a whore and I'm from beast stock."[103]

Off in the Puritan enclave of Boston, where social tranquillity was almost an obsession, Mistress Ann Hibbens was wreaking similar havoc. The imbroglio began when Mistress Hibbens became dissatisfied with the workmanship of some carpenters she had employed within her household. First, she complained to her husband, then consulted her minister about the alleged swindle, and finally sought retribution from the secular authorities. When no one proved sympathetic to the economic difficulties of the mistress of the household, Ann Hibbens made a general nuisance of herself, gossiping, grumbling, and blanketing the town with slander.[104] Woman's utility and aptitudes in the home economy could boomerang into social disorder when her powers were checked outside the household.

The aggressive temperament of colonial women often expressed itself in physical terms. One Anne Brown confronted all the highest authorities of Augusta County, Virginia, with her belligerence. When summoned to the court for abusing the local sheriff, she vented her rage against the judge himself, threatening "that on his coming off the Bench she would give it to him with the Devil."[105] The households and tribunals of every town were frequented by such troublesome and militant females. In one North Carolina village a man named James Warden fell victim of a woman named Margaret Briggs, who "with force and arms . . . did make and him beat wounded and evilly entreated and other Enormities to him."

The inspector of the Salem market was the victim of another aggressive colonial dame. The poor fellow alleged that an irate female trader "took me by the throat and with her fist punched me in the breast soe I was faynt for want of Breathe."[106] Other colonial men met violent death at the hands of such burly opponents. The colonial community was required to inculcate pacific behavior and restrain hostility in men and women alike.

Whether the culprits were men or women, accusations of sexual misconduct and perversion repeatedly disrupted the communications network of the agrarian village. Women assaulted one another as "common hoares" and "salte Bitches." Their tongues lashed out at the men of the town in such favorite epithets as knave, rogue, and cuckold. Two women of Virginia took direct aim at the virility of their neighbor: "Came to the cow pen and there did in a jeering manner abuse Grace Waltham saying that John Waltham, husband of the said Grace, had his Mounthly Courses as Women have, and that the said Anne Stephens should say that John Waltham was not able to gett a child."[107] The perpetrators of this slander, Anne Wilkinson and Anne Stephens, were ducked in the town pond. Although New England town clerks seldom were disposed to record episodes like this in such lurid detail, numerous incidents of slander, insinuations of dishonesty, drunkenness, and fornication indicated women's subversive effect on town tranquillity.

Although much of this squabbling can be laid to town gossip, it cannot be simply dismissed as a feminine foible. First of all, gossip served as a method of transmitting personal information of considerable significance to women: the moral failings, eccentricities, and general misbehavior of the men whom they were charged to obey. Informal verbal accounts were the only channels of such information open to women, who were barred from such public forums as the meetinghouse and the pulpit. Woman's household work, however, brought her into frequent contact with neighbors and servants and her trade took her into taverns, fields, and other homes. These associations among women undoubtedly provoked many opportunities for mutual support, sharing labor, and transmitting skills. The casual and disjointed conversations that ensued could, however, acquire the volatile, shrill, and cantankerous characteristics of gossip. Many a village controversy began when a group of women just happened to assemble along a village path. The frustration endemic to the contradictory nature of woman's place in agrarian society—invested with essential social and economic responsibilities but denied the right to pursue her self-interest and exercise power in public forums—led naturally to slander, character assassination, and gossip. The social disorder that issued from this contradiction ate away at the tight-knit bonds of small agrarian communities and tattered the Utopian hopes for creating a peaceable kingdom in the New World.

Thus it is not surprising that women played a major role in the most dramatic example of seventeenth-century community disintegration—the witchcraft hysteria that plagued the village of Salem in 1692. Till then, American colonists had prudently refrained from conjuring up the old demonic powers that had raged across Europe in the sixteenth century, and only a few isolated charges of witchcraft were made in the early years of American settlement. Still, most of those accused were women: Ann Hibbens of Boston, Anne Cole of Hartford, and Elizabeth Knight of Groton, Massachusetts, being the prime examples. It was not until the last decade of the seventeenth century, in the tiny agricultural village of Salem, that witchcraft led to a full-scale social crisis. Before the witchcraft controversy had taken its full course in Salem, nearly every element of the community had become involved, rich and poor, male and female alike. Nonetheless, the first to be accused, the major accusers, and the majority of those hanged for the offense of practicing witchcraft were of the female sex. In the deadly spotlight of a community rife with tales of witchcraft, women enacted the drama of their difficult social position, playing their complicated roles as victims, assailants, rebels, and conformists.

The fact that the majority of those accused of being agents of the devil were women invites the charge that the male authorities of Salem used the terror of witchcraft to exorcise unruly women from the community. Certainly some women were cruelly victimized by the trials before male judges, and many of them had been careless of keeping in woman's place. Mistress Hibbens' economic dealings in Boston had brought her excommunication for "usurping authority over him whom God had made her head and husband." Once an outcast, she developed an uncanny power of discerning the hidden import of social discourse. This womanly astuteness was judged the work of the devil, and Mistress Hibbens was executed as a witch. As one observer put it, she was hanged "only for having more wit than her neighbors . . . having . . . unhappily guessed that two of her persecutors who she saw talking in the street were talking of her."[108]

The first women accused in Salem were also town eyesores. Tituba, a West Indian slave, had indeed practiced the black arts; a trail of court cases and debts followed the accused Sarah Good, who was renowned as a town tramp and often chargeable to the town; Sarah Osbourne's relationships with her two husbands were the cause of town gossip, as was her irregular church attendance. The reputation of Bridget Bishop was also scandalous: she wore a red bodice, behaved seductively toward the young men of the town, and conducted rowdy entertainments in her home. At one time or another all these women became involved in economic squabbles with their neighbors. Rebecca Nurse, on the other hand, an aged and honorable mother, whose only eccentricity was deafness, was an unlikely candidate for witchcraft allegations. Rebecca and her husband, Francis, were parvenus in Salem, encroaching on the economic and social status of the powerful Putnam family, who played such an important role in conducting the trials. Perhaps even the prosperity reaped with the aid of an exemplary spouse could invoke community wrath amid the confusion and contagion of witchcraft trials. Yet, whatever the social transgressions of these women, witch trials were a circuitous and suicidal method of retribution, because the social turmoil and the curtailment of agricultural production left in its wake were hardly welcomed by the males of Salem.[109]

In fact, the role of women in colonial witchcraft was far more complicated than that of innocent victim of male supremacy. This is clearly demonstrated by the fact that the first accusing fingers in the Salem trials were pointed by a band of young, single women. The testimony of these girls, afflicted by hysteria that they attributed to agents of the devil, was the crucial evidence that sent members of their own sex to the gallows. At times, but only rarely, the young accusers seemed to carry out a vendetta against the opposite sex. The offenses that singled out George Burroughs, for example, included the suspicious deaths of his wives, from whom he had exacted a pledge to secrecy regarding his affairs. (This accused wizard had denied women an important privilege, the opportunity to gossip.) More often, however, the afflicted girls acted in the interest of their fathers and masters. Three of the most active accusers resided in the home of Thomas Putnam, Jr., a village patriarch and an opponent of many of the accused, including George Burroughs during his tenure as the local minister. Two other afflicted girls lived in the household of Samuel Paris, Burroughs' successor in the Salem pastorate. These daughters and servants of Salem most likely learned the names of those vulnerable to charges of witchcraft from the rumors and grumblings that circulated through the households of the small-town elite. They were well-versed enough in the social skills of colonial women to select as victims individuals against whom their household patriarchs bore a grudge. In other words, these young girls had not been sequestered from the social conflicts and power struggles of the small agrarian village.

In fact, there is some evidence that local political circles were particularly accessible to the women of Salem village. The village was an outlying precinct of the seaport town of Salem. Its only autonomous institutions were a parish and a village committee. Politics in this informal setting was largely a series of squabbles between neighbors and kin, in which women played an active part. For example, women signed petitions to oust the village minister during one heated and lengthy village conflict.[110] One of the most complicated and virulent struggles of the era occurred within the Putnam family, where a woman, in the stereotypical role of step-mother, played the villain. When such local controversies converged and created a community chaos in the 1690s, a cabal of young women stepped into the breach and set in motion the bizarre politics of the witchcraft tribunal.

The particular tensions that drove young women to this extreme course of action lay just beneath the surface of their own accusations. The affliction of the young women of Salem illustrates the psychological burdens of womanhood in the seventeenth century. The young accusers suffered palpable pain, the tortured symptoms of psychological disturbance. Fits characterized by swoons, contortions of the limbs, constriction of the muscles, and the recurrent sensation of being pricked, spread like an epidemic among Salem's daughters. The disease itself was often called the "suffocation of the mother." This terminology, coupled with the fact that the afflicted often attributed their hysteria to witches of approximately their mothers' ages, has prompted the observation that witchcraft fantasies were products of represssive weaning and oral fixations.[111] But why then were there no afflicted boys? Motherhood, it would seem, had a very special meaning for girls; it might symbolize the suffocating social position they would shortly assume, the probable enclosure of their adult lives within a patriarchal household.

The first outbreak of hysteria in Salem occurred when Elizabeth Parris and Abigail Williams had employed Tituba's assistance in evoking supernatural power to divine their futures. According to one report, "one of the afflicted persons who (as I am credibly informed) did try with an egg and glass to find her future husband's calling till there came up a coffin."[112] The New England girl whose future course in life was dependent on marriage and the stature of her husband might well be haunted by the possibility that lingered in that specter of a coffin, of being a widow or a spinster. The delirious conversations between Mercy Short and the devil give further evidence of the peculiar anxieties of young women in the seventeenth century. "Fine promises! You'll bestow an Husband upon mee, if I'l bee your Servant. A Husband! What? a Devil! I shall then bee finely fitted with an Husband: No I hope the Blessed Lord Jesus Christ will marry my Soul to Himself yett before Hee has done with me, as poor a wretch as I am! Fine Clothes! What? Such as your Friend Sarah Good had, who hardly had Rags to cover her! Pray, why did you not provide better for her Then?"[113]

When the afflicted girls lashed out at poor outcasts like Sarah Good, they may have projected the fearful possibility that through the accident of marriage they would meet a similar fate. The afflicted girls who resided in the Putnam household were granted special insight into the precarious status of women. Thomas Putnam, Jr., was beginning a long litigation regarding the conditions of his father's will, in hopes of wrenching property from his stepmother. The outcome of this struggle was not immaterial to the three afflicted women in the Putnam household, whose marriages and family security were dependent upon dowries and inheritances. The Putnam girls were especially aware of the cost of a lowered inheritance, for three of their aunts remained unmarried while they futilely awaited their legacies.[114] The afflicted girls were, in sum, at a decisive and anxious point in the female life cycle. Marriage and installation in a family economy were vital to their future well-being. A mistaken choice, however, could bring a lifetime of disaster; and should their mates be ideal, they still faced a sentence of unquestioning obedience. Understandably, premonitions of this adult womanhood could drive the girls of Salem to hysterical fits and accusations of witchcraft.

Their actions can also be seen as a disguised form of rebellion. For a few frantic months, eleven young women held an entire town in their power, making all of New England, even governors and their ladies, squirm. They received a degree of attention that children (as they were called) and women were seldom accorded by the assembled townspeople. Yet their glory was short-lived. The witchcraft hysteria was soon brought under control and within a few years the town repented, repudiating the whole bloody affair, leaving the once-afflicted girls to make their way through the same old labyrinth of difficult and constricting female roles. Even with the aid of demonic powers these girls could not extricate themselves from the frustrating contradictions of woman's place.

Once more, conjecture can be drawn from the debacle of Salem village witchcraft: the suggestion that the agrarian town and its gender system were in the process of transformation. In days past, a girl's future had been somewhat predictable if not ideal. In 1692, however, young, single women might have had particular cause for anxiety. They were part of a large generation coming into maturity at a time when the arable land in and around the colonial towns was slowly being exhausted. The possibility loomed that the young men and women of New England would not be able to obtain farmland on which to settle and raise families. Could it be that the witchcraft hysteria was inspired by what the future held in store—spinsterhood, the poverty of insufficient land, or migration to some distant city or frontier settlement? At some point the residents of the agricultural villages of the New World would have to confront these premonitions, which bespoke a new social and economic order and a new alignment of the sexes. The future beckoned to Salem Village from the thriving town to the east. As it turned out, residents of Salem Town and those with close ties to its manifold commercial operations were particularly liable to accusations of witchcraft. [115] Were the afflicted girls of the village of Salem, then, clairvoyants, espying new danger to their sex once their near-subsistence agricultural community became ensnared in the advances of commercial capitalism?

☐

For the moment, the women of New England towns, and as far as can be ascertained of the southern and middle colonies as well, had learned to live with the gender system peculiar to seventeenth-century America. The fundamental structure of womanhood as they knew it was the arrangement of household economies within small isolated settlements or scattered farm sites. This social and economic system had sundry, sometimes contradictory, effects on women. First of all, because most production transpired in the household, women were afforded a central and often respected economic role. Those who were ousted from the household, however— spinsters, widows, unwed mothers—were in very difficult straits. Second, the centrality of the household within colonial society also prohibited a refined segregation of males and females into different social spaces, where they might be assigned antithetical roles and traits of character. Third, both society and household were frankly patriarchal in the seventeenth century, based on the supreme authority of men as fathers. Women were subject to fathers and husbands within the household, and barred from positions of independence and authority outside it. Indeed, women were practically invisible within the official sphere; in no sense were they full citizens of any one of the thirteen colonies. At best, women found a measure of influence in the informal, face-to-face politics of the seventeenth-century community or neighborhood. Fourth, the subordination of women was only one example of an overall ideology and practice of social hierarchy and presumed inequality, among men as well as women. Gender, rather than standing out as one bold standard of social stratification in an otherwise egalitarian social order, was one of many gradations in a steep vertical ladder of inequality.

The position allotted to women in the agrarian settlements of early America was complex, multifaceted, and impossible to reduce to a single proposition about its advantages and disadvantages relative to other epochs in the history of womanhood. The course of women's history did not traverse through a sequence of golden eras and dark ages. Adam's Rib, like most gender systems, designated a secondary social status for women. But as always, the structure of womanhood was intricate enough to permit women to secure for themselves a measure of dignity, freedom, and power.

T W O

PATRIARCHY IN DISARRAY: WOMEN AND COMMERCIAL CAPITALISM: 1750–1820

n the annals of American history the years between 1750 and 1820 appear under the halo of independence and republicanism, and therefore invite a naïve question in the history of women: Did the female sex demand independence in 1776 and secure the full liberties of United States citizenship soon thereafter? The rights and privileges of Americans could not be kept secret from the nation's women. Abigail Adams was well aware of the ideological currents circulating through the Continental Congress when she taunted her spouse with the declaration that "If particular care and attention is not paid to the ladies, we are determined to instigate a rebellion, and will not hold ourselves bound by any law in which we have no voice or representation."[1] In the new nation a few female taxpayers, fortified by the principles of representative democracy, appeared and cast their ballots at the voting places of New Jersey. The catholic republican spirit of the new nation was at times hospitable to Mary Wollstonecraft's *Vindication of the Rights of Women*, which went through several editions in the United States in the last decade of the eighteenth century. The rights of women even found their way into ladies' magazines, where they were put to verse to be sung to the music of "My Country 'tis of Thee."[2]

This liberating theme in the history of American women cannot be pursued much further, however, for despite all the expansive talk of republicanism, women found no larger a place in the politics of the new nation than they had under the British Empire. Their names still remained absent from the ledger of voters and the lists of officeholders. Neither the Declaration of Independence nor the Constitution of the United States elevated women to the status of political beings. Relative to men, furthermore, women's political stature can be seen in decline after the American Revolution. For one thing, their disenfranchisement now stood out in bold contrast to almost universal white manhood suffrage. When young propertyless men went to the polls, leaving rich widows behind, sexual discrimination became a visible blemish on the republican complexion of the new nation. The centralization of political power stimulated by the Revolution and institutionalized by the Federal Constitution also fundamentally reshaped the context of women's politics. When political decisions were made at these higher, more formal and remote levels they became largely inaccessible to women. The old networks of kin and neighborhood rarely reached as far as the Constitutional Convention or the United States Congress. With the relocation of the national capital on the open landscape that would become Washington, D.C., the center of national politics became a male bastion, situated amid a ramshackle collection of men's boardinghouses. To put it simply, the federation of the United States created a remote public sphere that distanced women even further from political power. If participation in public affairs were the only means of being admitted to the history of the United States, the female sex would again be denied a past.[3]

Yet women's history was not held in abeyance while the Founding Fathers disengaged the colonies from British rule, designed constitutions, and squared off as Federalists and Republicans. On the social and cultural fronts, womanhood was undergoing a series of crucial changes. Some of the impetus toward the transformation of womanhood derived from the American Revolution itself. The independence movement had accorded women some opportunities to exercise their local political power on a grander historical stage; they formed the "Daughters of Liberty" to rival the famous "Sons," led boycotts of British goods, and joined in riotous resistance to imperial policies. When protest escalated to revolution, women found new glory in the performance of old roles. The household manufacture of cloth, for example, became a hallowed patriotic service, designed to foster American independence of British imports. In 1768, when the colonists' nonimportation pact was in effect, the *New York Journal* referred their readers to the "glorious example" of a woman and her daughter in Newport who "have spun fully sixty yard of good fine linen cloth nearly a yard wide, since the first of March, besides taking care of a large family."[4]

Women's responsibilities during wartime were more expansive than this. With colonial husbandmen off to battle, sometimes for months on end, many women learned to manage the entire household economy. For example, when John Adams was called away on public business he wrote his spouse: "I intreat you to rouse your whole attention to the family, the stock, the farm, the dairy. Let every article of expense which can be spared be retrenched; keep the hands attentive to their business and the most prudent measures of every kind be adopted." Mrs. Adams took this advice to heart, hoping "in time to have the reputation of being as good a *farmeress* as my partner has of being a good statesman."[5] She fulfilled the office most admirably, not only managing the farm but also manufacturing soap and saltpeter, and sewing blankets for the troops of the Revolution.

These wartime transmutations in woman's roles left their mark on both her public image and individual consciousness. One New Jersey woman, for example, sued for the repayment of state bonds, arguing "I have done as much to carry on the war as many that sett now at the helm of government."[6] The impact of the Revolution on women's status and self-esteem was registered in social records as well. In the Massachusetts divorce courts, for example, women appeared more aggressive and were granted more equitable treatment after the Revolution than before.[7] Women also received much more deferential attention from American writers after the Revolution. Patriarchal injunctions to obedience and subordination seemed to catch in the throats of republicans. Similarly, the wake of the Revolution brought a significant increase in the educational opportunities and literacy rates of women. Finally, as one historian reminds us, the first generation of American feminists, including the Grimké sisters, Elizabeth Stanton, and Lucretia Mott, was born of revolutionary mothers and fathers and grew up amid this more liberating American culture.[8]

Whatever changes in womanhood became apparent in the late eighteenth century should not, however, be attributed entirely to a discrete political event like the War of Independence. The Revolution and the building of the new nation coincided with (and in some ways derived from) fundamental changes in American society

and economy. The historical processes that would transform seventeenth-century womanhood were already discernible within three
generations of settlement. By the mid-eighteenth century they created a complicated pattern with four major interwoven motifs.

First of all, subsistence agriculture had been undermined by an
increasingly elaborate and extensive system of economic exchange
which reached from small towns to European capitals. Second, the
increase in trade spurred the development of regional economic
networks, which linked farms and plantations to a whole range of
commercial hamlets, towns, and cities. Hence, while urban residence was still very rare in eighteenth-century America, it had great
impact on the economy and on women. Third, the family system
characteristic of the seventeenth century lost much of the veneer
and the substance of patriarchy around the time of the American
Revolution. Finally, weaving through all these broken and tattered
social threads was a sharpened division of womanhood by class. In
the seventeenth-century agrarian village most male residents were,
or would become, propertied farmers, and the variations in wealth
among them were relatively small. By the mid-eighteenth century,
the distribution of wealth grew more disparate in commercial agricultural towns; cities harbored affluent and ostentatious merchants; and slave quarters grew up alongside mansions in the South.
The fledgling American elite, as represented by merchants and
planters, produced the most obvious and ostentatious fragment in
a new and disjointed mosaic of womanhood.[9]

Taken together, these historical processes spelled the steady
advance of capitalist commercial enterprise. By the mid-eighteenth
century, the simple, undifferentiated, family economy devoted primarily to subsistence, had been banished to the farthest reaches of
the frontier. And even there it survived only a fleeting moment.
The transformation occurred most painfully and slowly in the heart-
land of the little commonwealth, rural New England. By the mid-
eighteenth century the original land grants had long been exhausted
and the old town practice of distributing fields and meadows gratis
was discontinued. The farmland along the eastern seaboard became
prey to private enterprise, to be won or lost according to the relative
purchasing power of the townsmen. Economic power accrued to
those who raised surplus crops for a regional market, and then used
their profits to expand their landholdings, their output, and their
wealth. As the New England soil became increasingly exhausted,

the displaced farmers turned either westward or into diversified occupations—to trade, the professions, small-scale manufacture, and cottage industries such as weaving or shoemaking. In the process the disparity of wealth widened in these New England towns. Typically, the proportion of wealth controlled by the top 10 percent of the population more than doubled, rising within a century from 15 to 30 percent of the total community resources.[10]

A similar degree of income disparity characterized commercial agricultural centers farther to the west and the south, in such places as southeastern Pennsylvania or the Shenandoah Valley. These settlements were founded in the eighteenth century for the explicit purpose of reaping commercial profit. Farmers in these regions produced a substantial surplus and marketed it energetically. In fact, their livestock and grain were sold as far away as the West Indies and Europe.[11] Whether they dealt with international shippers or local tradesmen, the farmers of the eighteenth century were entangled in a complex network of economic exchange. The household economy was clearly no longer autonomous, but increasingly dependent on relations with other enterprises and reliant on money and credit to meet its needs.

COMMERCE, CLASS, AND WOMANHOOD

The growth of the commercial sector of the American economy and the consequent complication of the division of labor portended a variety of new economic possibilities for women. On the one hand, it opened up new outlets for their proven trading skills, which might foster a sense of enterprise, acquisitiveness, and self-improvement. On the other hand, a commercial economy dissolved the integral connection between production and exchange at the household level, and made possible the opening of a wider chasm between male and female economic activities. As the only fully legitimate property owners, American husbands had a headstart toward commercial investment, and should they prosper in farms, shops, shipping firms, plantations, and manufactories, they would be able to purchase the products and services that once had indebted them to female economic partners. Inequities among women as well as between the sexes could become exaggerated as the more privileged, talented, or avaricious wrenched from their fellows greater quantities of land and commercial wealth. Accordingly, by the late eighteenth century American women, either through their own enterprise or by dint of their husbands' status, went myriad separate ways into the rudimentary classes designated by such colloquialisms as the "better," "middling," and "lower sort."

On occasion, women were personally invited to join in the enterprising spirit of the era. A pamphlet printed in a New England village proclaimed that "a virtuous woman is a good economist. She not only labors with her hands to obtain the necessaries and conveniences of life; but she is provident and saving of her earnings."[12] One New England minister picked up on this refrain and built around it an oratorio of female entrepreneurship. In 1793 the Reverend John Ogden, of New Hampshire, lamented that "in so wise and civilized an age and country as we live in . . . young females have not partook of a greater share of the cares and prosperity of the community." To remedy this unfortunate state of affairs, Ogden advised the New England daughter to expand her household enterprise into a commercial operation; her homespun clothing, for example, could become "a means to open a merchandizer, which gives her the production of distant regions." Then Ogden planted even more grandiose ambitions in the young woman's mind. "She does not totally confine her cares to merchandise, but knowing the value of real property, the quality of land, and the importance of agriculture, she considereth a field and buyeth it." Thereafter, the female economist should strive to "improve all opportunities of increasing her wealth." John Ogden did not foresee that the stellar virtue of emergent American capitalism — individualistic economic achievement — would be recommended to males only: "So far from being masculine and improper for the delicate sex, it gives her health."[13]

Off in South Carolina, Eliza Lucas arrived at these principles of commercial economy independently. Left in charge of her father's plantation at the age of seventeen, Eliza speedily embraced the spirit of economic betterment. She wrote to a friend as follows: "I have planted a figg orchard with design to dry them and export them. I have reckoned my expenses and the profit to arise from the figgs, but was I to tell you how great an estate I am to make this way and how 'tis to be laid out you would think me far gone in romance." Eliza Lucas' subsequent marriage to Charles Pinckney did not curb her enterprising spirit but carried her further into the sphere of commercial agriculture as she pioneered in the American indigo trade.[14]

Yet Eliza Lucas Pinckney by no means spoke for all American women. The advancement of the commercial economy of Worcester, Massachusetts, portended quite a different fate for Millicent Goulding. In 1785 she petitioned the court as follows: "Gentlemen, I am in needy Circumstances, destitute of an house or Home to shelter me, but thank god am in a good degree of health and by my industry am able at present to support myself if I had a Room provided for me—I am loathe to put the town to any expense for my support and maintenance but necessity obliges me." Although the court granted Millicent Goulding's request for shelter, this did not assure her economic independence. Two years later she returned to the court, swallowing her pride and surrendering her hopes of self-support. "I am now Destitute of house or home or Decent clothing and Daily suffering for the Necessaries of Life." She begged the town to "support me during my natural life."[15] The advance of commercial capitalism could bode well or ill for the American woman, but it seldom left her old roles unchanged.

The vast majority of American women remained on small farms where the forces of commercialization changed their economic lives in subtler ways. The farmer's wife and daughters became acquainted to one degree or another with cash and commodities. The mistress of a commercial household was in a position to exchange her own surplus production for cash, or even to organize her work around the demands of the marketplace. For example, a farmer's wife named Grace Gessner who lived in Nyack, New York, at the turn of the century raised chickens for the New York City market and carefully kept her own accounts separate from those of her husband.[16] In the same period New England women took their poultry, dairy products, and needlework to nearby merchants for sale.[17] Throughout the Northeast, women were prodigiously marketing the staple domestic manufacture, textiles. As late as 1809 only 65,000 yards of cloth were produced in the factory, while 230,000 yards were manufactured in the homes of American housewives and traders.[18] Those women who controlled the income accrued from such home manufacturing might be able to accumulate enough resources to enter the commercial age as capitalists in their own right. At the very least, wives and daughters were becoming familiar with the ways of the market and acquainted with the elation that comes with possessing a little money all one's own.

Women were also present at the birth of the nation's infant industries. The early factory employment of women meshed neatly with the changing parameters of a basically agricultural home economy, taking up the excess labor power of widows, indigents, the old, and the young. In the first stage of this symbiotic relationship between manufacturing and the household, merchants simply solicited woman's home production—her yarn and cloth—for sale in their shops. Later they would delegate specific steps in the manufacturing process to home-bound women. Artisan manufacturers, such as shoemakers, followed a similar practice, giving the shoes stitched in their shops to their wives and daughters for finishing. Occasionally females organized their own collective workshops. In the fluid era of burgeoning industry, American women also played independent and inventive roles. In 1798 a twelve-year-old girl devised a method of making straw braid for bonnets and generated an industry that employed hundreds of women in her hometown of Dedham. As late as 1821 a Connecticut woman won a London Society of the Arts award for her inventive method of bleaching straw, and went on to organize another primitive American industry. All such manufacturing was an unsophisticated operation, the simple collection of workers under one roof where they manually plied a common trade. It transported women's manufacturing skills outside the home into more efficient and specialized economic institutions. This subtle but seminal transformation kept the female role of economist intact, and in effect declared that woman's place was not necessarily in the home but wherever she could be of economic service.[19]

At the same time the exhaustion of farmland sent many daughters out of the range of farming and home production and into cities and towns where the forces of commercialization held full sway. In the seventeenth century the towns of the Northeast were hardly urban. Boston's 6,000 residents, for example, were scattered along cowpaths in homes surrounded by garden plots and foraging livestock. A century later, however, Boston began to look and operate like a city, its population of 12,000 settled along marked-out streets and traveled to a commercial hub to exchange their specialized products and skills for coin and currency. New York eclipsed Boston as the premier urban center in the eighteenth century, and its population had increased no less than 500 percent by 1825.[20] Although less than 10 percent of America's population resided in these bustling towns, it was here that women acted their role in a commercial economy to the fullest.

One index of the commercial energies of the northeastern towns was the local press, with its advertisements for nearly every imaginable product. Some of these notices were placed by females and might read like this Philadelphia advertisement: "Elizabeth Perkins has for sale in her shop . . . glassware in every style and shape." The vast majority of Elizabeth Perkins' competitors were male. The city of Boston harbored the greatest number of she-merchants, but even there only 10 percent of the local advertisers were female and most of them were widows who were carrying on businesses established by their husbands. Nevertheless, the women who gave notice of their business enterprises in the city newspapers testified to the commercial skills of which their sex was capable. These women did more than barter their homemade goods. They managed a wide network of economic relationships that included purchasing, displaying, and selling goods from Europe and the American hinterland. The range of economic experiences open to women is illustrated by this notice in a Philadelphia paper: "All persons who are indebted to Anne Jones at the Plume and Feather in Second Street in Philadelphia are desired to come and settle the same . . . she designing to go for England in a short time." One Mary Jackson was a producer as well as a merchandiser: "The said Mary makes and sells Tea-Kettles and Coffee-Pots. . . . " A widow named Anne Page also combined the roles of artisan and merchant, selling tools and engaging in carpentry simultaneously.[21]

Newspaper advertisements cannot reveal, however, the extensive participation of wives and daughters in commercial enterprises owned by men. It is only in her husband's words, for example, that we learn of the contributions of Mrs. Alexander in New York: "The next day after my wife brought to bed of a daughter she sold goods to above thirty pounds value." As a child, Sarah Ripley of Greenfield, Massachusetts, casually noted her economic duties in her journal: "My father and sister Lydia departed for Boston—I am left with the care of the store, I hope I shall fulfill the duties incumbent on me in an acceptable manner."[22] Like Sarah's father, Benjamin Franklin did not climb the ladder to success alone, but with the aid of a wife who "proved a good and faithful helpmate, assisted

me much by attending the shop."[23] With Ben off with his kites
and philandering in France, Mrs. Franklin's responsibilities must
have exceeded simple assistance. Women also became the senior
partners of their sons. For example, "Mary Jackson and Sons" advertised regularly before the firm came under the management of
her male heirs. Other she-merchants consolidated their skills and
capital in "co-partnerships" or "companies" with other women and
men.[24] Whether as lone entrepreneurs, partners, widows, or the
wives and daughters of shopkeepers, these women retained a central
place in early American commerce.

The commercial towns also offered women a larger range in
which to practice their traditional skills, and now for monetary
profit. The services of a midwife or a nurse became paying occupations in the commercial towns where women solicited clients in
the press. More specialized skills could also be practiced in the
cosmopolitan setting. For example, one woman announced that she
"makes grave Clothes and lays out the dead." Other women turned
to teaching. A Miss Rodes, "newly arrived in Philadelphia," offered
to teach French, reading, writing, drawing, and embroidery to city
girls "in homes or at her place of residence." By 1757 even the
town of Dedham could employ eight women as teachers. As commerce flourished and towns grew into cities, a whole panoply of
new enterprises opened to women. Female economic life was enlivened with the possibilities of profit, diversity, and social exchange
with customers and middlemen as well as with their families and
neighbors.[25]

The liveliest of all commercial enterprises, rural or urban, was
the tavern, and there women found many opportunities for employment. As early as 1690, twenty-four of Boston's fifty-four taverns were run by women. One Mary Ballard opened a tavern "for
the entertainment of gentlemen and the benefit of commerce," where
"all the newspapers of the Continent are regularly taken in and
several English Prints and Magazines." The activities of some enterprising tavernkeepers were more extensive and less respectable
than simply the sale of liquor and literature. One proprietor of a
tavern, Alice Thomas, was brought to court for receiving stolen
goods, selling liquor without a license, entertaining children and
servants, profaning the Lord's Day, and, finally, providing "frequent
secret and unseasonable entertainment in her house to Lewd, Las-
civious and notorious persons of both Sexes, giving them oppor-

tunity to commit carnall wickedness, and that by common fame is a common baud." Alice Thomas taxed the liberality of commercial towns in 1672 and was rewarded with thirty stripes and imprisonment at the pleasure of the court.[26]

In the eighteenth century, when towns grew beyond the capacity of the Puritan magistrate to oversee public morality, tavernkeepers and dealers in "carnal wickedness" were allowed freer reign. An eighteenth-century British observer spoke of a woman in Newport who kept "a house of pleasure and has done so for a great many years past in a more decent and reputable manner than common, and is spoke of by everybody in town in a favorable manner for one of her Profession."[27] New York City authorities estimated that between 1,200 and 7,000 prostitutes roamed the city streets early in the nineteenth century.[28] Likewise, Ben Franklin found no scarcity of prostitutes in Philadelphia. He contended that the streets were thronged with women "who by throwing their heads to the right or the left of everyone who passed by them, I concluded came out with no other Design than to revive the spirt of love in Disappointed Batchelors and expose themselves to sale at the highest bidder." Franklin also had a good word for the economic and social contributions of prostitutes. In addition to contributing to the "health and satisfaction" of young men, streetwalkers stimulated the local economy by their exorbitant expenditures on shoe leather.[29] Franklin's satire was premised on the recognition of a new economic order, a network of specialized enterprises linked by monetary exchanges, expanding through private profit, and engaging men and women alike. This system permitted even the transformation of a woman's body into a salable item. Most American women did not market their sexuality on city streets, but she-merchants sold almost every other commodity and thus partook of the boom of a commercial economy.

Yet women entered all these commercial relationships shackled with the customary restrictions of the second sex. Commerce, after all, required legal privileges denied women by common law and American legal practice. To mount a successful commercial enterprise required access to credit, the ability to sue to collect debts, the right to possess personal and real property, all of which were severely restricted among women, especially wives. One would expect, then, that men would advance more quickly and farther in trade than would women. This prognostication of the decline of

women's economic freedom relative to men, is given some confirmation by the analysis of Revolutionary records. Loyalists' petitions
asking for compensation for property confiscated during the war,
for example, indicate that these largely urban and upper-class women
were quite ignorant of their husbands' financial affairs and unversed
in the language of capitalist enterprise. Women from families of
more modest means, where presumably capitalist accumulation and
commerce were less fully developed, had more knowledge of the
family business.[30]

Probate records indicate a similar relationship between the advances of commerce and women's economic roles. As the village of
Hingham, Massachusetts, matured into a market town, fewer women
were chosen as executors of their husbands' more complicated estates.[31] A similar trend was apparent in the wills of Petersburg,
Virginia, a southern town which served as an entrepôt in the tobacco
trade. A survey of the legal records of Virginia and New York
revealed that over the course of the eighteenth century the ranks of
female executors declined, along with female signatories to deeds
and economic documents of all sorts.[32] Women, it seemed, were
slowly losing their integral position in the economic life of America.
An increasing proportion of farm production was devoted to a single
cash crop, especially grains, which was cultivated and distributed
by men. The value of male and female labor was now measured by
separate price tags rather than the indivisible material welfare of
the family. In this accounting, the women of the commercial era
undoubtedly ranked second behind their husbands.

The eighteenth-century housewife was still a very busy woman,
whether she lived in town or on the farm. The social and economic
meaning of her labors was changing, however, in subtle but ominous
ways. While the goodwives of the past produced prosaic and essential goods—homespun clothing, simple foodstuffs, crude soaps,
candles and dyes—eighteenth-century women, and especially those
who resided in commercial centers, labored over more refined, if
not ornamental creations—chintz curtains, decorative rugs, em-
broidered coverlets. The diaries and correspondence of urban middle-class women also indicated that they were less involved in both
their husbands' business activities and the neighborhood barter system than were their foremothers. The economic consequences of
household labor were becoming softly shaded with connotations of
domestic amenities.[33]

The advances of commercial capitalism also meant that women's relation to the economy began to shift slowly along the spectrum from production to consumption. A rise in per capita income in about the mid-eighteenth century made possible a significant increase in the volume of sales among American merchants, large and small. Country stores kept their accounts in the names of household heads, testifying to the continuing patriarchal control over the allocation of family resources. Yet women undoubtedly played some role in the selection and purchase of a growing array of household commodities.

As the eighteenth century drew to a close, the economic activity of shopping played an increasingly prominent role in personal accounts of how American women spent their days. The diary of Mrs. Mary Holyoke, for the years 1760 to 1800, found her busily employed salting hogs weighing up to 188 pounds and making butter in quantities of nearly 90 pounds, as well as manufacturing candles and soap. As time went on, however, this wife of an eminent doctor found more and more time to visit "the shops" and purchase stockings, mantuas, fashionable shoes, spices, coffee, and other imports. The diaries of Mrs. Holyoke's daughters, Mary and Susanna, plot the subsequent eclipse of home production by a profusion of such shopping expeditions.[34] In the same era Mrs. John Amory, the wife of a wealthy merchant, experienced shopping as a time-consuming avocation. For example, she spent the entire morning of September 16, 1775, "in going to the shops,"[35] the only memorable event of the day. Eunice Callender, a less affluent young lady, spent May 27, 1808, in a similar fashion: "Caroline and myself called on Mrs. Henry in the forenoon and went a shopping in the afternoon."[36] These women were the clientele for many of the she-merchants of the seaboard towns, but they themselves embraced a role that was increasingly peripheral to production, a more passive contribution to the distributive sector of the economy.

For another class of women, those who were not securely attached to households of the middling or the upper sort, commercial society promised neither shopping sprees nor financial achievement. In growing numbers the wives of the poor and propertyless, daughters without a patrimony, unwed mothers, and widowed family-heads entered the urban labor market to earn a livelihood. Only one occupation was particularly eager to receive them—domestic service. Laments over the scarcity of good servants rang through the fashionable social circles. An English observer in 1710 described the American "help" problem this way: "All women's work is very dear there, which proceeds from the smallness of the number and the scarcity of the workers, for even the meanest single women marry there, and being without want are above work."[37] In 1748 supply and demand did not seem so favorable to female servants in Philadelphia, whose standard wages were only eight to ten pounds annually in excess of room and board. This wage, furthermore, was only 50 percent of what a male servant might expect to earn. Women's other choices of employment were seldom better-paying or more attractive. They included nursing, laundry, needlework, menial chores in hospitals or asylums, and occasional industrial piecework such as making cartridges during the War.[38]

By 1800 sizable numbers of women were unable to find any position whatsoever. The expanding economy unceremoniously deposited them in the class of paupers, simply judging them incapable of earning a living. By 1811 the town of Worcester allotted thousands of dollars a year "For the support of the poor (they have greatly increased in number and expense)."[39] New York City administrators estimated the number of dependent poor in 1816 at 15,000. The city's relief baskets were reserved for women with such notations as these: "husband in prison," "husband has broken his leg," "husband bad fellow," "her husband abandoned her and she has broke her arm," "husband at sea."[40] Disruption of the family and its distressing economic consequences for women were particularly frequent in port towns, which sent men off to sea and often to untimely deaths. The seaboard town of Marblehead, for example, listed 459 widows and 869 orphans (500 of them female) on the relief rolls of 1790. Sailors were also wont to leave unwed mothers in American ports. One of Marblehead's unwed mothers was renowned for her exemplary "neatness, prudence, and love of her children." Yet the chances for a single woman or a widow to support her family in such dignity were few, and as Marblehead swarmed with unemployable persons, the city fathers grew intolerant of the poor of either sex. By 1815 they were grumbling that "the women are lazy and of consequence dirty creatures" and opining that "nothing but a characteristic want of economy, even in the worst state of the fishery, can be the cause of such suffering."[41]

The increase in the poor overtaxed the old welfare system and compromised the ideal of Christian stewardship. At the turn of the century New York City deported as many as 1,000 paupers a year, while the ranks of the strolling poor increased throughout the Northeast, swollen by the many widows of eighteenth-century soldiers. Towns throughout the colonies were hard pressed to devise new methods of dealing with the poor. One Margaret Page was summarily ushered into the new social shelter for the poor, the Boston jail, where she was identified as "a lazy, idle, loytering person" and ordered "to work for a living."[42] Soon specialized institutions were constructed for the incarceration of the town's paupers. New York established its first almshouse in 1736, and in 1816 constructed the massive walled edifice of Bellevue to house its teeming population of indigents.[43] By the early nineteenth century even Worcester, Massachusetts, was setting aside the bulk of its tax monies for a "house for the reception and employment of such persons as are or may become Chargeable to the town."[44] The almshouse served a dual purpose, removing the poor from public view and forcing them to contribute to their own support. More than 60 percent of Bellevue's inmates were women in 1821, and they were put to work at traditional female tasks: cleaning, sewing, spinning, cooking, and nursing. The men at Bellevue were employed at such skilled tasks as carpentry and shoemaking as well as common manual labor.[45] Private citizens also designed institutions to employ the poor. In Boston, for example, a "society for encouraging industry and employing the poor" gathered idle women and children in a clothmaking workshop that was organized by local merchants.[46]

Calvinists and capitalists alike chafed at the sight of idleness in men, women, and children. To the proponents of American manufacturing, like Alexander Hamilton and Tench Coxe, unemployed women were seen as a potential industrial labor force. These men calculated that poor women, as well as wives and daughters with time on their hands, could be employed in manufactories and workshops without disrupting the agricultural production on which the nation still depended. According to Hamilton, women, "doomed to idleness and its attendant vices . . . are rendered more useful by manufacturing establishments." Tench Coxe added "that the portents of time of housewives and young women which were not occupied with family affairs could be profitably filled up" by periodic stints in the manufactory. George Washington observed the female employees of a textile workshop with satisfaction: "They are the daughters of decayed families and are girls of character—none other are admitted."[47]

By the close of the eighteenth century, America's first large mechanized factories were taking in poor and deracinated families en masse. The Rhode Island textile firm of Samuel Slater was the first to utilize machinery on a scale that demanded a large, permanent labor force. Slater recruited families as his labor supply, removing entire households from farm to factory. Once a family had been transplanted to the factory, its inner hierarchy became translated into a wage scale. A Massachusetts father contracted with Slater under the following terms: $5 a week for himself; $2.33 for his sister; $2 for his sixteen-year-old son; $1.50 for a son and a nephew, both thirteen years old; $1.25 for a twelve-year-old daughter; 83 cents and 75 cents for two girls, ten and eight years old respectively.[48]

When the contributions of each man, woman, and child to the sustenance of the household were translated into specific monetary terms, the labor of the family was proven to be divisible into individual shares—portending clear inequality for females. The advances of technology exacerbated this process, as Tench Coxe observed in 1814: "Women, relieved to a considerable degree from their former employments as carders, spinners, and feeders by hand, occasionally turn to the occupation of weaver." In this textile plant women usurped the role customarily occupied by the male. Yet within the factory, weaving was a simple machine operation which did not confer an elevated status or a larger wage on women. Rather, as Coxe went on to demonstrate, it freed men for more highly skilled and rewarding occupations. With "improved machinery and implements the male weavers imploy themselves in superintendence, instruction, supervision or other superior operations and promote their health by occasional attentions to gardening, agriculture and the clearing and improvement of their farms." As the new nation's factories grew more sophisticated and more numerous, the distinction between superior and inferior, male and female jobs became more and more blatant. As the operation of factory equipment became simpler, it commanded lower wages and was increasingly delegated to women and children. An 1816 report on the United States cotton industry listed 66,000 women operatives,

24,000 boys, and only 10,000 adult men.[49] These women trod a treacherous path—out of the home economy and toward full exploitation within a capitalist labor market.

THE AMERICAN DEBUT
OF THE LADY

The era of commercial capitalism escorted other American women far afield of any direct economic activities. Within a small class of wealthy Northern merchants and Southern planters the productive responsibilities of women all but disintegrated. The merchants who conducted America's foreign trade were the major component of that upper class in northeastern port towns. The sea captains and the scions of old mercantile houses were all males and were well enough off to dispense with a female economic partner in the conduct of their business affairs. In the 1690s a handful of women appeared among the stockholders of Boston's shipping fleet, but as a few wealthy families came to monopolize the import business in the early eighteenth century, the female presence among the city's merchant elite was entirely erased.[50] The wives and daughters of these business leaders played only indirect and symbolic roles in the making and maintaining of their family fortunes. The female's most important service was to consolidate her family's wealth and power through a well-calculated marriage. The merchant elite of Salem, for example, was an exceedingly inbred circle, with no less than forty-two marriages between cousins within a single generation. The merchants' daughters carried into marriage the name, trade connections, and capital of their fathers, thereby attaching great economic consequences to their matches. The marriage of cousins, and the use of brides as conduits of family capital was also common among wealthy southern planters.[51]

In wedlock these women served, like the Georgian mansions with their costly furnishings, as an objectification of their husbands' wealth and status. A merchant's wife exhibited the social and economic status of her family by the conspicuous display of personal adornment and social graces. These could be very exhausting duties. The upkeep of her appearance, for example, might involve preparation of the cosmetic base, aqua vitae, a potion requiring thirty ingredients, two months' cultivation, and an impossible final step:

"shake the bottle incessantly for ten to twelve hours."[52] As early as 1721 Mrs. Van Rensselaer described the daily routine of New York society women in which all household chores were completed by 11 A.M., with the rest of the day devoted to reading, dressing, visiting, and entertaining.[53] Two generations later, Mrs. John Amory devoted most of her time to social events. Entries in her journal typically played on a single theme: "At home with Company," "dined out," "a large company at home."[54] The Southern lady's daily schedule was much the same, according to Elizabeth Dulaney. "As soon as my breakfast is clearly down my throat away I go—and generally make an engagement to spend the evening before I return so that I am very little at home except with company."[55] For this select class of women the geography of gender took a novel and distinctive shape. The decline of household production did not strand them in domestic isolation but invited them into a whirlwind of activity in an enlarged circle of kin, friends, and members of their elite class. Neither was the life of the eighteenth-century lady given over to indolence and irrelevance. By maintaining extensive social ties, organizing lavish entertainments, adorning her house and her person, she exhibited and shored up the class status of her mate.

This was the social meaning and context which nurtured the ideal of the lady. This elite class was so small and of such recent vintage, however, that American ladies took their cues for public and private behavior from abroad—from etiquette books written by foreigners and American publications that parroted the mores of the fashionable classes of Europe. When an upper-class woman picked up these volumes and magazines from her dressing table, she was greeted with a foreign language of femininity. "Give ear oh daughter of beauty attend to the voice of your sister. . . . My father was brother of tenderness, my mother was sister of love." That the authors of such lines were men impersonating women would not disturb the reading lady, for she was wooed with the most extravagant compliments. "The whiteness of her bosom transcendeth the Lily, her smile is more delicious than a garden of roses, the innocence of her eye is like that of the turtle, the kisses of her mouth are sweeter than honey. The perfumes of Arabia breathe from her lips."[56]

A farmer's helpmeet or a she-merchant would most likely respond to such a ludicrous mode of address with a quizzical guffaw.

Such sentiments were offered to the American lady, however, as adulation to her sex. John Gregory outlined the elevation of women to civilized status in his American publication dated 1775: "I have not considered your sex as a domestic drudge, not the slave of our pleasures, but as our companions and equals as designed to soften our hearts and polish our manners."[57] Household utility was reduced to drudgery and in its stead the American lady was offered the narrow role of polishing male manners. The exponents of the new femininity also made use of the rhetoric of the age of reason: "Remember thou art man's reasonable companion, not the slave of his passions, the end of thy being is not merely to gratify his loose desire, but to assist in the toils of life, to soothe him with tenderness and recompense his care with soft endearments."[58] Women were rhetorically equipped with reason and equality but summoned to employ them only in soothing, civilizing, and comforting men. An insidious formulation of sexual stereotypes underlay the paean to the white-bosomed, sweet-lipped American daughter of beauty.

American publishers moved haltingly at first to insinuate the new femininity into the culture of the new nation. The United States publication of *The Lady's Pocket Library* in 1792 was prefaced by a polite apology. The author hoped that her American readers "will not be offended if she has occasionally pointed out certain qualities and suggested certain tempers and dispositions as peculiarly feminine, and hazarded some observations which naturally arose from the subject, on the different characters which mark the sexes. And here again she takes the liberty to repeat that these distinctions cannot be nicely maintained."[59] By the turn of the century, however, the American lady's library was littered with ecstatic endorsements of distinctly and exclusively feminine characteristics. In addition to beauty of face and form, upper-class women were flattered by celebrations of their modesty, innocence, sweetness, softness of manner, and gentleness of voice—a whole catalogue of refinements, which could be summarized in the simple aphorism "submission and obedience are the lessons of her life, and peace and happiness are her reward."[60] A natural tendency toward submission was now regarded as integral to the personality of woman and adjudged the source of her personal happiness and her self-fulfillment.

Still, additional incentives were required to seduce women into the new femininity. The fashionable writers of the eighteenth century employed a now familiar device for this purpose: the flattering assurance that women were different and superior to men. A French author whose treatise was published in America late in the eighteenth century displayed the basic principle of this casuistry: "Many [women] rival us in the endowments of the mind and in the qualities of the heart they generally surpass us." The celebrated qualities of the feminine heart included an overabundance of love, a refined sensibility, a timidity that prompted frequent blushes—and a heightened moral sense. The latter characteristic was defined as a "great innate sense within, more than a conscience—a certain instant faithful monitor which holds a residence in special in the female breast."[61] All these feminine qualities neatly complemented the newly designed concept of masculinity: "Man is designed for deeds of strength and courage, has a toughness in his temper, which women alone can soften."[62] Within the libraries of the upper class, humanity was vivisected into male and female parts and then patched together again in a symbiotic union.

It should be clear that the female member of a fashionable couple was more severely crippled by this surgery. Women were endowed only with the capacity to quietly cultivate their accomodating personalities, not to accompany men into the world, to acquire, achieve, and produce. Within the private sphere, the passive woman became the humble servant, and the active man became her grateful master. Female identity came as an afterthought to masculine endeavor, designed to solace, please, and refresh the world-weary male. The need to please, it was said, was lodged deep in the nature of women. While the male half of the sexual pair might survive very well without the blandishments of femininity, his female counterpart was helpless apart from her stronger partner. She would languish without male company, support, and earnings.

As a consequence of this unbalanced arrangement, some hectic maneuvering was required to bring the two maimed sexes together again. In fashionable social circles, the drawing rooms and ballrooms of the wealthy provided the arena for this process. The writers of the era often posed as distraught young men who rushed to balls, teas, and salons to find repose in the salubrious company of females. Women were to take up their stations there in order to "tame the young man's wildness," "civilize him," and exert their "instinctive conscience." Coincidentally, the young gallants might feast upon the physical beauty of the opposite sex as well. "Now view the maid, the love-inspiring maid / with virtue and with modesty array'd / Survey her matchless form . . . Survey and Re-survey from feet to head." The author of these lines, James Bowdoin, poetically transversed the entire female body, lingering with a special awe over her "tempting breasts."[63]

Such attentiveness to the female form was but one example of a general preoccupation with the physical attributes of the lady. Even English Puritan writers of the era, most notably John Milton, delighted in describing the sensual qualities of Eve. This trend is graphically illustrated by eighteenth-century American portraiture. Plain, unadorned representations of goodwives gave way after 1750 to highly idealized portraits of American ladies, draped in satin, endowed with ample and amply-displayed bosoms, surrounded by fruits and flowers and other natural symbols. Companion portraits of males favored darker hues, more sedate attire, and symbols of commerce and learning, sailing ships and libraries. A bridal party in the South displayed similar fashions in masculinity and femininity: the bride "elegantly dressed in white satin and the bridegroom in a lead color lined with pink satin." The fashionable costumes of the nineteenth century boldly exhibited the sexual characteristics of both sexes, the woman's tiny waist and full bosom, as well as the man's muscular thighs and calves. When American upper-class culture turned the spotlight on gender divisions, it employed a familiar ideological device—an exaggerated emphasis on the physical differences between male and female—with particular focus on the natural and bodily symbolism of femininity.

While the fashionable woman might amply expose her body, she was advised to be more niggardly in the display of certain attributes of her mind. John Gregory, for example, instructed young women that "if you happen to have any learning, keep it a profound secret, especially from the men, who generally look with a jealous and malignant eye on a woman of great parts and cultivated understanding."[64] The female protagonist of Charles Brockden Brown's *Alcuin* refrained from political discourse, on the principle that such topics were beyond the propriety and capacity of women. When a relentless young dandy continued to invite her opinions, he unleashed a tide of angry accusations against the male sex. The prescriptive literature of the period, however, repeatedly advised women to suppress such outbursts as well as the intelligence that underlay them. They were admonished to move gingerly through the social circle, exerting their civilizing influence on the assembled men without giving the slightest appearance of calculation. The French author of *Essays on the Character of Women* put it this way: "The woman in society by being continually upon the look-out, from the double motives of curiosity and of policy, must have a perfect knowledge of man. . . . They must know how far one may direct without appearing to be interested. How far one may presume upon that art, even after it is known; in what estimation they are held by those with whom they live, and to what degree it is necessary to serve them, that they may govern them."[65]

Such duplicity, intrinsic to the maintenance of artificial sexual differences, transformed the fashionable social circle into a hotbed of suspicion and intrigue, amply illustrated in the fashionable literature of the era. American publishers gave generous circulation to a treatise entitled *Female Policy Detected*, wherein "the art of the designing woman is laid out." The author of this humorous diatribe against women, and many others like him, alerted the young Boston bachelors to the peculiar stratagems of harlots, widows, husband hunters. Even those females who wished no more than a sexual liaison were to be distrusted: "He that serves the lust of a woman makes himself her monkey, for she admires him no longer than while he is playing with his taile." English literature of the eighteenth century abounded with references to the nearly insatiable sexual appetites of women. One Englishman warned that "the sensibilities of woman are not limited as ours. . . . Truly women do not feel themselves exhausted, even if they suffer the amorous attacks of a multitude of men successively."[66] This interpretation of female sexuality merely compounded male suspicion of the opposite sex.

Women writers had some suspicions of their own. The most popular American novel of the era, Susanna Rowson's *Charlotte Temple*, was built around the innocent maiden's liability to seduction and abandonment by the predatory males of the upper class. As Rowson made clear in the following lines from another work, perfect female innocence was a poor adaptation to the fashionable coterie. "No sooner did the tyrant see woman from every blemish free, / Than heedless of his guardian part / He strove by mean seductive art / To rob her of her brightest charms."[67] One character in an American short story did not mince words in confronting a male predator: "You are a man . . . and I dare not trust you."[68] Women were also advised to be on the alert for the chicanery of their own sex. Popular tales of seduction customarily portrayed jaded females as accomplices to the acts of a lecherous villain. Didactic books and magazine articles directed young women of the upper classes to choose their female friends with care, and to share the secrets of their hearts only with their mothers.

Yet it was only in this circle of intrigue and distrust that a fashionable woman could seek out a mate. Her very nature, it was said, necessitated her matrimony. "That Providence designed women for a state of dependence and consequently of submission I cannot doubt when I consider their timidity of temper, their tenderness of make, the many comforts and necessities of life which they are unable to procure without our aid. Their evident want of our protection upon a thousand occasions impels us to help and protect them."[69] Woman's happiness as well as her survival were now proclaimed to be contingent upon marriage: "Her family is the source of all her joy."[70] Matrimony, furthermore, consigned her to a private and dependent and isolated sphere; "The proper spheres of the sexes are distinctly different." While the upper-class husband took up his position in "the widely differing professions and employments into which private advantage and public good require that men should be distributed," his wife was relegated to the "care of the family."[71]

The wife of a wealthy businessman or planter would still find many occasions to make her fashionable way through a large social circle. At the same time, however, a special woman's place was being set apart from this wider social sphere. The role of wife, pure and simple, gained new significance. The exclusively wifely function was described as follows: "When ruffled with the busy cares and scenes of the world [the husband] flies to his home, where the engaging smiles of the friend of his heart dispel the gloom and restore the ease and comfort of his heart."[72] At the rarefied apex of the American social order a novel and ominous concept of woman's place began slowly to take form. The home appeared, albeit indistinctly, as a private refuge set apart from society and the economy, from which women dispensed domestic comforts to husbands whose major activities transpired outside its boundaries.

The routine absence of the husband from this domicile undercut the mutuality upon which earlier and more down-to-earth concepts of conjugal affection rested. The sentiment of love lost its equilibrium in the fashionable literature of the eighteenth century as the balance of conjugal affection tilted awkwardly toward the female. "Love is without dispute the passion which women feel the strongest and they express the best . . . it is their soul."[73] Supposedly, love not only occupied a larger place in the female psyche, but consumed her entire being: "For a woman of delicate sentiments to bestow her heart is properly to give up her whole self." Put another way, "Love in one sex is Conquest, in the other a Sacrifice."[74] Needless to say, women were cast in the sacrificial role in this scenario of love among the upper classes. In order to play it adequately, married women were instructed to render unto their spouses their entire stock of love, warmth, and solace.

In point of fact, members of the female leisure class did run the risk of considerable personal sacrifice, for the wife who failed to meet her marital obligations could be easily dispensed with by a rich and powerful husband. The town records of Newport tell of one woman who suffered this fate, the wife of Timothy Dexter, merchant. "Whereas Elizabeth my wife has become an intemperate, quarrelsome and troublesome woman, inasmuch that it is impossible to live with her in peace and decency I am therefore determined not to cohabit with her any longer, while she continues her present evil courses." The local press put a different construction on this event: "Timothy [Dexter of Newport] has now parted from his wife because she is old, upon a contract paid of 2,000 pounds [sterling] and the horse and chaise and is looking out for a young wife."[75] Those men who rose to the pinnacle of power and wealth in the American commercial economy had the wherewithal to divorce a spouse who was not to their liking and support another. Their wives, furthermore, lacked the power inherent in a practical economic partnership that might deter their mates from dissolving a marriage. Accordingly, the social role of the upper-class wife could be narrow, subordinate, and precarious as well.

The comforts of wealth and leisure, moreover, were counterbalanced by the wife's subjection to the insidious influences of fashionable training in womanhood. Nancy Shippen, daughter of a prosperous Philadelphia merchant, was fated to translate the new literature of womanhood into a real-life melodrama. In 1777 Nancy's father sent her to Miss Rogers School with instructions to educate herself for the upper-class social circle, "in holding your head and shoulders, in making a curtsy, in going out or coming into a room, in giving and receiving, holding your knife and fork, walking and setting. These things contribute so much to a good appearance that they are of great consequence." Miss Shippen learned her lessons well, and upon entrance into Philadelphia society quickly won many suitors, including Henry Livingston, a scion of New York aristocracy. When, against Nancy's romantic predilections, a marriage was arranged by the two lofty families, Nancy's mother sent her to the altar with this piece of advice: "Never forget that it should be your first care to please and make your husband happy."[76]

Nancy Shippen Livingston had little time in which to practice these wifely virtues. Her husband turned out to be an utter fop and a compulsive philanderer. They separated within two years. Henry Livingston was vindictive as well, refused his wife a divorce, and repeatedly barred her from seeing her daughter. The belle of Philadelphia society had no other recourse but to return to her parents' home and immerse herself once again in the diversions of the fashionable coterie. Her days often went like this:

> This morning I gave orders to the servants as usual for the business of the day, then took a little work in my hands and set down before the fire to think how I should dispose of myself in the evening. The morning I generally devote to working and reading, and I concluded to go to the concert. Then I considered what I would dress in, and having determined this important part, I felt light and easy.[77]

The rest of her days typically entailed a round of social engagements interspersed with attention to her toilet.

Before the dissolution of her marriage Mrs. Livingston had one additional avocation, attention to her daughter. "Dress'd my Angel Child, kiss'd her a hundred times, thought her the most beautiful Child in the world and sent her to be admir'd by Miss Tilghman who said a thousand things in her favor in which I perfectly agreed." The devoted mother seemed intent upon transmitting the vanities of femininity unto another generation. Her ecstasies of maternal delight would meet with approval from some spokesmen for fashionable womanhood. One treatise written in 1788 maintained that "maternal affection was inherent in the nature of women."[78] Other writers saw fit to take no chances and actively inculcated this supposed attribute of feminine nature: "Art thou a mother, let they children be the darlings of thy tenderness."[79] Such references to maternal qualities were relatively infrequent in the literature of femininity, however, merely brief addenda to the virtues required of the status symbol and the wife. The practical duties of motherhood were given even shorter notice, limited to occasional injunctions to suckle the infant and mold its mind in the early stages of its growth. Most upper-class women could delegate the physical care and education of their offspring to wet nurses, servants, governesses, and schools. Motherhood remained a poorly articulated and ambiguous role for upper-class women, for American ladies were still advised: "Dote not on the idol of thy womb, for the extreme fondness of a mother is as dangerous as the violence of her hate."[80]

In sum, the lady was a unique image of womanhood, drawn in vivid contrast to both Adam's Rib and the domestic icons that would be worshipped by the nineteenth-century middle class. Unlike the goodwife of the past, the eighteenth-century lady was an emblem of exaggerated and idealized femininity, set on a pedestal far above mundane economic activities. Unlike her Victorian successor, however, she was not noted for her domestic or maternal attributes; she preferred the social circle to the hearth, and the toilet to the nursery. This particular model of womanhood was mounted on the social foundation of the merchant and planter elite. It symbolized a set of female roles which served as a social display of elite class position. Those men who succeeded in converting family ties and social connections into merchant capital were able to install their wives and daughters in a position of opulent display and apparent leisure. These same men installed their sons at the helms of lucrative and demanding business enterprises. The specialized role of the lady, in other words, was a testament to the preservation and enrichment of patriarchal power, at least within a select class of Americans.

THE DECLINE OF PATRIARCHY AMONG NEW ENGLAND'S MIDDLING AND LOWER CLASSES

The position of the merchant patriarch was well beyond the reach of most Americans, who were openly disdainful of the pretensions of the lady. Reverend Ogden, for one, regarded the fashionable construction of femininity as an odious and contagious English disease. Of the removal of women from productive activity, he said, "the American heart revolts at the idea."[81] Other homespun authors made the fashionable female the butt of their satire. Mason Locke Weems concocted a humorous brew of American backwoods manners and English pretensions entitled *The Lover's Almanac*. Its subtitle reduced the sublimities of romance to the ridiculous: "A very seasonable and savory dissertation on love, courtship, and marriage—with a most enchanting flourish on beauty, admirably calculated to disclose those two most delectable and desirable of all secrets, how the homely may become handsome and the handsome angelic." The female characters in Weems' little farce displayed the American's severely retarded sense of gentility. One was renowned for "picking her teeth with her fork, snuffing up her nose, picking it with her fingers, blowing it and looking in her handkerchief." The more refined heroine of the piece was nonetheless a very down-to-earth young lady. "From the time she was ten years old, she took the keys and became her mother's little housekeeper. The dairy, the manufactory, the garden, her books and harpsicord are continually visited by the dear angelic bee."[82] Indigenous genres of American writing, like this Virginia almanac or Yankee sermons, were not in the business of manufacturing paragons of femininity. The best they could manage was the occasional creation of an awkward, almost schizoid image like "the dear angelic bee." Only a very select group of women, pandered to by the fashionable ladies' magazines, lived suspended in the rarefied sphere of the leisure class.

Even among the lower strata of American society, however, the social position of women was subtly changing. The transformation is most well documented in the North, and especially New England. The incipient transformation was manifest in the growing numbers of women who escaped patriarchal surveillance by fleeing to the cities of the new nation. A New York matron observed:

> I know this age has so great a contempt for the former, that 'tis but a matter of scorn to allege any of their customs. Else I should say the liberties that are now taken would then have been startled at. They that then should have seen a young maid rambling abroad without her mother or some other prudent persons would have looked at her as a stray and thought it but a neighborly office to have brought her home, whereas

now 'tis a rarity to see them in any company graver than
themselves and she that goes with her parents thinks she does
but walk around with her jailor.[83]

Such observations cannot be dismissed as the perennial complaints of an older generation, for the commercial era actually expanded the social freedom of women in a variety of ways. For one
thing, advertisements in city newspapers often recruited female
workers independently of their parents. One such notice offered
employment to a woman between eighteen and twenty-three, resourceful, attractive, and "possessed of 3 or 400 pounds entirely at
her own Disposal, and where there will be no necessity of going
through the tiresome Talk of addressing Parents or Guardians for
their consent."[84]

There is also some evidence that young escapees from the patriarchal household were reluctant to form homes of their own. A
Providence, Rhode Island, census, for example, recorded the fact
that 23 percent of the city's residents over the age of sixteen were
single. Statistics like these were likely to alarm the conservative
fathers of the town. In 1752, the Reverend Thomas Humphrey felt
called upon to write and publish a sermon entitled "Marriage as an
Honorable Estate." He was prompted to do so by the fact that the
institution of matrimony "hath in the last century more than in
any precedent age, been deprecated and villify'd by the scurrilous
inventions of ludicrous and pretending wits, and been made the
common subject of railery and ridicule."[85] Edward Ward's treatise
certainly fit into this category, vilifying those "millions two by two
that fall into misery by matrimony and are deadly wounded by the
plague of poverty for want of virtuous preceding in themselves."[86]
Ward and other writers on the subject implied that marriage could
be a hindrance to a young man's rise to wealth in a commercial
economy. The skeptics regarding marriage were many and well
placed. Matrimony was one of Ben Franklin's favorite targets for
satire. He went so low as to advise young men to conduct liaisons
with elderly, and hence infertile, women if their inclinations or
finances deterred a wedding. Even worse, he honored Miss Polly
Baker for the patriotic service of supplying the new nation with
five children without ever going through the formality of acquiring
a husband.[87] Of course, jokes at the expense of marriage could not
deal a fatal blow to the time-honored institution. This literary

leitmotif did, however, indicate that the meaning of marriage was changing and with it the social role of American women.

Although most women would continue to work out their adult roles within the family, they embarked upon wedded life in a more erratic and unpredictable fashion. As the eighteenth century progressed, the age at marriage became more random; weddings, in other words, were not concentrated around one modal age such as twenty-one. Rather, women were marrying at a more individualized pace and one that was no longer determined by the order of births within their families. Beginning in the mid-eighteenth century fewer women patiently waited for their older sisters to marry before they proceeded to the altar. Fathers, it would seem, were unable or ill-disposed to impose the old hierarchical order of matchmaking. Be it the effect of strong-willed children, or of powerless or soft-hearted fathers, this element of the patriarchal family system had dissipated with the commercial era.[88]

Independent evidence of increasing self-direction among the young men and women of the Revolutionary era is found in eighteenth-century baptismal records. Young couples were clearly impatient with the slow-moving family cycle of the patriarchal household. In towns North and South, as many as one in three couples conceived a child before their wedding day.[89] The rate of early births was equally high in once Puritan New England. Indeed, even in the center of revitalized piety during the Great Awakening, ministers reported that their congregations were teeming with bastards.[90] It would be rash, however, to label the youth of the Revolutionary era insouciant hedonists. Bearing an illegitimate child still conveyed a social stigma and incurred considerable economic risk, especially to women. Therefore, most young women remained very cautious about sexual matters. All those early births, after all, were conceived under such circumstances that a marriage soon followed. The young men and women seemed to be walking a fine line between rigid repression and open defiance of the sexual code of their fathers and mothers. They may, in fact, have become rather calculating about sexual matters. This was apparently the case with a young woman from Concord, Massachusetts, by the name of Lucy Barnes, whose father forbade her to marry the man of her choice, Joseph Hosmer. The patriarch could not restrain the young lovers for very long, however, for Mr. Barnes consented to a wedding after his daughter became pregnant with Hosmer's child.[91] Perhaps Lucy

Barnes Hosmer was not the only young woman who maneuvered so cleverly around the waning authority of the patriarch.

The decline of the New England patriarch was clearly a result of dwindling land resources. By the mid-eighteenth century very few fathers had nearby fields on which to settle all their sons, nor sufficient personal estate to supply their daughters with enticing dowries. In town after town as many as half of the native sons left their villages and their fathers to find land on distant frontiers or jobs in distant cities.[92] As new avenues of employment opened up within the more diversified economy, young men and women could plot out their futures alone, and women could negotiate directly with their prospective spouses.

The resultant marital relationships generated one substantial and highly significant social change, a decline in fertility. The first wholesale downturn in the nation's birthrate occurred at the turn of the nineteenth century. This demographic transformation, which began in agricultural New England in the late eighteenth century, was linked to the diminishing land supply. Philip Greven has charted the stages of this population implosion in the Massachusetts village of Andover. By 1764 Andover had grown from a settlement of a few young families to a town of almost 2,500 residents. The rapid rate of growth continued into the next decade, when Andover's population peaked at almost 3,000. Then, by 1790, the number of Andover residents actually declined to less than 2,800 persons. This watershed coincided with the exhaustion of Andover's land supply. While part of the decline in population was due to the emigration of young men and women to more lucrative frontiers, the major factor in the reduction of population growth was the constriction of the birthrate. By the last half of the eighteenth century, the women of Andover were bearing on the average two fewer offspring than did their grandmothers—five or six rather than seven or eight children.[93]

Other New England towns faced this demographic crisis at times appropriate to their own economic history. In Hingham, Massachusetts, for example, the number of children per married woman began to fall significantly between 1691 and 1745. The depression of the fishing industry in the town of Ipswich produced a similar drop in the birthrate before 1750. A study of comfortable Quaker families in Philadelphia, New York, and Salem revealed that the fertility of women in the Society of Friends declined by an average of 1.4 offspring in the era of the American Revolution.[94] In short, women in such diverse segments of the commercial economy as urban shops and New England farms and fishing villages saw the size of the family decline significantly in the late eighteenth century.

In its earliest stages this decline in fertility was the result of an older age at marriage. By marrying a few years later than the preceding generations, in other words, women reduced the number of births by one or more children. By the early nineteenth century, however, family size was declining independently of age at marriage.[95] It would follow that husbands and wives were taking direct and conscious action to curtail fertility. The most conclusive and early evidence of this change comes from a study of the Quakers, whose fertility declined so sharply in the Revolutionary era. These women were not marrying less or later, or dying earlier, in the post-Revolutionary era. Such factors did not cause the drop in the birthrate. Women who married late in life, furthermore, bore approximately the same number of children as young wives, who somehow curtailed childbearing well before they reached menopause. This pattern clearly suggests that these Quaker men and women had determined an ideal family size, substantially lower than that of their parents.[96] They might implement this ideal size through the ancient practice of coitus interruptus, through sexual abstinence, or perhaps induced abortion. But whatever the means they used, select groups of American parents had determined that a large family was a liability rather than an asset. In the burgeoning commercial economy, and particularly in those rural towns that had reached the saturation point for farm population, the value of unchecked fertility came under question and woman's reproductive labors slowly began to diminish.

Further details of this demographic transformation are supplied by a study of Sturbridge, Massachusetts, between 1760 and the first decades of the nineteenth century. During this time span, when the agricultural village was first introduced to commercial production and a proliferation of shops and cottage industries, the average family size declined by more than two persons. Approximately half of the reduction in the number of children was due to the delay of marriage. The change in fertility that was accomplished after marriage was due in large part to an earlier termination in childbearing. The women who married between the years of 1760 and 1769 bore their last children at the average age of 39.47, while those wed four decades later, between 1800 and 1819, terminated childbearing at the age of 37.82. As the family cycle approached maturity, it would seem that husbands and wives began to see an additional child as a burden rather than a resource.[97] The couples of Sturbridge acted decisively and early in the nineteenth century to prevent further growth of their families. A similar decline in fertility coincided with the exhaustion of the land supply and the advances of commercialization throughout the Northeast.[98] The diminution of woman's burden as the bearer and caretaker of infants was only one vital consequence of this shift in the birthrate. It also affected her most intimate relations with her mate and her most basic way of thinking. Sexual behavior, childbearing, and family size were no longer matters left to tradition and nature; now they were subjects for rational, individualistic, and often monetary calculations.

The fragmentation of the family into individual and perhaps self-interested economic agents led to a small epidemic of runaway wives, children, and servants at the turn of the nineteenth century. It was clear that the impudent mobility of wives caused considerable havoc in the household economy, for deserted husbands instructed merchants in far-flung regions not to trust their errant spouses for debts incurred in the family name. A woman of the busy commercial town of Newburyport, Massachusetts, for example, had "privately undertaken to buy sundry merchandise unknown to her husband" and proceeded to offer it for sale. Promptly her spouse gave public notice that he would not be held responsible for the debts of this wayward merchandising wife.[99]

Still, most wives remained by their husbands' sides through the turbulence of early commercial capitalism. The basis of their conjugal ties, however, had altered to such an extent that contemporary writers had to adopt a whole new language when they discussed family matters. First of all, the terms "patriarch" and "household" gave way to a concept of marriage in which increasing importance was attached to the marital pair as detached from the larger unit of kinship or residence. Couples, furthermore, were less frequently portrayed as the building blocks of society or the "first links of Human Society to which all the rest are formed," as William Secker once put it. When the conservative New England minister Timothy Dwight rose to defend marriage against the assaults of advocates of divorce, for example, he described the family as merely the *"source of all subordination and government and consequently of all peace and safety in the world"* (italics mine). The American family was now hailed as the fountainhead of social order, not a microcosmic society in itself. Marriage, according to Dwight and many of his contemporaries, was valued as the seat of private and personal services. It fostered the "comfort" and the "happiness" of the couple.[100]

These American writers seldom bathed the concept of marital happiness in sentimental and romantic euphoria. More often, they couched their endorsement of marriage in the language of the age of reason. One widely circulated treatise on courtship and marriage portrayed an ideal match as "a union of mind and a sympathy of mutual esteem and friendship for each other."[101] "Rational friendship" and "mutual respect" were the touchstones of marital propriety in the urbane literature of the new nation. The duties and manners incumbent upon the female parties to such alliances were trumpeted as far west as the Tennessee frontier, where a Nashville paper exclaimed in 1811: "What is more agreeable than the conversation of an intelligent, amiable and interesting friend? But who is more intelligent than a well educated female?"[102] Such enlightened views on marriage were something more than rhetoric at a time when vital family decisions, such as the timing of marriage and the number of children, were increasingly matters of rational, joint decisions between husbands and wives.

As if to underscore and advance this domestic enlightenment, the post-Revolutionary era occasioned major reform in women's education. The 1780s witnessed a great rush of women students into local secondary schools once reserved for males. The Founding Fathers themselves spawned several proposals for female education. Benjamin Rush's blueprint for the education of women commingled old and new ideas regarding the household obligations of wives. American women still needed to be trained, he thought, to become the "stewards and guardians of their husbands' property." But Rush also added the less prosaic skill of music to the curriculum of woman's education. This accomplishment, he maintained, would equip women to perform at public worship and to "soothe the cares of domestic life." In addition to providing domestic comfort for her husband, the educated woman would be better prepared to serve her sons. Instruction in history, geography, politics, and religion would assist American mothers to populate the republic with wise leaders and patriotic citizens.[103]

Rush was expounding on the theme of the "Republican Mother," the contribution of the patriots of the Revolutionary era to the museum of female iconography.[104] The Republican Mother as described by Rush altered previous notions of womanhood in two important ways. On the one hand, women are being granted access to intellectual training and discourse but, on the other, this education was being directed into specifically feminine channels. Women's intelligence was designed for domestic uses, for the private services of husbands and, especially, children. Thus the rudiments of a more narrowly private and domestic sphere of womanhood also date from this period. The essential responsibility of the Republican Mother was to instruct and socialize her male children for democratic citizenship. Women were urged to socialize their offspring in the spirit of the Enlightenment. One sermon of 1800 instructed mothers that "as soon as the blossoming flowers of reason begin to shoot forth, while yet in the bud, the opportunity to form them to virtue is seized upon with avidity and improved with care."[105] In the education of her children, a woman was to employ the methods of the American rationalist.

Motherhood also came to connote certain parental duties predating the blossoming of the child's reason. The infant became the topic of the first child-rearing manual to be published in America, portentously entitled *The Maternal Physician*. It was written by an upper-middle-class Boston woman, well versed in European literature on her subject, who chose to remain anonymous. This brief volume injected the spirit of science into woman's customary roles of nurse, midwife, and overseer of household health. The author of *The Maternal Physician* informed women about the latest methods of diagnosing and treating childhood diseases and providing for the general health and well-being of the young. Simultaneously, she clothed these instructions in an emotionally evocative rhetoric heretofore unheard of in the annals of American motherhood:

> And believe me, my fair friends, this is not a labour. What can so sweetly relieve the tedium of three or four weeks of confinement to a sick room as to watch with unremitting care, and mark with enraptured eyes, the opening beauties of the dear innocent cause of such confinement. Or what can equal

a mother's ecstasy when she catches the first emanations of mind in the mantling smile of her babe?

The Maternal Physician went on to celebrate "the thousand raptures" that thrill a mother's bosom "before a tooth is formed."[106]

Two new principles have been introduced into the maternal role, both of which, if put into practice, would greatly expand the purely domestic functions of American women. First of all, this scenario of motherhood called for a great expenditure of woman's time, constantly overseeing her infant's health and comfort. In addition, *The Maternal Physician* summoned prodigious emotional energy from the infant's mother. Although it was acknowledged that the child would require "comparatively less attention" after the age of two, this intense relationship between a mother and her babe left a lasting imprint on the character of woman. Its import was fully elaborated by the *Ladies' Literary Cabinet*.

Is there a feeling that activates the human heart so powerful as that of maternal affection? Who but woman can feel the tender sensation so strong? The father, indeed may press his lovely infant to his manly heart, but does it thrill with those feelings which irresistibly overcome the mother?[107]

By 1822 when these words were printed, the American woman was being invited to accept a specialized domestic function, one that not only was labeled "woman's work," but also distinguished between maternal feelings and "the manly heart."

This expanded concept of maternity, although far removed from the sober, largely asexual colonial idea of parenthood, was but a rare and subdued hint of the extravagant celebration of motherhood to come.

Even those privileged females who entered the domain of higher education during the American Enlightenment succeeded only in buying time before household roles would all but enclose them. The students who enrolled at the Young Ladies Academy of Philadelphia, for example, were promised that they would no longer be excluded "from the discussion of subjects calculated to strengthen and expand the mind." The academy's graduates in 1794 stood before an audience that included the First Lady of the new nation and several congressmen, to exhibit the results of their initiation

into the intellectual regimen previously reserved for men. The sal-
utatorian oratorically proclaimed that "In the age of reason . . . we
are not surprised if women have taken advantage of the small degree
of liberty that they still possess, and converted their talents into
public utility." Then, without a stammer, the young scholar announced, "In opposition to your immortal Paine we will exalt our
Wollstonecraft." Yet this graduate of the female academy did not
intend to apply her intellect nor her pride of sex in the way an
educated man would. She registered her compliance with the fact
that "custom and nature teach the propriety of [the sexes] being
suitable to the different situations and employments of life to which
they are allotted."[108]

These customs decreed that men could engage in war, politics,
business—all the "more active scenes of life"—and that women,
no matter how well educated, were not to desert their stations in
the home. Thus, when the valedictorian of the Young Ladies Academy of Philadelphia rose before the assembled dignitaries, she delivered an epitaph for the educated women of her generation:
"Anticipating soon to be called upon to fill their various domestic
stations in society, [the students] will, it is probable, never more
be required, or never more have opportunity of delivering their
sentiments in public."[109] Even the beneficiaries of the best that the
American Enlightenment offered to women were escorted only within
eyeshot of equality, and then were ushered swiftly into private life.
Their education would be applied to the direction of their servants,
the care of children, intelligent conversation with husbands and
friends.

The daughters of the American Revolution, newly liberated
from colonial patriarchy, did not fall compliantly into line with
this domestic program. Women still found it possible to move quite
freely through the familiar spaces of commercial villages and towns.
The compact size and accessibility of places like New York, Boston,
and Philadelphia still justified the title "walking city," and during
the Revolution allowed women frequent opportunities for political
action as well as casual socializing. In the busy commercial city,
public debate and conflict often spilled over from the orderly channels of church and state. In fact, in the immediate pre-Revolutionary
era, the span of fifteen years between 1760 and 1775, there were
no less than forty-four full-scale riots. Violent collective action in
the streets remained a popular mode of political action well into

the nineteenth century, and one in which women participated frequently and actively. The comment of an English journalist in 1800 might apply to the United States as well: "All public disturbances generally begin with the clamour of women." Women mingled with the crowds of rebels who sparked the War of Independence, and played a leading role in riots of special interest to their sex. When, in the heterogeneous ambience of the city, women could no longer rely on the church or town meeting for protection, they often took to the streets in their own defense.

There were at least three riots in the 1760s (in Providence, Newport, and New York City) that publicly shamed and physically punished unfaithful husbands. In Boston in 1707 a crowd of men and women demanded retribution from a wife-beater. "Seven or eight persons of both sexes," went the news report, "lured a man out of his house, and tore off his clothes and whipped him with rods to chastize him for carrying it harshly to his wife." Elsewhere, women took to the streets to defend their economic interests. In Pennsylvania in 1780 "several hundred of the weaker sex tore up all the posts and fence rails around a grain field [and] severely beat the owner over the shooting of three foraging hogs." This was neither the first nor the last time that women would violently protest an infringement on their rights and responsibilities as producers of their families' meat supply. They repeatedly made the same political point in flour riots, demanding that the price of bread be set at a reasonable level.[110]

Neither ladies nor wives of the bourgeoisie were likely to participate in this rowdy street politics. But these women also found some new social contacts outside the home during the eighteenth century. For one thing, ladies of relative leisure had time to cultivate strong bonds with their peers. A long and loving correspondence between Esther Burr and Sarah Prince, during the eighteenth century, was one of the early manifestations of this embryonic society of women. The diary of Sarah Stearns of Greenfield, Massachusetts, recorded a whole series of such friendships, which spanned into the nineteenth century. The same document illustrated that female social circles often trafficked in more than emotions and private companionship. Mrs. Stearns was actively involved in her local church, which in the early nineteenth century was becoming largely a coterie of females. When a revival occurred in her village in the 1810s, Mrs. Stearns professed her faith with special fervor. Her religious enthusiasm did not exhaust itself in personal introspection, however, but drove her instead into more frenetic social action. She formed her neighbors into a "little band of associated females" and spurred them on to such projects as a maternal association, a school society, and a juvenile home. Her proudest creation was a local female charity: "Our Benevolent Society is in a flourishing state, many destitute children have been assisted and taught many things. I can truly say it affords me one of my chief sources of pleasure."[111] Sarah Stearns, for one, was not about to relinquish the broad social contacts and extensive social responsibilities of the old-fashioned mistress of the household.

Although the women of the new nation were barred from the countinghouse, the council chamber, and the militia, they were by no means confined to their homes. The doors to the church and their neighbors' parlors were still open to them, and when these proved too narrow, women created new avenues to social activity. Between 1800 and 1830, women organized themselves into benevolent societies throughout the United States. They formed religious associations like the Female Missionary Society, whose chapter in western New York State was active in at least forty-six different towns as of 1818. New York City's Society for the Relief of Poor Widows with Small Children was founded by Isabella Graham in 1797, and in the next three decades similar female associations for the assistance of the needy proliferated through the Eastern United States and all along the pioneer trail. One association of Boston women aided more than 10,000 families and distributed more than $22,000 in the thirty years after its founding in 1812. Women were also active in establishing new social institutions: orphan asylums, charity schools, and homes for the indigent.[112]

The congregation of women in these extrafamilial groups served several purposes. First, benevolent associations allowed women to perform some of their traditional social-welfare functions outside the home. Second, they provided women with company, simple access to more lively social intercourse than was available in the less populous households of commercial society. Once women went outside the family unit for social action and companionship, furthermore, they were able to master some of the procedures of commercial economy. Women could collect large sums of money, chair business meetings, and cultivate a far-reaching organizational network, all for the cause of religion and charity. Finally, the female members of benevolent societies served notice that they would not let the course of history pass them by as it portended the removal of economic and social activity from the home. In the first decade of the nineteenth century, ministers came to recognize, with some bafflement, that the world of charity and religious benevolence had been thoroughly infiltrated by women.

At the same time that women were beginning to lay claim to this sphere outside the home, however, many of the traditional female functions were exiting from the household, and perhaps at a faster rate. The proliferation of prisons, almshouses, orphan asylums, and hospitals absorbed the social services once performed by the mistress of the household. These specialized institutions were more often supervised by city fathers and salaried male commissioners than by women, who were remunerated by the town. Simultaneously, schools usurped the educational functions of women, and hired day laborers supplanted the indentured servants they had once trained and supervised. Servants, the poor, abandoned children, the sick, and the criminal were being evicted from the household and American women were increasingly left with only their husbands and children to care for.

In sum, the social roles and spaces allocated to women, like their economic position, while clearly changing in the late eighteenth and early nineteenth centuries, were moving in a maze of different directions. These were the myriad nuances of womanhood that coincided with the rise of commercial capitalism in America. While the glamorized parasitism ascribed to the fashionable lady was perhaps the most dramatic innovation of the era, it was practicable for only a few American women before 1820. Meanwhile, other women plummeted to poverty and exploitation in the almshouses and the slums of the new nation. At the same time, the prospects of she-merchants paled before the opportunities open to enterprising males, while the productive duties of helpmeets changed and sometimes dwindled as men took the reins of a more complicated economic system. The middle-class wives of commercial farmers, shopkeepers, and professionals were stranded in somewhat narrower households, where strictly domestic functions like adorning the home and caring for children were granted new stature and importance. Clearly, the rigid sexual stratification of the patriarchal household had not survived the dismemberment of the subsistence family economy. The more individualized ethic of early American capitalism and the egalitarian standards of the new republic had penetrated into the family and affected women as well as men.

Yet all these signs of change did not line up to form a clear road map to the gender system of the future. This was a moment of promise, risk, and ambiguity in the history of American women. Something of the tenor of this transition is revealed by the diary of Sarah Ripley Stearns.[113] The daughter of a shopkeeper in a small market town of New England, Sarah Ripley grew up at the crossroads of commercial capitalism. The early entries in her diary chronicled the active but leisurely social life of a young woman early in the nineteenth century. Sarah's days were occupied with intermittent visiting, country walks, boat trips, and shopping sprees, often in mixed company. Her parents sent her to boarding school, where her social activities became more formal—balls and assemblies and "many of those amusements of which young people are fond." Upon the completion of her education, Sarah returned to her home where she assumed the economic responsibility of assisting in her father's shop. In busy mercantile seasons, she had little time or incentive to consult her diary, for she confessed that "time passes on in the same dull round of domestic occupations and I seldom go out or see company, consequently the incidents of my life at present afford but few materials to commit to writing." If Sarah engaged in any mode of home manufacturing she did not feel this was noteworthy enough to mention either. It was clear, however, that in her youth Sarah Ripley was enjoying some of the new freedom and new opportunities the era offered women: a relaxed social life, the chance to engage in commerce and to get an advanced education.

As matrimony approached, however, a new set of priorities seemed to close in on her. The private journal of Sarah Ripley contains few references to courtship, almost none to romance. The young woman occasionally alluded to a "friend," the focal point of mysterious difficulties too delicate or painful to detail. Then in 1812 she announced without warning, "I gave my hand in marriage to Mr. Charles Stearns of Shelburn and accompanied him immediately home—I have now acquitted the abode of my youth, left the protection of my parents and given up the name I have always borne to enter upon a new and untried scene. May the grace of God enable me to fulfill with prudence and piety the great and important duties which now dissolve on me." Thus ended a courtship, which had been drawn out for five years and yet left hardly a trace in the repository of a young woman's deepest thoughts—her private diary. Once settled in what she called the "still and peaceful scenes of domestic tranquility," Mrs. Stearns seems to have contracted a slight case of ennui. Why else would she quote at great length from the memoirs of one Hannah Hodges, a shopkeeper who retired at age eighty-five to complain that "I have not so much comfort not even in religion as when I was bustling half the day behind the counter. I need more variety than I now get. I become stifled for want of something to rouse me."

Mrs. Stearns herself was not to rest idle for long, however. Within four years of marriage she had given birth to three children. With the birth of her first child, a daughter, she resolved to take "assiduous care" to cultivate her "infant reason." She assumed the same responsibilites for her subsequent offspring as well as for two children, one a pauper, the other orphaned, whom she took into her home to raise. Now Sarah Stearns was busy enough but not altogether content. She acknowledged to her diary that "I have little time for working on serious reflections with my little family." She did, however, as reported earlier, make the time to become an active member of her church and a leader in female benevolent organizations.

Mrs. Stearns' diary recorded yet another newfangled concern on the part of its author: a sharpened consciousness of personal feelings and emotional ties. This acute emotional sensibility engulfed the pages of Sarah's journal whenever the idea of death entered her consciousness. While in her teens, Sarah was moved to poetry by a newspaper account of the untimely demise of a stranger: "But Death's cold hands the hopeful youth destroys." When her infant brother died shortly thereafter, her elegy included the consoling observation that he had gone to "happier scenes" where they would be reunited. Sarah's musings about death amounted to more than a religious preoccupation with the afterlife. They also occasioned a heightened consciousness of her own earthly bonds. Sarah poured out her innermost feelings when a young friend died in 1808. "I can scarcely bring it home to my imagination that my Rachel is gone forever, and that I shall no more behold her loved countenance, meeting me with the smile of welcome no more to hear her soft voice, or soothing gentle accents, speaking from the feelings of her heart and assuring me of a good reception—but it is too true!!!"

Sarah Ripley Stearns was to experience many other painful separations: her brother's move to the West, her departure from her parents' village, the uprooting of her family three times in the course of her married life. The most devastating blow came in 1818 with the death of her husband. Prior to this event Mrs. Stearns had not recounted her feelings toward her husband in any detail. Now she devoted nine full pages of her journal to this theme. She confided: "I did love him alas but too tenderly. We lived together in such terms as man and wife ought to live, placing perfect confidence in one another, bearing one another's burdens and making due allowances for human imperfection." The bereaved woman's diary ends on this note of loneliness: "I am now a widow, I have no bosom friend to go to in seasons of perplexity for advice, no one with whom I can unreservedly share all my griefs and sorrows, all my joys and pleasures." Sarah Stearns' reactions to her husband's death and to death in general seem to suggest an intensification of domestic affection and dependence among the women of her generation.

It is unlikely that American women of this era experienced deaths in the family more frequently than did their mothers and grandmothers. They did, however, inhabit a more unstable social environment. The community and the little commonwealth were splintering into individual fragments; young men sought more lucrative frontiers; young women married away from the parental homestead; vital manufactures relocated outside the household; trade moved out into the commercial marketplace; social services were lodged in specialized institutions. The family and close friends were the primary buoys in a sea of social change, and the sundering of these ties by death took on added significance. Simultaneously, women were placed at a greater distance from the central processes of social and economic life, and were left in the relative solitude of home with time to cultivate their emotional responses.

This process did not affect all American women in the early nineteenth century. But it did touch the lives of women like Sarah Stearns, located in the middle-class center of the commercial economy. The diaries of such New England women are peppered with maudlin descriptions of death. Sarah Ripley Stearns' friend Eunice Callender left a private journal steeped full of sentimental visions of death, touching her family, friends, and total strangers. The most devastating emotional breach for Miss Callender was the death of her mother: "From this bleeding heart a Mother! A parent—the

Author of my being . . . dearer to me than my own existence."[114] Catharine Maria Sedgwick, another Boston spinster, also filled her journal with the anguish of separation. Every object on which she fixed her affection—parents, siblings, nieces, and nephews—ultimately departed, leaving her to grieve in later life, as she had from the tenderest age, "who can see the dreaming that brings tears to my eyes from a world of memories and mourning."[115]

These preoccupations with personal feelings and emotional attachments were not unique to New England women. Neither was their sentimental expression. Westward, in the town of Montrose, Pennsylvania, a local poetess wrote graveyard verses: "Not for the dead but for the woe of sever'd bliss, these sorrows flow; / For sleep the good on sweeter bed, / Than this world's love can ever spread."[116] Off on the Tennessee frontier the newspapers harbored the same genre of poetry, devoted to such themes as "The Dead Twins" ("Within a little coffin lay, helpless babes as sweet as May," etc.).[117] Such sentimental preoccupations quickly seeped out of diaries into newsprint and little gilt volumes. By 1820, Lydia Huntley Sigourney of Hartford, Connecticut, had made a national reputation on paeans to dead children and their weeping mothers.

This curious blossoming of sentimentality must be added to the myriad nuances of womanhood whose appearance roughly coincided with the rise of commercial capitalism. It suggests that the volatile conditions of womanhood and commerce were also stirring up a storm in the minds and feelings of American women. The responses, thoughts, and actions of women like Sarah Stearns would play a critical part in shaping a new womanhood to come.

T H R E E

CREATING WOMAN'S SPHERE: GENDER IN THE MAKING OF AMERICAN INDUSTRIAL CAPITALISM: 1820 – 1865

The variety and fluidity that characterized images of womanhood at the turn of the nineteenth century was to be short-lived. By mid-century, woman had been escorted to a definitive place in American culture. She was to be the faithful guardian of the home fires, nestled by the hearth while the great common man conquered the West, built the railroads, and championed democracy. The American democrat during the age of Jackson was loath to call the female sex unequal or designate her sphere as inferior, subordinate, or servile. Woman's place was only different, as she was. Her assigned place was deemed a far better one than the rough-and-tumble world of war, work, politics; and woman's superior nature—pure, pious, and gentle—entitled her to reign there. It was between 1820 and 1865 that this familiar set of sexual stereotypes and role divisions was firmly imprinted on the American popular mind. By the time war broke out between the North and the South, another bold gash had cut across American culture, one which bluntly divided national life, and human character as well, into two seemingly inviolate spheres labeled male and female.

These prescriptions for what was called "true womanhood" were propagated even in the most remote corners of the continent. Because of the development of cheap printing and the expert salesmanship of powerful publishing companies during the 1820s, the circulation of ideas had become a thriving national industry. Books and magazines, printed in northeastern cities by such publishing moguls as the Harper Brothers, were circulated throughout the country via canals, railroads, steamboats, and covered wagons. When this literary baggage was unloaded in the Ohio Valley or in the trans-Mississippi West, the new frontier became littered with evocations of fragile femininity, paeans to "Rose of a Western Bower" or "Fair Flowers of the West."[1] The American West in the nineteenth century was not particularly hospitable to the sturdy helpmeet and brash virago of the seventeenth-century Atlantic seaboard, the first American frontier. The mainstay of the national publishing industry was books for, about, and by women. For the first time in American history the topic of womanhood was among the central preoccupations of the national culture and had been standardized to obliterate local and regional variations. By the 1850s female readers were imbibing directives in femininity through the vicarious experience of sentimental novels. A score of writers, including the prolific Mrs. E. D. E. N. Southworth, Augusta Jane Evans, and Maria Cummins (a literary circle that Nathaniel Hawthorne dubbed a "d----d mob of scribbling women"), turned out books at a frantic rate and sold them in editions of 100,000. Each was a gilded literary package of domestic piety and pathos: heroines, writers, and readers were caught in a whirlwind of familial emotions, anxieties, crises, and resolutions.

The pioneer medium of this woman's culture was *Godey's Lady's Book*, which achieved a vast national audience in the 1830s under the skillful editorship of Sarah Joseph Hale. *Godey's* eschewed the aristocratic lady of the federal period and celebrated instead the wholesome American woman who dedicated herself to the service of her family. This lady's magazine did not present the ideal woman to her public surrounded by the homely details of managing a household, however, but in a regal hyperbole: *Godey's* put forth Queen Victoria as the archetype of femininity; "Victoria we consider as the representative of the moral and intellectual influence which woman by her nature is formed to exercise." The moral and intellectual qualities that the English monarch typified included "all that is majestic, all that is soft and soothing, all that is bright, all that expresses the universal voice of love in Creation." Invested with love and gentleness (not energy or power), women were suited to reign only in the domestic circle, on "The throne of the heart." From their little kingdoms, however, women were assured that they could dictate national morality, preside over the tone of American culture as surely as Victoria reigned in England.[2]

Godey's Lady's Book conceived and propagated a whole new scheme of gender differentiation, one which would be stamped on American popular culture. First of all, this gender theory prescribed an exact and exclusive segregation of character traits by sex. One writer described the ideal distribution of a personality this way:

> The characteristic endowments of women are not of a commanding and imposing nature, such as man may boast of, and which enable him to contend with difficulties and dangers, to which both personally and mentally, he is liable. They consist in purity of mind, simplicity and frankness of heart, benevolence, prompting to active charity, warm affection, inducing a habit of forbearance and self denial, which the comfort or good of their human ties may demand.[3]

This theory also ordained that male and female would continue to play distinct social roles. The "commanding" male could fight, politick, and scrape for his income; the wife would oversee the world of "human ties," particularly within the small circle of her immediate kin. Victorian writers visualized these sex roles in spatial rather than functional terms. The male operated in wide-ranging public places, the female was secluded and almost immobilized in the private spaces of the home. In other words, gender created its own geography during the antebellum period, allocating two disparate spheres of influence to male and female.

The spheres were separate but complementary, so the theory went. Women's stable home base was an anchor to the peripatetic male. Whether in a frenetic eastern city or along the western prairies, she provided the essential "home calm" that restrained the "restless rover" from excessive antisocial individualism.[4] It was by putting in check the wilder nature of the male that woman as wife and as mother acquired her celebrated societal power. This was her pretension to the throne of Victoria. "The influence of woman is not circumscribed by the narrow limits of the domestic circle. She controls the destiny of every community, the character of society depends as much on the fiat of woman as the temperature of the country on the influence of the sun." This influence of woman, the crowning dogma of the doctrine of the spheres, was often presented in the beneficent natural similes of sun and stream.

Other proponents of the dogma resorted to more coercive and political metaphors. To a major architect of this gender system, Catharine Beecher, women's influence was the only means of preventing an American social "earthquake" of the magnitude of the French Revolution. Writing from the Midwest, one Margaret Coxe called on women to play the role of "national conservatives in the largest sense." Off in the raw masculine settlement of San Francisco, a newspaper editor likened women's influence to "God's own police." The notion of woman's sphere, in sum, not only assigned distinctive roles, characteristics, and spaces to the female sex, but also construed this sexual division as a principal safeguard of social order. The inflated rhetoric of Victorian culture, in other words, signaled the emergence of a whole new gender system.

This widely and highly touted theory was not without its basis in social history. First, there is no doubt that males and females were veering off into distinctive social spaces during the antebellum period. The decades before the American Civil War marked the most rapid development of industrial production and urbanization in the nation's history. Economic historians generally regard this period as a crucial era of transition to industrial capitalism. The mill towns that grew up along the streams of the Northeast and the steam-powered factories of the cities clearly demonstrated that the once integral home economy could be dismantled, sending male and female, young and old into separate spheres of work. The old commercial cities would grow at a gargantuan rate until the premier city, New York, housed more than half a million people by 1850. In the large city, whose expanding territory was now crosshatched with street railroads and omnibus lines, some affluent and even middle-class men could locate their homes miles away from their places of work. The distinctive sphere of the male sex in the antebellum city was apparent to everyone; it was the basic premise of the major municipal publication, the city directory. Each entry in this catalogue of urbanites identified a citizen's place of work and his home address, the two poles of urban life that were now almost always separated from one another. As home and workplace became detached, woman's connection with the family's economic identity was obscured, absorbed into the private home. Females accounted for only a tiny percentage of the listings in the nineteenth-century directories, and most of these were widows without an occupation. Woman's status was presumably incorporated in the occupational title of her spouse.

This more distinct outline of the male's sphere—his occupation or career—can be discerned even on the nation's farms. Although the vast majority of American women and men still resided in rural areas in the antebellum period, they were not removed from the process of industrialization. Only during the initial pioneer stage of Western settlement were nineteenth-century farmers so isolated from the market that they relied on the simple sexual division of labor typical of subsistence economies.[5] Agriculture itself most often required major capital investments. The average farmer at mid-century was equipped with reapers and threshers, dependent on the railroads and steamboat transportation, prone to speculative land dealings, and eager to employ hired men to assist in his labor. This intensive and mechanized production was commonly concentrated on a small number of cash crops; vegetables on the truck farms of New England, corn or wheat in the prairie states, and, on a much larger scale, cotton in the South. The business of agriculture now placed greater emphasis on field work and market relations, largely male responsibilities according to the usual division of farm labor. Hence, even on the farm the male occupation was given more definition during the antebellum era. Furthermore, the expanded male enterprise would bring larger amounts of cash into the farm household, cash that could be exchanged for commodities formerly produced in the home and by females. The old symbol of domestic production, the spinning wheel, was seldom loaded onto the covered wagons that headed westward after 1830. The typical farmer's wife could buy cloth, soap, candles, even an occasional ready-made dress, "in town." Hence, by mid-century even the agricultural journals contained their women's pages full of accolades to the domestic accomplishments of the farmer's wife.

In mill town, city, and farm, the male work sphere had become significantly more specialized with the advances of industrial capitalism. It had become a job or a business clearly set apart from the activities of the rest of the family. Women made their way into this sphere of specialized, income-producing work in far fewer numbers than men. As of 1860 only about 15 percent of the adult women enumerated on the United States Census were said to be gainfully employed outside the home. This statistic earmarks the antebellum era as a pivotal period in the history of American women. A larger proportion of the female population was placed at the margins of production than at any time before or since. This fact gave foundation to the doctrine of the spheres, and impetus to its rhetorical extravagance and wide circulation throughout American culture.

The home, which the antebellum male deserted during his workday, was also the terrain of significant historical development. When males evacuated the home they left onerous responsibilities for their wives to shoulder alone. The care and socialization of children, for one thing, were now left in women's hands. This social responsibility became especially onerous in an industrializing society. The young men reared in the antebellum period would face a complex occupational structure, uncertain economic prospects, and a very high probability of living far from the place of their birth. A few statistics convey the extent of this precarious world that awaited young men outside their homes. In Boston in the 1830s nearly half of all adult males changed their social status, and their movement was just as apt to be downward as along the upward path to riches. Even in the prairie frontier in the 1850s, 80 percent of the residents moved on again within ten years. Similar indices of social and geographical mobility can be assembled from towns, farms, and cities across the country. Everywhere they set the stage for a major role for home-bound women: to prepare the sons and repair the husbands who were buffeted about in this unsettling universe. In this context the veneration of the loving, calming, stabilizing influence of womanhood takes on concrete historical meaning. However ephemeral and immaterial those specialized female virtues might seem, they do identify actual psychological services performed by women within the home, for their sons and husbands, and in behalf of the social order. Thus the woman's sphere itself, however remote from the paid labor force, must be taken very seriously, for much of the work necessary to the making of industrial capitalism transpired there.

The doctrine of woman's sphere does not, however, illuminate the halting historical process whereby women made a place for themselves in industrial society. The blunt ideological dichotomy between male and female camouflaged considerable variation in the allocation of sex roles within an American population that was increasingly divided by class and ethnic origins, as well as by race. It also failed to comprehend the elasticity of the boundaries of woman's sphere. In actuality, women often stretched the doctrine of the spheres and escaped its confinement in regular and patterned ways. First, many women spent a portion of their life cycles, particularly in the time before marriage, employed outside the home. Second, large numbers of women secured a special place for themselves just on the boundaries of woman's sphere, in female circles devoted to reform or charitable activity. Finally, no sooner had the doctrines of true womanhood been formulated when a small but vocal class of dissenters organized the first women's right movement. All these apparent contradictions went into the making of a woman's sphere within early industrial capitalism.

Between 1820 and 1860 women and men worked out their new roles and relationships in a haphazard, erratic fashion, without any foreknowledge of the ease with which subsequent generations would mouth the cliché that woman's place is in the home. As a matter of fact, it remained undecided for some time just what direction the course of gender differentiation would take. When *Godey's Lady's Book* first unveiled the Victorian pedestal to American view, there were still a variety of options open to young women. Not all of the nation's respectable daughters could be found by the fireside in the 1820s, '30s, and '40s. Some were in factories, others heading up revivals or on public podiums pleading any number of causes. Women's history would dally outside the home at places such as these, before it arrived at a clearly marked border of woman's sphere.

WOMEN IN THE FACTORIES AND SHOPS

Women's assignments in the traditional household economy were actually among the first productive activities to be transferred to the factory: the spinning of yarn was industrialized long before the planting of corn. When, in the early decades of the nineteenth century, American entrepreneurs undertook the mass manufacture of cotton textiles, they pictured young women at the helms of their machines. Thus when a group of Boston businessmen drew up elaborate plans for cotton mills along the New England waterways in places like Lowell and Waltham, Massachusetts, they designed female boardinghouses as well as spinning, weaving, and warping rooms. This model of early American industry recruited a work force of young farm girls from throughout New England. The

Hamilton Company at Lowell was typical. By 1835, 85 percent of the machine tenders were female, 86 percent were native-born, and 80 percent were between the ages of fifteen and thirty. In the large and small textile mills that grew up throughout New England and the Middle Atlantic States, women workers were almost always in the majority.[6]

Only one antebellum industry rivaled textiles in scale of organization and level of productivity. This was shoe manufacturing, and here again many women found employment. In Lynn, Massachusetts, for example, women had only to move a few steps outside the home to enter the industrial world. Wives and daughters had always been delegated the role of binding "uppers" to soles in the artisan process of shoe manufacture. Advances in technology and industrial organization in the antebellum period seemed only to expand opportunities for women's work, both at home and in the factory. By the 1850s women were the dominant labor force in the full-scale factory operations of Lynn. In the 1860s the invention of heavier machinery would mean the replacement of many of these workers by the opposite sex, but for the time being women were granted an unquestioned place in this important industry. Shoe manufacturing, moreover, was still not judged to be entirely remote from the home sphere. Cheap machinery for shoe stitching was put on the market in the early 1860s and recommended particularly to "lady operatives." It seems that women were eager to adapt this technology to home production, for it was said that a sewing machine was nearly as commonplace as a hog around the households of Lynn.[7]

Shoemaking and textile factories accounted for the bulk of the large-scale, highly mechanized industry of the antebellum period. Both employed women in numbers equal to or in excess of men. The development of the heavy industries that employed great numbers of males, especially mining and metalworks, would await the postwar period. In the meantime, male industrial workers were concentrated in smaller workplaces, in traditional artisan shops with their almost domestic scale of organization. As late as 1860 the typical manufacturing unit employed only a dozen workers. Men in industry were more likely to follow the ancient routine of the blacksmith or cooper. It was women who were first exposed to the modern imperatives of fully rationalized factory production.

At first the architects of the New England cotton mills attempted to adapt the factory system to the moral and social preferences of female workers of rural origins. Hence came the celebrated amenities of the Lowell girl: neat brick boardinghouses with freshly painted white cupolas, mandatory church attendance, devoted housemothers, and a panoply of cultural fringe benefits—libraries, lyceums, and the company literary journal, the *Lowell Offering*. In the early years at Lowell, furthermore, the pace of production was slow enough to allow for cooperation and socializing among the workers, or even an occasional pause to read the Bible or scan a book of verse. Yet from the first, and more brutally with time, these pioneer industrial workers would bear the brunt of the factory organization: the pace of the machine and the imperative of expanding productivity soon assumed control over the conditions of woman's labor. Lowell workers were roused from their sleep as early as 4 A.M., and by the toll of a factory bell, not by the rays of the sun. They would work fourteen hours a day or more, at a pace that was calibrated by the ever-advancing speed of the machines. First the mill operative would tend one machine, then two, three, or four. Power looms were redesigned in the 1840s to weave at many times their former speed and produced a geometric increase in the level of noise and tension in the factory. The mill girls were witness to a disconcerting change in the rhythm of labor. One of them described it this way:

> They set me to threading shuttles and tying weaver's knots and I have improved so that I can take care of one loom. I could take care of two if only I had eyes in the back of my head. . . . When I went out at night, the sound of the mill was in my ears, as if crickets, frogs, and Jew harps, all mingle together in strange discord. After it seemed as though cotton-wool was in my ears. But now I do not mind it at all. You know that people learn to sleep with the thunder of Niagara in their ears, and the cotton mill is no worse.[8]

In the American case it was largely young women who were first exposed to this inexorable reorganization of the work process. It was women, in other words, who first passed through that painful initiation into the industrial mentality that E. P. Thompson has called "work-time discipline."[9]

Factory girls were rewarded for their labors in an equally modern and ominous fashion—by the receipt of a wage. After she had paid her room and board, the factory girl had a surplus of cash to spend as she pleased. Her wages could be a passport to a measure of autonomy and independence. The reward of the factory worker, unlike that of the farmer's daughter, was not eaten up by the immediate needs of her family. Because most factory girls had journeyed some distance from their farm homes to seek employment, they were free to spend their wages without even bothering to consult their fathers. Women used this newfound freedom in a variety of ways. Some sacrificed to pay off a father's mortgage or send a brother to school, others impulsively exchanged their wages for bonnets and sweets. Some saved for their own dowries, schooling, or business investments. Whatever the destination of their weekly pay, the mill girls were exercising the freedom of choice inherent in the control of their own cash income.

Similar experiences were in store for female workers in other sectors of the antebellum economy, thousands of whom left rural homes for employment in cities as well as mill towns. Both sons and daughters continued to be evicted from the stagnating farm economies of the Northeast. While sons found their way to the western frontier, women often congregated in the cities closer to home. By the middle of the nineteenth century even the new western cities of Chicago and Milwaukee harbored more females than males, especially among young adults. These young female migrants were clearly attracted to the employment options of the urban area: factory jobs, skilled trades, and above all, domestic service. Every antebellum city had at least a small economic sector operated by and for women. This was the world of the dressmaker, milliner, and purveyor of fancy goods. Many towns could boast of at least one woman who had made a modest fortune for herself in one of these trades, employing a string of apprentices and pieceworkers and serving an array of fashionable customers. As many as one in ten city women found employment in the clothing trade, somewhere along its finely graded female hierarchy, from shop owner through seamstress to pieceworker. Here too women were learning the lessons of the marketplace, the uses of profits as well as wages. [10]

The first lesson of the female wage earner was simple and unpleasant: her wage did not command a great deal of power and freedom in the marketplace. The prospects of a seamstress in the city of Philadelphia in 1829 were perhaps the most dismal. Even with diligent application from dawn to dusk, her piecework seldom earned more than $1.25 in a six-day week. After paying her rent and fuel, she was left with 50¢ for food, clothing, and medical expenses. Surely she had nothing to spare for luxuries or to save for her future. The factory worker, in the meantime, seldom earned much more than $2 a week, again scarcely above the price of individual survival and well below typical male wages. At Waltham in 1821, for example, a common mill girl received from $2 to $2.50 a week, while the male foreman received $12. A decade later at Lowell the typical male worker took in from 85¢ to $2 in a single day; women earned from 40¢ to 80¢ for the same time spent in factory labor. Those women who remained employed at Lowell for more than a few years rose somewhat in level of skill and rate of pay. Yet even for this privileged minority, woman's social mobility lagged way behind that of male workers. Already in the antebellum period industrial capitalism had served notice that while women were welcome in the factory, they could expect an excess of exploitation in this sphere outside the home.[11]

At the same time, women workers served notice on their employers that they would not quietly submit to this oppression. In fact, they repeatedly met inhumane conditions and exploitative wages with collective defiance. As early as 1824 women walked out of a mill in Pawtucket, Rhode Island, to protest a wage cut and worsening working conditions. Four years later women workers organized a protest in Dover, New Hampshire. Several hundred women filed out of the factory, refusing to consent to a regimen of time-discipline that included fines for being late and the prohibition of conversation during work hours. Twenty years later in a cotton mill near Pittsburgh, women struck in behalf of the ten-hour day and proclaimed their solidarity in militant crowd action. A mob composed chiefly of women pelted scabs with eggs, stormed the factory, and damaged its machinery. By this time the protests of workingwomen were something more than spontaneous localized acts of resistance; the demand for a ten-hour day was part of a concerted movement begun in Massachusetts and associated with the energetic labor leader and Lowell operative, Sarah Bagley. Bagley was the veteran organizer of the Female Labor Reform Association, which in the 1830s had sponsored a series of militant strikes in the Massachusetts textile mills. Women would also play a central role in the first cohesive organization of shoemakers. When the shoe workers mounted a major strike in Lynn in the 1860s, it included large numbers of female workers. One in four of the Lynn women workers were formally enrolled in their own union, the Daughters of St. Crispin.[12]

In the course of their participation in the antebellum labor movement, American women adopted a democratic ideology that is commonly associated with the male public sphere. First, striking women claimed as their own the political tradition of the Founding Fathers. During a strike in 1834, the Lowell girls solicited the support of "All who imbibe the spirit of our patriotic ancestors, who preferred privation to bondage, and parted with all that renders life desirable—and even life itself—to procure independence for their children." Second, at least some of these Yankee daughters also subscribed to the feminist tenets of the Enlightenment tradition. According to the *Boston Evening Transcript*, "one of the leaders mounted a pump and made a flaming Mary Woolstonecraft [sic] speech on the rights of women and the iniquities of the 'monied' aristocracy which produced a powerful effect on her auditors." The reference to "monied aristocracy" revealed still other contemporary political associations. This protest and Sarah Bagley's diatribes against "drivelling cotton lords" and the "mushroom aristocracy" were undoubtedly inspired by the rhetoric of the Jacksonian and Workingmen's parties.

Finally, the concerns of abolitionists and of the Free Soil Party intruded into the ideology of laboring women. The striking women at Lynn, for example, proclaimed in 1860 that "American Ladies will not be Slaves: Give us a Fair compensation and We Will Labour Cheerfully." Indeed, workingwomen seemed particularly receptive to invitations to the political sphere. Lowell girls, some 1,500 strong, provided one of the largest audiences ever to applaud the controversial public addresses of the abolitionists Angelina and Sarah Grimké. Sarah Bagley and the members of the Female Labor Reform Association carried their protests directly into the political arena; they entered the Massachusetts legislature carrying copious petitions, while Bagley gave public testimony before the official assembly.[13] In short, the workingwomen of the antebellum period seemed to have found a gateway into the larger public sphere.

At the same time, all these new options for women seemed to flush nicely with the continuing attachment of male and female to the home sphere. The complicated interchange between home and work is illustrated by Thomas Dublin's analysis of the living arrangements of those Lowell girls who participated in the strike of

1834. Those workers who lived in the company boardinghouses were more likely to go out on strike than were women who lived with private families. From this it would seem that detachment from family loyalties, and everyday intercourse with fellow workers, nurtured the "unity and exertion" of the Lowell girls and their strong sex solidarity and class consciousness. Yet at the same time, the workers' families supplied essential if indirect support during the course of the strike. Protesting women went to their rural homes to obtain free room, board, and sustenance during the duration of the strike. Without this alternative mode of survival, it would have been very difficult for women to have sustained their militance.[14] The family also encouraged and accommodated striking women in single-industry towns like Lynn. There, women shoe workers joined their husbands, sons, and kin on the job and at the turnout. The family reinforced worker-consciousness and solidarity in this instance as well.

Finally, neither at Lowell nor at Lynn did women's worker-consciousness detract from the fulfillment of home responsibilities. The Lowell women were almost entirely single or widowed. Less than 20 percent of the wives of Lynn were workers, and these were unlikely to be the mothers of young children. The married women of native birth who became industrial workers were few, primarily widows and employees of factories whose hours and working conditions were the least disruptive of family life.[15] Accordingly, work and even public protest were not necessarily seen as antithetical to women's place in the home. Thus, in selected local economies like that of Lynn, and in much of American industry in the 1830s and '40s, women could find a respectable if lowly place for themselves. Women's utilization of these opportunities also suggests that they had acquired habits of independence and aspirations toward public roles that might lead them on an autonomous course in the future.

WOMEN AS REFORMERS

During the epoch of the Lowell girls, native-born women appeared in public in a variety of other roles. Perhaps their most notable public appearance was in the ranks of the antebellum reformers. The 1830s and '40s were particularly ripe with crusades to rehabilitate mankind and reorder American institutions. Most of these associations of reformers were somehow associated with Protestant Christianity and in particular with the cycle of revivals called the Second Great Awakening. The evangelical enthusiasm that began in New England in the late eighteenth century spread into upstate New York in the 1820s where, under the masterful direction of the Reverend Charles Finney, it achieved the heat and velocity of a brush fire, earning the territory its title as the "Burned-Over District." Finney was especially successful with the young women of the district. In fact, some of his richest harvests of souls were among mill girls. In one cotton factory young female workers burst into tears of repentance at the very sight of the evangelist. Elsewhere women factory workers participated more actively in the Second Great Awakening. Salome Lincoln, a Massachusetts weaver, not only led a turnout but also personally recruited souls for Christ after her conversion as a Freewill Baptist. The revival church as well as the factory must be counted among the spheres of womanhood in the antebellum period. Females reportedly outnumbered males among the converts by a ratio of three to two, and most of them were young.[16]

Historian Nancy Cott has suggested that these young women were in the throes of an identity crisis. The decades of the revival had clearly presented the young women of New England and upstate New York with unsettling rearrangements of their roles and expectations. Factory girls experienced the most direct impact of the process of industrialization, but migrants to the city and farmers' stay-at-home daughters stood on shifting economic ground as well. Their old roles in cloth production had been forfeited almost entirely to the factory, while the West began to seduce their potential husbands. The conversion experience could at least give expression to these dislocations of womanhood and the accompanying anxiety. The revival ritual might also resolve some of the tensions of women on the precipice of industrialization, if only in the pious acceptance of whatever history and the Almighty held in store for them. The classic Calvinist conversion was characterized as an abject submission to the will of a superior God, coupled with a commensurate distrust of the converts' self-efficacy. In fact, the converts of the Second Great Awakening continued to castigate themselves as wicked, worldly, and vile. The female convert commonly described her Christian rebirth as an act of self-surrender and obeisance before the will of God.[17]

Yet during the Second Great Awakening the act of conversion was situated within quite another social and ecclesiastical context. Organized collective action, often among women, was the keystone of this episode in the history of evangelical Protestantism. The revivals were preceded by the congregation of women in prayer circles where they begged grace for themselves, their families, and their church brethren. Women were, in other words, actively and collectively intervening in the evangelical process. In fact, for decades they had been organized for revival in the female missionary societies that numbered in the hundreds and by the 1820s had spread deep into the frontier. The Second Great Awakening expressed, confirmed, and legitimized this growing role of women in the church. Finney and his ministerial followers were in some ways at the rear guard of religious and social change, endorsing the rights that women had long practiced in local churches: to speak in mixed congregations, for example, and to carry on benevolent enterprises without male sponsorship, or to play the leading role in the religious practices of their families. Thus it would seem that the Second Great Awakening would resolve women's religious identity crisis in a positive manner, confirming her proud and active role in Protestant churches. [18]

Women emerged from the revival cycle of the early nineteenth century poised to play an expanded social role as well. A new crop of female societies grew up in the seedbed of the revivals. New varieties of religious benevolence were spawned, among them Sunday schools, infant schools, schools for the poor and black children. It was in the wake of the Second Great Awakening, furthermore, that women began to join together for the explicit purpose of "reform," that is, to attempt to guide historical change in the direction they had chosen. Their ends were most often moral in nature: the regeneration of slave masters, drunkards, and libertines. Most of the female reform associations were originally auxiliary to male groups, but in the end, women came to almost overshadow their brothers in number, in tenacity, and in dedication.

The first Female Anti-Slavery Society was founded in Boston in 1832 and became a chapter of the American Anti-Slavery Society led by William Lloyd Garrison. Similarly, the female temperance associations that sprouted up in almost every town, city, and hamlet in the 1840s were modeled after their male predecessors (as revealed by such names as the Daughters of Temperance or the Martha

Washington Union, in dutiful parody of the Sons of Temperance and the George Washington Union). At any rate, female associations followed very quickly on the heels of most male crusades. The American Physiological Society was established in 1837 to propagate higher standards of health care; Ladies Physiological Societies appeared around the country within the year. In one case, however (and this was indeed a notorious exception), women took the lead and set the course of reform. This was the American Female Moral Reform Association, founded in 1834 and boasting more than 400 chapters within the decade. Males later formed a parallel association, the Seventh Commandment Society, and clearly took the secondary role in this campaign to reform American sexual behavior. [19]

Whatever the cause, reform in the 1830s and '40s enrolled large numbers of women throughout America and especially in the smaller towns and secluded rural settlements. The constituency of the reform movement came from a broad spectrum of the middling classes. The wives and daughters of artisans, shopkeepers, and farmers joined in profusion. Almost all the activities of reform associations, male and female, were directed toward the education and persuasion of individuals, aimed, that is, at changing public opinion and policy. The women reformers often perceived the strategy of moral persuasion in immediate personal terms. They sought first to exert influence on their very closest associates, the members of their families, Abolitionist women began by "entreating their husbands, fathers, brothers and sons to abolish the institution of slavery." When the American Physiological Society resolved to sponsor ladies' associations, they had the same domestic strategy in mind: "That woman in her character as wife and mother is only second to the Deity in the influences that she exerts on the physical, the intellectual and the moral interest of the human race." The first obligation of the female missionary was to practice reform in her own home—to forswear intoxicating beverages, goods manufactured by slaves, unsanitary health practices, and sexual innuendos and indulgences. By converting husbands and sons to her cause she could send emissaries of reform out into the public sphere as well. [20]

The influence of female reform by no means stopped at the garden gate. However retiring their methods and domestic their rhetoric, these women had formed associations that circumvented the boundaries of the home and whose goals were ultimately of a political nature. It is well-known that the "parlor talks" of such female abolitionists as Sarah and Angelina Grimké metamorphosed gradually into public addresses before "promiscuous," or mixed sex, congregations and led to appearances before the legislature. The same dialectic that propelled the two sisters from South Carolina from abolitionism toward feminism was working its way through the grass roots of sundry women's associations. A flourishing, well-organized female reform association was often a force to be reckoned with in city hall. The Philadelphia Female Anti-Slavery Society characterized its political transfiguration as follows: "The little circle imperceptively widens until it may embrace a whole town." The embrace was not always loving and gentle. In the 1830s scores of American cities were wracked by anti-abolition riots, incited in part by the forceful effect of female associations on public opinion.[21]

Female associations had considerable success with one more direct strategy for achieving public attention and political leverage. This was the petition campaign, which inundated legislatures with a tide of paper in the 1830s and '40s. Abolitionist petitions numbered in the hundreds of thousands, and probably the majority of the signatories were female. Temperance women mounted similar campaigns in state after state, calling for prohibitions on the sale of intoxicating beverages. The Female Moral Reform Society appealed to the New York State Legislature to outlaw seduction, and with the power of some 20,000 signatures behind them, they succeeded. The petition movement seemed on the surface to be a proper and feminine tactic. It did not ask women to step out of the normal circle of their private lives, and required only that "every woman with pen and ink in hand armed with affectionate, but unconquerable determination go from door to door 'among her own people'; that everyone of them may have an opportunity of affixing her name to the memorial." Still, the means cannot disguise the consequences: these women, acting in consort with their neighbors and sisters, had made a powerful impression on the nation's legislators.[22]

Many female reformers were half conscious of the daring implications of their actions. At times, as in this antislavery appeal dated 1837, women reformers seemed to assume that their sex was entitled to full political rights. "Are we aliens," the Female Anti-Slavery Society asked, "because we are women? Are we bereft of citizenship because we are the *mothers*, *wives*, and *daughters* of a mighty people? Have women no country—no interest staked in public weal—no liabilities in common-peril—no partnership in the nation's guilt and shame?" This bold argument was merely intended as a rhetorical ballast to the petition drive; it did not culminate in a call for women's suffrage. Yet many members of female associations were acting as if their sphere extended well into this public arena. Off in the tiny Ohio town of Austinburg in 1834, for example, the members of the Young Ladies Society for Intellectual Improvement were acting for all the world like potential voters, discussing the merits of the Bank of the United States as well as the qualifications of Jackson and Adams for the Presidency. The steady protofeminist undercurrents of the early reform associations were also readily apparent in the abolitionist movement. One woman wrote to Garrison's *Liberator* asking how anyone could "grant for a single day that doctrine to be true that inferiority is stamped upon our sex by the hand of nature?"[23]

Other female reformers dared to question whether men were qualified for the superior reputation and status they enjoyed. Almost all the female reform associations were implicit condemnations of males; there was little doubt as to the sex of slave masters, tavern-keepers, drunkards, and seducers. One women's crusade, Female Moral Reform, made this assumption explicit and often in a virulent manner. It directed women's ire toward the American male and shouted as its battle cry, "Level your artillery at the head and heart of the debauchee." Just as surely, the members of the Female Moral Reform Society were acting in defense of their own sex. All their tactics—the education of the populace on sexual morality, the public exposure of notorious libertines, attempts to reform prostitutes—were aimed expressly at making the world safe for their daughters, sisters, and friends who might now be walking unchaperoned into factory towns and along city streets. Like the other reform groups of the era, these women had slowly and half consciously widened the social habitat of their sex. The transformation was a fait accompli by 1837 when the association's journal, *The Advocate of Moral Reform*, announced: "If the sphere of action is limited to private life exclusively, then we have long since left our province and entered that of the other sex. . . . Women have organized associations, held meetings, published reports, appointed solicitors and resolved themselves into communities without alarm-

ing the guardians of the public welfare or outraging public sentiment."[24]

The female moral reformers, like the striking factory girls of
the same era, seemed to anticipate a stalwart march of women into
industrial society, advancing even into the male sanctums of political
power. They pushed forward blissfully ignorant, it would seem, of
the restrictive domestic sphere into which so many of their contemporaries had begun to invite, cajole, and banish their sex. The
proponents of woman's sphere often spoke from more lofty podiums.
To the *New York Commercial Advertizer*, the female moral reformer
was guilty of "forgetting the delicacy and reserve of her sex." The
leading clergymen of Massachusetts banded together in 1837 to
condemn the incendiary actions of the Grimké sisters and the female
abolitionists. Women's proper influence, according to the clergymen's spokesman, the Reverend Nehemiah Adams, must remain
"private and unobtrusive." It would be a woman, however, who
issued the shrewdest denunciation of the social and political vagaries
of female reformers. Catharine Beecher, unmarried daughter of the
renowned New England clergyman, rebutted the emerging feminism of the Grimkés by drawing a tight veil of privacy and explicit
inequality around her sex. Unabashedly, she championed the "divine
economy" that assigned to "one sex the superior, to the other the
subordinate station." Women would, in Beecher's estimation, find
their happiness in dependent domestic relations. From that social
place they could exercise a salubrious conservative influence upon
American society, prohibiting rather than provoking such disruption as the abolitionism that "shakes this nation like an earthquake."
In short, Beecher had clearly formulated the doctrine of the spheres
in 1839. She and countless other writers of both sexes would elaborate that ideology endlessly in the decades to come. Thereafter,
women would hesitate before they ventured outside the home in
search of direct income, influence, or power.[25]

Indeed, the female sex did not obtrude so aggressively into
American public life after the 1840s. Native-born women surrendered their positions in the cotton mills to immigrants of both
sexes, and the militant labor reform associated with Sarah Bagley
and her sisters disappeared. Female Moral Reform also assumed a
quieter public image, dedicated more to exalting feminine purity
than to pursuing male libertines. The American Female Anti-Slavery

Society did not sponsor a national meeting after the 1830s, and its local chapters slowly disbanded. When abolitionists resumed petitioning Congress in the 1850s, female signatures were in a clear minority.

It would be a mistake to conclude that American women retreated from the borders of the public sphere out of docile compliance with the wishes of Nehemiah Adams, Catharine Beecher, or their own husbands. Their apparent retreat was facilitated first by changing social and economic conditions. Certainly the textile tycoon was happy to replace the demanding Yankee daughters with cheaper immigrant workers, and accordingly withdrew his offer of relatively genteel working conditions to these young women. The social and political geography of America also shifted after 1840 in ways that obstructed women's access to the public arena. Female reformers had been particularly rampant in the smaller cities and rural villages of the Northeast. Women were in easier reach of power in these more intimate polities than in the larger cities that grew by leaps and bounds after 1840, absorbing a larger and larger portion of the nation's population and gaining greater sway over American public opinion. At the same time, reform movements began to focus their attention on the more remote citadels of political power. Both the abolitionists and the temperance movement looked to state and national government and to the exclusively male electoral process for the fulfillment of their goals. Conditions peculiar to America in the early stages of industrialization—the demand for female workers, the social freedom of small-town republican government, and the relatively sex-blind ideology of hard work and moral vigilance—had fostered an unusual amount of experimentation with women's roles. After the 1840s these conditions would change, and the range of women's action would narrow accordingly.

It should also be underscored that the women who tested the limits of their sphere in the work roles and the reform groups of the 1830s and '40s were always a minority of their sex and tended to be concentrated in evangelical churches, small towns, and Yankee lineages. More important, these women shared common demographic characteristics, that is, they were of similar ages and marital status. The labor-militant woman worker was almost always young and single. The female agents of the American Anti-Slavery Society were, to a woman, unmarried and usually very young. The rank and file of these movements may have been middle-aged matrons, but a closer look at the demographic profile of reform leaders would probably reveal an overabundance of childlessness, domestic help, and otherwise diminished family responsibilities. Even then, the dashing activism of reformers and workers was enacted on the temporal margins of the domestic sphere. It seldom consumed an entire lifetime.

In other words, women's social activism of the 1830s and '40s was undertaken in addition to, not in defiance of, the duties of the household. No one, male or female, presumed that it could be otherwise. In fact, most of the reformers had consistently honored, even exaggerated and elaborated, the importance of women's role in the home. Reform societies repeatedly informed their members of all that women could do as wives and mothers to outlaw drunkenness, disease, lechery, even slavery. One association of the era was dedicated to the single-minded pursuit of these responsibilities. Women gathered throughout the Northeast and Midwest in groups called maternal associations. They met weekly to renew vows of devotion to their children and to devise ever more elaborate and demanding methods of child care. Many would argue that a reformed motherhood was enough to rid an entire generation of all the sins and crimes that plagued the conscience of an antebellum Protestant. To some extent, abolitionists, moral reformers, and temperance workers all agreed with this evangelical rendition of the doctrine of the spheres. The theories of Catharine Beecher would not appear as a novelty to most women reformers.

Finally, most American women were too consumed with household responsibilities to be recruited by the reformers or annoyed by the preachers of women's place. From where they were situated in antebellum society, the doctrine of woman's sphere could be very attractive. The positions in the female labor force had proven ill-paid and arduous, and grew ever more dehumanizing with the advances of industrial technology. Assuming public and political power required energy and time available to few busy housewives. The doctrine of women's influence promised women that rarest of delights, having one's cake and eating it too. They could remain at home and still achieve accolades from popular culture and a real but indirect power in society, as mediated through their relations to husbands, children, or brothers. Thus the majority of American

women would continue to plot out their lives within the boundaries
of the home, but after the 1840s they would have a finely wrought
ideology to justify and to honor that sphere.

THE DOMESTIC LIFE CYCLE

The women who came of age in that decade would plot their life
courses with the directives of the cult of true womanhood and
domesticity in mind. This ideology screened out some of the opportunities that the mill girls, converts, and reformers had stumbled
upon less than a generation before. Thus the life cycle of the native-
born, literate women who grew up in the two decades immediately
preceding the Civil War could assume a classic Victorian aspect.
The children's literature that became so popular in these decades
conspired to set even little women upon this retiring and feminine
life course. Stories for girls pictured model little ladies "so quiet
and so affectionate and looked so much like a dove." The girls'
literary universe was cluttered with flowers, kittens, and of course,
dolls. The latter invention was designed to give little girls a playful
apprenticeship in the adult female role. "The dressing of dolls is a
useful as well as a pleasant employment for little girls. If they are
careful about small gowns, caps and spencers, it tends to make
them ingenious about their own dress when they are older." More
importantly, playing with dolls was practice for motherhood. "When
little girls are alone, dolls may serve for company. They can be
scolded, advised and kissed and taught to read and sung to sleep,
and anything else the fancy of the owner may devise." The childish
occupation of "playing house," complete with toy tubs, brooms,
and cookware, was also a creation of antebellum culture.[26]
 Games for girls were carefully differentiated from boys' amusements. A girl might play with a hoop or swing gently, but the
"ruder and more daring gymnastics of boys" were outlawed. Competitive play was also anathema: a "little girl should never be ambitious to swing higher than her companions." Children's board
games afforded another insidious method of inculcating masculinity
and femininity. On one boys' game board of the era the player
moved in an upward spiral, past temptations, obstacles, and reverses
until the winner reached a pinnacle of propriety and prestige. A
girls' playful enactment of her course in life transpired on a flowery,

pastel game board and moved along a circular, ever-inward path to the "mansion of happiness," a placid tableau of mother and child. The dice of popular culture were loaded for both sexes and weighted with domesticity for little women. The doctrine of the spheres was thereby insinuated into the personality of the child early in life and even during the course of play.[27]

In other instances, however, boys and girls followed similar courses of socialization. Both sexes left home in the nineteenth century to enter the growing public school system. As a consequence, females achieved the same high rate of literacy acquired by their brothers in the Revolutionary era. Most daughters and sons of the Protestant middle classes would continue in the same school system until their mid-teens. If education should be continued beyond this point, however, it would diverge again by sex.

Beginning in the 1820s, coeducational academies were supplanted by secondary schools designed expressly for females. These institutions were created by ambitious women such as Emma Willard, Mary Lyon, and Catharine Beecher, each equipped with an acute sense of business as well as pedagogy. Willard's Troy Seminary, Lyon's Mount Holyoke, Beecher's Hartford Seminary, all became models for the advanced but expressly feminine education of women. Along with erudition in anything from philosophy to astronomy, the seminarians acquired preparatory training for the home sphere. The female seminaries played down the female accomplishments favored by the fashionable private schools of the past. Instead, they supplemented academic study with practical training in what Beecher called domestic science. Female seminaries were particularly concerned about providing their students with a moral education, or the training of the heart. They took great pains, in other words, to cultivate the emotional sensitivity whereby women could nurture children and influence husbands. Most women, if ever granted the privilege of attending a female academy in the first place, were likely to spend only a term or two there. Then, scarcely past their mid-teens, they would return to the parental home where, like the majority of young American women, they would complete their domestic education at their mothers' sides.[28]

At this point in the life cycle the historical outlines of womanhood become rather fuzzy. The young woman's formal education was complete. She had passed puberty. Yet it would be at least a half-dozen years before she would marry. In times past, a young woman in this predicament might have been bound out to another family as a servant or kept busy at home caring for siblings or engaged in domestic manufacturing. Just decades before, she might have traveled to the cotton factory or a milliner's shop during this domestic hiatus. Yet after 1850 very few native-born women seemed to be exercising these options. A glance at the census schedules of city after city reveals that only a small minority of American-born women ever assumed the occupation so common among immigrants—domestic service. Other jobs were even rarer. In Buffalo, New York, for example, only 5 percent of native-born females found gainful employment outside the servant quarters. In 1860 in Poughkeepsie, New York, where the daughters of skilled workers and artisans quite often sojourned in local millinery shops and garment factories, 70 percent of native-born girls aged sixteen to twenty still remained unemployed. At this juncture of the life cycle many women were occupied neither as wives, workers, nor students. In Hamilton, Ontario, at mid-century, for example, this was the status of 50 percent of those in their teens, and one in three of those aged sixteen to twenty. This measure of relative idleness was undoubtedly much higher for the native-born daughters of the middle class. In a predominantly white-collar district of Chicago several decades later, two out of every three fifteen-year-old females were neither in school, at work, nor married. These women remained in the parental home, it should be added, at a time when smaller families and the advances of the consumer economy had probably diminished the amount of labor that transpired there.[29]

The young women of the Victorian middle class did find one significant alternative to this comparative idleness—school teaching. In the state of Massachusetts, for example, 2 percent of all women claimed the occupation as their own. In itself this may not be an impressive figure. Yet it refers to primarily young women who taught school for very short periods. Therefore, if extended over time, it might apply to large numbers of women, however briefly. In fact, it has been estimated that one in four native-born women of Massachusetts had spent some time in front of a classroom. The schoolmarm had secured not only a relief from idleness but a more remunerative, quiet, safe, and prestigious position than had mill girls and servants.[30]

They did not, however, achieve a status or income that their brothers would envy. The wages of female teachers were consistently and shamefully below those of their male counterparts, rarely more than half. Such wages seriously inhibited the exercise of independence for women teachers. Most of them were forced to remain at home or board around with the families of their students. Few women teachers experienced any occupational mobility, because the job of principal was usually reserved for males. During her quiet and brief tenure in the classroom (about two years on the average), the woman teacher was valued for her domestic qualities. Such school reformers as Horace Mann venerated the maternal influence that a woman brought to the schoolroom, while stingy school commissioners relished her limited career ambitions and docile manner. The Boston School Committee praised female teachers as follows: "As a class, they never look forward as young men almost invariably do, to a period of legal emancipation." Preferences aside, young unmarried women were not capacitated by the meager wages of schoolteachers to challenge the hegemony of fathers, brothers, and grooms.[31]

Emancipation, of sorts, would come to most only with marriage. Yet the young women of the Civil War era had reason to fret about this eventuality. They could no longer expect to marry according to the predictable timing of their birth order. Large numbers of women would have to wait an extended period before they marched down the aisle. In some cities 40 percent of the native-born women remained single between the ages of twenty-six and thirty. Other women would never find mates at all. A full 13 percent of the women born in Massachusetts in the 1830s would live out their lives in this predicament. This statistic probably represents significantly greater chances of remaining unmarried than in generations past, a result in large part of the unbalanced local sex ratios created by the continuing western migration of men. Marriage was as important as ever to the livelihood of women. Yet its coming was less assured than ever before, and something beyond a woman's direct control. The young women of the antebellum era faced quite a quandary. They might well get a bit skittish as they passed their mid-twenties and contemplated the ludicrous popular image of the old maid.[32]

American popular culture offered abundant advice and numerous palliatives to women during this nervous stage of the life cycle. In a collection of homilies called *Girlhood and Womanhood*, Mrs. Margaret Graves alerted her readers to all the pitfalls of courtship. The snares of drunkards, gigolos, and heartless businessmen could be just as perilous as spinsterhood. In order to avoid these and to escape the odium of being an old maid, this typical literary guide advised young women to maintain a warm, demure, and chaste demeanor ("No man not even the most dissipated and reckless" would choose a flirtatious female "as the wife of his bosom and future mother of his children").[33] Above all else, the young women of the ante-bellum era were admonished to marry not for money, status, or parental approval, but for love. The exact meaning of this injunction was seldom specified in the essays addressed to young ladies. The elaboration of the mysteries of heterosexual love was left to the novelists.

A character in *Clarence*, a novel written in 1830 by Catharine Sedgwick, introduced the be-all and end-all of courtship in this way: "Ever since I first thought of it at all, though I can't remember when that was, I have always said that I would never marry any man that I was not willing to die for." In this instance, love paraded as a craving acquired in childhood and so intense that a woman would give up her life to satisfy it. The rites of love were spun out more ornately in the sentimental novels of the 1850s. Here young love was so mysterious, fated, and elusive that it can only be labeled romantic. Romantic love required lengthy and convoluted plots. For example, an epic love story by Mrs. E. D. E. N. Southworth typically introduced the destined lovers in the first few pages, but took several hundred more to bring them together in connubial bliss. The love story became a staple of popular culture by the mid-nineteenth century and was meant for the special delectation of women. As Lydia Sigourney put it, "A Woman's nature feeds on love. Love is its life."[34]

The voracious appetite for love stories undoubtedly stemmed from some real craving among women readers. Perhaps this literary initiation into the world of heterosexual love functioned as the privatized puberty rite of the industrial age. Throughout her child-hood the Victorian girl had been cloistered in a female world and deeply attached to her mother. The emotional extravaganza of the love story might have the psychological force to break these bonds and affix a young woman's affection to the increasingly alien opposite sex. Prohibited from actively seeking out a spouse, the demure ingenue might rehearse her courtship in romantic fantasy. As marriage was delayed to a later age or its probability became doubtful, those fantasies might well approximate the sundry delays, misunderstandings, and catastrophes that intercepted heroes and heroines on their way to the altar.

Neither is it farfetched to draw some connections between romantic novels and the political economy of marriage. For Victorian young ladies, matrimony was often a risky business, infused with some of the high-pitched drama of a Gothic adventure. Marriages were rarely negotiated in such a way as to consolidate the productive resources and skills that had, in the past, provided a secure foundation for a functioning home economy. Middle-class brides now entrusted their material destiny to the business acumen of their grooms. Few married women (generally less than 5 percent) would ever enter the labor force and thus contribute a sizable portion of the household income. As wives surrendered control over the economic status of the family, husbands encountered precarious prospects themselves. The native-born women of the Victorian era married into a new middle class: artisan production would be eclipsed by factories; farmers and shopkeepers were now fully implicated in capitalist relations of credit, price fluctuations, mortgages; property owners gave way to salaried employees—clerks, cashiers, managers. In the antebellum period these occupations did not guarantee the security commonly associated with the middle-class today. The rate of foreclosure was notoriously high in the Farm Belt. Bankruptcy was routine in the city. According to the credit records compiled by Dun & Bradstreet, the majority of small businesses conceded failure within five or ten years.[35] The arrival of industrial capitalism was punctuated with depression, first in 1837 and again in 1857. With these turns in the business cycle, many a loyal wife watched her economic security disintegrate in some financial wizardry that she scarcely understood. This combination of risk, dependency, and passivity might well create nervous excitement among brides, matrons, and novel readers of the nineteenth century.

The bride might best turn to matters she understood, to the business of her own sphere. Indeed, she had little choice; within a year or two of the wedding most women would begin a long career of mothering. The spacing of subsequent births was such that she would still have an infant at her breast late in her thirties. The delayed marriage of her children would ordain that a woman in her late fifties still had her offspring to care for. In sum, child care occupied almost as large a portion of a woman's life cycle as in her grandmother's day. Using another measure of reproductive activity, however, motherhood was becoming less demanding than in generations past. The average fertility of all white women had fallen from 7.04 children in 1800 to 5.21 in 1860. Native-born middle-class women had reached levels of fertility that rivaled the twentieth century in their conservative proportions. Few of these women bore more than three or four children. Thus Victorian mothers seemed to have a more relaxed role, bearing and rearing fewer children over the same lengthy reproductive cycle.[36]

Reproduction itself was hardly a relaxed aspect of marital relations in the nineteenth century. Maintaining that low rate of fertility was a very exacting and frustrating enterprise, achieved without any improvement in the technology of contraception. Furthermore, the decline in the nineteenth-century American birthrate was not due to societal measures; it could not be traced to later and fewer marriages, for example. Rather, the onus of fertility control now fell on individual couples. In addition, husbands and wives did not wait until they reached a maximum family size after a decade or so of wedlock to begin to put their reproductive powers in check. Even young couples were having fewer children, spaced wider apart.[37]

A good portion of this burden of sexual restraint was carried by husbands, who in the nineteenth century probably practiced coitus interruptus with new regularity and self-control. Certainly, urban middle-class fathers had their own incentives to limit the number of their offspring. Rearing a child could be very expensive in the city and even Dun & Bradstreet's agent was known to deny credit on the grounds that an otherwise frugal businessman had a "large and expensive" family. Yet women had also assumed a measure of rational control over their reproductivity. They expressed it decisively by employing another time-honored technique of birth control, abortion. The rate of abortion rose dramatically between 1840 and 1880 until some estimated that as many as one in five pregnancies was terminated by abortion. Abortion prior to "quickening" (the clear evidence of fetal life at about the fourth month of pregnancy) was within the law during this era and was increasingly resorted to by middle-class, native-born, married women. During the same period, the popular health movement, including its Ladies' Physiological Societies, was educating women regarding their reproductive biology. Women such as Paulina Wright Davis and

Mary Gove Nichols took to the popular lecture circuit, often illustrating their talks to females with mannequins that graphically portrayed woman's reproductive system. All in all, more and more men, and women, too, were subjecting reproduction to conscious deliberate control during the antebellum period.[38]

On the eve of the Civil War a few men and women, notably Davis, Nichols, and fellow reformer Henry C. Wright, articulated birth control as the peculiar right of women. They maintained that a woman alone should determine if, when, and under what circumstances to bear a child. Their determination to prevent the birth of "the unwanted child" would be called "voluntary motherhood" later in the century. These early advocates of fertility control did not recommend such methods of birth control as withdrawal or abortion. Neither did they endorse the sundry ineffective devices recommended in marriage manuals and folklore: a faulty rhythm method, chemical douches, sponges, and prophylactic potions. Rather, they put forward one tried-and-true method, sexual abstinence. In this, Victorian culture concurred: abstinence was deemed the only moral, healthy, and respectable mode of birth control. In fact, demographers now rank frequency of intercourse as one of the major correlates of fertility, suggesting that chastity was indeed a common method of birth control in the nineteenth century.[39]

Abstinence was more than a means of birth control; it was a basic element in a Victorian sexual economy, and like most everything else in the culture was cut through with gender distinctions. According to Victorian sexual theory, ejaculation expelled the vital energies that were concentrated in a man's semen. Hence excessive intercourse was profligacy, destructive to a man's health, offensive to bourgeois frugality, and, by extension, detrimental to the national economy. Accordingly, marriage manuals were very miserly in their prescriptions of the optimal frequency of intercourse; once a month, nineteen times in a lifetime, at twenty-one-month intervals, were among the recommended intervals. Victorian women were asked to play a decisive role in this sexual economy, to be watchguards of the male passions. According to most physiologists of the time, the normal woman had no sex drive per se, only the generosity to submit to coitus out of love for her husband or in anticipation of motherhood. Female sexuality was subsumed under woman's affections and her spirit of self-sacrifice: "When a delicate, exhausted woman lies on the bosom of a strong man with his loving arms around her a new life is instilled in her." This asexual characterization of the female made her the ideal candidate for policewoman of the bedroom. Nineteenth-century writers had a more elegant metaphor for this role: "It is the part of the woman to accept or repulse, to grant or to refuse. It is her right to reign a passional queen." Sexual abstinence, whether in deference to feminine purity or not, undoubtedly contributed to the decline in nineteenth-century fertility.[40]

Still, family limitation remained a hit-and-miss process, relying on a confusing array of methods, few of them entirely effective: coitus interruptus, abortion, abstinence, and the apothecary's concoctions added up to a frustrating campaign to control fertility. Conjugal relations must have been particularly tense for Victorian wives. Fear of the pains of childbirth, or the dangers of abortion, loomed over their sexual encounters. The practice of withdrawal probably inhibited the satisfaction of female sexual needs. Unlike their mates, Victorian women could not seek relief from sexual frustration at the brothel. They were, however, susceptible to the venereal disease their mates might contract there. Little wonder then that femininity and the female reproductive system were commonly associated with disease, both mental and physical. Catharine Beecher reported that scarcely a single married woman of her acquaintance was completely healthy, a judgment that the manufacturers of patent medicines had arrived at independently. The single largest advertisement in an antebellum newspaper was likely to be for "female pills," which promised to prevent pregnancy and cure "sick headaches" in the same swallow.

Ironically, this Draconian campaign to limit fertility coexisted with the absolute veneration of motherhood. By the mid-nineteenth century maternity had assumed its honored position in the center of popular culture, right alongside a familiar variety of American pastry. At this point, however, the cult of the mother did not have deep roots in American mythology. During the colonial period, a mother's love was slightly suspicious, often equated with the overindulgence of her offspring. It needed always to be scrutinized and moderated by patriarchal surveillance. As late as the 1830s an occasional "father's book" appeared and reminded males of their continuing responsibility as the superior parent. Such literature was soon lost in a flood of mothers' books and mothers' magazines, which informed women that, because of the father's absorption in business affairs outside the home, the female parental role had been expanded. Instead of just the physical care of infants, mothers were now delegated the major role in the childhood socialization of both sexes. Motherhood was invested with a new glory. "What a delightful office the creator has made for the female. What love and tenderness can equal that existing in the mother for her offspring?" Motherhood was proclaimed the essence of femininity, "woman's one duty and function . . . that alone for which she was created." Expectant mothers were forewarned that this female role would absorb the bulk of their time and energy: "It truly requires all the affection of even a fond mother to administer dutifully to the numerous wants of a young child."[41]

Both the rigor and the bliss attached to maternity stemmed from a novel interpretation of child rearing. *Godey's Lady's Book* defined mothers as "those builders of the human temple who lay the foundation for an eternity of glory or of shame." The mother encroached upon the Almighty's power to dictate salvation and create human beings. She was, in fact, granted "entire, perfect dominion over the unformed character of [her] infant." The "empire of the mother," as defined by nineteenth-century writers, was more than a feminine mystique. It conferred upon women the function of transforming infant human animals into adult personalities suitable to the culture and society into which they were born. Parents could not fully articulate this process of socialization during the preindustrial era, when childhood was brief and enmeshed in the routine practice of adult roles. In the nineteenth century, however, middle-class and particularly urban children were removed from the nexus of social and economic activity and left with only vague notions of the occupational and social situations in which they would find themselves as adults. In the intervening years, parents had time to deliberate about a child's future. If they could not dictate the life course of the next generation, they could at least strive to instill in their own offspring those general traits of character deemed conducive to success in the bourgeois world: propriety, diligence, conscientiousness. The task of implanting these virtues in human minds while they were young and malleable was allocated to mothers, conveniently cloistered with children in antebellum homes. America's female agents of socialization collectively molded "the whole mass of mind in its first formation." This was the preeminent social function carried on within woman's sphere.[42]

Mothers were initiated into this role by a long list of highly detailed instructions in infant care: feeding schedules, balanced diets, cleansing rituals, complicated wardrobes and equipment. The mother's manual also attuned women to such childhood crises as teething, constipation, and masturbation. This regimen of physical care, however, was secondary to the task of socialization. Each maternal gesture toward the child, no matter how trivial it seemed, conveyed a moral message. This hybrid of physical care and moral training was termed "gentle nurture" and constituted a total system of child rearing. Its goal was primarily negative, to suppress all the immoral and antisocial passions of the infant. Its first injunction was to begin early, with the first spark of human consciousness. Its principal vehicle was the emotional exchange between mother and child, out of which was woven an environment of perfect trust, untarnished purity, and complete tranquility. In essence, gentle nurture merged mother and child in one morally antiseptic and love-saturated unit, deemed the cradle of national health and social order.

The first crèche of socialization was the mother's body. Pregnant women were advised to furnish the environment of the fetus with all the salubrious qualities of femininity—no lust, anger, aggression, mental or physical overexertion should disturb the embryo's nest in her womb. Carrying a child ordained living a stereotype. A pregnant woman was not expected merely to mimic the plastic feminine icon, but to mold her whole being to its contours, donning a cheerful, composed, and altruistic nature. The biological bond between a mother and a suckling child prolonged this self-abnegation another year; "her passions calm, her being serene and full of peace and hope and happiness," she breast-fed her babe. Nursing an infant was one of the most hallowed and inviolate episodes in a woman's life. "She must not delegate to any being the sacred and delightful task of suckling her child." Breast-feeding was sanctified as "one of the most important duties of female life," "one of peculiar, inexpressible, felicity," and the "sole occupation and pleasure" of a new mother.[43]

This occupation entailed more than nourishing the infant, for a mother's milk and the warmth with which she offered it also conveyed the child's first moral lessons. Nineteenth-century child-rearing experts assured mothers that a four- to six-month-old infant was morally cognizant, as evidenced by his or her ability to emulate the smiles and frowns of others. This was the opening wedge of social control: "While the tenderest affection beams from her own eye and plays upon every feature of her countenance she contrives by the soft and winning tones of her voice to overcome the resistance of the child, too young indeed to know why it yields but not too young to feel the power by which its heart is so sweetly captivated." The infant marionette of a mother's moods would not only be a good-natured child but would be inextricably bound to the values she represented. All a mother's actions should be calculated to draw the reins of her "invisible control" even tighter. "As the infant advances in strength its religion should be love. Teach it to love by your own accents, your whole deportment." Once the child's physical and psychological well-being had been intertwined with a mother's love, it was said that her disapproving reaction to misbehavior would trigger pangs of guilt and genuine pain in the youngster. Therefore, the favored punishment of the nineteenth-century child-rearing manual was the withdrawal of love, exercised by the curtailment of a mother's smiles and kisses or ostracism from the warmth of the family circle. The penitent child would be quickly restored to his mother's good graces, embraced once more by loving intimacy.[44]

If the mechanics of love were securely established during infancy, assiduously nurtured in childhood, and later reinforced by female schoolteachers, they were expected to retain control for a lifetime. The most crucial test of gentle nurture would come just as young men and women took leave of the parental home. Child-rearing literature assured mothers that a well-bred adolescent would be shielded from every temptation by his mother's loving image and gentle instructions. Literature addressed to young men and women assisted mothers in exerting this uncanny power. One parable for adolescents pictured a brokenhearted mother consigning her daughter to a house of correction. The moral of the tale was this: "Her own daughter was the serpent which had stung her bosom. Such is the grief which children may bring upon themselves and their parents. You probably have not thought of this very much." The pious young reader was advised: "Soon you will leave home and will sit down and weep as you think of parents and home far away. Oh how cold will seem the love of others compared with a mother's love." Mother's abiding love would steer young men clear of brothels, saloons, gambling tables, shady business enterprises, and disruptive social and political causes. If gentle nurture was even half as effective as its exponents guaranteed, the domestic machinations of mother love had substantial social consequences.[45]

The same might be said for the gentle services of the model wife. One popular male writer conjured up this fantasy of her magic ministrations: "Your wants are all anticipated the fire is burning brightly; the clean hearth flashes under the joyous blaze; the old elbow chair is in its place. . . . If trouble comes upon you, she knows that her voice beguiling you into cheerfulness will lay aside your fears." Another fictional husband (created by T. S. Arthur, master of domestic parables and author of *Ten Nights in a Barroom*) begged his spouse to "strengthen [my] hand and I will press onward with pride and obtain high places; oppose me and I may sink into oblivion." In other words, the personal services and psychic support that a wife alone could provide were accounted among a man's business assets. They acted as incentives to success and salves in case of failure. More than this, a loving wife could enforce ethical and conservative business practices. "If all is well at home we need not watch him at the market. One will work cheerfully for small profits if he be rich in the love and society of the home." Wives were responsible for eradicating that common male vice, ambition. They were taught that "true wisdom consists in being contented with that station that providence has allotted thee."[46] This shibboleth of the ladies' magazine also gained credence in the business ledgers, where a "man of family" was judged a reliable creditor. A wife was a buoy in the choppiest financial seas. After the expansion of married women's property rights, beginning in the 1830s, shrewd businessmen routinely avoided ruin by placing debt-ridden property in their wives' names.

Not all the social and economic functions of married women were mediated through husbands and children. She superintended a whole complex of essential activities within her own sphere. In the 1840s Catharine Beecher spearheaded the campaign to rationalize and upgrade the whole field of housework. Under Beecher's tutelage, the housewife would master a complex body of knowledge and skills. Domestic science included the physics of ventilation, the chemistry of home remedies, the esthetics of furniture, the architecture of domestic space, the psychology of child care. All had to be employed with "order and system" and on schedule. Housework as engineered by Catharine Beecher was hardly a throwback to the casual, leisurely rhythm of preindustrial labor. Rather, it was tightly organized, methodical, intricately timed.

Nonetheless, Victorian housewives also continued to practice many of the domestic arts inherited from their grandmothers. Many household items were still manufactured domestically: medicines, dyes, cleaning fluids, varnishes, not to speak of the family wardrobe. Most homes still had gardens attached, even in the larger cities. Just north of 42nd Street in New York City, women raised a portion of the family food supply even as late as 1890. Farmers' wives probably took the produce of gardens, chicken coops, and pigpens to market and returned with a personal cache of coin and paper currency. For urban wives, however, home production was normally consumed within the family. Indeed, marketing domestic produce was not considered genteel for middle-class women. Sarah Hale of *Godey's* denounced the involvement of women in such market activity, for it "encourages avarice by all members of the family . . . our men are sufficiently moneymaking."[47]

One simple stratagem allowed middle-class women to routinely circumvent this tenet of the cult of domesticity. They earned cold, hard cash without ever leaving their homes, entering the marketplace, or adopting masculine roles. Income came into their own sphere in the person of a boarder. The practice of taking in boarders was seldom acknowledged in domestic literature, except to disparage it as an intrusion on family privacy. Yet its incidence was very high, especially in the households of the urban middle-class. In city after city from 20 percent to 30 percent of all households contained boarders.[48] Because boarding was most common relatively late in the family cycle when children were grown and parents had purchased homes of their own, this figure underestimates the proportion of families who would take in boarders at one time or another. Boarders' rent money could be put to a variety of uses—paying off the mortgage, or sending children to secondary school or college, for example. Whatever comfort or status it bought for the family was generated by women, by the wives and daughters who supplied the boarder with many services in addition to shelter: cooking, cleaning, and laundering among them.

These extensive contributions of women to the material well-being of their families did not go entirely unrecognized. Changes in legal statutes and inheritance practices acknowledged these alterations in women's status. It was during the antebellum period that slowly, state by state, married women were first granted property rights. New York was the pioneer, in 1848 granting wives control over property acquired prior to marriage, and in 1860 to that acquired thereafter. During the same time period, the will books of New York State revealed a trend toward leaving larger portions of family property to wives, without restrictions to their lifetime or widowhood. The same trend was found in Virginia where women were also increasingly appointed the executors of their husbands' estates. The significance of these changes can, however, be exaggerated. A married woman's property rights, it will be recalled, were often used simply as a device to avoid a husband's bankruptcy. Women were made the heirs and executors of small estates composed primarily of consumptive property—houses, personal belongings, and small amounts of cash—rather than land or capital. If the perpetuation of a farm or business was at stake, sons would probably remain the major heirs. Still, these laws and legacies indicate a degree of trust and reliance on the middle-class wife—a man's silent business partner, specializing in the consumptive, psychological, and non-market activities still necessary to family survival.[49]

By the mid-nineteenth century the vast majority of native-born women had found their place in partnerships like these. Only a small minority of their husbands occupied the ranks of unskilled or manual workers in industrial society. Most were relatively comfortable farmers, shopkeepers, managers, clerks, and professionals. They were middle class. Yet women did not simply marry into this status. They helped to create and reproduce it. The domestic duties of Victorian women all came together to create the patina of respectability that usually identifies this all too amorphous social rank. She was responsible for the neat bungalows, lace curtains, and starched collars that announced a middle-class reputation. The income she acquired by keeping boarders might educate sons and ensure a second generation of nonmanual employment. The sexual repression practiced in her name was central to middle-class psychology and helped to limit family size as well. The ideal mother inculcated the values that underwrote middle-class character as well as economic and social status. She played a major historical role within the domestic sphere as she worked to shape the American middle class into its nineteenth-century mold.

At this point it might be tempting to suggest, as have some historians, that women's detour into a more isolated sphere in the nineteenth century was a circular but sure route toward enhanced power and status. Victorian women had achieved, after all, a larger jurisdiction over children, a modicum of control over their reproduction, and a measure of autonomy within their own homes. Surely, the nineteenth-century urban household was without a patriarch for most of the working day. Even after hours, the male presence in the Victorian home was often shadowy and elusive. Writers as popular as Ike Marvel and as perceptive as Herman Melville created male characters who were timid, even besieged, in their homes. Observers of one middle-class neighborhood described the husbands of the district as a goaded, henpecked, and spineless crew.[50] Within her sphere, it seems, woman may have reigned triumphant, a possibility that has been labeled domestic feminism by historian Daniel Scott Smith.[51]

There were other advantages of domestic segregation as well. Retired within a common sphere, women could cultivate their ties to one another. The intense female friendships developed by eighteenth-century ladies like Esther Burr continued to grow in the nineteenth century, nurtured in the congenial feminine environments of female seminaries, Victorian parlors, and pious ladies' circles. This marked tendency toward strong attachment between women, labeled homosocial bonding by Carroll Smith-Rosenberg, is poignantly portrayed in nineteenth-century correspondence. For example, Sarah Alden Ripley wrote to her recently married daughter, "You do not know how much I miss you, not only when I struggle in and out of my mortal envelop and pump my nightly potation and no longer pour into your sympathizing ear my senile gossip, but all the day I muse away since the sound of your voice no longer rouses me to sympathy with your joys or sorrows. . . . You cannot know how much I miss your affectionate demonstrations." Mary Halleck Foote shared the same heartfelt sympathy with a friend made at school: "I wanted so to put my arms around my girl of all the girls in the world and tell her . . . I love her as wives do their husbands, as friends who have taken each other for life. . . ." Indeed, it is highly likely that women found greater support, sympathy, and understanding among their female friends than with their husbands. Some may have found erotic pleasure there as well. This was some compensation, at least, for the restrictions of woman's sphere.[52].

Still, those restrictions should not be dismissed too readily. Domestic feminism grasped for autonomy only within a narrow social space. Homosocial bonds, in the case of women, did not create alliances with the powerful nor open doors to diverse experience. The fundamental question still remains: Just how much societal power and how much positive freedom was possible in the confines of woman's sphere? The answer for the nineteenth century may be "less than ever before." Control over economic resources was clearly departing from the household, while political decisions were transferred from intimate local circles to city hall, the voting booth, Washington, and Richmond. It was more important than ever, therefore, for women to find a realm of independent action outside the home. Had the cult of domesticity and the disrepute of the reformer of the 1830s foreclosed on women's opportunities in the larger sphere?

WOMAN'S SPHERE
IN THE MUNICIPALITY

There were, however, select places outside the home to which women flocked in such numbers that they were conceded to be within the female sphere. One was, of course, the church, and the other the local charity organization. Once the civic duty of town fathers and poormasters, subsequently the charge of the welfare state, the care of dependent populations was known as charity in the nineteenth century, and became the province of women. By 1820 most major cities and numerous small towns could count on benevolent matrons to care for their poor. New York, Boston, Newburyport, Philadelphia, Salem, Concord (New Hampshire), Bedford (Massachusetts), to name only a few municipalities, had female-sponsored orphan asylums or homes for indigent women.

These early charities emerged quietly out of existing female circles, especially in the church, and they mushroomed in the wake of revivals. This report, issued from New York City in 1813, exemplifies the process: "A few ladies moved with compassion associated themselves for the purpose of relieving the necessities and distresses of aged females." By this method of association, women took up a larger and larger share of the responsibility for the care of the urban poor. By the 1830s female charities could be found all along the Ohio Valley, deep into Virginia, and as far west as Illinois. Chicago, Illinois; Trempealeau County, Wisconsin; Hamilton, Ontario, all had their female charities within a few years of settlement. The larger cities offered women sufficient benevolent activity around which to build a full-time career. A young Boston woman named Susan Huntington, for example, belonged to the Female Orphan Asylum, the Graham Society, the Corban Society, the Female Bible Society, The Widow Society, the Boston Female Education Society, and the Maternal Association. She served as an officer in at least three of these organizations.[53]

Thus, by 1830 female charity had become a major component of the urban social system. It would grow more comprehensive and entrenched as time went on. Yet it is unlikely that these charities ever enrolled more than a minority of the female population. Analysis of the rosters of charitable institutions in such places as Providence, Rhode Island; Utica, New York; and Petersburg, Virginia, reveals a uniformly affluent and elite membership. The officers, trustees, and the bulk of the members of benevolent associations were the wives and daughters of prosperous merchants, financiers, and professionals. The philanthropic women formed a very tight and interlocking circle. Membership lists of local charities were laced with kin ties. The managers of the Orphan Asylum of Petersburg, Virginia, for example, were almost a family circle; 50 percent of them had relatives on the board. In their activities outside the home, upper-class women had formed, almost literally, a benevolent sisterhood.

What began in informal association and familial intimacy became more rational and bureaucratic with time. In the beginning, the magnanimity of women might be expressed by ceding the contents of their sewing baskets to the poor or holding a fair to raise funds to assist the needy during a cruel winter. But slowly, women constructed a solid institutional base for poor relief. By mid-century the local asylum often stood among a city's more impressive public buildings, housing hundreds of homeless children and operating on a budget in five figures. If a city had a hospital at all it had most likely been established by females—by Catholic nuns if not Protestant matrons. The dispensing of alms had become a very calculating and intricate operation by the 1850s. Groups like the New York Association for Improving the Condition of the Poor were administered by committees composed of both sexes and relied on a mass of female volunteers. The NYAICP devised an intricate system of canvassing the city to discover the worthy poor. In 1844 they divided the city into 236 districts; three years later they visited more than 5,000 poor families.

The New York Association called their voluntary agents, who numbered over 400 in 1853, family visitors. The family visitor who performed the nitty-gritty welfare work in many cities was usually a female. She left home to trek through the most unsavory districts of the city. Other women tried to create a woman's space in the heart of the slums. The most notable example of this method of antebellum charity was The Ladies Home Missionary Society of the Methodist Episcopal Church, founded by the noted female revivalist Phoebe Palmer. Palmer and her associates transformed an old brewery in the notorious New York slum of Five Points into a pioneer settlement house, complete with training schools, classes in child rearing, day-care centers, and homes for working women. In this larger house outside the home, Victorian women had begun to redesign urban space according to their own altruistic specifications.[54]

By the mid-nineteenth century, then, women were operating a whole welfare system in cities and towns across the country. In so doing they undoubtedly performed Herculean service for American society and for the class their husbands represented. Female benevolent associations had lifted a heavy financial and civic burden from the shoulders of busy businessmen. One of the first official acts of a female charity was to acquire a corporate charter that specified that the husbands of the benevolent society's officers would not be liable for any debts that their wives incurred. Most associations also took care to appoint a single woman as treasurer, that is a *femme sole* capable of independently managing the society's finances. Once they had acquired this financial autonomy, the female charities proceeded to accumulate substantial sums of money, from subscriptions, legacies, fairs, bazaars, by whatever device at their disposal.

It would take a major accounting project to measure the amount of welfare funds generated by the unpaid labors of antebellum women. The total would most likely exceed the amount of the city's budget for the poor. Thanks to the active benevolence of upper-class women, the entrepreneurs of the age of laissez-faire were not obliged to divert large sums of capital from business investments to care for the poor. In fact, they could rely on their wives and daughters to supplement the income of ill-paid, underemployed workers. At the same time, the charitable activities of the financier's wife could add a luster of generosity to his reputation. In Hamilton, Ontario, for example, 40 percent of the entrepreneurial class could point with pride to a wife in the Ladies Benevolent Society.[55]

This is not to say that philanthropic women of the antebellum era were simply pawns of city fathers and financial leaders. More often they found space for autonomous action in this select sphere. Female charities often chose to minister to women and to offer support and sympathy to the most downtrodden and disreputable of their own sex. They brought instructions in housekeeping and child care into the most miserable hovels of the slums. They formed boardinghouses that took in lowly workingwomen and even prostitutes. Some women even began to question the treatment of women in the male-dominated world of the paid labor force. The Boston Seamen's Aid Society called for the equalization of male and female wages as early as 1836. The ladies of this society quickly established a strong loyalty to workingwomen and soon felt called upon to ally with their sisters against the men of their own class. They attacked head on, saying: "Combinations of selfish men are formed to beat down the price of female labor; and they call this diminished rate the market price." After several decades of work among the laboring females of the city of Providence, the members of the Employment Society took a similar course of action. They took as their avowed and leading principle the slogan "fair wages for women's work." Again these benevolent women aimed their social criticism directly at the opposite sex: "If either sex is disqualified to judge of these matters, and is apt to judge wrongly and act oppressively it is not our own."

Within such charitable institutions as the Seaman's Aid Society and the Providence Employment Society, women found ample space in which to flex their minds and muscles. It allowed them to exercise their abilities outside the home, brought them into contact and sympathy with workingwomen from another class and culture, and led them even to criticize industrial capitalism and the men who managed it. They had, in sum, significantly remodeled the sexual division of social space. In justification of their demand for better wages for females, the women of the Providence Employment Society proclaimed, "There are spheres which ladies ought never to enter. . . . But this is not one."[56]

IMMIGRANT WOMEN
OF THE LOWER CLASS

As an upper-class woman went about her charitable rounds in Five Points, Murderers' Row, or the slums of any American city, her sphere inevitably intersected with women of different classes, cultures, and gender systems. At mid-century, one-third to one-half of the population of most American cities had been born abroad — in the British Isles, French Canada, and most notably Ireland and Germany. Like the shifts in the native population that had sent farmers' sons westward and their daughters to town and factory, this global migration often sent men and women in different directions. On the one hand, emigrants tended to set off from the provinces of Germany in pairs, families, or equal numbers of men and women. Even the highly domesticated Germans, however, scions of artisans and peasant families, began to uncouple at the portals of American cities. In the premier German town, Milwaukee, Wisconsin, women outnumbered men in the years of young adulthood. It was not uncommon to find some young, single women among the German pioneers. Among the Irish, on the other hand, the urban and industrial pioneer was very likely to be a female. In fact, after the Civil War the Irish would become the only major nationality to send more daughters than sons across the Atlantic.[57]

Hence Irish-American women present a very special case study in the history of the nineteenth-century gender system. In Ireland itself sexual differentiation was built into a peasant economy. While male and female alike might till the fields and tend animals, only males could inherit the old sod. Thus women were accustomed to being the more wayward sex, breaking up roots and moving to the farms of their grooms or, if they remained unmarried, journeying to Dublin or an English city in search of employment. The devastating crises of nineteenth-century Ireland — population explosion, enclosure, depression, and the *coup de grâce*, famine — sent the rates of Irish migration soaring and scattered disinherited sons and daughters around the globe. In the wake of the famine, 1.5 million Irish men and women arrived in the United States.[58]

One imperative drove men and women alike across the Atlantic: the need to make their daily bread. Thus it was predictable that many Irish would be found in centers of female employment. They flocked into textile towns, constituting the bulk of the labor force in Lowell by 1850. Nearly half the working families in this former bastion of Yankee maidens were headed by females, chiefly widows of foreign birth. Another mill town, Warren, Rhode Island, was almost a feminine colony. In this settlement of immigrants, chiefly Irish and French Canadian, there were only 64 men for every 100 women. On the western flank of the textile industry, the northern New York town of Cohoes was populated by female-headed families and their working daughters. In Cohoes four out of five teen-age Irish girls could be found tending textile machinery.[59] Whether she arrived in America singly, as a daughter or a widowed mother, the first thought of the Irish immigrant woman was to make a living. Victorian notions of woman's sphere were not prominent in her mind. Irish immigrants had a relatively poorly developed sense of private household space. Peasant families seldom occupied a more elaborate domicile than a dirt-floored cottage, which they were apt to share with livestock as well as relatives.

Factory towns offered one answer to the need for immediate employment. Any city of reasonable size also beckoned women workers, as seamstresses, washerwomen, and, above all else, domestic servants. The rate of immigrant employment as domestic servants was truly extraordinary. Be it in New York City, Milwaukee, Wisconsin, or Hamilton, Ontario, the majority of both Irish and German immigrant girls would spend a portion of their youth as domestic servants. In Buffalo, New York, for example, Irish girls began leaving home to work as servants at eleven years of age. In the age group eighteen to twenty-one, one-half to two-thirds of all Irish daughters could be found working in another household. Recent immigrants were the most likely to go into service. Three-quarters of all Irish teen-agers who were new to the city became domestic servants. In the case of Irish immigrants, the role of domestic service was an exacting new occupation, one for which the shanties of Erin provided little preparation. One immigrant girl, recalling her thatched hut in the old country, allowed that "There was no housework done in our house." "When a green girl comes in a house," she continued, "she don't know what half the things is for." The immigrant girl had to master a whole fund of skills and knowledge if she was to make her living as a domestic in the new land. These accomplishments were not lost on her immigrant brothers. Servant girls were highly valued on the marriage market of immigrant Milwaukee, for example, where it was said that German men sought domestics because of their superior command of English and knowledge of American customs.[60]

After this rapid apprenticeship in the sphere of the middle-class woman, immigrant daughters entered homes of their own. German women married particularly early in life. In Milwaukee it was said that girls went as fast as lager beer. Most immigrant wives would remain close to home through the bulk of their married lives. Only a tiny minority, around 5 percent of all immigrant wives, were enrolled in the labor force at any single point during the antebellum period. Domestic womanhood did not go unheralded in immigrant cultures. The nineteenth-century Catholic Church, where so many immigrants worshipped, paid special homage to the virtues of the Virgin Mary. Local churches instituted Young Ladies' Sodalities and Societies of the Holy Family where the same domestic graces were enshrined. Thus a Catholic funeral sermon could honor womanly accomplishments similar to those proclaimed from a Protestant pulpit. One Catholic priest had special praise for the mother of ten: "Not one to this day has ever died, or now lives out of the belief and practice of their mother and grandmother's faith." This pious mother was not entirely atypical, for on one score immigrant women performed the duties of the domestic sphere more diligently than anyone, typically bearing two or three more children than did native-born women. Immigrant women often shouldered a particularly heavy domestic burden regardless of the size of their families, for they frequently reared their children alone. Widowhood was most frequent among the Irish. As many as half of all Irishwomen in their fifties were without a spouse because of widowhood, desertion, or temporary separation. Thus, if anything, a woman's duties in relation to her family were even more onerous among this immigrant and lower-class population.[61]

Not all women of immigrant background lived in poverty and squalor. In the higher circles of immigrant and Catholic families women enlarged their sphere in the same fashion as had their native-born peers. New York City had its Catholic Orphan Asylum by 1817. Soon thereafter the Ladies' Society of Charity at Transfiguration Catholic Church could boast of sewing 350 garments for the poor of the parish. Among Catholics, however, unmarried women were responsible for much of the charity in the immigrant community. Catholic women could devote their entire lives to benevolence by joining a religious order. The Sisters of Mercy set up a multifaceted welfare system among New York's Irish. In one five-year period they reported finding jobs for 8,000 needy girls. They certainly were a match for the Protestant missions of the city in the extent and energy of their benevolence.[62] Immigrants as well as Yankee women set up their own peculiar symbiosis between the needy and the idle of their sex. Upper-class and middle-class women, regardless of ethnic origin, did not live in perfectly segregated cultures or sanitized spheres.

To immigrant women, often recently uprooted from peasant economies, however, the boundaries between home and society, family and work, did not constitute particularly formidable barricades. Immigrant, and particularly Irish, women seemed to move in and out of the labor force whenever family emergencies warranted it, which was quite often, given their high rates of widowhood. They met their domestic obligations on the job as well as in their kitchens. Many immigrant women played out their social and economic roles in the streets as well. Poor Irish girls, some ten years old and younger, conducted an arduous business in the streets of New York—scavenging, ragpicking, prostitution—to support themselves and their kin. Immigrant women also readily took to the streets for political purposes. In 1842 in New York they participated in a riot provoked by municipal attempts to prohibit the free reign of pigs on the city streets. In this not infrequent urban drama, work and family, public and private life, all mingled together as women made a raucous public defense of the right to produce their family's supply of protein. In other times and places immigrant women resorted to street violence in hopes of bringing down the price of flour. In Utica, New York, in 1859 women physically dismantled the municipal pest house, because it threatened to expose their families to smallpox. The women who participated in riots such as these committed every possible offense against the doctrine of the spheres. They left their homes, raised their voices, and exerted direct physical force against public male authority. It is doubtful whether even the most emphatic lady of mercy would endorse this altogether unfeminine behavior.[63]

Indeed, the different versions of womanhood enacted by the rich and the poor, the native and foreign, cannot be blithely reconciled. They erupted into open conflict during the New York City Draft Riots of 1863. The major protagonists of that open urban warfare were predominantly lower-class Irishmen, who, outraged by the conscription law, rampaged through the city for four days, viciously assaulting blacks and attacking symbols of wealth and power. Yet just off center stage, the poor women of the city took this opportunity to express their own antagonism toward their "betters." The Protestant missions came in for their own share of abuse. Several charitable institutions, which Protestant women had so carefully built, were the targets of arson. Amid the din of the riots, more personal and vitriolic abuse of upper-class women could also be heard. One Irishwoman, on observing a rich matron mourning the charred ruins of her mansion, coldly barked, "Serves you right you long-necked yankee bitch."[64]

SLAVERY AND GENDER

The Draft Riots also brought grisly testimony to another deep fissure in American womanhood, one that divided black and white women. The free black women of New York City were terrorized for four days, assaulted, tortured, and raped without the least deference to the fragility of Victorian womanhood. Even under normal conditions, the black females of northern cities lived on the margins of woman's sphere. They came to the city in search of a livelihood and found a facsimile thereof as servants, laundresses, and scullery maids. They were routinely widowed, deserted, and left to rear their children alone. In Philadelphia in 1839, for example, 37 percent of all blacks lived in single-parent households, a figure substantially above even the Irish rate of incomplete families. These free black women of the antebellum period had an acrid taste of what northern urban capitalism held in store for their race and sex.[65]

For the time being, however, most black women were bound to the plantations of the American South. Their womanhood was inextricably entangled with their status as slaves. With the widening of international markets and the invention of the cotton gin, southern agriculture expanded rapidly in the early nineteenth century. Vast new territories in the Deep South were brought under cultivation, and the slave system expanded apace. Although large numbers of black women still lived on small farms where they might work quite casually alongside a poor-white master and mistress, the majority were now part of the more rigid and regimented labor system of the large plantation. Here only a minority of women held the relatively privileged position of house slaves. Most, if they were over ten years of age, went to the fields six days a week, to plant, plow, and pick cotton from sunup to sundown. Nor did southern entrepreneurs hesitate to put women to work in grueling and menial jobs outside of agriculture. Slave women built canals and labored in factories. In agriculture or industry, black women were first and foremost slave laborers. [66]

Slave women hardly inhabited a domestic sphere; they merely pieced together a semblance of family life along the margins of their workday. A female field hand might be granted a month off for childbirth, or be allowed to return from the fields three or four times a day to nurse a newborn infant. Occasionally, women were permitted to leave the fields early on Saturday to perform some chores around the slave quarters. Their homes were small cabins of one or two rooms, which they usually shared with their mate and their children, and perhaps another family secluded behind a crude partition. They might also tend a small garden plot whose produce they could claim as their own. Slave women were often responsible for manufacturing soap, candles, and clothes for their families, as well as cooking crude meals. [67] Clearly, hard labor, whether in the field or in the slave quarters, was the defining characteristic of black womanhood in the South.

At the same time, slave women performed many tasks that were unique to their sex. Most importantly and fundamentally, slave women worked to reproduce the slave labor force, a task of crucial import after the end of the slave trade in 1808. Black women were remarkably prolific, bearing seven children, on the average.

The central role of women in southern production and reproduction is readily acknowledged. The extent to which women's roles were organized around the institution of the two-parent nuclear family, however, is the subject of much debate among historians. The strength of bonds between black men and women are particularly at issue. Writing in the 1930s, the black sociologist E. Franklin Frazier argued that the slave family was a truncated institution, reduced to the relationship between the slave mother and her children. In the absence of a strong father, the black family was proclaimed a matriarchy by Frazier. His choice of terminology was unfortunate and has caused scholars considerable confusion and fruitless altercation. An enslaved woman was hardly invested with the scepter of a reigning matriarch. Still, the obverse of Frazier's argument is equally dubious. An enslaved male was hardly in the position to act as a patriarch or even to exercise the kind of authority assumed by the Victorian father. Even if the slave father was not sold away and remained in the same cabin with his growing children, many of his traditional male prerogatives actually belonged to the slave master, who controlled the labor and provided the subsistence of the slave family.[68]

Recent historians have uncovered evidence that slave husbands and fathers did, despite all these obstacles, maintain a position of some status in the slave family. The records of several large plantations, which listed the fathers as well as the mothers of slave children, indicate that a slave woman commonly bore her children by one man who remained her mate through most of the family cycle. Furthermore, slave culture paid special homage to patrilineage. Slave children were often named after their fathers and grandfathers, less often after female ancestors. Male slaves also found concrete ways of demonstrating some of the superior status associated with masculinity. For example, they had more opportunities than did their wives to acquire special skills, stature within the plantation labor force, and a modicum of cash rewards. Male slaves also had some prospects for upward mobility. They might be apprenticed to a skilled job, be promoted to driver, or be granted a cash bonus for loyal service. The songs and stories heard around the slave quarters also indicate that women were relatively marginal and subordinate within antebellum black culture. There is even some evidence that Victorian notions of woman's sphere had penetrated to the slave quarter. With emancipation came complaints from freedmen that working wives wounded their masculine pride. There can be no doubt, then, that the nuclear family did exist under slavery, along with a sexual division of labor and status, and at least a primitive distinction between the male and the female spheres.[69]

Still, the slave family was far from a facsimile of the white middle class, whose womanhood differed only in complexion. Slave marriages were clearly fragile institutions. In the upper South one-third to one-half of the slave family units did not contain an adult male. The sexual division of slave labor was decisive enough to send male and female into different economic sectors and geographical locations. Southern towns and cities, with their needs for the personal services of domestic workers, often had an excess of women, while the demand for heavy field work on plantations created larger numbers of unattached male slaves. Even on those plantations where stable marriages were the dominant domestic arrangement, as many as one in four slave families were female-headed. Whether by choice or because of the coercive power of the slave system, marital bonds were considerably weaker among slaves than anywhere else in Victorian America.[70] The more relaxed conjugal ties were manifest in the sexual behavior of slaves, as well. An adolescent woman was often free to experiment with a variety of sex partners and settled into a monogamous relationship only with the birth of her first child. Even then, partners would be exchanged with some regularity. On one plantation, one in three slave women bore children by different husbands. Neither can the frequency of sexual relations between master and slave be discounted. Miscegenation was common enough to make an estimated one in eight to one in three slaves mulattoes by 1865.[71] It is indisputable, in sum, that an enslaved woman was far less likely than most of her sex to be under the lifelong domestic power, or protection, of a single male. This is a variation in the gender system of major significance.

Slave men were also denied the superior status that accrues from a position of political authority. In the absence of a male-dominated political structure, the slave community organized itself in less formal ways, through face-to-face and kin relationships. Females as well as males could participate in this social system. These more diffuse bonds of the slave community competed with the family for social hegemony, beginning even during childhood. Slave children were commonly reared collectively, often in groups of twenty or more. While their parents were in the fields, infants might be placed under the care of an elderly woman and supervised by older siblings. Extensive bonds among peers endured into adulthood.

When for example, a Georgia slave sent a message back to her old plantation she acknowledged a complicated latticework of friends and relatives:

> Clarissa your affectionate mother and father send a heap of love to you and your Husband and my Grand Children Phebea, Mag, and Cloe. John. Judy. Sue. May aunt Aufy sinena and Minton and Little Plaska. Charles Nega. Fillis and all of their Children. Cash. Prime. Lafatte. Rick Tonia sends their love to you all. Give our love to Cashes Brother Porter and his wife Patience. Victoria gives her love to her Cousin Beck and Miley.

Throughout the slave community the titles aunt, uncle, brother, and sister were used to convey a sense of intimacy, fellowship, and mutual sharing that transcended biological ties. Slaves worked out their collective lives in this extended but closeknit social network. Anthropologists have observed that social systems of this nature grant a relatively large share of power to women.[72]

The relative equality of the sexes under slavery was written into the marriage vows recited on one plantation. While the groom pledged simply to perform the "duties of an affectionate and faithful husband," the bride did not vow obedience, but recited the same pledge, to be "an affectionate and faithful wife."[73] In sum the interplay of slavery and gender was riddled with contradictions, and heavy with irony. It was within this most brutal and oppressive American institution that women came the closest to obtaining social and economic symmetry with men, that is, with their fellow slaves, hardly with their white masters.

The interaction between white southern womanhood and the slave gender system introduces an even more snarled skein of relationships, which historians have hardly begun to unravel. Standing out from all this confusion, however, is the stubborn image of black women summoning the strength of survival and even resistance within the slave system. Her image was recalled by a proud daughter: "My mother was the smartest black woman in Edes . . . she would do anything. She made as good a field hand as she did a cook. She was a demon, loud and boisterous, high-spirited and independent. I tell you she was a captain." The sons of a slave named Sally Thomas had cause to recall their mother with pride and gratitude. They made their way to freedom before the Civil War, thanks to the encouragement and hard labor of this slave woman, who reared her children and ran her own laundry in Nashville, Tennessee, without the assistance of a mate.[74] Images like these speak to the real strengths of slave women. They do not, however, dispel the oppression of women under slavery, nor override the margin of male dominance that existed within the slave quarters as well as the Victorian cottage.

THE WOMEN'S RIGHTS MOVEMENT

The image of the strong black woman is also prominently displayed within the history of the women's rights movement. It was Sojourner Truth, raising the rugged arm of a field hand and shouting "Ain't I a Woman," who gave courage to one of the first nervous gatherings of women's rights advocates. Even before that, a black abolitionist, Maria W. Stewart by name, was the first American woman who dared to speak in public before audiences composed of members of both sexes. And, of course, the female abolitionists were the first to mount a direct campaign for sexual equality. Angelina and Sarah Grimké were hardly habituated to the lecture circuit when they were required to defend their sex as well as the slave. Sarah Grimké responded with the clearest enunciation of feminist consciousness yet heard in America: "I ask no favor for my sex. I surrender not our claim to equality. All I ask our brethren is that they will take their heels from our necks and permit us to stand upright on that ground which God designed us to occupy." It was over a decade later that an independent movement for sexual equality was inaugurated. Even then, the call to the celebrated meeting at Seneca Falls, New York, was issued by seasoned abolitionists, Lucretia Mott and Elizabeth Cady Stanton.

This gathering of approximately 100 men and women in a small village in the Finger Lakes district of New York State was a strangely prescient event in the history of women. The segregation of the sexes into the sharply distinct spheres typical of early industrial capitalism had hardly been established when this little band of women put forth a series of proposals for the moral, economic, and political equality of women. Their ninth and most controversial resolution pronounced the demand that would consume the women's movement for more than seventy years—female suffrage. The declaration of sentiments and resolutions drawn up at Seneca Falls, however forward-looking, was not a fortuitous occurrence. It arose, first of all, out of the network of female reforms that had been particularly strong in the environs of Seneca Falls, the now smoldering burned-over district.

Attendance at the Seneca Falls meeting was partly a habitual response of well-organized women, many of whom chafed at the obstacles of gender that had impeded their earlier reform efforts. When called upon to provide a theoretical justification for women's rights, Stanton reached even further back into history, to the Declaration of Independence, with its principles of equality and its promise of a political voice for all. These women also drew strength from some elements in the emerging doctrine of the spheres. Woman's reputed moral superiority, they implied, made it imperative that she be granted access to the political arena. All these ideals and experiences commingled in such a way as to give birth to an organized feminist movement and generated a score of subsequent women's rights conventions throughout the Northeast and the Ohio Valley.

The women's rights advocates, some of whom took to wearing pantaloons or bloomer costumes in the next decade, were considered cranks by most of their contemporaries, men and women alike. Comments on the Seneca Falls Convention, usually hidden in the back pages of the local newspaper, went something like this: "We respect woman as woman. She fills a place higher, more useful and far more appropriate when she acts in the sphere she has already enabled than she could in any other capacity."[75] The murmuring of rebellion at Seneca Falls served in part to provoke a clearer and more rigid definition of women's proper sphere. In fact, not even the women's movement explicitly countermanded the imperatives of woman's sphere. Demands for equal pay, equal work, the vote, and an independent identity might seem to contradict the notion that woman's place was in the home. But most feminists did not see it that way. Before the Civil War, none proposed that women surrender their home responsibilities or even that men shoulder a significant part of their domestic burdens. The feminist's pride in her own sex, furthermore, often led her to extol the Victorian wife and mother as a select and superior species of human being, and to confer special honors on her home station.

Neither were antebellum feminists freed from the practical restrictions of the domestic sphere. Only Susan B. Anthony, a spinster, devoted a lifetime to the women's movement. The activities of

Elizabeth Cady Stanton were severely curtailed until her children were grown. Other early leaders of the movement, including Angelina Grimké, Antoinette Brown, and Lucy Stone, all but retired after marriage and childbirth. Stone bore only one child, but still motherhood removed her to the periphery of the movement for a full ten years. On gazing down at her sleeping child, she confessed, "I shrank like a snail into its shell and saw that for these years I can be only a mother." When Angelina Grimké went into domestic retirement she took her sister Sarah with her as well. By the 1850s even Sarah Grimké seemed to have succumbed to the seductive pronouncements of woman's sphere. She celebrated the "beautiful differences" between the sexes, and "the great moral power" of women. She wrote to a friend in 1856 that "I feel not haste, no anxiety to see my sex invested with their rights."[76]

☐

Thus feminists and conservatives alike were hemmed in by the antebellum gender system. For the native-born white middle class, womanhood took on a distinctive spatial character during the early stages of industrial capitalism. The social roles and workplaces of the two sexes became segregated: men journeyed away from the household to secure cash income, while women's work, influence, and consciousness moved centripetally inward toward a tight nucleus of relations to her husband, children, and perhaps a boarder. Even when women found a position of authority and power outside the home, it was within a primarily female space, most notably the urban welfare system or the public schools. Woman's role in antebellum history, while confined to a narrow space, was by no means diminished in importance. Within her sphere woman performed all those essential social tasks that existed outside the factory, the marketplace, and the reach of capital. The development of a woman's sphere during the antebellum period had its compensation. Women were given exorbitant praise for the loyal performance of their home duties. They went about their domestic work without the interference of males, who were preoccupied with the world outside. Finally, women found support and a common identity with their sister inhabitants of woman's sphere. These more positive implications of the nineteenth-century gender system would become more apparent in the years to come.

F O U R

THE BREADGIVERS:
IMMIGRANTS AND REFORMERS:
1865–1920

The class of 1881 of the Female Seminary in Rockford, Illinois, took as its model of womanhood "the saxon lady whose mission it was to give bread unto her household." The seminary's most illustrious graduate, Jane Addams, went on to explain her classmates' appreciation of this ancient meaning of the term *lady*: "We have planned to be Breadgivers throughout our lives, [and] believing that in labor alone is happiness, and that the only true and honorable life is one filled with good works and honest toil, we will strive to idealize our labor and thus happily fulfill woman's noblest mission."[1] In 1925, at a time when Jane Addams' breadgiving had gained her an almost sainted national reputation, the term appeared in another document of women's history. *Bread Givers* was the title of a novel of immigrant life written by Anzia Yezierska. The Yiddish title referred to the selfless, long-suffering women of a Jewish immigrant family. Yezierska described the mother and elder daughters of the Smolinsky family as they toiled in sweatshops, stores, and kitchens to support themselves as well as a father, who preferred the idle and unremunerative role of the Talmudic scholar to the American norm of masculinity, breadwinner.[2]

Both the immigrant working-class women, among whom Anzia Yezierska grew up, and the educated middle-class reformers represented by Jane Addams, were hard workers whose sense of social and economic responsibility took them frequently outside the home. In this respect they seemed to have broken free of woman's antebellum sphere. Yet the activities they pursued outside the home were still more in the nature of breadgiving than breadwinning. Jane Addams, and the millions of women who joined ranks behind her in a veritable army of reformers, clothed even their most forceful social and political actions in the rhetoric of feminine altruism and motherly sacrifice. Similarly, immigrant wives and daughters went to work not to win their fortunes but to feed their families, and seldom coveted any individualistic sense of achievement. The term *breadgiver*, then, is an appropriate symbol for womanhood in the late nineteenth and early twentieth centuries. It denotes a significant movement of women into a larger world of economic and social action, but one that remained hemmed in by domestic associations.

This genuine progression in the history of women occurred during the most vigorous and aggressive stage of industrial capitalism, when the United States became the most powerful national economy in the world. It was the age of steel, steam, and then electricity. Tons of brick and mortar went into building the cities, which by 1920 sheltered the majority of the American population. Powering the industrial machine required massive amounts of human muscle from mine, metal, and construction workers, most all of them male and the majority imported from abroad. It was also the age of the Rockefellers, Carnegies, and Vanderbilts, who consolidated this industrial power into a few monumental national corporations. In sum, American economic history seemed its most masculine during this period, characterized by the brute muscular strength of the steelworker and the arrogant aggressiveness of the robber baron.

Yet, as always, women were integral to this historical process, standing not to the rear but right beside the men at an essential place in the soial system. First of all, the low wages and erratic employment of working-class men were not sufficient to support families and replenish the supply of industrial workers. Women's work, at home and increasingly in the labor market, remained necessary to the survival and reproduction of the working class. Furthermore, while the businessmen of the gilded age were building their trusts and monopolies, the women of the upper and middle classes were creating equally impressive national organizations and formulating some ideas of their own about the organization of industrial society. Operating through settlement houses, women's clubs, and welfare agencies, women became the backbone and inspiration of the Progressive movement and thereby helped to shape the political economy of the era. These two species of breadgivers, the women of the largely foreign-born working class and the female social reformers, together remade American womanhood.

THE BREADGIVER
AS IMMIGRANT WORKER

The rate of female employment outside the home began to rise from its Victorian nadir in the 1870s. Between 1880 and 1910 the proportion of adult females enrolled in the labor force rose from 14.7 to 24.8 percent.[3] Of the one in four women on the job, however, very few were native-born. Almost every one of the immigrant groups to arrive in the United States during the second great wave of immigration, however, sent large numbers of women to work. The new female immigrants, often coming from rather patriarchal cultures such as the Italian or Jewish, were only slightly more shy of the labor force than were the hardworking Irish lasses of the antebellum period. If demographic and economic conditions were suitable, Italian, Jewish, and Slavic immigrant women all flocked into the labor market. The percentages of female immigrants among the Slavs and Italians were quite low, as was the rate of permanent residence within the United States. Among Jewish immigrants, women constituted 40 percent of the new arrivals, most of whom departed Europe as families.

When women disembarked at Ellis Island, American employers were eager to hire their cheap labor, regardless of national origin. The large metropolitan areas of the Northeast were particularly greedy for women workers in such thriving light industries as garment making, cigar rolling, laundering, and food processing. In diversified economies like those of Philadelphia and New York, large numbers of women of all the major immigrant groups found their way into the labor force.[4]

At the same time, xenophobic reaction to the entry of oriental workers into the Western United States led to the near exclusion of Asian females. The sex ratio among Japanese and Chinese immigrants was extremely unbalanced at the turn of the century, with men outnumbering women by as much as 100 to 1. The rare woman who disembarked in San Francisco arrived either as an indentured servant, "picture bride," or piece of contraband. The Asian immigrant community extracted a heavy cost of labor from these female pioneers. Perhaps the majority of them were employed, or enslaved, as prostitutes before they married and went to work in family businesses—typically laundries, restaurants, and small farms.[5]

Meanwhile, more traditional forms of female employment remained open to immigrants old and new, from Asia and Western Europe. By 1890 when the rate of female employment stood at slightly more than 20 percent of the women of working age, the Census Bureau counted 1.5 million domestics, which accounted for nearly 60 percent of America's workingwomen. These women, who entered the work force at a very primitive level, were confined to homes nearly twenty-four hours a day and were awarded only minuscule wages beyond their room and board. More than 30 percent of these servants were foreign-born, and in heavily immigrant states like Massachusetts, the figure rose to more than 60 percent.[6] Young Irishwomen, who continued to stream into the United States on their own and in excess of their brothers, had something of a monopoly on jobs in domestic service.

Still, many recent immigrants from elsewhere in Europe found domestic employment. One maidservant wrote home to her family in Poland that "I do well. I have fine food only I must work from 6 o'clock in the morning to 10 o'clock at night and I earn $13 a month." This Polish girl, Aleksandra Rembienski by name, quickly moved to more lucrative posts. Her second job paid $16 a month, for which she and another woman cleaned eighteen rooms, cooked three meals a day, washed 300 pieces of linen a week, and ironed for periods of up to four days. In short order Aleksandra earned a wage of $22 a month in return for which she single-handedly cleaned sixteen rooms and cooked for a large family. Such meager wages in exchange for exhausting services were coupled with the particular discomforts of servant status: constant attendance, limited free time, isolation from family and friends, and residence with strangers who often spoke a foreign tongue. Consequently, the average tenure of a servant in one job was very short, and many women obliged to earn their own living gravitated to other occupations. The proportion of immigrant women employed as household workers declined steadily after 1890, leaving this less than inviting occupational opportunity largely to black women. Barred from anything but the most menial industrial jobs, black women became a servant class, a status many of them ranked only a notch above slavery.[7]

Meanwhile, white immigrant women streamed into the second largest occupational group of the era, manufacturing. By 1890 all but nine of the 369 industries listed by the U.S. Census Bureau employed women.[8] Many of these were particularly eager to hire "greenhorns," women just off the immigrant vessels, eager for work and unversed in the ways of industry. From 1890 to 1920 these vulnerable women came from Southern and Eastern Europe in great waves, courted at times by such promises as this: "For girls there is work in America, but not for men." Although men far outnumbered women in the immigrant steerage, millions of women landed in America, alone, penniless, and begging for work. Between 1912 and 1917, for example, 500,000 women under thirty disembarked on America's shores. Two-fifths of the immigrant women working in the industrial districts of Pennsylvania had traveled to the United States alone, and three-fifths of them were under eighteen at the time.[9] Work was not a novel experience to these women, but in Europe they had been employed in agriculture or alongside their husbands and brothers in construction or handicraft, and only occasionally in industry. In America they sought and found work almost immediately, often in factories or sweatshops. The European peasant girls were swiftly deposited right in the vortex of nineteenth-century urban industrial society.

These "green" women entered a segment of the industrial work force that was clearly labeled female. Although a great variety of industries employed them, their status, wages, and working conditions were designated for women only. The division of labor in the cigar factories of Pittsburgh at the turn of the century illustrates the kind of opportunities available to immigrant women. Many of the recent arrivals had skill and experience in rolling cigars, traditionally a woman's task in Slavic countries. In America, however, the well-paying job of hand-rolling expensive cigars had become a male monopoly. The second echelon of the cigar industry, mechanized rolling, was reserved for men and women of American birth or long experience in the United States. The raw immigrant women were exiled to the damp and putrid basement rooms to strip tobacco. One Pittsburgh shop employed 523 strippers, including 18 men, 4 of them black, 2 feebleminded, 3 boys, and 9 elderly.

The rest of the workers in this most odious post in the factory were immigrant women, largely Polish. One Slavic woman acknowledged this pattern of discrimination with the simple phrase, "Greenie not wanted in nice clean places."[10]

Women could find work in a variety of industries in the late nineteenth century. But whatever their place of employment the pattern of sexual segregation was likely to be the same. The first principle of the sexual division of factory work decreed that women would be assigned to relatively unskilled tasks. In the garment factory this meant that men would cut and usually press, while women finished garments, sewed on buttons, or worked with inferior materials. In the National Biscuit Company's Pittsburgh plant in 1906 the baking was done by a handful of men, while 1,100 women packaged and frosted cakes. The sexual division of labor was not necessarily based on relative muscle power. In the Pittsburgh metal trades, for example, women heaved sand cores (devices used in molding steel) weighing 10 to 50 pounds and hauled them through dusty shops to fuming ovens. Men in the same factory worked only with lighter but more intricate sand cores, having been apprenticed to acquire this high-paying skill.[11] In the printing industry women were also excluded from apprenticeship and denied the acquisition of skilled jobs. As early as 1856 a Boston union ruled that "this society discountenances any member working in any office that employs female compositors and that any member found doing so be discharged from the society."[12] Whether the result of custom or of the jealousy of male craftsmen, the exclusion of women from skilled employment worked to the benefit of the factory owner, assuring him of a large pool of female workers consigned to the monotonous repetition of simple tasks.

Of course, such labor also came cheaper, as indicated by the wage scale in Pittsburgh factories in the first decade of the twentieth century. Tobacco strippers, usually recent immigrants of the female sex, seldom earned more than $5 per week, while the operators of rolling machines, more likely to be either men or women of native parentage or long tenure in the United States, took home up to $10 per week. The garment cutter received $16 a week, the average female needle worker $6 to $7. Master bakers were awarded salaries of up to $100 a month, the female packager averaged $22 a month. In the Pittsburgh metalworks, male core carriers made $3.50 a day on a union scale, while the nonunionized and unskilled female core carrier made $1.25.[13] In New York State during the same period it was estimated that female industrial workers made one-half to two-thirds of the typical male wage.

Women, furthermore, were more often in those segments of American industry where earnings were determined by the piece-rate rather than a standard wage. Piecework proved a convenient method of accelerating women's output, which involved the repetition of a simple manual process in which speed was at a premium. Women workers, well aware of the few pennies earned with each collar stitched, each bottle scrubbed, or each tobacco leaf stripped, sped on relentlessly to earn a living wage. Only speed could possibly win them economic betterment. Sarah Cohen, a deft cigar roller, worked her way up to making $12 a week by the age of sixteen. The nervous strain overtook her soon thereafter, however, and at twenty-one she was back in the stripping room, where she made a mere $4.20 a week. When a female core maker's Herculean efforts brought her wage up to $2 a day in another Pittsburgh factory, she and her peers were punished by a reduction in the piece-rate.[14] Upward economic mobility was as elusive and frustrating for women workers as was the labor of Sisyphus.

Women's hours were also subject to the iron will of the employer. One immigrant woman reported this procedure: The boss would say, "Rosy, are you doing anything tonight?" When she replied in the negative, he would respond with the politely phrased order: "I guess you can work until half past six."[15] Commonly, the boss or foreman did not resort to such formalities. In the busy season, women would be expected to work late into the evening and through the weekend or forfeit their jobs. When the season was slack, on the other hand, desperately needy workers would be summarily informed that no work and no wage would be forthcoming for days on end. Elizabeth Hasanovitz, an immigrant dressmaker, held no less than fourteen jobs in her first four years in America. She reeled from "that eternal repetition—slack, busy; busy, slack! My head grew over-burdened with heaping up broken thoughts."[16] Tattered nerves and unrelenting anxiety were part and parcel of female industrial labor, subject to seasonal unemployment, piecework, and unskilled jobs.

The greenhorn worker was also victimized by special manipulation of her paycheck. It was common to initiate the unskilled worker into the sweatshop routine with nominal or nonexistent wages. In 1905 one eager young girl worked two months without pay for the privilege of learning to operate a sewing machine. Countless women like her, unfamiliar with industrial practice and often ignorant of the language of the boss, were ill-prepared to question this practice. Others, without basic arithmetic skills, were vulnerable to the bosses' chiseling on the weekly wage checks. It took one Philadelphia worker a year to summon the courage to resist the conniving boss: "Last year I was shy, too, and I never fuss for anything under $1, but now I get tired telling him all about 25 cents. I copy in my book all the amounts on the work slip before I take them back to the factory, so I know what I due just like a bookkeeper."[17]

Some sweatshop managers carried this routine exploitation to the extreme of outright theft of a woman's production. An Italian girl, a greenhorn in the garment industry, sewed coats for three weeks and built up credits with the shop owner amounting to more than $30. Her boss kept saying, "I pay next week"; "I pay after Sunday," until she returned to work one morning to find the shop locked, the machines removed, and the boss absconded. Her wages were never recovered and she was deep in debt and without the carfare to look for another job. "Then what I do? I get married. He want me; he help me pay my ship card. I help him buy nice things."[18]

Even in the absence of such a melodramatic turn of events, few working girls were comfortably self-supporting. Studies of working girls in industrial cities from the 1880s to 1920 revealed that a woman's wage was rarely a living wage. In Pittsburgh, for example, 60 percent of female workers made less than the $7 a week essential for subsistence in 1906–07.[19] The Boston working girls were in a similar predicament in 1885.[20] Elizabeth Hasanovitz budgeted her greenhorn's wages of $2.55 a week as follows: $1 for rent, 60¢ for carfare, 6¢ for the newspaper, and a variable sum for her diet of sugar, bread, milk, butter, and beans. Hasanovitz saved the remainder toward bringing her family to America. After nine weeks in the United States she spent New Year's Day clutching $2 and muttering in bewilderment: "Does it pay to live, after all. Work, work, and never earning enough for a living! Eternal worry how to make ends meet."[21] The immigrant woman's work was not only alienating in itself, but it often failed to earn her a decent living. Still, she had no choice but to struggle on. As one tobacco stripper expressed it, "I must live. What I eat, if I not work?"[22]

IMMIGRANT HOUSEHOLD INCOME

The exploitative industrial use of female labor could reduce immigrant workers to individual atoms denied economic self-sufficiency. The surest means of survival in this predicament was to pool wages in family units. Three out of five of the workingwomen of Boston lived with families in 1885.[23] The majority of Pittsburgh's workers two decades later did the same.[24] A survey of immigrant workingwomen in Pennsylvania in 1925 revealed that 90 percent of them resided in families, with an average of 2.4 workers per household.[25] In essence, women's paltry wages were but one component of working-class family income. In the first decade of the twentieth century, a Senate investigation of workers in mining and manufacturing found that a mere 38 percent of the foreign-born families surveyed relied solely on the income of the male head of household.[26] The provider role in the immigrant family was shared by parents and children of both sexes. While women's work might be far removed from the home and her wages won as a solitary individual, her economic status, her very survival, was a function of the combined labor of her family. Thus female immigrants were not simply workers, but women of the working class and, as such, they played the vital social and economic role of mediating between the family and industrial society.

Before 1920, the majority of the women in the industrial work force related to the family unit as daughters—young, single women living with their parents. A Bureau of Labor study in 1887 revealed that three-fourths of female industrial workers in America's large cities were under twenty-five years of age, and 96 percent of them were single. As late as 1920, approximately 90 percent of the entire female labor force was unmarried and most women workers were under twenty-five.[27] Immigrant girls customarily entered the work force at a very early age. The typical immigrant working girl entered a Pittsburgh factory in her mid-teens and retired early in her twenties. In Providence, Rhode Island, 80 percent of the Italian daughters over the age of eighteen were actively employed.[28] Immediately upon her arrival in America, a twelve-year-old immigrant from Russia named Rose Cohen was placed in a garment shop and put to work alongside her father to earn passage money for her mother and siblings. Needlework was no novelty to Rose Cohen. She recalled that as a child in a Russian village, "as soon as we were able to hold a needle we were taught to sew." Within a year of her arrival in America, however, Rose was sent to a shop without her father and placed in the company of workers whose ways and language were foreign to her. At this juncture in immigrant womanhood she was "eager to begin life on my own, but also afraid."[29]

Although immigrant daughters like Rose Cohen might work at a physical distance from their families, they remained bound to their kin by custom, experience, and the concrete social ties that spun through and around the homes and the factories of the immigrant community. In a Jewish neighborhood the small garment manufacturer often shared an ethnic background if not direct kinship with his employees. Thus in keeping with tradition he would deposit a daughter's pay with her father, his *landsman*. Italian businessmen often practiced a similar payroll policy. Even in the absence of such procedures, informal pressures and sanctions would propel immigrant daughters to dutifully hand over their pay envelopes to their fathers or mothers. If a young worker withdrew a small portion of her wage to purchase sweets or finery, she would pay an additional price in paternal anger. An Italian woman recently interviewed in Providence, Rhode Island, for example, still recalled her father's sullen response to such chiseling: he threw the remaining pay in her face.[30] Another woman recalled her participation in the immigrant family economy in a more positive fashion. "My father was a stonemason, you know how it is. He didn't have steady work and my mother used to talk all the time about how poor we were. So I had my mind on work all the time. I was thinking how I could go to work and bring money home to my mother."[31] Some mixture of family loyalties, subtle coercion, and simple necessity compelled working-class daughters to wed their labor to the welfare of their parental families.

Most working girls did not expect to remain in the labor force for very long. Their own weddings most often spelled retirement from the paid labor force. As of 1890 the average tenure of women's work outside the home was only eleven years. In New York City, for example, fewer than one in twenty Italian wives were gainfully employed outside the household; among Jewish immigrants the figure was a paltry one in fifty.[32] Still, marriage did not promise a permanent retirement to all women. A Hungarian girl named Anna, for example, entered the cigar factory almost the minute she arrived in America in 1912, and left the factory a year later when she married. Her spouse's wage proved insufficient, however, and he was recurrently unemployed, so Anna was forced to return to the factory. In the next ten years her working life was interrupted only by the births of her six children, several of whom she took to the factory to nurse.[33] When Anna recounted her employment history in 1925, working wives had become more common. Although only one in ten immigrant families contacted by the Pennsylvania study (of which Anna was a part) contained women workers, the majority of them were wives and mothers. Wives began to supply the supplementary income once earned by daughters who were now being sent to school and were barred from the factory by child labor laws. The wives resorted to the factory for familiar reasons: "Greenhorns need their wives to help them," "If woman does not help, bad for men," "Husband sick; nobody give me eat, I work." To their families, these wives and daughters were essential breadgivers, but to the employer, they were merely women workers and entitled only to a wage that fell well below the level of subsistence.[34]

Participation in the industrial labor force, furthermore, did not excuse females from woman's work in the home. Daughters like Rose Cohen left the factory early on Saturday in order to clean the tenement apartment. Working wives in the industrial districts of Pennsylvania, whose factory hours were often longer than those of their husbands, were given some assistance in housekeeping by their spouses and children. Investigations of working-class homes in Philadelphia often found husbands and wives engaged jointly in housework. In one home the wife washed the clothes and her husband wrung them, while a brother-in-law did the dishes.[35] Rose Haggerty, the fourteen-year-old breadwinner for a family of siblings, was assisted by a five-year-old sister who did the dishes, the cleaning, the shopping, and ran errands.[36] Still, the chief responsibility for home labor fell to the wife. One factory wife described a typical day as follows: "Everything I do—wash, iron, cook, clean, sew, work in the garden, make bread, if time. Get up at 4:30, feed the

chickens, make the breakfast, get ready the lunches and it is time
to start work. 6 o'clock home, make eats for the children, washing
at nighttime, and make clothes for children."[37]

The responsibilities of a working mother were particularly burdensome. Few workingwomen could afford to provide reliable care
for their children while they were at the factory. They left their
children under the casual supervision of fathers, siblings, neighbors,
or alone. One worker described her routine procedure as follows:
"I give them their breakfast, put the meal on the table for them,
lock the front door, and the gate in the backyard and go away."
Other working mothers had to take jobs at hours when their child
would be cared for or out of mischief, typically menial work, scrubbing offices and shops at night. Such unpleasant devices were necessary if working-class women were to balance their manifold roles—
housewife, mother, industrial worker. No wonder investigators from
the U.S. Women's Bureau described working mothers as "wearing
out," "languid and very tired," "nervous and tired all the time."[38]

Most wives and mothers would not invite twofold oppression
by entering the work force if it could possibly be avoided. Yet the
economic contribution of the vast majority of married women who
remained at home was not by any means negligible. A Chicago
social worker at the turn of the century encountered in Mrs. Nowicki, a Polish mother, an adamant determination to bring income
into the home: "She wishes to help by taking in work which she
can do and still care for the seven weeks' old baby." Previously,
Mrs. Nowicki had milked cows, opened a home dairy, and started
a grocery store in a vain attempt to support her family and remain
at home. Only as a last resort did she ask "for night work, providing
it comes at such hours that she could be home to see the boys are
not on the streets."[39] Whatever home work immigrant women acquired tended to be less profitable than selling their labor power
in the industrial marketplace. Still, the home mother grasped at
any chance to earn a mere pittance of cash income. Immigrants soon
learned that in America "nothing is to be had without paying."
They knew, in other words, that they had traded a rural European
setting, which still provided opportunities for home and subsistence
production, for an advanced industrial urban economy where dollars
as well as the sweat of the brow were essential to maintaining a
household.

Italian wives were particularly dextrous at producing income while remaining in the home. Piecework, chiefly finishing the products of the garment industry, was a mainstay of their immigrant households. Even as late as 1925, Italian mothers could be regularly found in their tenements finishing cloaks, cutting carpet rags, and stringing tags. Ambitious labor contractors, called padrones, set whole neighborhoods of women to work sewing for a single garment manufacturer. The pennies awarded for each little job seldom totaled more than $3 a week. Thus women had to maintain a frantic pace and often put the whole family to work. Even a little tot could paste an artificial flower. Other children were sent to school with bits of piecework to occupy them during recess. Some women turned to their piecework only intermittently—"whenever the baby sleeps." Others worked steadily, without interruption. A Philadelphia woman named Jennie, for example, reported that she stopped working only to have a baby, and even this curtailed her labor for a mere two weeks.[40] Jennie reported one additional vacation from home work: for one summer she pursued the alternative employment of picking tomatoes on a New Jersey farm.

Seasonal agricultural labor was a second major source of income for Italian wives. It was especially popular in cities with few female industries and thus little opportunity for either piecework or sweat-shop employment. Buffalo, New York, was such a town, and hence its Italian district was depopulated during the summer months when women and children went to work in the fields and canning factories outside the city. Seasonal employment such as this could be a very lucrative mode of breadgiving; with the aid of her children, a mother might bring in $350 to $450 a summer, a sum that would compare favorably with her husband's income, often in another seasonal occupation, construction work.[41]

Italian women, and indeed almost every immigrant group, also resorted to a third method of bringing cash into the home, taking in boarders. In the working-class districts of New York City, for example, almost every other household contained a boarder. This method of producing income was particularly common in those immigrant groups with unbalanced sex ratios, where hoards of young, single men were without wives to provide them with do-mestic services. Polish immigrants of this sort commonly took up residence in large households where their meals were cooked and rooms cleaned by the wife of one of their number. The husbands in these makeshift boardinghouses were fortunate indeed. One young man wrote his parents in Poland of his brother's good fortune: "In the beginning he did not do very well, but now every thing is going very well with him. His wife keeps eight persons boarding in his home and he earns $2.50 a day."[42] Other immigrant women managed to at least cut down their own home expenses by living in cooperative households, sharing kitchen facilities with neighbors, or doubling up with their kinsmen. When Rose Cohen's family was hit by the depression of 1893–94, they boarded with two male relatives, sharing both the rent and the housekeeping labor of the womenfolk.[43]

Jewish families, where wives had a particularly low rate of employment outside the home, were especially eager to take in boarders. The prevalence of boarding in Jewish households prompted Jacob Riis to observe that the lodger was the equivalent of the pig among the Irish, the reliable and well-regarded source of supplementary income. Jewish families were known to rent out every available space, even crowding a few beds into the kitchen after the evening meal.[44] By the late nineteenth century, keeping boarders was no longer the monopoly of middle-class homeowners, but had become a common economic strategy among tenement families.

Immigrant and working-class wives routinely played at least this final economic role: stretching the income of others to make ends meet. The wives seem to have been customarily placed in charge of the household budget. Margaret Von Staden's working-class family in San Francisco is a case in point. Three male wage earners—her father, who was a longshoreman, and two brothers, who were employed by the ironworks—brought home the family income. Of her father, Margaret reported, "He drank once in a while. Most of the time he brought all of his money home to my Mother." Mrs. Von Staden then doled out the family finances in the tightfisted manner that kept a roof over the heads of seven people. "My mother always put so much a week in a cup in the closet to save for rent. Many a time we had to do without butter when she didn't have money enough. But she would never touch that blue cup."[45]

A Jewish wife recounted her singular method of apportioning family income. "I worked and worked mightily and have gone without food days so that he could have it and then I would maneuver different ways to pay our way so that he always should have a little change in his pocket."[46] This role was also a cherished source of woman's self-esteem in the Irish family of Mary Kenney. Even after her marriage to Jack O'Sullivan, she deferred to her mother in budgetary matters. "I had always given my salary to Mother. I wanted her to feel she was still running the house. After I married, Jack brought his salary to her too."[47] As fiscal agent of the family, the woman of the immigrant working class played a highly significant role: she eased the transition into a complex money economy and kept families with meager dollar-power from financial disaster.

HOUSEWIVES AND MOTHERS
OF THE WORKING CLASS

The role of housewives in the working-class family was physically arduous as well as crucial. It was a formidable task to keep families of working-class neighborhoods alive, healthy, and fit for work. The ramshackle houses of the slums, the crowded quarters of the tenement, the dense neighborhoods and cluttered streets, were hardly propitious to family hygiene. Nor were the starchy, meatless diets that the workers' frugal budget allowed particularly nutritious. The most meticulous mother would be hard pressed to keep her children clean in the New York City tenement district of the 1890s, where only 306 of 225,000 residents had access to bathtubs, and only 51 of nearly 4,000 tenements had private toilets.[48] As late as 1925 only one in three immigrant homes in Bethlehem, Pennsylvania, had indoor toilets, and three-quarters of the families had no bathtubs. In the most squalid areas, whole blocks shared a solitary water hydrant. No wonder, then, that in these districts as many as one in three children died in infancy.[49] An investigation of working-class homes in New York City, completed in 1909, revealed that shelter, diet, clothing, and health care were repeatedly substandard. Neither "the habits of the fathers" nor "the managing ability of the mothers" was responsible for this dire situation, according to the investigators. Rather, these families were caught in a vise between low wages and high prices.

Against all these odds, the housewives of the slums managed to keep most of their children and husbands alive. The Jewish residents of the Lower East Side, as a matter of fact, had one of the lowest mortality rates in the city of New York.[50] These mothers of the slums lugged pails of water up stairways several times a day, slaved in primitive kitchens to get a frugal meal on a crowded table, and devoted a day each week to washing and ironing. Since such amenities as sewerage and running water had to be purchased by private property owners, few slum landlords provided their tenants with this costly service. Accordingly, working-class women had to invest more physical energy in domestic work than did the most meticulous middle-class housewives.[51] When a social investigator registered amazement at the ability of one Irish woman to work full-time in a meat-packing plant, raise two children, and keep her house "immaculately clean," she was given a lesson in highly efficient working-class household management. This housewife labored until 10 P.M. each week night, and until 5 A.M. on Saturday, carefully allocating different household tasks to each work stint.[52] In the rural immigrant community of Hannibal, Missouri, Mary Kenney's mother had a full day's work in keeping her family fed, clothed, and cleaned: "Mother made soap, boys waists and pants, my dresses and father's shirts. Every night when he had gone to bed, she would scrub the kitchen floor."[53]

East and West, day in and day out, the wives of the immigrant working class toiled to replenish the labor power of the husbands and children who composed the industrial work force.

Simultaneously, working-class women were reproducing the industrial labor force. Once the immigrant population had settled into a balanced sex ratio and high marriage rate, foreign-born women achieved a fertility rate substantially higher than that of the native-born middle class. As of 1910, for every 1,000 married women of native parentage there were 3,396 births; the comparable figure for foreign-born women was 4,275 births. In regions of concentrated immigrant population, the fertility differential was even larger. In the immigrant districts of Boston, for example, the birthrate among the foreign-born was 64 percent higher than among natives. The Italian women of Buffalo had an astounding fertility rate: women aged forty-five and over had mothered eleven children on the average.[54]

The immigrant woman usually brought her offspring into the world with only the assistance of a midwife. Two women who assisted in these home births, Emma Goldman and Margaret Sanger, observed the fear and fatalism that surrounded childbearing in the working-class home. Mothers entreated them to perform abortions and supply contraceptive information. Goldman described childbearing in the slums as follows: "Most of them lived in continual dread of conception; the great mass of the married women submitted helplessly, and when they found themselves pregnant, their alarm and worry would result in the determination to get rid of their expected offspring. It was incredible what fantastic methods despair could invent: jumping off tables, rolling on the floor, massaging the stomach, drinking nauseating concoctions, and using blunt instruments." According to Goldman, both Irish Catholics and Jewish women referred to pregnancy as "a curse of God."[55]

Immigrant and working-class parents seldom articulated their method of rearing these heirs of poverty. They bequeathed their values to children through the daily exemplification of the principles of survival—hard work and frugality. The child was educated as much by practice as by instruction, mostly through the seldom gentle nurture of joining the labor force at an early age and living in the slum streets. At times it seemed that the immigrant youngster was more worker than child. In the factory town of Lawrence, Massachusetts, for example, half of all children were in the labor force. Italian parents were especially assiduous in utilizing the full labor power of their children. Some Buffalo mothers, for example, responded with a near-riot when the manager of a canning factory proposed to send their children to school rather than allow them to earn a few dollars alongside their mothers.[56]

At the same time, working-class culture assigned women the larger parental role and invested females with a hallowed maternal feeling. Both the taverns and the show halls of immigrant districts hummed with sentimental songs to mother. When a settlement worker questioned one immigrant mother about her solicitude for the souls of her children, the logic and the ethic of child rearing in the slums were revealed amid the rancor of her answer:

Who's got time to think about souls grinding away here 14 hours a day to turn out contract goods? Tain't souls that count. It's bodies, that can be driven an' half-starved an' driven still, till they drop in their tracks. I'm driving now to pay a doctor's bill for my three that went with the fever. Before that I was driving to put food into their mouths. I never owed a cent to no man. I've been honest and paid as I went and done a good turn when I could.

The major objective of this lower-class mother was simply to keep her children fed and alive. Her central values were honesty, hard work, and being a good neighbor. Yet she was not optimistic about maintaining her own dignity nor that of her children. She went so far as to question the basic virtue of bourgeois maternity, Victorian purity: "If I'd chosen the other thing while I'd a pretty face of my own I'd had ease and comfort and a quick death. Such a life as this isn't worth living."[57]

This extreme fatalism points up the quandary of parentage for the immigrant poor. Fathers and mothers hoped their children would find the good life in the promised land of America and be able to "live like folks." The gulf between the glamour of the gilded age and the gloomy environment of the immigrant, however, could engender despair and defeat. It could also tempt their children to shirk their arduous responsibilities to contribute to family income. Mothers of the working class could not insulate their children in cozy cottages and antiseptic classrooms nor immunize them from the contagious allure of American materialism. Throughout the nineteenth century immigrant children flocked to neighborhood theaters, where visions of romance and wealth tantalized them from the stage. The nickelodeons and the silver screen made these fantasies even more immediate and appealing. Immigrant boys, impatient to taste the fruits advertised in America's popular culture, took to thievery and flooded the juvenile courts of industrial cities. Similarly, working-class daughters were often sorely tempted to squander their paychecks on clothes and entertainment. The affluent and acquisitive surroundings of industrial capitalism did not provide a supportive environment for selfless devotion to the immigrant family, its needs and values.

Hence, not every immigrant daughter toed the mark of family loyalty. Some immigrant girls saw prostitution as a shortcut to glamour. Jane Addams told of a Chicago girl who went directly from the theater to the brothel. After hoarding her wages to finance a whole week at the theater, she could not bear to return again to the reality of the sweatshop.[58] Margaret Von Staden told a similar story in her own words. She went off to her first job at age twelve full of excitement. "I thought all the time of the money I could make and the fine clothes I could have." The nerve-racking work of the garment factory and $3 a week in wage brutally shattered her fantasy. As she went from one menial, low-paying job to another, however, she still dreamed of "classey" men, "real swells," and the fine clothes and good times they would buy her. Margaret

In a recent poll,
Abigail Adams
(1744–1818) and
Eleanor Roosevelt
(1884–1962) were
voted America's
most outstanding
First Ladies.

The Senate Chamber
as It May Be

American Woman and
her Political Peers

According to two
political cartoonists
of the 1800s, if women
were not kept in their
place, things could really
get out of hand.

Suffragist and first woman member of Congress,
Jeannette Rankin (1880–1973) opposed entry into
both World War I and World War II.

Teacher, social reformer, humanitarian,
Dorothea Dix (1802–1887) inspired legislators
to establish state hospitals for the mentally
ill. Opposite: Journalist Ida Wells-Barnett
(1862–1931) fought for the causes of racial
equality and women's rights.

Women acquired physical and social grace
at Smith College in 1904.

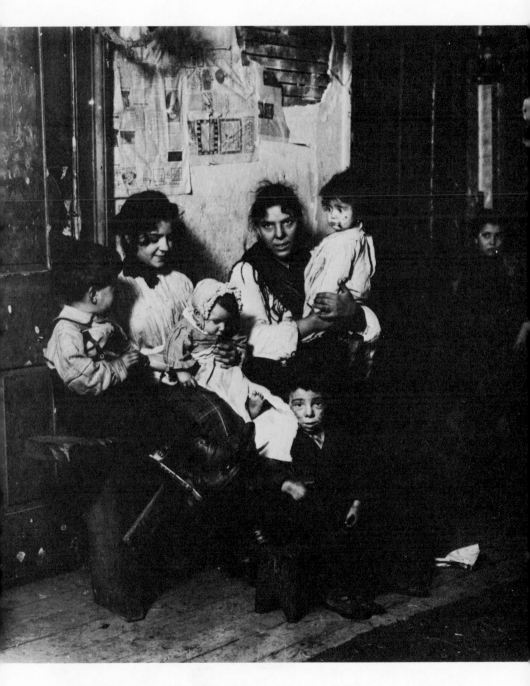

In the slum tenements of Chicago in 1910,
the immigrant housewife's role was arduous.

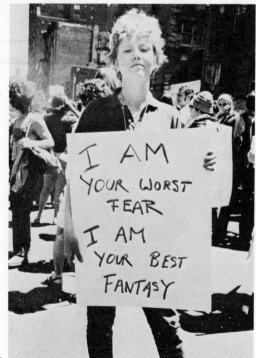

Above: by 1973, living,
as well as education, had
become coed at Harvard.
Opposite: A member of the
"Now Generation" attempts
some consciousness-raising.

soon found herself in a circle of devil-may-care youths and showered
with presents by a devoted beau. When this flood of riches ebbed,
she could not return to living on $4 or $5 a week. She became a
prostitute instead.[59]

In the brothel, Margaret Von Staden lived out the sharpest
contradictions of class and sex, serving the lust of the husbands of
model Victorian women. Von Staden observed that nearly all the
men who visited the brothel were married: "They would not dare
to even mention such practices to their wives, so they came to us."
At the same time, Von Staden retained the belief that almost every
prostitute was at heart a true woman, steeped in maternal instincts.
Her full bitterness erupted only once, but with ferocity: "But oh,
to be just once the animals [men] think us, so as to turn on our
tormentors, sinking sharp, vengeful teeth in their flesh and glory
in their agony as the blood is drawn."[60]

During an immigrant's first years in America, visions of a land
of milk and honey often gave way to such angry cynicism. One
Polish immigrant, for example, called his adopted land "the great
golden whore." The dreams of another, Wladek Wiszniewski, gave
way to the reality of trying to survive on the $3 a week earned by
his wife. Then Mrs. Wiszniewski became pregnant and left her job.
"I cannot even now take a walk with my wife, for she has not even
shoes to put on her feet but wears my old shoes. And she must
bear all this through me for I brought her to this. . . . She suffers
for me like a slave and nobody pities her."[61] This Polish couple
could not even afford to visit with their relatives, but clung only
to one another in despair.

WORKING-CLASS
WOMEN'S ORGANIZATIONS

Most of their fellow immigrants, however, were insulated from such
anomie by extensive kinship networks and a tight-knit ethnic community. In Providence, Rhode Island, for example, half the Italians
and one-third of the Jews lived near their relatives. Working-class
neighborhoods were riddled with mutual-benefit associations and
ethnic clubs, while extensive informal socializing took place in the
slum streets. Male social life centered in the neighborhood tavern—

the workingman's club where everything from camaraderie to banking services could be acquired in an atmosphere of casual good humor. It has been estimated that working-class districts in the late nineteenth century supported one saloon for every 50 adult males. Taverns, unions, mutual-benefit societies, Jewish *chevrahs*, and clubs named for Italian patron saints might take immigrant men outside their homes nearly every night of the week. Most of these groups excluded females. In the tavern, womanhood was represented by a back-room prostitute and perhaps a buxom nude that adorned the wall above the bar.[62] Nineteenth-century workingman's culture, in other words, was highly sex-segregated and probably characterized by distrust and disdain for women.

Formal social organization among working-class women seems to have been more rudimentary. The few organized associations of women were often centered in the church or synagogue. Sodalities to the Blessed Virgin among Catholic immigrants and the *mitvah* where Jewish women cleansed themselves after menstruation, for example, suggested male objectification of woman, be she pure or contaminated. Women also lacked an institution, like the saloon, where they could congregate in relatively large groups on a routine basis. The social life of working-class and immigrant women took a less formal, more private shape. It was in the home and on the front stoop that their social networks centered. Men vacated that space for women's use during most of the day and much of the night. These women's networks often snaked their way through the whole immigrant community. They showed themselves in a familiar event, the urban riot.

The most celebrated instance of this mode of women's politics was the kosher meat riot that spread from Brooklyn to Manhattan, Newark, and Boston in 1902. It was a typical case of women's resistance: bands of housewives ransacked butcher shops and destroyed merchandise in order to force lower prices. The strength and breadth of this women's network was such that thousands of women joined in this demonstration of collective protest. Five years later the Jewish women of Providence, Rhode Island, also succeeded in lowering the price of kosher meat by using pickets, persuasion, and a door-to-door survey of the women in the community. In 1914 Italians of the same city staged their own ethnic variation on the food riot — violent street action to control the price of pasta. This kind of crowd politics suggests a community organization that granted women some informal access to public influence.[63]

Isolated public actions such as these are among the few tracks that immigrant wives and mothers have left in the historical record, and they have not been pursued very far by historians. They are enough to suggest, however, something of the distinctive way the immigrant working class carved out social spaces for the two sexes. While all ages and both sexes were obliged to cooperate in one household economy, males and females seemed to seek social and emotional support in segregated spheres. Through it all, finally, ran the superior authority of men, be it in defending the name of the Italian family or wielding the scepter of the Hebrew patriarch.

These basic elements of the immigrant gender system—the family economy, sex segregation, and male dominance—impeded the development of labor organizations among women workers. There were sporadic outbursts of militance in the years after the Civil War, among such female trades as laundry workers, collarmakers, typographers, and cigarmakers, but these acts of resistance seldom resulted in the formation of enduring labor organizations. In the 1880s, women workers did find a relatively commodious institutional base in the Knights of Labor, where 10 percent of the membership was female. The Knights became moribund soon thereafter, however, while the industrial work force was inundated with difficult-to-organize foreign-born laborers. Women's place in the unions dwindled apace and had fallen to less than 3 percent of the total membership by 1900.[64]

The collective consciousness of women workers was deflected by a sense of temporary employment, fragmented by ethnic differences, atomized by an irregular wage scale, and dispersed through a multitude of small shops. Furthermore, union men did very little to encourage women to overcome these obstacles. The custom of holding union meetings during the evening, in smoke-filled taverns, was not particularly welcome to working girls. Furthermore, after 1890 and the demise of the more sympathetic Knights of Labor, the male leaders of American unions were by no means eager to organize women. The American Federation of Labor, under Samuel Gompers, focused its energies on skilled laborers and expediently ignored the weakest links in the industrial labor force, women and blacks. A.F.L. affiliates, such as the Bakers, Carpenters, and Mold-ers unions, explicitly barred women from membership as late as 1918. In 1921 the national A.F.L. was still resolving, in a halfhearted fashion, to abolish sexual discrimination. Yet even the International Ladies' Garment Workers' Union ignored the female segments of an industry where women workers outnumbered men two to one. [65]

The left-wing social movements of the era were not much more alert to the needs of working-class women. Nineteenth-century socialists conceived of the proletariat in masculine garb, while the female role in the movement was primarily to supply refreshments at socialist picnics or to preside over genteel parlor meetings. The left-wing labor movement had its radical heroines like Mother Jones, but she devoted her organizing skills to her "boys," notably miners. It was not until the 1910s that explicitly feminist issues were raised within radical labor organizations such as the International Workers of the World, by the likes of Elizabeth Gurley Flynn. By that time female membership in the Socialist Party had risen to its peak of about 15 percent. Occasionally the Party held a "Women's Night," characterized by condescending political education for the weaker sex. When Margaret Sanger raised the issue of sexual hygiene and contraception among Socialists, she received a cool reception from her comrades, especially those who held tenaciously to nineteenth-century standards of female purity. One male Socialist accused Sanger of presenting women as mere "animal beings" and feared subversion of "mother love" and the exquisite loyalty of the eternal female. Only when the suffrage movement threatened to entice females away from the party, and pit the wives of Socialists against their husbands, did the party grant women a larger organizational role. Yet this concession was halfhearted and short-lived. By 1920 female membership had declined to around 10 percent. [66]

Unorganized and divided, immigrant women were prey to the most brutal conditions of industrial capitalism. The garment industry was especially bald and arrogant in its exploitation of women. The hours in New York City's shirtwaist factories were 8 to 6 Monday through Friday, and 8 to 5 on Saturdays. Twenty-five percent of the women workers were making $3 to $4 a week, and the average weekly wage ranged between $7 and $12. Seasonal unemployment was endemic. Petty regulations rubbed salt in these wounds: fines for breaking equipment, being late, even talking; worker purchase, at a profit to the company, of needles, electricity, chairs, and lockers. At the turn of the century there were sporadic protests against this state of affairs and several major strikes in 1909. The leaders of the ILGWU toyed with the idea of calling an industry-wide strike. When 20,000 workers gathered at Cooper Union to discuss the course of action, a young worker named Clara Lemlich rose and announced in Yiddish, "I am tired of listening to speakers who talk in general terms. What we are here for is to decide whether we shall or shall not strike. I offer a resolution that a general strike be declared now." The audience reportedly rose en masse, shouted their approval, and took the Jewish pledge: "If I turn traitor to the cause I now pledge, may the hand wither with the arm I now raise." The "Up-rising of the 20,000" had begun, and 80 percent of the strikers were women, 75 percent of them under twenty-five years of age. In the next year a similar eruption of militance occurred in the Chicago garment industry where the majority of workers were male. Yet once again the strike was triggered by the angry protests of women.[67]

It is customary to emphasize the spontaneity of these epic events in labor history and to extol the naïve courage of the anonymous women who, like Clara Lemlich, assumed "emotional" leadership, worked unselfishly in the emergency, and then were heard no more. The strike is also remembered in condescending references to genteel participation on the part of the wives and daughters of the rich, such as Anne Morgan, Olive Belmont, and students of Wellesley College. The women's garment workers' strike of 1909–10, however, constituted far more than the visceral reaction of young workers and the noblesse oblige of upper-class ladies. Clara Lemlich, for example, was educated at anarchist meetings as well as the New York Public Library, and had organized a local of the ILGWU three years before the strike. Solid organizational support came from the Women's Trade Union League and its seasoned working-class organizers, Mary Kenney O'Sullivan and Leonora O'Reilly. The WTUL leadership had long included upper- and middle-class women like Margaret and Mary Dreier and Mary McDowell. A relentless champion of workingwomen, Mary Dreier was among the first to support the striking garment workers, join the picket lines, and be arrested. By 1910, women from all classes had acquired organizational abilities and experience in the rugged ways of the industrial world. Something of major consequence in the history of American women had taken the mothers of civilization into such unlikely places as union halls, picket lines, and jails.

SOCIAL HOUSEKEEPING AND THE PUBLIC WOMAN

Certainly many women passed the last half of the nineteenth century secluded in middle- and upper-class homes, oblivious to the advances and the hazards of industrialization. Some of them were collecting the symptoms of the fashionable female diseases. Alice James presented one of the most poignant examples of the destructiveness of domestic seclusion. While her equally "neurotic" brothers, William and Henry, won laurels in psychology and literature, Alice utilized her acute perceptions in bantering with her maid and recounting the foibles of mankind in her diary. Oscillating from lucidity to madness, gentility to violent fantasies, she consigned herself to "the glorious role" of standing for "sick headache to mankind."[68] So many women were in similar predicaments that this catatonic condition of the sex acquired a name all its own — neurasthenia — and scores of physicians designed cures and built sanitariums for its treatment. Charlotte Perkins Gilman was taken with this dread disease in a "charming home," with a "loving and devoted husband, an exquisite baby, healthy and intelligent and good; a highly competent mother to run things; a wholly satisfying servant — and I lay all day on the lounge and cried." The consulting physician recommended the standard cure: "Have as domestic a life as possible, have your child with you at all times . . . have but two hours of intellectual life a day." Compliance with this advice merely drove Gilman further into madness.[69]

Charlotte Perkins Gilman did not recover until she left her small family, and then part of her recuperation occurred at Jane Addams' Hull House, a center of rehabilitation for many disgruntled daughters of the antebellum cult of domesticity. Jane Addams herself began very early to stretch the boundaries of woman's spheres. She reported in her autobiography that as a child her precocious maternal heart went out to the poor who resided in her hometown of Cedarville, Illinois. She resolved: "When I grow up I should, of course, have a large house, but it would not be built among the other large houses, but in the midst of horrid little houses like these."[70] Simultaneously, many women were discovering an enlarged arena for their maternal influence in the Sanitary Commission, the female, benevolent flank of the Union Army. There was the nurse who "rarely rendered any service to those poor fellows that they did not assure me that I was like their mother, or wife, or sister." There were the women who sent hand-knit stockings to unknown soldiers with notes like this: "You are not my husband or son; but you are the husband or son of some woman who undoubtedly loves you as I love mine."[71] Such maternal rhetoric would suffuse female social action for half a century.

Motherhood was used to justify a multitude of extrafamilial activities. Jane Addams clothed settlement work in maternal metaphor, an expression of "the great mother breast of our common humanity."[72] Women's clubs were founded under the motto "Now show a more glorious womanhood . . . a new unit, the completed type of the mother-woman working with all as well as for all."[73] The suffrage movement resorted to maternal rhetoric, asserting that "the mother of the race, the guardian of its helpless infancy," must keep watch over the ballot box.[74] The union organizer Leonora O'Reilly surmised that "the labor movement must be purified by a woman's movement."[75] The most honored woman in the labor movement was "Mother" Jones, whose route of agitation was littered with sentimental images of the plight of angelic children.[76] The heroine of the women's temperance movement in the 1870s was a "Mother" Stewart, while the leader of the Women's Christian Temperance Union, Frances Willard, advertised her militant and consciously feminist crusade as a campaign for "home protection." When Willard endorsed socialism in the 1890s she continued to clothe her politics in maternal rhetoric. Socialism, she said, was "the womb out of which the coming civilization we believe will be born."[77] Even anarchism could be rhetorically related to maternity: Emma Goldman chose *Mother Earth* as the title of her magazine, proclaiming her intention to "find an outlet for my motherliness in the love of all children."[78]

This enlargement of the promise of motherly power was recognized and tacitly approved by the pioneer social scientists of the late nineteenth century. Social Darwinism had identified sexual differences as the driving force of progressive evolution. By selecting her mate, it was said, the female of the species determined the course of future generations. Furthermore, the female, equipped with mammary glands and a larger amount of adipose tissue, was by nature the more social sex, formed to nurture and serve the race, rather than to scrap and fight for personal gain. The Social Darwinist posited these sexual differences in temperament: "The male as extreme egotism or selfishness, . . . a female as altruism or care for other individuals outside of self."[79] Such anthropologists as Henry Lewis Morgan and Johann Jakob Bachofen were simultaneously describing the point in primitive history, when the male sex had by animal force usurped social hegemony from women. Pioneer American sociologists Lester Ward and William I. Thomas held this to be a retrogressive stage in sexual history, which lamentably still endured. Writing in 1883, however, Ward espied with approval a new turn in the evolutionary cycle. "Even in our own times we are beginning to observe the most unmistakable signs of the eventual resumption by woman of her lost sceptre and of her restoration to that empire over the emotional nature of men which the female of nearly all other animals exercises."[80] This was an update on the maternal stereotype which assumed an aggressive and expansionist female posture as it summoned women into the public world.

As women emerged from their homes to enter clubrooms, settlement houses, and reform groups, they absorbed some of the spirit of the scientific era which soon replaced the religious roots and justifications of antebellum female altruism. The women of the Sanitary Commission deployed as much tough-mindedness as maternal sentiment. The nurse in a Civil War hospital had to hold herself "in iron control" until she had become "habituated to the manifold shocking sights that are the outcome of the wicked business men call war." The female leaders of the Sanitary Commission, in charge of a nationwide system of collecting and distributing medical supplies, quickly developed "administrative talent" and came to value the female who was "erect and decisive, quick of comprehension and prompt in action." The exemplary personality of the Sanitary Commission, "Mother" Bickerdyke, symbolized the dual personality of the new woman reformer. To the soldiers she tended, Mary Bickerdyke was "more to his army than the Madonna to a Catholic," but to hospital administrators, doctors, and generals, she was "energetic, resolute and systematic." Women's exposure to modern warfare made it clear that tearful appeals for moral reform would not serve to civilize industrial society. Lessons in executive ability, practical stamina, and rational organization would have to be assimilated by the feminine temperament.[81]

In her graduation essay at Rockford Seminary, Jane Addams contended that more than feminine intuition was called for in the civilizing mission of her generation. The woman's mind must "grow strong and intelligible by the thorough study of at least one branch of physical science, for only with eyes thus accustomed to the search for truth could she detect all self-deceit and fancy in herself and learn to express herself without dogmatism."[82] As Addams spoke, women had already taken up a vocal position in the American Social Science Association. As a teen-ager, Charlotte Perkins Gilman also resolved to pursue the study of physics, anthropology, sociology, and history and thereby equip herself to guide the course of human evolution. The same principles of intellectual discipline were instilled in such institutions as Vassar, Smith, and Wellesley, originally dedicated to the cultivation of the softer feminine virtues. The fortunate women who acquired this broad education had only begun the struggle to escape feminine confinement. The most difficult trial came after college when the young woman searched in vain for an opportunity to put her hard-won education to work. At this point Gilman was sidetracked by an unhappy marriage and Addams floundered for eight full years, "absolutely at sea so far as my moral purpose was concerned, clinging only to the desire to live in a really living world and refusing to be content with a shadowy intellectual or aesthetic reflexion of it."[83]

The gilded age found more and more upper-middle-class daughters educated beyond the roles available to their sex. As of 1890 there were only 3,000 female college graduates, fewer than one in four of the total baccalaureates. By 1900 females accounted for 40 percent of the graduates of American institutions of higher learning. These women received their sheepskins either from coeducational public universities or the prestigious female colleges that had been founded after the Civil War. The rising aspirations of this class of educated women were described by a Smith student in the 1880s:

We were talking last night about what the girls were going to do who were to be at home next year. Of course they would not settle down to a mere hum-drum existence after our busy systematic work here. They would get restless and discontented as so many do. We have been discussing temperance, hospitals, and all sorts of training schools and industrial and charitable works in which we could interest ourselves. And there are so many things of that sort that I never heard of which need women who are dedicated and know how .to plan and carry out such ideas.[84]

Within a few years, college-educated women could add one major career opportunity to this rather vague list of pastimes. In 1887 seven graduates of Smith College met at a class reunion and launched a direct assault upon the real world, founding the College Settlement Association. A week after these women and their recruits set up America's first settlement house, Jane Addams and Ellen Star chose an old Chicago mansion as the site of Hull House. All these young women were driven by what Addams called "the subjective necessity of social settlement" to provide "cultivated young people with an outlet for the sentiment of universal brotherhood." At the same time, however, Addams directed prospective settlement residents to develop a "scientific patience in the accumulation of facts and the steady molding of their sympathies as one of the instruments for that accumulation."[85] By 1910 more than 400 settlement houses had been established, and thousands of young people, three-fifths of them women, gathered there, assured of a chance to put their talents as well as their compassion to work.[86]

Within the settlement house, maternal sentiments were further sifted and leavened until they became an entirely new variety of social reform. Initially, Jane Addams and her comrades set out to civilize their immigrant neighbors through literary evenings, art classes, genteel entertainments, and kindergartens. Soon Miss Addams found herself sweeping the slum streets, dramatizing to her neighbors that good housekeeping in the industrial city required that a woman enter the public sphere and sacrifice her gentility. The next step in Addams' industrial education took her to city hall, where she won the appointment of another college-educated woman as district sanitation director. About the same time another settlement house resident, Mary McDowell, left the kindergarten for the Chicago stockyards where she organized workingwomen into unions. Florence Kelley went far afield of the settlement house to investigate child labor.

By 1915 this wide range of female reforms was commonplace and quasi-legitimate: "Women by natural instincts as well as long training have become the housekeepers of the world, so it is only natural that they should in time become effective municipal housekeepers as well."[87] By this time, however, social housekeeping entailed more than wielding a broom and dustrag. For Florence Kelley it meant heading a state board of labor, compiling statistics, and lobbying with legislators. For Mary McDowell it meant organizing unions and leading strikes. For Jane Addams it meant blazing the long, steep trail from the social housekeeper of Hull House through national political conventions and international peace organizations, to become one of the most famous and honored women in American history.

A similar transformation was occurring in other segments of woman's world. The little bands of women's reading groups across the country were organized, in 1890, into the massive General Federation of Women's Clubs. Within a few years the GFWC leaders were asking, "Is there not room in the clubs for outlook committees, whose business it should be to investigate township affairs, educational, sanitary, reformatory?"[88] By the turn of the century, women's clubs were not only investigating social conditions but conducting social reforms—forming corporations to build sanitary housing in the slums, reconstructing the judicial system for juvenile offenders, and endorsing factory inspection and child labor legislation. Already in the 1880s groups like New York's Working Woman's Protective Union brought middle- and upper-class women into reformist associations with their sisters from less genteel backgrounds. The Woman's Trade Union League, founded in 1903, devoted less and less time to bringing middle-class culture to working girls and became deeply embroiled in union activities and strikes.

Meanwhile, traditional women's groups had become careless of their ladylike ways. As early as the 1870s, the Women's Christian Temperance Union resorted to the vulgar antics of Carrie Nation, entering saloons and destroying the tavernkeepers' property. By the turn of the century the WCTU had become a broad social-service organization, embracing labor legislation and suffrage, and known to debate such questions as "Is housework incompatible with the higher life?" By the 1890s women were even sloughing off the outer crust of Victorian purity and joining the social purity movement, where they openly discussed sexual issues like prostitution even as they proselytized in behalf of what Frances Willard called "the white life for two."[89]

Whatever the specific direction upper- and middle-class women took as they emerged from domestic confinement, it led them to mass organizations headed by members of their own sex. By the second decade of the twentieth century, women had formed a veritable army composed of many well-organized divisions, strategically linked, and positioned on the outer flank of the home. By 1920 it was estimated that the General Federation of Women's Clubs had perhaps 1 million members; the Women's Christian Temperance Union 800,000; the YWCA 500,000; there were 400,000 women union members; and as many as 2 million women participated in the suffrage campaign. The seeds of most major contemporary women's organizations, from the PTA to the American Association of University Women, were planted before 1920. Organized women chaired business meetings, were nearly obsessed with writing constitutions and formulating resolutions, and traveled the country to give lectures and attend conventions. Most of the major women's groups had interlocking directorates, supported one another's pet causes, and pooled their resources for the cause of suffrage. Between 1890 and 1920, women built a national organizational network that was nearly as sophisticated in its own way as the corporate business world.[90]

The social housekeeper was more sophisticated and more wide-ranging than those angels of mercy who operated the local charities of the antebellum period. Benevolent women quickly grew restless within parochial associations. When Frances Willard joined the Women's Christian Temperance Union, for example, she had no intention of staying within its original constituency—the narrow circles of women who had waged a rebellion against small-town saloonkeepers in the 1870s. Immediately she directed the Union toward an expressly political and broadly national goal: "To influence those strongholds of power, the national Congress, State Legislatures and Municipal Councils."[91] Willard, like most social housekeepers of the Progressive Era, as well as women's rights advocates like Stanton and Anthony, sought affiliation with major political parties and labor unions. Similarly, Jane Addams moved quite naturally from a local to a national political arena. When her campaign of urban reform was repeatedly stymied by the venal interests of Chicago's ward politicians, Addams quickly sought broader avenues to power. In the end, she would place Theodore Roosevelt's name in nomination for President at the Progressive

Party convention, and preside over international congresses. Addams intended to exert a pacific influence of global proportions.

The avowed goals of most of these women's organizations remained essentially altruistic—to serve the needy, weak, and defenseless—rather than to conquer wealth and power for either themselves or the female sex. At the same time, professional women were among the first to form secular, sex-segregated organizations. Sorosis, founded in 1868, brought together journalists, writers, and physicians united by their frankly professional aspirations. Countless individual women were pursuing their personal, educational, and professional objectives. When M. Carey Thomas was Jane Addams' age, she did not weep for poor children but at the thought of being denied a college education. Thomas pursued her personal goal with as much diligence as Addams directed to her social dream. She struggled, begged, and blackmailed her way into Cornell, to a Ph.D. in Zurich, and finally to the presidency of Bryn Mawr in 1894. M. Carey Thomas strove to carry the next generation of educated women with her on her upward climb. She urged Bryn Mawr students to imitate their brothers and disparaged marriage and motherhood as detrimental to professional success.[92]

Schools like Bryn Mawr, and coeducational state universities, cleared the way to professional careers for women between 1890 and 1920. During that period the number of professional women increased 226 percent, almost triple the rate of male advancement. While the majority of professional women were teachers at the elementary-school level, some women made substantial inroads into traditionally male spheres. By 1920, 5 percent of the nation's doctors, 1.4 percent of the lawyers and judges, and 30 percent of the college presidents, professors, and instructors were women. The route of social housekeeping also led women to prestigious posts. By 1920 women headed three state wage boards, five industrial commissions, and eleven children's bureaus. Florence Harriman sat as chairwoman of the U.S. Industrial Commission, Ida Tarbell headed the Tariff Commission, Julia Lathrop the Children's Bureau, and Mary Anderson the Women's Bureau. These were some of the hardest-won jobs in American history: women had organized, propagandized, and lobbied to create the bureaus and commissions that they later headed.[93]

By the second decade of the twentieth century, social housekeepers were aligned in an impressive formation alongside male structures of public and political power. The women who went to Washington during the Progressive Era were not simply assimilated into the male political establishment. Rather, they were part of a parallel female infrastructure with its own hierarchy and own independent base of support. When someone like Julia Lathrop went to head the Children's Bureau, for example, she was not marooned among Washington politicians and bureaucrats, but could still draw strength from her first lieutenants in similar state agencies, and from the vast rank and file of women's clubs and settlement houses. In other words, women moved into the public limelight at the turn of the century but did not disband their female social network in the process.

In manifold ways the organization of social housekeepers is more adequately defined by the term "sisterhood" than by the military metaphors used above. The concept of sisterhood, first of all, registers the fact that these reformers inhabited a social circle that included very few fathers, brothers, or sons. The leadership of the progressive women's organizations was largely a group of spinsters, sprinkled with a few divorcees and widows, and a small minority of married women. These leaders, furthermore, were drawn from the largest generation of single and childless women in American history. The cohort of women born between 1865 and 1874 married later and less frequently than any group before or since. At the turn of the century nearly one in five married women were childless.[94] This marked trend away from domesticity was most prevalent among educated women. The female graduates of the era had a strikingly low marriage rate, while those who eventually wed did so relatively late in life. As of 1915 more than 42 percent of the graduates of eastern women's colleges were gainfully employed, and almost 70 percent of them had spent some time in the work force. Overall, 75 percent of female professionals were single as of 1920.[95] This is but one of the ironies of social housekeeping. This supposedly feminine and motherly service to society was made possible by a significant decline in the rate of actual family formation and childbearing.

The prominent women of the Progressive Era, although single, did not lead emotionally barren and lonely lives. Rather, they developed their own system of personal support and mutual responsibility: they created their own kind of families within woman's sphere. The self-sufficiency of the female world was so complete that it assumed a physical and architectural form. The residences of college students and settlement workers, even the offices of the Women's Trade Union League, were all called "houses," living spaces adapted to the domestic needs as well as the working lives of predominantly female families. The late-nineteenth century also produced a flurry of utopian schemes and practical experiments in cooperative or socialized housekeeping, all premised on the growing power and autonomy of woman's sphere.[96]

The female sphere also fostered the formation of families of a more intimate sort. A chart of the emotional networks of social housekeepers would reveal countless pairs of women who lived together like conjugal couples. June Addams shared a home, and probably a bed, with Mary Smith for some forty years. Vida Scudder, Frances Willard, and M. Carey Thomas, to name a few notable women of the era, lived with a series of devoted women friends. This homosocial coupling was also commonplace around the halls of academe. For example, the president of Wellesley, Mary Woolley, maintained an intimate relationship, lasting no less than 52 years, with the head of the college's English Department, Jeanette Marks. These loving friendships and cohabitations were so widespread and acceptable in the late nineteenth century that they introduced a new kinship term into American parlance—the "Boston Marriage."[97] All these couples showed intense affection for each other, which usually found some form of physical expression. Like intimate relations between males and females, these relations also generated their share of petty jealousies. Sometimes the less famous partner was asked to play the role of selfless housekeeper or personal secretary. Still, these women had carried sex segregation to its fullest, creating an almost perfect insularity of womanhood, in emotional and erotic as well as political and social terms.[98]

Frances Willard wrote of the homosocial bonding characteristic of her generation this way:

> The loves of women for each other every day grow more numerous, and I have wondered much why these things were: that little should be said of them surprises me for they are everywhere. In these days when any capable and careful woman can honorably earn her own support, there is no village that

has not its examples of "two hearts in consort" both of which are feminine.[99]

As Willard suggests, these female partnerships were based in part on the ability of professional women and social housekeepers to support themselves and one another (to assume, that is, the male role of breadwinner). Yet they were also rooted in a gender system that starkly differentiated male and female temperament. The presumption of female purity, for example, allowed women to live celibately or even in sexual intimacy with other women without inviting suspicion, scorn, or stigma. These homosocial ties were also protected by women's distance from males and their disdain for the masculine culture presumably drenched in liquor, tobacco, and sexual vice. It was the doctrine of the spheres, in other words, which permitted homosocial bonds to mature into a sex-segregated social system. They were, as Willard put it, "the token of a transitional age" before the barriers between male and female had been breached by a "finer more unified humanity."

In fact, the fates of both social housekeepers and eager careerists were in many ways closely intertwined with the remnants of domesticity. The traditional female home functions interacted in an intricate symbiotic fashion with the extrafamilial advance of women between 1860 and 1920. On the one hand, the honorable tradition of woman's sphere could be a source of strength to social reformers. For the mass of members of reform groups, rather than the leaders, middle-class motherhood could be an incentive to social activism, nourishing their humanistic impulses and leaving them reserves of talent and time for social benevolence. In fact, mothers of small families were more prone to join the ranks of social reformers and suffragists than were childless wives, single women, or more prolific mothers.[100] At the local level, the leaders of women's clubs and temperance organizations were usually married and mothers. In addition, the Victorian age granted both dignity and incentives for full-time social mothers, unmarried women like Jane Addams and her peers who could not be castigated as Lesbians or dismissed as sexually frustrated. Leaders and followers alike found in the antebellum doctrine of female moral influence a stimulus to serve civilization outside the home. This dialectic of woman's sphere propelled their movement into clubs, settlements, and conventions.

Still, that dialectic did not take many women fully outside the domain of housekeeping. Despite the systematic, forceful, and in-novative methods that brought women into the center of the Pro-gressive movement, they remained the social charwomen of the industrial system. They tidied up the man's world, removing the most unsightly evidence of corrupt politics, smoothing over the ugly clash between the rich and the poor, and cleaning up around the slums. Jane Addams saw her role as "socializing democracy," bringing the classes into harmonious relations with one another without disturbing basic differences in wealth and power. "The dependence of the classes on each other is reciprocal, it gives a form of expression that has peculiar value," she wrote.[101] The Women's Trade Union League was also perfectly explicit about its intention to pacify class conflict: "If the burden of remedying unfair industrial inequalities is left to the oppressed social groups, we have the crude and primitive method or revolution." Progressive women remained guardians of social order and enemies of class conflict. Furthermore, they became so engrossed in the immediate goal of ameliorating slum and factory conditions that they sometimes lost sight of the inequities built into the capitalist industrial system. Florence Kelley was an avowed Socialist and onetime friend of Friedrich Engels, but once she became absorbed in the efforts to ameliorate factory con-ditions, her Marxism was drowned in the day-to-day exigencies of social housekeeping.[102]

Most career women were also either social housekeepers or as-sistant professionals. Women congregated in professions of social service, public-health medicine, legal aid, public-school teaching, and social work, rather than attempting to storm the citadels of financial and industrial power. The vast majority of even the grad-uates of prestigious women's colleges never obtained a higher profes-sional status than that of schoolteacher. As of 1920 the term "businesswoman" did not refer to executives and tycoons but to professional secretaries, clerks, and telephone operators. These jobs did not lead to the power at the center of the male business world. Social work had also been certified a profession by 1920, declared closed to "vaguely benevolent persons" and open to the college educated who were especially trained for casework and social re-search, 62 percent of whom were women. Yet women were less likely than men to advance to high positions in this new profession. In Minneapolis, for example, more than 30 percent of the male social workers and only 7 percent of the women held executive positions. Pioneer career women were advised of the difficulties they would face in the male-dominated professions. "They will have to learn not to ask nor to expect any concessions whatever on the grounds that they are women, nor even sometimes that they are human, since any weakness is likely to be considered feminine." Beneath the excitement of careers for women lurked the dangers of being integrated into the man's world at endemically subordinate levels.[103]

The social housekeepers and career women of the nineteenth century raised the doctrine of separate spheres to the highest level possible without assailing the boundaries of gender themselves. Rather than invading male territory directly, this remarkable generation of women built a separate female domain in the public sector—a world which they designed to stand apart from but parallel with, at times superior to, the male sphere. This preferred geography of gender was expressed in repeated attempts to found women's congresses and parliaments. At one such meeting, the International Council of Women held in Washington in 1888 and attended by representatives of 53 organizations and ten nations, "Mother" Zarelda Wallace of the WCTU proposed that "A republic of Women" be established "within the national government as carried on by men." This second public sphere would, according to Wallace, "train for the next great step in the evolution of humanity when women shall sit side by side in government and the nation shall learn war no more." Frances Willard used this same language when she dreamed of "the rule of a joint world by the joint forces of the mothers and the fathers." Women remained, in other words, distinct from men, and still molded in the domestic fashion of pacific motherhood. When they entered the realm of public authority it would be as a separately organized governmental institution.[104]

AT THE BORDER
OF PUBLIC WOMANHOOD

Yet as the nineteenth century gave way to the twentieth, and in the height of the Progressive Era when Jane Addams' generation nurtured the public woman to maturity, a few murmurs of dissent could be heard along the borders of woman's sphere. Skepticism regarding the cult of the home-based mother acquired a powerful voice with the publication of Charlotte Perkins Gilman's *Women and Economics* in 1898, and *The Home* in 1903. Gilman directly challenged the assumption that women were natural child-rearers. "Who but mothers," she asked, "raised our huge and growing crop of idiots, imbeciles and cripples and defectives, and degenerates, as well as the vast number of slow-minded, prejudiced, and ordinary people who clog the wheels of progress?" Gilman shattered the icon of domesticity, declaring that it hindered progress "by keeping woman a social idiot, by keeping the modern child under the tutelage of the primeval mother, by keeping the social conscience of the man crippled and stultified in the clinging grip of the domestic conscience of the woman." In *Women and Economics* Gilman contended that the home was an archaic vestige of preindustrial society and proposed that its essential functions be mechanized, collectivized, or surrendered to other institutions. Still, Gilman couldn't entirely free herself from the seductive aspects of the maternal stereotype of woman. As late as 1911 she wrote: "The mother instinct throughout nature is one of unmixed devotion, of love and service and defense, with no self interest."[105]

From women slightly younger than Gilman came more pointed questions about the doctrine of the spheres. At the turn of the century, coeducational graduate schools, most notably the University of Chicago, fostered research that put notions of stark gender differentiation to scientific tests, and found them wanting.[106] The voice of a new generation of women was also heard within the Socialist Party, uttering such blasphemous opinions as this: "The virtues that were once deemed distinctly womanly were in reality the virtues of the slave."[107] Some more recent recruits to municipal housekeeping began to propose that daughters be reared away from the sacred womanly duties of the past century. Mary Beard nonchalantly asked: "Why should girls not be taught the principles of machinery? Such knowledge would be useful to them in energizing as in enervating occupations. It is only a matter of getting used to the idea. . . . Women swing golf clubs, hockey sticks and tennis rackets. Why shouldn't girls swing hammers?"[108]

It is obvious from Beard's analogy that young women had already been introduced to activities inappropriate to the passive, fragile feminine ideal. The *Ladies' Home Journal* had been presenting its readers with models of active and athletic women for two decades.

In the 1890s the *Journal* recommended a panoply of "Out-door Sports for Girls," bicycling, gymnastics, badminton, tennis, golf. The fashion pages sketched apparel for the active woman: divided skirts, sports frocks, looser corsets, and lightweight girdles. As early as 1894, this youthful cast of female characters was given a name, "the new woman."[109]

In the 1910s the *Journal* saw fit to print a Cornell student's report on "How Can a Girl Work Her Way Through College?" and a long series on two young women touring Europe alone. The *Ladies' Home Journal* endorsed an interval of independence before marriage. The editors were more ambivalent about a career in the work force. As early as 1890 they wrote of "The Aspiring Girl of To-day": "She is bright and ambitious. She looks out at the workers in the world and thinks that if she were among them she would make a great success." While the *Journal* writers did not want to "say one word to discourage young women intent on pursuing such a course," they asked the reader to consider the old-fashioned ways: "May not the life work for you be in the home?" Thereafter the *Journal*'s policy toward workingwomen fluctuated with the state of the national economy. The editors lost their qualms about working outside the home during World War I, for example. Then they boldly proclaimed: "Thousands of women are wanted practically at Men's Pay," and praised "Women Who Have Blazed New Trails" in law, investment, and construction.[110]

Before 1920 advertisers in the *Journal* were not particularly attentive to feminine manners. Car companies posed women behind the wheels of their own automobiles, and gun manufacturers pictured armed women capturing burglars. From the 1890s on, these images of plucky, self-sufficient women competed in the *Journal*'s pages with maternal symbols of an earlier era, and by 1920 it seemed clear that the newer image would triumph.

At the same time, the *Ladies' Home Journal* quietly recommended some alterations in the domestic sphere itself. In the December 1899 issue, *Journal* readers found an article entitled "Let the Children Live Their Own Lives," in which mothers were advised against watching their children too closely and smothering their individuality. In the next issue one article asserted that a child "must be taught independence early," and another recommended that fathers play a larger role in the rearing of children. At the turn of the century, in short, the predominant American magazine suggested that modern motherhood was no longer an obsessive and exclusive woman's role. As late as March 1910, the "Mother's Guide" in the *Ladies' Home Journal* reiterated that it was a sacred obligation of womanhood to breast-feed her infant. Yet on the very same page Nestlé's prepared food was advertised as "The only substitute for Mother's Milk." Other advertisements heralded a transformation in the role of the housewife. Van Camp's soup, for example, detailed "How a Million Housewives Have Created a Cooperative Kitchen." An increasing number of manufacturers of food products and home appliances presented themselves as the housewife's liberators, freeing them from exhausting, time-consuming, domestic labor. The advance of industrial production had in fact begun to ease women's domestic burdens. The number of canning factories, retailers of ready-made clothing, department stores, and restaurants grew twenty-fold between the Civil War and the 1920s, and the drudgery of housework declined apace. The cult of domesticity was quite frayed by the turn of the century, exposing a few narrow openings through which women could escape from the strictures of nineteenth-century stereotypes.[111]

Many of these new opportunities represented hard-fought gains, won by women themselves in the arduous campaigns of social reform and professional striving. These daring women were often propelled into battle by the dialectics of motherhood, in search of expanded outlets for nurturance, surrogate homes, and foster children. Other women of the middle class seized upon the antithesis of true womanhood, rejecting domesticity entirely for a career defined in spartan masculine terms. Simultaneously, the social alignment of home and the marketplace was slowly changing and leaving its imprint on popular culture in the form of more various images of women, invitations to spend at least some time in the work force, and promises of mechanized households. Still, few female leaders of the era, neither social housekeepers nor career women, mounted a direct attack on woman's sphere: they seldom questioned the delegation of domestic responsibilities almost exclusively to wives and mothers.

The same criticism can be brought against the suffrage movement, whose triumphant phase coincided with the maturation of industrial society and of social housekeeping. It has often been noted that the suffragists actually exploited and often endorsed the doctrine of woman's sphere. They were quite capable of arguing that the morally superior sex would bring a purifying influence into the voting booth and stand maternal watch for the nation's children. The proponents of suffrage occasionally donned the ugly garb of racism and xenophobia. Some educated white women claimed qualifications for citizenship superior to blacks and immigrants—"Ex-slaves, illiterate and semi-barbarous" and the "Riff-Raff of Europe."[112]

The use of these arguments from the Victorian notions of pure womanhood was not, however, simply a case of naïve sentimentality and blind conservatism. The suffragists of the late nineteenth and early twentieth century were very wise to the ways of American politics. These slogans were part of an arsenal of expedient devices suffragists used to achieve their goal. After decades of division and infighting, which dated from Reconstruction, the Stanton-Anthony faction joined with the more conservative wing of the women's movement to form the National American Woman's Suffrage Association. With Carrie Chapman Catt as president, NAWSA took to pragmatic politicking in the 1910s in order to enact a national suffrage amendment. The new suffragists courted political parties and made political hay even out of World War I. When war became imminent, Catt and her fellow leaders carefully withdrew from women's peace organizations and jettisoned their rhetoric about the innate pacifism of their sex. By supporting the war effort, NAWSA courted public opinion, President Wilson, and Congress, simultaneously installing themselves in Federal offices and incurring political debts that could be repaid with the endorsement of the Nineteenth Amendment. The suffragists were not blushing Victorians, but seasoned politicians who had learned how to beat males at their own game.

The special experience of organized women also helps to explain the focus of the women's movement on civil and political rights. The members of the Sanitary Commission acquired this preoccupation in the 1860s. One of the commission's leaders, Mary Livermore, was utterly shocked when a builder would not accept her check for the construction of a hospital. "Here was a revelation. We two women were able to enlist the whole Northwest in a great philanthropic money-making enterprise in the teeth of great opposition, and had the executive ability to carry it forward to a successful termination. We had money of our own in hand, twice as much as was necessary to pay the builder. But by the laws of the State in which we lived our individual names were not worth

the paper they were written on." Such practical affronts to the
enterprising women of the nineteenth century were not easily forgotten. Mary Livermore "registered a vow when the war was over
I would take up new work—the work of making law and justice
synonymous for women."[113]

By 1890, state legislatures had removed the most egregious
legal bars to women's property rights, but disenfranchisement remained as a glaring insult and obstacle to female equality. The
denial of the vote to women was particularly offensive to women
in the Progressive movement, whose reform efforts inevitably took
them before city councils, state legislatures, and the U.S. Congress.
It was demeaning as well as inconvenient to be rebuffed time and
time again by male public officials whom the energetic reformers
had no role in electing. Mary Beard put it this way: "Women who
have experienced these political reverses have often become ardent
suffragists because they realized that the direct way to work for
sanitary municipal housekeeping is through elected officials, and
having been unable to influence the votes of men they have acquired
the desire and determination to cast the ballots themselves."[114] The
vote was not simply a panacea for all injustice. To organized women
it constituted an immediate and practical instrument of reform,
another step toward efficient participation in the man's world.

The ratification of the Nineteenth Amendment not only testified
to women's adroitness in manipulating the American political system, but also finally raised the second sex to the full status of
United States citizens. In and of itself, then, the successful conclusion of the suffrage movement is a landmark in the history of
women and an unprecedented political triumph. After more than
eighty years of struggle, American women convinced the majority
of American men to open up their ranks to a once totally disen-
franchised and politically invisible population. Even in the immigrant stronghold of New York City, the majority of voters supported
female suffrage. It was championed by such working-class leaders
as Clara Lemlich, Leonora O'Reilly, and Rose Schneiderman.

Woman's new status as citizen, finally, did not sit well with
the notion of breadgiver. A voter, after all, was honored for his
independent judgment and expected to act in his own self-interest.
He, and now she, was expected to assume public responsibility and
could not cower in particularistic family relationships. On this score,
as historian Ellen DuBois has argued, the vote was the most radical

and far-reaching demand of the nineteenth-century women's movement. Suffrage, unlike most reforms of the era, struck a decisive
blow against the walls of woman's sphere, for it brought her directly
into the public sphere to a place she would share with men, and
called upon her to act as an individual agent and autonomous
decision maker.[115] Now, at least on this all-important front of citizenship, male and female were to be regarded simply as equals.

□

Official admission to the American political system, however,
had some short-term liabilities. As outsiders working from the
sidelines of the system, women had acquired acute social and political perceptions and built their own organizations and institutions
through which to implement them. In their truly heroic struggles
to break free of nineteenth-century constrictions, women created an
enlarged sphere all their own, where women could plan, organize,
and lead without the interference of men. With the passage of the
Nineteenth Amendment, women were admitted to a political universe where the rules were made and the positions of power were
held by the opposite sex. Having won the battle for suffrage, women
would have to begin another steep upward climb, now from inside
male-dominated spheres.

F I V E

THE EROSION OF WOMAN'S SPHERE: HETEROSEXUALITY AND THE STREAMLINED HOME, 1910–1940

Jane Addams titled her autobiography for the years between 1909 and 1929 *The Second Twenty Years at Hull House*. Yet the later chapters in her career took her far afield of that enlarged home in the slums into national and international politics and a variety of benevolent projects, all pursued with the hard-nosed efficiency of a veteran social housekeeper. Forty years' immersion in the sordid conditions of industrial America had purged much of the sentimental ethics with which Jane Addams disguised her career in the first volume of her autobiography. She still retained the conviction, however, that the female sex had a distinctive and segregated role to play in public life. In 1930 she issued a caveat against the political "masculinization" of women, that tendency to "dovetail into the political themes of men [rather] than to release the innate concerns of women which might be equivalent to a revolutionary force." Truly feminine political values, she surmised, might have been an effective counterforce to World War I, for woman's social conscience "rebelled against the destruction of their own children, the waste of life they had nurtured." At this point Addams' reiteration of the doctrine of social motherhood was clearly defensive and became more so as she confronted the "contrast in the Post-War Generation." She observed remorsefully that the young women of the 1920s were too concerned with personal freedom and self-development to devote themselves to the cause of societal reform and justice for all Americans.[1]

Other social reformers of Addams' generation echoed her anxiety, admitting to a "surging despair" in the 1920s, which was well-founded in fact. Ironically, woman's official admission into the political arena seemed to retard rather than enhance the social power of women. Acting without benefit of the vote, the women's organizations of the presuffrage era had pressured state legislatures and the U.S. Congress into enacting literally hundreds of child-labor, woman's equity, and social-hygiene laws. The women's lobby consolidated into the Joint Congressional Union and kept up the momentum of female social influence into the 1920s, bringing some of the most cherished projects of female reform to legislative fruition immediately after suffrage was granted. By 1925, however, this crescendo of Progressive legislation had been stilled to a murmur. Even the operations of the Women's Bureau were curtailed without concerted feminine protest. Election studies revealed that women did not vote in a bloc, in greater numbers, or in opposition to their husbands.[2] The Republican and Democratic parties, which had scurried to recruit women members after the passage of the Nineteenth Amendment and had written the resolutions of the League of Women Voters into their platforms, soon began to ignore women, with impunity.

The organized phalanx of female reformers was no longer a force to be reckoned with. When the National American Woman's Suffrage Association reconstituted itself as the League of Women Voters its membership dropped to one-tenth of its original size. Veterans of the suffrage campaign exhausted much of their energy in factional quarrels over the Equal Rights Amendment, introduced before Congress by the Woman's Party in 1923 to the disapproval of Progressive women who feared it would endanger protective legislation. Some organizations, like the Women's Trade Union League and the Consumers League, slowly disintegrated. Others, such as the General Federation of Women's Clubs, retrenched into privatized and conservative positions. In the late '20s the GFWC mixed reformist policy with such resolutions as the recommendation that women should seek a physician's advice before going on a diet, and such reactionary concerns as rooting Communists out of American schools. The colleges of the '20s no longer sent large numbers of young women into settlement houses and reform organizations.

Few rose from the ranks of the new generation to claim the mantle of Jane Addams. The only remote competitors for her title were Frances Perkins, New Deal Secretary of Labor, and Eleanor Roosevelt, both residents of settlement houses in the waning days of social housekeeping. The circle of women surrounding Eleanor Roosevelt managed to carry the banner of social housekeeping into the 1930s and saw their long labors bear fruit in such major New Deal reforms as the Social Security Administration. Yet, the ranks of public women had dwindled to a handful of old friends fighting to win a few token appointments of females to the Roosevelt administration. The fate of enfranchised women was to be integrated at a secondary level into the male-dominated political system. Postwar reaction, red-baiting, and the obstinacy of male power combined to check the advancement of the second sex.[3]

Jane Addams added a subtler factor to the explanation of the disintegration of the women's movement. It was, she surmised, "associated in some way with the breaking down of sex taboos and with the establishment of new standards of marriage." The young, educated women of the '20s seemed to Addams to be preoccupied with sexual gratification and self-fulfillment through marriage, an observation that was confirmed by attitude surveys of college women, 90 percent of whom aspired to the role of wife above all else. Jane Addams found this emphasis on the heterosexual relationship both alarming and perplexing. She surmised that "Perhaps this astounding emphasis upon sex was less comprehensible because of the unique element in the social situation during the last half century regarding the role played by the educated unmarried woman."

The centrality of sex and marriage in the new woman's consciousness also boded ill for women's advancement in the professions. Emily Greene Balch, whose last twenty years had been spent as chairman of the economics department at Wellesley, felt that the new mores would undermine single-minded devotion to careers. While Balch welcomed relief from the sexual frustration suffered by Victorian women, she could not help but feel a bit resentful of the connotations of neurosis now visited upon the spinster. She feared that the celebration of sexual fulfillment might go too far. Balch, like Addams, balked at "the reinterpretation of life, in novels, plays and psychological treatises, that represents sex as practically the whole center of life."[4] These reactions to the roaring '20s were not simply prudery and paranoia. Sex-consciousness had in fact been used against the social housekeepers. One of the charges leveled against their favorite project, the child and maternal welfare programs funded by the Sheppard-Towner Act, was that it was devised and administered by "female celibates."[5] This federal program was defeated in Congress in 1929, proclaiming the demise of Progressive womanhood.

THE FLAPPER:
SIGNAL OF A NEW WOMANHOOD

Already by the middle '20s, celibate careerism and social motherhood were clearly out of fashion, eclipsed by the antithetical image of the flapper. The slim figure of the new woman seemed designed for play and pleasure, energetic self-expression rather than altruistic service to mankind. The exposure of the flapper's legs rose to the knees, betokening a disdain for the purity that had once justified both spinsterhood and social action. The new woman entered into the sporting world with her male chums, smoking, drinking, dancing lasciviously, and necking openly. It was old-fashioned to gather with one's own sex and pledge mutual dedication to the cause of the poor. The flapper symbolized a gay abandonment of social housekeeping, women's organizations, and dogged professionalism.

The flapper was only a symbol, and a very ephemeral one at that. The *Ladies' Home Journal* proclaimed the "Flapper Is Dead" as early as 1920. The celebrations of the roaring '20s (which more properly spanned the mid-teens to the late 1920s) loomed larger in the public imagination than in the everyday life of the average American. This symbol, however, effectively erased the nineteenth-century ideal of the mother of civilization. The icon of the flapper was also a more fitting representation of woman's place in twentieth-century America than the traditional portrait of Jane Addams, with immigrant children clustered around her ample form. The social mother of the period 1890 to 1920 had helped to create her own obsolescence. The female social activist was central to the construction of institutions and professions—government bureaus, urban services, organized philanthropies, and social work—which usurped and rationalized the process of social housekeeping. Simultaneously, the flight of second-generation immigrants into more comfortable homes and regulated factories, followed by the Federal restriction of immigration in the 1920s, depleted the social mother's supply of adoptive children. The highly specialized and bureaucratized new century had less use for creative humanitarians than for self-absorbed service workers, whom it rewarded with a paycheck. In short, flappers were preferable to social mothers.

The cherished nineteenth-century ideal of feminine purity had also outlived its usefulness. For one thing, improved technology of contraception eliminated the need to practice sexual abstinence in order to curtail the birthrate. The social-psychological function of the chaste female—internal control of the economic lust and antisocial tendencies of the middle-class male—was also outmoded. By the twentieth century the advantages of middle-class upbringing and education could secure young men a predictable job and a post so highly routinized that individual passion had little destructive potential. A self-employed, risk-taking capitalist was now very rare among the salaried organization-men of the twentieth century. Finally, sexual repression, operating as deference to the wishes of pure wives, had lost its economic usefulness by the 1920s. The intensive capital accumulation required by industrialization was completed, and corporate financing methods had become so sophisticated that private saving, be it of cash or semen, was no longer of great social or economic significance.

In fact, the role the middle-class American was asked to play in the advanced stage of capitalism was basically antithetical to either sexual or economic frugality. Twentieth-century industry shifted from producing iron for railroads to steel for cars, from power for factories to electricity for homes. Those industrial products were designed not to build a public transportation network or to mechanize factories, but to be purchased by private individuals. This consuming (rather than saving) habit was sufficiently far advanced by 1929 that there were more than 25 million automobile registrations in the United States, and almost 70 percent of American homes were equipped with electricity to power a panoply of home appliances. In the mid-'20s, 76 percent of the cars and 90 percent of the washing and sewing machines were purchased on credit. American economic expansion depended on the cash purchase of a growing variety of nondurable goods as well—apparel, food products, and articles of personal hygiene. By 1920 the majority of American homemakers purchased bread manufactured by large baking companies and bought ready-made clothing from mail-order houses or department stores. By the turn of the century, the appropriate economic practice had become spending rather than thrift, and in the '20s frugality gave way to a devil-may-care quest for material goods. The Chamber of Commerce in one Indiana town made the message patently clear: "The first responsibility of an American to his country is no longer that of a citizen, but of a consumer. Consumption is a necessity."[6]

American businessmen rushed to inform the public of the virtues of immediate material gratification. Advertising first became the colleague of big business late in the 1880s, when producers used the press and magazines to announce the availability of certain goods to a nationwide audience. These early advertisements were quite matter-of-fact, simply acquainting the public with national brand names and with the functional superiority of a particular product. For example, a car manufacturer early in the twentieth century promised that "The Oldsmobile Goes." The commonsense advertisements of the Fair Soap Company even resorted to feminism, picturing Elizabeth Cady Stanton extolling the virtue of their pure, simple cleansing product, unadulterated by perfume. By the 1920s, however, businessmen had concluded that the advance of the consuming sector of the economy demanded a more extravagant advertising campaign. One executive described the function of advertising as the cultivation of a healthy "dissatisfaction with what they now have in favor of something better. The old factors of wear and tear can no longer be depended upon to create a demand. They are too slow."[7]

In the '20s, then, advertising agencies set out to create demand for consumer goods, to instill a greater and greater appetite for things. Advertising itself became a major industry, accounting for 2 to 4 percent of the national income up through the 1950s. American advertising business, which amounted to $95 million in 1890, reached $1 billion annually in 1920. Advertising had become the handmaiden of the consumer economy, "almost the only force at work against Puritanism in consumption."[8] Clearly the sexy flapper was a more propitious emblem of the sales mania than the pure mother. The women's organizations that survived the '20s were integrated into the market network as well: The General Federation of Women's Clubs offered its members as subjects for surveys of both sexual behavior and patterns of domestic consumption.[9] Concurrently, the Consumers League, the agency through which social housekeepers like Florence Kelley had attempted to establish sober and socially responsible habits of consumption, failed to attract a second generation of enthusiasts and become moribund. These trends hailed the arrival of the sexy saleslady, a provocative new model of femininity that symbolized new patterns of behavior in both private relations and the public marketplace.

THE SEXY SALESLADY

Once the producers of consumer goods had determined that expansion of their business depended upon the constant escalation of popular demand, they looked to advertising for assistance. As one businessman put it, "I want advertising to rouse me . . . to create in me a desire to possess the thing that is advertised, even though I don't need it." In order to induce such irrational behavior, psychologists of advertising recommended that consumer products be associated with the gratification of more fundamental human appetites, the most basic of them being sexual. The deep-seated cravings of female consumers were expanded to include romance, marriage, and domestic security. Subliminal promises of sexual fulfillment, love, and a happy home life—all the prizes at stake in the marriage competition—were attached to everything from automobiles to toilet paper, in the hope of engendering compulsive buying habits. One advertiser readily admitted that this tactic was suitable for a public whose average intelligence approximated that of a "14-year-old human animal."[10]

The male animal was customarily enticed into consuming by the most undisguised sexual stimuli. Advertisements for male-oriented products—cars, liquor, cigarettes—were adorned with female bodies. An attractive girl even turned up inside the rim of an automobile tire. Often the association between sex and purchase was made explicit, as in an automobile advertisement that pictured a woman beside an Oldsmobile above the inscription "A Man Is Known by the Car He Keeps." Well before 1920, the liquor industry had discovered its characteristic ploy, posing its product in the hands of an attractive woman with the inscription "a bottled delight." The tobacco industry followed suit, combining sexy models with such slogans as "Reach for a Lucky when you crave something sweet." Occasionally men and women were jointly informed of the sexual power of a product. For example, a perfume was advertised during World War II as follows: "He will if you wear it. She will if you give it." Relatively straightforward invitations to make major purchases were last addressed to women in the early '30s, when the automobile industry occasionally recommended their latest model to career women—"Women Know Success and Know Buick." Thereafter, most products and advertisements were clearly typed according to conventional sex roles.[11]

The most frequent message to women was that love and romance could be acquired in the consumer marketplace. The manufacturers of cleansing products formed the vanguard of this marketing practice. Woodbury began its pioneering advertising campaign before 1920 with the promise "You too can have the charm of a skin he loves to touch." When the *Ladies' Home Journal* announced in the 1920s the advent of "the Cosmetic Age" (and recommended that cosmetology be taught in the nation's high schools), an avalanche of new products was declared essential to sexual and romantic fulfillment. Shampoo companies insisted you "must have beautiful well-kept hair to be attractive" and a deodorant manufacturer proclaimed that a "woman's instinct tells her" that body odor will deny her romantic canoe rides in the moonlight. The Palmolive company carried the sexology of advertising a step further by displaying the testimonials of movie stars who reputedly used their facial soap, and by touching the sensitive nerves of competing females with such queries as "Will others he meets outdo you in natural charm?" In the 1930s the sexual connotations of advertising grew more and more explicit. By then, Woodbury ads featured very scantily clad female bodies.

In general, however, the depression subdued the sexual daring of American advertisers. Rather than escalating the promises of fulfillment, the advertisements of the '30s played on women's fears of marital and financial disaster. One advertisement asked, "I love you but how can we afford to get married?" The illogical answer was: Use Lux soap. Increasing attention was given to the pathology rather than the pleasure of the body. A distraught woman in a deodorant ad asked, "What's wrong with me?" and Listerine put a warning of domestic disaster in the mouth of a little girl: "He didn't kiss mummy yesterday either." In the '30s, consuming was portrayed to women as a simple method of keeping the family healthy and intact through the crisis of the Great Depression. Bran flakes would remove the frown from the worried face of the workingman; aspirin would relieve the nervousness of the mother; hot cereal would protect children from the pangs of hunger.

The twentieth-century interplay between sex and sales created yet another more substantial and expansive role for women. The businessmen who reminded Americans of their patriotic duty to consume, spoke particularly to women. They spoke with the authority given to them by the market researchers who produced evidence that two-thirds of the $70 billion of consumer purchases were made by women.[12] Some said that the women of America propelled economic expansion by purchasing $1,000 worth of goods every minute.[13] Studies of shopping patterns in New York City indicated that husbands were responsible for only 12.2 percent of the family consumer decisions and were consulted on only about 23 percent more.[14] As early as 1922, American home economists introduced women to their important new role of routine extravagance. "That we want more than we have is the very foundation of progress, whether what we want is material or spiritual." High-school home economists in the same decade set about "equipping the girl to be an intelligent consumer."[15]

When the frenzied consuming and installment buying of the '20s ended in the debacle of the stock-market crash and the Great Depression, women were chastised for their profligacy and admonished to restrain their lusts for goods. Eleanor Roosevelt chastened American women to "see that they live within their incomes, that they buy as fairly as possible from the fair merchant and buy only such goods as are manufactured by fair merchants."[16] In the next decade Mrs. Roosevelt recited her message of frugality in the pages of the *Ladies' Home Journal*, whose editors shamed and cajoled women to ration and conserve for the good of the war effort. In the marketplace as in the bedroom, the appetites of the sexy saleslady were supposed to be passively responsive, turned on and shut off as the economy careened from prosperity to depression, and back again.

Sex and sales were so tightly conjoined with the female gender that women themselves began to resemble marketable commodities. Female bodies paraded through the popular culture and advertising copy like standardized, interchangeable parts coming off an assembly line. The resemblance between the female form and a product in a display case became ritualized in the beauty pageants of the '20s, which have been annually reenacted ever since.

One of the most crass and explicit presentations of women as sexual commodities was enacted on the movie screens of the '30s and '40s in Busby Berkeley's dance extravaganzas. In a single film, *Footlight Parade*, Berkeley lined up scores of female bodies to project such images as mechanical dolls wound up by male dancers, slaves of old Africa, occupants of honeymoon suites, Singapore prostitutes and, of course, water nymphs. The waterfall number in *Footlight Parade* can hardly be rivaled as a fantasy of sex objects en masse. At one point the camera passes between a formation of thighs, pointing up at a long line of bead-covered crotches. The gold digger musicals of the '30s attested to the marketability of these assemblages of sex objects, appropriately costumed in jingling coins. Under the direction of Busby Berkeley, the image of the sexy saleslady was fully unveiled, her body molded into one standard, infinitely replicable shape, displayed en masse, and put up for sale. Berkeley was Hollywood's Henry Ford, the master manufacturer of the sexy feminine image.

It was the medium of the cinema which brought the sexy image of woman to a mass audience and infused it with a vivid and captivating authenticity. Even the greenest immigrant girl could decipher the message of the silent screen. Estimates of the size of the weekly film audience ranged from 60 million to 100 million up through the 1940s. Even in the depths of the depression, according to a study by the Connecticut Consumers' League, young workingwomen whose wages hardly reached the subsistence level attended the movies regularly, 66 percent of them once a week or more.[17] The immediacy of sex in the movies was revealed to one sociologist by a waitress's reference to Rudolph Valentino as her personal "boy chum."[18] The same women aped the hairstyles, apparel, and gestures of screen heroines. The silver screen demonstrated the new priority of twentieth-century women—attracting the male through sexual allure—and very few women could escape exposure to this message.

The American movie industry was at first ambivalent about the treatment of sexual topics. Certainly its most accomplished director, D. W. Griffith, was steeped in Victorian values. Yet many of the sweet roles in which he cast Lillian Gish betrayed the fragility of her pure, delicate ways and the vulnerability of the ethic of chastity. For example, in the 1919 production *True-Heart Susie*, Gish's values were placed in deadly combat with the mores of the "fast crowd." In fact, Susie lost her childhood sweetheart to the audacious Bettina, with her painted face, short skirts, and provocative walk, Only after Bettina exposed her vile cooking, cosmetic-free visage, and marital infidelity, and then died of pneumonia for good measure, did True-Heart Susie win back the hero.

From the very first, innocents like Lillian Gish and Mary Pickford were rivaled at the box office by the likes of Theda Bara, whose gluttonous sexuality demonstrated the etymology of the term "vamp," and Clara Bow, whose fashionable sex appeal labeled her "the 'it' girl." The odds against the nineteenth-century heroine surviving through the '20s were raised in 1919 with the release of Cecil B. De Mille's *Male and Female*. De Mille dared to show Gloria Swanson bathing, and focused in on her scantily clad thighs and breasts in a notorious shipwreck sequence. All these films employed that curious Hollywood representation of lust, the clinch. The box-office success of *Male and Female* led to relentless replication of the sexy formula for movie-making, under such titles as *Married Flirts, Sinners in Hell, The Price She Paid, Queen of Sin*. The movies were perhaps the most effective school of the new female sexuality. One young woman described her sexual education as follows:

> No wonder the girls of the olden days before the movies were so modest and bashful — they never saw Clara Bow and William Haines. They didn't know anything else but being modest and sweet. If we didn't see such examples in the movies when would we get the idea of being hot?[19]

One glance at the starlets of the 1920s is enough to demonstrate that a great change had swept through the museum of feminine stereotypes. The model of the new femininity was not Jane Addams, but the favored Hollywood ingenue of the moment. The slick surface of the celluloid image exuded an aura of female sexuality that shocked social housekeepers and purity crusaders, but it conformed nicely to the ambitions of the producers of consumer goods and their advertising agents, legitimizing as it did impulses for personal gratification, be they material or sexual.

THE FLAPPER'S
DECLARATION OF INDEPENDENCE

The movie moderns, for all the titillation of their screen images, were something more than simple sex symbols. The new woman as enacted by the stars of the 20's, Clara Bow, Joan Crawford, Janet Gaynor and many others, was also full of a zestful, energetic and fun-loving youth. She seemed deliriously liberated from the corsets of the Victorian age. Above all else she declared her independence and a crystalline sense of individuality. In *Our Dancing Daughters* Joan Crawford greeted the arrival of a new generation of women with this toast: "Here's to myself, I have to live with me all my life."

The movie screens of the 1920s provided the visual expression of this definition of the flapper, culled from a college newspaper: "Any real girl . . . who has the vitality of young womanhood, who feels pugilistically inclined when called the 'weaker sex,' who resents being put on a pedestal and worshipped from afar, who wants to get into things herself is a flapper." She was as much an athlete, prankster, and buddy as a sex partner, prompting another college journalist to say of the new model of womanhood, "If man has lost his ideal he has gained a pal."[20]

This new image and new freedom had some grounding in social fact. Even in the movies the flapper was commonly situated in one of two congenial habitats, either at a job in the city or in a dormitory in some college town. Both movie locales were situated at some distance from a girl's parental home. The ingenue traveled to the first cinematic location from her rural home and took up residence among her peers, usually in some crowded city apartment. In fact, the 1920s brought a rapid depletion of the nation's farm population, and women led the exodus. Surveys of the young women migrants revealed that they were drawn to the city by the chance to be on their own in an exciting and variegated environment. Even those young women who worked in the same city as their parents were increasingly likely to reside independently. While nineteenth-century surveys of young female workers found the majority residing with their parents, studies conducted in the '20s found two-thirds of these young women on their own, many of them no doubt residing in the working-girl flats so fondly depicted in the movies.[21]

Far fewer women congregated in the flapper's second cinematic habitat, the college. Yet the American educational system in general was the locus of an important shift in the experience of womanhood. By the 1920s secondary schooling was widespread and typically extended well into the teen years. A full 80 percent of the nation's children between the ages of five and seventeen were attending school in 1928, as opposed to 59 percent in 1900. During approximately the same period, high-school enrollment alone went up 650 percent and included more females than males. Going to school, like the move to the city, provided an exercise in independence for women, a moment of liberation from familial government. While in school, furthermore, a young woman was excused from making a selfless contribution to the family income, and was free to think about her own interests and prospects of personal mobility.[22]

It was not the classroom nor the apartment, but the job, that was the most widespread and sympathetic environment for cultivating the spirit of independence exhibited by the flapper. By the 1920s the young female who spent her late teens and early twenties idly awaiting a suitor was a rare and archaic specimen. Whereas before 1900 over one third of America's women aged sixteen to twenty-four were neither in school nor on the job, that figure had been reduced to a mere 5 percent by 1930.[23] The increase in employment over these years was due in large part to the legitimacy newly accorded work among native-born, middle-class daughters. Yet the drafts of female independence were also invigorating the daughters of the immigrant poor and working class, long accustomed to laboring for their daily bread and that of their families. In such traditionally patriarchal cultures as the Italian neighborhoods of lower Manhattan, for example, the custom of forfeiting wages to parents had gone out of vogue by 1930. Rather, working girls began to contribute only a portion of their weekly pay envelope to their parents, in lieu of rent. This alteration in family economics, which transferred financial control from parent to daughter, was described by one young working woman as follows: "She used to open the envelope and take a few dollars for herself if she needed it. And then one day my sister wanted to pay board. She was eighteen. My mother asked what do you mean board? 'I give you so much and keep the rest.' So my mother said alright do as you please."[24] Control of one's own wages, even if they were squandered at the nickelodeon or department store, bred a heady sense of autonomy. In Anzia Yezierska's novel it set her young heroine apart from her breadgiving elders. With her first earnings in her pocket, Sara Smolinsky felt the elation of being "independent, like a person."[25]

Such young women were likely to find a position within the labor force which was also less socially constricted than in times past. A diminishing proportion of women workers, first of all, were confined to the household as domestic servants. The relevant figures declined from the majority of women workers in 1870 to only one in four by 1920. At the later date, domestic servants were outnumbered by both white-collar and industrial workers. The 1910s saw the most dramatic increase in white-collar jobs for women; they rose by 64 percent to surpass manufacturing as the major sector of female employment.[26] In taking up her position at the desk or behind the counter, a young woman often escaped not only the household but also the supervision of her kinsmen or ethnic subculture, so characteristic of the sweatshop. The female pioneers of white-collar employment, furthermore, were granted not only more comfortable working conditions and shorter hours, but also a wage that could be as much as two to three times that of a female industrial worker. Movement into the new jobs of the twentieth century was experienced as upward mobility, a new and exhilarating experience for women, and another contributor to the high spirits of the flapper.

Such elation could, however, prove ephemeral, as the case of the telephone company will illustrate. Before 1920 women had occupied 99 percent of the seats at Ma Bell's switchboards. Their advancement into this once male job sector was orchestrated by feminine stereotypes (woman's special aptitude for service with a smile), but it had its clear compensations: good pay, flexible, safe, and sanitary working conditions, and possibilities of climbing to supervisory post. The corporate drive to cut costs and rationalize service systematically undermined all these benefits of white-collar employment during the 1920s. Pay and chances of mobility declined as the work process itself was transformed into a sequence of routinized tasks accompanied by rigid and insulting instructions such as these: "In a clear, distinct tone with the rising inflection on the word 'please' she says, 'number please.'" The scientific managers at the telephone company subjected workers to a hydra-like system of supervision which one woman described as "everybody watching somebody else and the whole gang watching the poor operators and trying to get more speed out of them."[27]

The audacious young women of the flapper era did not submit quietly to the deterioration of working conditions at the telephone company. With the assistance of the Women's Trade Union League and the International Brotherhood of Electrical workers, they mounted a series of militant strikes during the 1910s. Thousands of women from Boston to California walked off their telephone company jobs demanding better hours, wages, and benefits. Yet the company's campaign of harassing strike leaders and buying off workers with paternalistic reforms, combined with the growing indifference of male unions, successfully squelched this resistance. Work at the telephone company soon rigidified into a female occupational ghetto, in which women surrendered their spirit of independence to a highly bureaucratized organization of the work place. In the end, young women workers responded to this turn of events with individual rather than collective action: they left their switchboard jobs in droves, seldom staying at their posts for more than two years. The case of the telephone operator was a gloomy omen of things to come in the female sector of the labor force.[28]

SEX AND FEMALE PSYCHOLOGY

The event that occasioned a woman's exit from her job at the telephone company, or most any other sector of the labor force for that matter, was most often her wedding. The flapper image and its real-life facsimile may have proclaimed young women's independence from patriarchal fathers and Victorian mothers, but they hardly disclaimed contact with males of their own generation. In fact, the twentieth-century gender system fostered closer ties between the sexes than ever before. That, after all, was the purport of the revolution in sexual expectations, which were always directed into heterosexual channels. At the outset, exponents of the doctrine of sexual fulfillment contributed their share to the flapper's spirit of liberation, but once again the promise of emancipation soon gave way to another set of constricting gender rules and renewed support for conventional marital relations.

□

The relaxation of Victorian sexual morality was already evident in the 1890s when G. Stanley Hall and his disciples at Clark University began to speak of something called "sexual fulfillment." About the same time Emma Goldman, embittered by the sexual frustrations of her Russian Jewish upbringing, took to touring America and lecturing on the merits of free love. Pioneer writers on female sexuality such as Havelock Ellis championed the "love-rights" of women, who, according to clinical observations, suffered immensely from sexual frustration. In fact, 55 percent of the women in his highly select study claimed to have strong sexual desires but rare orgasms. Nearly one-fourth of his subjects accused their husbands of being "undersexed." Ellis urged women to assert their rights to sexual satisfaction and described a variety of sexual techniques whereby they might be fulfilled.[29] Sigmund Freud himself was sensitive to the sexual frustrations of Victorian women. He wrote plaintively to an American psychologist in 1909: "What would you have us do when a woman complains about her thwarted life, when with youth gone she notices that she has been deprived of the joy of loving for merely conventional reasons?" Freud pledged himself to help change "other social factors so that men and women shall no longer be forced into hopeless situations."[30]

The mere announcement of the legitimacy of female sexual needs did much to relieve the frustrations of women. Robert Latou Dickinson, whose gynecological practice spanned forty years, recalled that prior to the '20s his patients had been trained to repress their sexual desires by mothers who said such things as "No good woman ever has pleasure, passion is for the vile," or, "If you love enough, you can stand it." Another woman reported to Dickinson that it was only after six years of marriage, and then by masturbating, that she learned that women could reach sexual climax. By the '20s, young women in Dickinson's practice, largely upper-class college graduates, had been informed that sex was wholesome, pleasurable, and essential for health.

The daughters of the immigrants also benefited from the demise of sexual reticence. Few second-generation girls displayed the total ignorance of menstruation, intercourse, and reproduction that had been so common among their mothers. Sexual freedom was also incorporated into a new breed of feminism in the teens and twenties. Chrystal Eastman put the matter directly: "Feminists are not nuns. That should be established. We want to love and be loved . . . but we want our love to be joyous and free and not clouded with ignorance and fear."[31]

A woman's sexual enjoyment was further enhanced in the '20s and '30s by the greater availability of more reliable methods of birth control, among them the condom, an accurate rhythm method, and the diaphragm. Prior to these innovations, Dickinson's patients told hair-raising tales of contraceptive failure. One woman's childbearing history went like this: "The first was intended; the second was withdrawal; the third was a Lysol douche." Another mother admitted she had had eight abortions following nine failures of douching as a method of birth control. By the '20s, 70 to 80 percent of the upper-middle- and upper-class women used some more or less reliable means of birth control. By the 1930s, approximately one-third of the lower-class women used some method of birth control, then available from Planned Parenthood Clinics and from most doctors. By the 1950s, rich and poor, black and white, and Catholic, Protestant, and Jewish women were regularly employing relatively reliable methods of birth control. Contraception was by no means foolproof, but it was effective enough to remove much of woman's anxiety from the act of sexual intercourse.[32]

Some writers of the 1920s were so exuberant about the awakening possibilities for sexual pleasure that in its pursuit they trampled on once sacrosanct marital conventions. V. F. Calverton concluded that marriage was a bankrupt institution; unwed mothers were courageous, almost heroic; monogamy and the bourgeois home were obsolete.[33] Calverton's contribution to *Woman's Coming of Age* was entitled "Are Women Monogamous?" and his answer was negative. Calverton and several other writers also dismissed romantic love as an ephemeral by-product of sexual sublimation. Meanwhile, the father of American behaviorism, John B. Watson, predicted with scientific assurance that monogamy would disappear in fifty years;[34] Suzanne La Follette, speaking as a feminist, did not go quite that far but did put marriage in perspective. She saw it not as a dictate of God and nature but as a deep-rooted habit that was conducive to social order and the retention of private property.[35] At any rate, many alternatives to marriage were posed in the '20s: open promiscuity, divorce and remarriage, or serial monogamy, and Judge Ben Lindsay's suggestion of companionate, or trial, marriage. Even homosexual relationships were granted legitimacy by some writers. Katherine B. Davis, in her survey of female sexual practices, reported a high incidence of homosexuality (one-fourth of the college women she questioned), without great alarm.[36] Lesbianism became a quasi-legitimate literary theme in Radcliffe Hall's *The Well of Loneliness*, while early sexologists such as Havelock Ellis were tolerant of homosexuality.

The proponents of sexual freedom in the '20s observed and applauded the sense of independence that new ethics could engender in young women. Judge Ben Lindsay in *The Revolt of Modern Youth* quoted with sympathy the marital philosophy of the young workingwoman engaged in premarital sex. "He's crazy about me. But I'm not sure I want to marry him. I haven't any too much confidence in Bill's capacity. Why I'm earning more than he is right now."[37] Sociologist Robert Park took note of a "new type of woman evolving, a woman sophisticated, self-reliant, competent—a woman of the world." In the lives of workingwomen, he maintained, "marriage plays a considerably less important part than it has in the past and still plays in the lives of most women who have not achieved economic independence."[38]

Economic independence for these avant-garde women could also nurture sexual freedom. For example, a saleslady who was interviewed by the sociologist Frances Donovan in one of her studies of female employment, considered a series of short affairs more convenient than marriage as a means of sexual release for the workingwoman.[39] V. F. Calverton judged from his observation of the mores of the roaring '20s that women had become the more liberated sex. "Men are more sentimental than women. When a woman grows up, she grows up. And she comes up simply and says to the man— 'If you feel like coming up today and spending the night, come. But tomorrow don't bother me with your heartaches. Out, don't interfere with my useful work.'"[40] The new sex mores, combined with contraceptive progress, laid open the possibility at least of a more satisfied, self-sufficient, and worldly wise womanhood.

The breakdown of reticence about sex did result in a proliferation of surveys on sexual practice, which suggested that one significant change in the sexual activity of women occurred around 1920. In G. V. Hamilton's sample of middle- and upper-class women, for example, 24 percent of those born before 1891 had sexual experience outside of marriage, while 61 percent of the women born after that year reported illicit sexual behavior.[41] Kinsey's massive study of nearly 8,000 subjects also indicated that the generation of women whose sexual experience began around 1920 engaged in sexual intercourse outside of marriage at about double the rate of their mothers. In the next three decades the incidence of extramarital sex remained practically stable for the college-educated population, according to a relentless barrage of sociological questionnaires. Another method of gauging the sexual practices of the population at large, encompassing more than the upper classes, is the compilation of statistics on illegitimate births, which continued to rise in the twentieth century, most sharply after 1940. This apparent increase in the incidence of extramarital intercourse, however, does not mean that the sheer quantity of women's sexual experience was increasing. In fact, the majority of twentieth-century women followed the sexual routine of the 1890s, engaging in intercourse approximately twice weekly, a frequency governed by the desires of their husbands.[42]

These compilations of statistics, furthermore, do not measure the quality of a woman's sex life. Kinsey's exhaustive survey did suggest that the sexual practices of the '20s were somewhat more sophisticated than in previous decades. Prior to the '20s, sex was described by Dickinson's patients as merely a brief intromission without foreplay, and with the man on top and in control. Understandably, few women achieved orgasm in the process. Ninety-four percent of the women born after 1900 and interviewed by Kinsey in the 1930s and '40s had explored less conventional coital positions and saw their chances of reaching orgasm increased 10 to 15 percent. Still, these relatively minor increases in the variety and quality of women's heterosexual experience were insufficient to satisfy many women. The majority of subjects confessed that they resorted to masturbation to assure sexual release. Furthermore, the most contented women in his survey were homosexuals, who seldom failed to reach orgasm in their sexual relations.

If sexual revolution is gauged by such simple measurements of physical gratification, the 1920s did not mark a great divide. In fact, one sexual survey that drew on the experience of nineteenth-century women found comparable, if not higher, levels of expressed sexual fulfillment before 1920. In the Victorian era, however, many women took a sense of reciprocated affection and diffuse pleasure as sexual satisfaction. Their daughters would be asked, however, to pass a clinical and physiological test of sexual accomplishment— the achievement of orgasm.[43] In fact, almost as soon as the existence of female sexuality had been acknowledged, physicians and psychologists began to register alarm at the appearance of "a new and alarmingly prevalent female disease," frigidity. According to Dickinson, 10 to 15 percent of his patients were affected with the malady.

If the sexual revolution did not pay off in the sheer multiplication of the incidence of sexual pleasure among women, it still had a profound impact on the social meaning of womanhood. It was swiftly put in the service of new standards of femininity. By 1920 the *Ladies' Home Journal* had a new rationale for ushering women into homes and nurseries: not only the dictates of biology and "divine purpose," but "sex psychology" as well. When in the same year an anonymous woman was interrogated about her sex life she had already mastered the new jargon, rhapsodizing about the "deep psychological effect" of intercourse, "making possible complete mental sympathy."[44] Clearly, the sexual revolution was not just a matter of genital mechanics.

The earliest sex theorists set eagerly to work rekindling consciousness of all differences between the sexes, in temperament and behavior as well as physiology. Havelock Ellis's work *Man and Woman*, published in 1894, began with the observation that as contemporary women entered the social and economic spheres once reserved for men, "we are brought face to face with the consideration of those differences which are not artificial and which no equalization of social conditions can entirely remove, the natural character and predisposition which always inevitably influence the sexual allotment of human activities."[45] At the same time, G. Stanley Hall saw fit to recount the distinctive features of female physiology, impelled by the alarming evidence that nearly one-half of all American girls "choose male ideals or would be men."[46]

So inspired, Hall and Ellis began to scrutinize once again the biological differences between the sexes. Ellis set out to measure and compare every bone, sinew, and ligament in the male and female bodies. He concluded that "a man is a man even to his thumbs and a woman is a woman down to her little toes." This potpourri of statistical trivia provided the foundation on which Ellis's scheme of mental and behavioral differences was built. "While the man's form seems to be instinctively seeking action, the woman's falls naturally into a state of comparative repose, and seems to find satisfaction in an attitude of overthrow." After determining by the haphazard comparison of the skeletons of the two sexes that women had failed to rise to the completely erect stature of her male counterpart, Ellis concluded that women were designed for the posture of giving birth and were similar to children in their anatomy and character. They were made for motherhood. The cult of maternity was wrestled from the clutches of feminists. Ellis felt he had proven that "the realization of the woman's movement in its largest and completest phases is an enlightened motherhood in all that motherhood involves, alike the physical and the psychological."[47] G. Stanley Hall took a different path to the same conclusions. He focused on the menstrual cycle and built around it a theory of woman's temperamental periodicity, which was conducive to piety, dependence, and passivity. Hall regarded his biopsychology as a justification for the emancipation of women from "the man-aping fashions now just beginning to wane and will no doubt sometime be wrought out."[48]

The ideological implications of the psychology of sex were abundantly clear. After reading *Male and Female*, Alice Beale Parsons complained, "All I was sure about was that I was stunned by another one of those Olympian bolts that are hurled at woman everytime that she is almost convinced that she is a person like man." As she wrote in 1931, however, Parsons had evidence with which to refute Ellis's "Alice-in-Wonderland science." Dr. Helen Thompson and Professor C. L. Thorndike had conducted their own review of the differences between the sexes and concluded that "individual differences within one sex so enormously outweigh the difference between the sexes in these intellectual and semi-intellectual traits that for all practical purposes the sex differences may be discarded." The concept of the statistical normality, the standard male and female as determined by the collection and averaging of data, could not withstand the test of logic, and certainly did not justify the segregation of every man and every woman into two different compartments of human personality and endeavor. Surveys published in the 1920s further revealed that the sexual appetites of men and women were remarkably similar, differences in anatomy and reproductive functions notwithstanding. By 1931 even Havelock Ellis was somewhat chastened, convinced by simple empirical studies that there need be no distinctly feminine psychology of sex.[49]

Just as these primitive theories were being refuted, however, the path of female psychology took another devious turn. In 1918 H. W. Frink launched a new kind of psychological attack on feminism. He dismissed one feminist this way: "Upon analysis, this patient's violent warfare against all forms of subordination of women was revealed to be very largely a compensation for a strong but imperfectly repressed masochistic tendency." Of feminists in general he said, "A certain proportion of at least the most militant suffragists are neurotics who in some instances are compensating for masculine trends, in others, are more or less successfully sublimating sadistic and homosexual ones."[50] R. L. Dickinson attributed all sorts of feminine ills as well as unfeminine behavior, including involvement in "social and political causes," to "compensation neurosis."[51] By the 1920s, social reform as well as feminism was being dismissed with the appellations "neurotic," "masochistic," "sadistic," "homosexual," terms derived from the field of psychoanalysis.

Whether Freudian or behaviorist, the psychology of sex did have the effect of casting a shadow of disapproval over erotic relationships between women. At the outset, the relaxation of sexual taboos and the expansion of sexual knowledge might have had some positive implications for lesbians: giving their practice a name, teaching techniques of sexual gratification, proffering a modicum of clinical legitimacy. Yet the sexologists conferred a stigma upon same-sex relationships along with this soupçon of toleration. Homosexuality was seen as a pathology if not a perversion, an irremediable but diseased and inferior form of sexuality. For women who had once enjoyed the romantic friendships of the nineteenth century, including erotic pleasures that stopped short of genital sex play, the psychology of sex could foster new inhibitions and self-doubts. Mary Woolley, for example, the president of Wellesley, would spend her autumn years living with her companion of a half-century, Jeannette Marks, yet at the same time she warned her students against intimate relationships with their classmates; such bonds were "unwise," "abnormal," "unpleasant or worse."[52]

THE HETEROSEXUAL IMPERATIVE

The psychology of sex was merely one instance of a more general diversion of social relations into heterosexual channels. In the course of the twentieth century the American woman's attention was focused more and more intently upon her private interaction with men. While the nineteenth amendment worked to integrate male and female within the political arena (at least in theory), popular psychology strived to bring the two sexes closer together in their emotional relations. Both ideology and institutional changes conspired to break down the homosocial bonds of the nineteenth century and erect in their place a tight union between pairs of males and females.

This heterosexual bonding was judged so imperative that a whole stage of the female life cycle was devoted to its cultivation. The period of adolescence was designed especially for this purpose: "development toward heterosexual attraction."[53] At the turn of the century G. S. Hall advised young women to devote this era of their lives to the contemplation of their motherly nature. In 1916 Caroline Wormeley Latimer updated the concept of adolescence, defining it as the epoch in a woman's life that brought to the fore "the great elemental instinct, sex, which henceforth is to be one of the most powerful agencies in her life."[54] The popular enthronement of sexuality in the '20s decreed that teenage girls move out into a circle of their peers to acquire training in heterosexual relations. As Latimer put it, "It is through a girl's intercourse with the other sex that she receives the one most valuable part of her social training, namely the knowledge of how to accept [men's] attention and also to protect herself against them when necessary to do so."[55]

The development of a teenage subculture provided girls with ample opportunities for heterosexual contact. In the 1920s approximately 50 percent of the nation's teenagers were attending high school, largely public coeducational institutions. Robert and Helen Lynd discovered that the high school was the cradle of modern mores, where intellectual training took a back seat to social life. Middletown's youth flocked to dances, sports events, and parties in the '20s. Approximately half of them spent less than four evenings a week at home. Relationships with his or her peers, in other words, became the center of a teenager's social life. Within peer culture, furthermore, heterosexual contacts were given the place of greatest honor. Admittance to the major social events of high school was granted to couples only, and rumor had it that petting parties were rampant among the "in crowd." Middletown's mothers expressed alarm at the precocious heterosexuality of their daughters: "Girls have more nerve nowadays—look at their clothes." "Girls are more aggressive today. They call the boys up and try to make dates with them."[56] By the '20s, the American high school had become a fitting environment in which to undertake training in heterosexual relations. Psychologists applauded the teenage subculture: "This conformity to the manners of her own age group is the result of a wholesome impulse. For the final adjustment of the girl must be with her contemporaries and not with the older generation if she is to be successful in her adjustment to work, play and marriage."[57]

American popular culture also provided ample food for adolescent romantic and sexual fantasies. The *Ladies' Home Journal* published "girls' issues" as early as the first decade of the twentieth century, packed full of bridal fashions and wedding pictures. These literary depositories of girls' culture harped on the importance of heterosexual attractiveness and peer-group conformity, and doled out copious advice on how to deal with boys. The "Sub-Deb" column of the *Ladies' Home Journal*, which first appeared in the '30s and endured through the '50s, dispensed such advice as this: "He Loves Me, He Loves Me Not—How to Detect" and "The Boy Watcher's Guide."[58] In short, popular culture followed the instructions of the sociologists and psychologists of adolescence, teaching the "A.B.C.'s of the New Language: how to impress a certain boy or girl, how to be liked by many, and how to know when one is getting ahead with one's chosen groups."[59]

Proponents of adolescent heterosexual norms had an even more effective ally in the movies. In Middletown the majority of high-school girls frequented movie houses at least once a week.[60] A study of suburban adolescents in the '30s revealed that, while they went to movies less often than boys, girls spent a larger proportion of their leisure time—26 to 44 percent—before the silver screen, while males were out on football or baseball fields.[61] Studies of popular taste, furthermore, indicated that women preferred the themes of romance and love, "the woman's picture," while males delighted in adventure films: Westerns and war stories.[62] As adolescents flocked to the neighborhood theaters they imbibed potent doses of feminine and masculine stereotypes, while the love stories nourished the romantic fantasies and heterosexual consciousness of young girls.

There is ample evidence which suggests that the propaganda campaign of the new womanhood was successful. As early as the '20s, girls began to display their anxiety about popularity. One girl wrote to a newspaper columnist asking, "Please help me out. I am not very popular and yet according to people I have met I am pretty, I am five feet eight, with short brown hair, greenish eyes, good color and inclined to be fat. I do not use cosmetics and don't talk much. It is hard for me to make friends, but I have some. How can I become popular?"[63] Young girls worried about standards of sexual behavior as well as personal attractiveness. Advice columns to teenagers were bombarded with questions as to whether a girl should engage in necking and petting. Ben Lindsay's experience in the juvenile court of Denver, Colorado, led him to project that 90 percent of the fashionable high-school set engaged in at least hugging and kissing. The judge quoted one popular girl as saying "there is something wrong with boys who don't know how to love me up."[64]

The heterosexual imperative also held sway outside the high school and beyond the middle class. A survey conducted in 1920 revealed that 18 percent of both college women and working girls thought that the willingness to pet was essential to winning popularity. At the same time, sociologist Frances Donovan observed that the waitresses of Chicago "always talked about men," while others noted that the most frequent topic of conversation among factory operatives was "Who is she going with . . . who is her steady beau?" Social housekeepers like Mary Dreier of the WTUL were confounded and disappointed by these modern women, "giggly girls whose sole interest in life was boys and how to attract them." Dreier found them "sort of oversexed and unwholesome."[65]

Yet this heterosexual consciousness should not be mistaken for sexual promiscuity. Adolescent girls and single working women were seldom loose in their sexual mores. Boundaries were quickly imposed on the range of permissible sexual behavior. In the 1920s the teenage peer group set up rules for necking and petting: when, where, with whom and how far it should proceed. For teenagers, the sexual revolution meant primarily an increase in foreplay. Both sexes and all ages still held to the principle that brides should be virginal, and a young couple who engaged in premarital coitus was a prospective husband and wife. Most single women remained very cautious and calculating in their sexual relations, and ever attentive to their prospects for marriage.

The major effect of the heightened interest in female sexuality came down to this in the end: matrimony became more imperative than during the preceding decades. Single women interviewed by Katherine Davis in the '20s suffered from psychic distress as well as a social stigma. One of Davis's subjects said that "the single woman must always be bothered with questions of sex. Her life is stunted." Another took the modern disdain for sexual abstinence so seriously that she declared "I have never lived."[66] Such attitudes would consign the lives of renowned social housekeepers to oblivion. In the '30s the indictment of celibacy was brought against single workingwomen by Frances Donovan. The unmarried schoolteacher, Donovan surmised, had probably in her youth been too devoted to study to engage in "the childish love affairs that educate the emotions." Denied adolescent training in the techniques of winning male approval, these romantically retarded women were unlikely to ever catch a husband. Their sexual frustration gave rise to the sternness, tyranny, and moodiness that characterized the "queer teacher."[67] The ideal girlhood, the apprenticeship in heterosexual relations, on the other hand, led directly to the altar: "Developed to a mature heterosexuality, love will be given first place in her dreams of happiness, and she will not think of sacrificing marriage for any prize."[68]

The imperative of matrimony was inscribed in social statistics as well as popular culture. The proportion of never-married women fell precipitously after 1900, from as high as 20 percent for women who came of age in the late nineteenth century to well less than 10 percent for women born after 1900. College-educated women were quick to adapt to the new mores. At Vassar, for example, only two in five graduates of the 1870s were married by age twenty-seven. By the 1920s the majority, or three in five, of the graduates of that decade approached the altar before that age. Successive generations of women also entered upon marriage with greater haste; the mean age of marriage fell steadily after 1890 until in the 1950s it reached an all-time low of 20.2 years.[69]

The pursuit of the prized object of twentieth-century womanhood, a husband, could put women in ruthless sexual competition with one another, and further unravel the ties of sisterhood. When the painted girls at the drugstore flirted with the beau of *True-Heart Susie*, even the sweet countenance of Lillian Gish contorted into a squint-eyed, jealous snarl. According to Donovan, a woman must begin the husband hunt early or "she will find the matrimonial prizes have been carried off" by women who have "concentrated upon what it takes to get men to give up their liberty." The autobiographical writings of women like Mabel Dodge Luhan, Anaïs Nin, and Zelda Fitzgerald are spiced with acute calculations of the sexual powers of their opposition, both before and after they had won a groom. The ordinary wife's sexual competition was hardly as glamorous as that of Mrs. Scott Fitzgerald, but she too had her own little worries.

The *Ladies' Home Journal* repeatedly issued "Warnings to Wives" about the captivating girls in their husbands' offices, and printed stories of spouses enticed away by younger women. Admonitions to maintain sexual attractiveness and thus her husband's interest peppered ladies' magazines, and by the 1950s the anxieties of being a wife in a sex-charged culture were catered to by regular features such as the *Journal*'s "Can This Marriage Be Saved?" The nervous energy entailed in winning and keeping a man was brilliantly captured in Clare Boothe Luce's play *The Women*, which was made into a film by George Cukor in 1939. The film pulsated with wit, aggressiveness, and stamina. The all-female cast mobilized these resources in a "war" to win, steal, or recapture husbands. The campaign ended when a covey of acid-tongued, scheming women (bonded together by their joint trip to Reno) retrieved the former husband of the heroine from the clutches of his duplicitous second wife. The energy and highly developed skills needed to protect the heterosexual relationship were seldom exercised in collective manner. In fact, the comic vitality of *The Women* resulted from the cutting insults passed between the female characters, which culminated in a most vicious "catfight." The heterosexual imperative fostered a degree of distrust and competition between women such as had never been seen before.

Once she had won exclusive rights to one male, the woman of the twentieth century was expected to retreat into a relationship of unprecedented intensity. The prescribed heterosexual bond of the twentieth century was so different from the marital partnership of the past that a new term was required to denote it. That watchword of modern marriage was "intimacy." Something of the nature and operation of this new marital priority is suggested by this description of the modern conjugal unit:

"The family has become an end in itself and one that is essentially the development and satisfaction of personality. If success is realized, it has to be by at least partial fulfillment of the individual's union with the other self. The woman has become less a helpmate and more a comrade in an adventure which proves hopeless, unless it is a reciprocity not so much in services as in responses."[70]

Aside from documenting the emergence of a new academic specialty called the sociology of marriage and the family, this novel and opaque language seemed to suggest that marriage was no longer alloyed with such practical concerns as exchanging economic and social services. It was now elevated to a rarified plane of feeling;

its business was the raw interaction of personalities. As Ernest Burgess put it, the family was a "mere unity of interacting personalities." Women, more than men, were educated to this new ideal of coupling, which was presented in high school home economics textbooks as well as college courses in the sociology of the family. Young women who had been instructed in the new ideology of the family looked to marriage for a "fuller richer life," "sharing joys and sorrows," or simply "companionship." The newlyweds took up residence in an intimate social space whose function was to produce neither social services nor material goods, but an illusive commodity called "happiness."[71]

A social relationship based on the pursuit of individual satisfaction, an object which women as well as men were now taught to prize, turned out to be rather fragile. Marriage vows were rescinded with growing alacrity as the nineteenth century gave way to the twentieth. The divorce rate skyrocketed between 1867 and 1927, increasing by 2,000 percent, or at five times the rate of new marriages. By the 1920s one in six marriages were being dissolved. After 1900 the causes for divorce altered as well. In the nineteenth century, the most common grounds for divorce were the failure of either partner to live up to conventional sex roles: to be a good provider, or efficient housewife. After 1900, suits for divorce, increasingly initiated by women, were frequently justified by the failure of marriage to live up to expectations of personal fulfillment, including the wife's craving for "excitement," "change," and "independence."[72]

THE STREAMLINED HOME
AND PREMONITIONS OF THE
DUAL ROLE

Still, most marriages survived the hedonism of the 1920s, and although they may not have been havens of perfect intimacy and ecstatic personal gratification, most of the new households of the twentieth century did entail less drudgery for wives and mothers. The simplification of family functions was reflected in the transformation of even the physical space of the house. A movement to streamline domestic architecture had emerged before the close of the nineteenth century when, for example, leaders of the craftsman school (including Frank Lloyd Wright) gathered at Hull House to exclaim against the gingerbread excesses of the Victorian home. By 1920, simplified home designs were in vogue across the country and implemented in row upon row of tidy bungalows with clean lines, uncluttered floor plans, and roomy, antiseptic kitchens. The bungalow style was recommended to housewives as a blueprint for efficient and expeditious domestic management.[73]

To further relieve the housewife of her Victorian burdens the model home of the early twentieth century was stocked full of technological aids. By the '30s the majority of homes were supplied with running water, central heating, and electricity which powered such labor-saving devices as vacuum cleaners, electric irons, stoves, and refrigerators. The immediate impact of the new domestic technology was to reduce the time and energy devoted to housework. When social scientists investigated the organization of housework in the 1920s, they discovered that domestic chores typically consumed fifty hours of women's labor per household per week. This accounting of the time spent in housework, while it remained substantially unchanged until the 1960s, was no doubt well below the labor-time required to manage a Victorian household. For example, the time devoted to clothing and linen care was cut almost in half between 1926 and 1936 as homes were increasingly equipped with indoor plumbing, mechanical washing machines, and electric irons.[74]

Time-budgets calculated for the typical household of the 1920s identified something called "family care" as another category of housework that occupied a relatively small portion of women's working hours. This category, which consisted primarily of the care and training of children, demanded about five hours of work per week during the '20s and '30s. In other words, mothering as well as housework had become streamlined in the early decades of this century. Motherhood demanded less woman's labor time mainly because there were simply fewer children to care for. The birth rate fell dramatically and steadily, from 3.17 per woman in 1920 to 2.45 a decade later, and 2.10 in 1940. Simultaneously, alarming numbers of women remained childless, as high as 20 percent for some birth cohorts. Even the mothers of small families found their maternal responsibilities lessened as children spent larger portions of each weekday and their life span in schools, kindergartens, and day nurseries.[75]

Not only the state and the municipality, but private enterprise as well, were encroaching on the mother's turf. Reproduction itself became a lucrative frontier of the consumer market in the 1920s and '30s. At the turn of the century, childbirth was still quite firmly situated within woman's sphere. Half of all American women still employed midwives, most always female, who for a small fee helped with nursing and housekeeping chores as well as assisting at a birth. Only a tiny minority of women, of any class, gave birth outside their own homes. By 1930, however, midwives had been effectively banished, and 75 percent of all births took place in hospitals under the supervision of obstetricians, mostly males. The cost of reproduction increased more than tenfold in the process. Birth control also grew expensive after 1920, becoming the monopoly of well-paid medical experts, who alone were legally permitted to dispense the more effective modes of contraception. In sum, even women's basic reproduction function had become imbricated in the marketplace and converted into something more, and less, than domestic labor.[76]

This modernization of maternity was also well underway on the plane of domestic ideology where it was overseen by a growing coterie of professional experts, many of whom were careless about the prerogatives of mothers. On the one hand psychoanalysis, and especially the concept of the Oedipal complex, placed unpleasant, incestuous connotations on the ties between mother and son. On the other, behavioralists warned that doting mothers could retard the advances of the younger generation, encumbering them with archaic values and constricting ties to the home. The child, it was said, belonged to the future and "parents should never expect their own highest ideals to become the ideals of their children." Disregard for the icon of motherhood reached its apogee in the work of John B. Watson, who contended that excessive maternal affection rendered children incapable of assuming self-reliant positions in the adult world. Accordingly, Watson would limit parental demonstrations of affection to a kiss on the forehead at bedtime and a handshake in the morning. Behavioralist child-rearing manuals also recommended feeding on a rigid schedule (and by bottle), early toilet training, and such hardening techniques as moderate exposure to heat, cold, and pain. The objective of this regimen, to foster the child's independence, also required that mothers send their offspring to preschool, kindergarten, summer camps, and other extrafamilial institutions to be "emotionally weaned" from mothers.[77]

Some authors of advice on childrearing expressed more concern for the independence of mothers themselves. A manual of infant care written and issued by the female leaders of the children's bureau recommended that mothers seek regular respites from the demands of childcare. "If you have not tried putting your children to bed at six o'clock," wrote this empathic advisor to mothers, "you have no idea what a relief it will be to you." A college text on marriage and the family, written by Ruth Lindquist, proposed that mothers take off at least one day per week. The provision of preschools, recreation facilities, and other public services would, in her opinion, not only improve child development but relieve mothers' fatigue.[78]

Writing in 1931, Lindquist carried her concern for the welfare of mothers yet a step further. She dared to suggest that even mothers were entitled to interests outside the home. The question of "occupational opportunities for married women," wrote Lindquist, "is no longer one which can be lightly dismissed."[79] The possibility of combining marriage, motherhood, and paid employment had occurred to many women well before this time. In fact, countless women had put the principle quietly into practice. A visible minority of social housekeepers, among them labor leader Mary Kenney O'Sullivan and journalist and women's club founder Jennie Cunningham Croly, had managed to raise families and serve as public women as well. The elite ranks of working wives and mothers expanded after 1900 with the addition of many academic women such as psychologist Elsie Clews Parsons, anthropologist Margaret Mead, and educational reformer Lucy Sprague Mitchell. Even with such advantages as sympathetic husbands, flexible work routines, and sufficient income to purchase child care and household help, the adjustment of family and career was not an easy one. Still, enough couples were "working out the problem" to give substance to a new set of feminist aspirations during the 1920s.[80]

The new feminists argued that the dual roles assumed by a privileged few should be made available to the mass of womankind. The popular press picked up the idea in the '20s in articles with such titles as the "Two-Job Wife," "Fifty-fifty Marriages," or "The New Triangle: Women, Home and Business." While feminists, and many popular writers as well, championed the need and right of married women to work outside the home, even they faltered at the notion of combining careers with motherhood. A woman might continue working after her wedding day, and resume employment after her children were grown, but a career could not be comfortably alloyed with the responsibility for young progeny. One writer described the ideal adjustment of the female life cycle in a particularly colorful metaphor: "Two bites of the cherry,—A career, a period of child-rearing and a career again."[81]

Mary Ross offered a more sober exposition of the ideal adjustment of women's work and home roles. Eschewing the "self-assertive and antagonistic feminism of the past" (where women "worked against heavy odds and usually had to buy success at the price of marriage and children, sometimes charm and personal appearance, of being considered queer—as some of them undoubtedly were"), Ross asserted that the modern woman would pursue her career only at the intervals allowed by her marital and childbearing history. No, the women of the twentieth century would not compete with men nor usurp the dominant position of their husbands in economic affairs. The new feminist balked at the radical notion of reconstructing the gender system so as to allow mothers the same career opportunities as fathers.[82]

At the same time that the new feminists shied away from demands for the full-time employment of wives and mothers, others were working to shore up women's traditional domestic roles. Veterans of the earlier women's movement, especially those involved in trade unions and concerned with the plight of poor and lower-class women, worked at cross purposes with the new feminists as they strove to relieve mothers from the necessity of working outside the home. This was a major thrust of protective legislation, the chief concern of the Women's Trade Union League after 1912. Laws which restricted the hours and conditions of women's work were justified as a defense of woman's chief function, mothering. Male trade unionists supported protective legislation as one mode of segregating female workers and averting what they saw as potential threats to their jobs and wage rates. Neither were union men above more direct resistance to female employment, including strikes, legal suits, and harassment on the job. With only slight abatement in the '20s and '30s, unions remained staunch supporters of a single domestic role for women. As one AFL official put it: "It is in the interest of all of us that female labor should be limited so as not to injure the motherhood and the family life of the nation."[83] Progressive women also concurred with male trade unionists in endorsing a correlative notion: that every husband and father was entitled to a wage large enough to allow his wife and children to retire from the labor force. The notion of the "family wage" was even accepted by some entrepreneurs. When Henry Ford introduced the $5 day in 1914, he advertised this famous wage increase as one that would support an auto worker, his children, and his *unemployed* wife.[84]

The powerful combination of corporations, unions, and reformers, not to speak of the timidity and paucity of feminist counterproposals, contained the advances of married women into the labor force within modest proportions. Despite the streamlining of their home roles, the employment rate of married women grew quite slowly. Members of the paid labor force accounted for 6 percent of America's wives in 1900, and 12 percent in 1930. The numbers of working wives continued to increase during the 1930s but still accounted for only one in seven married women at the end of the decade. The majority of these women were poor, black, or foreignborn, and worked not out of some feminist principle or desire for personal fulfillment, but out of sheer necessity.[85]

The effect of the Great Depression on gender roles was complex and inconclusive; it failed to disturb this tenuous adjustment of women's work and home roles. On the one hand, the steep rise in male unemployment and the sharp decline in individual income pushed many desperate wives into the labor force. That increasing numbers of women could find jobs during the depression testified to the tenacity of the sex segregation of the labor force. While the male-dominated industrial sector experienced chronic unemployment, white-collar jobs for women, in the clerical and government sectors especially, were actually expanding. The recruits into these positions were not entirely the wives of the unemployed, or other women driven by economic necessity. The 1930s also witnessed the entry into the labor force of increasing numbers of women from middle-income families. The wages these women earned made it possible for their families to maintain, even in the midst of the depression, the standard of living and consumer habits established during the affluent 1920s. This new species of woman worker accounted for nearly 40 percent of the wives who entered the labor force during the '30s, and seemed to be a harbinger of a major shift in the sexual division of labor.[86]

Yet in the last analysis, the public response to the depression conspired to suppress any radical alterations of the gender system. Restrictions on the employment of wives were actually written into state and federal statutes during the depression. Some thirty states enacted laws inhibiting the employment of women, while the majority of the nation's public schools and over 40 percent of all public utilities enforced a curb on hiring married women.[87] Not even the lobbying of Eleanor Roosevelt and her New Deal women's network could prevent the institutionalization of job discrimination at the federal level. Section 213 of the Federal Economy Act of 1932 barred from government employment any person whose spouse held a federal job. The statute was clearly directed against working wives, who constituted the vast majority of the more than 1,500 individuals fired by order of section 213.[88]

Discrimination against women workers could be found littered throughout New Deal agencies: in the unequal pay provisions written into the wage codes of the National Recovery Administration, in the disproportionate allotment of public work funds to construction projects which employed men only, in the relegation of women to a paltry number of sex-stereotyped work programs (such as sewing groups or hot lunch programs for school children). The New Deal had the ultimate effect of shoring up the traditional division of labor at a more fundamental structural level, as well. Such reforms as unemployment compensation, social security, minimum wages, and the legalization of collective bargaining operated, by and large, to buttress the male's ability to support a wife and children. By making it possible for increasing numbers of working-class as well as middle-class men to provide the sole source of family income, the welfare state, in effect, democratized the male role of breadwinner.[89]

The conservative impact of federal policy on the gender system was clearly consistent with public opinion during the '30s. A poll conducted in the midst of the depression put this question to both men and women: "Do you approve of a married woman earning money in business and industry if she has a husband capable of supporting her?" Eighty-two percent of those questioned answered a definitive "No."[90] Even men who could not secure jobs to feed their families sometimes held tenaciously to the traditional prohibitions against wives' employment. One unemployed man went so far as to say "I would rather turn on the gas and put an end to the whole family than let my wife support me."[91] When wives did enter the labor force, furthermore, they continued to defer to male authority in financial matters and carefully refrained from attempting to convert their economic contributions into superior domestic status. Meanwhile the sons and daughters of the beleaguered workers of the 1930s were being socialized in the traditional gender roles. Girls were less likely than their brothers to take odd jobs outside the home, were more likely to surrender a large portion of their earnings to the family, and were more frequently saddled with unpaid domestic chores.[92] Compared to her flapper predecessor, the adolescent female of the 1930s seemed tame and domesticated. The Great Depression had trimmed the sails of the new woman, and it appeared that times of economic crisis were not conducive to feminist changes in the gender system.

THE FATE OF THE FLAPPER

A series of critical changes in the structure of womanhood were set in motion early in the twentieth century. Beneath the dashing symbol of the flapper and coincident with the rapid advance of consumer capitalism, women embraced a variety of new roles. The first three decades of this century found young women, including the daughters of the native-born middle class, entering the labor force in growing numbers and conquering more advantageous white-collar jobs for their sex. For their part, older married women curtailed their fertility, claimed the right to sexual pleasure, streamlined their housekeeping and maternal roles and, in small but significant numbers, embarked upon paid labor outside the home.

All these changes slowly eroded the women's culture which germinated during the nineteenth century and then matured and stagnated in the age of the flapper. The new woman eschewed notions of sacrifice, purity and service, and instead held high the banners of individuality, independence, and self-fulfillment. She entertained higher expectations of finding emotional satisfaction and intimacy through her relations with men. The slim, energetic image of the flapper, as well as scientific studies of sex differences, cast suspicion on gender asymmetry itself. At the same time, the women born into the new century were taught to be suspicious of intense friendships with other females. With few second thoughts they began to abandon women's culture along with the vast public spaces their foremothers had struggled so hard to create. Even the self-proclaimed feminists of the 1920s identified private life and personal relations, not formal politics, as the locus of gender reform.[93] They failed, furthermore, to develop any institutional or organizational base for their new consciousness. A new epoch of womanhood was truly if slowly dawning.

Yet all these genuine changes in the experience of women stopped short of a revolutionary transformation of the structure of womanhood. The women of the early twentieth century balked at the idea of surrendering their own preeminence within the home, however streamlined it had become. They seldom questioned that reproduction was still a female sphere. Secondly, the women who married and bore children (an increasingly popular choice) forfeited positions of power and pecuniary status outside the home that might potentially rival those of their husbands. If mothers labored in the public sphere it would be only part-time, or for a portion of the life cycle. The place of women within the gender system no longer took the exact, bold shape of a separate sphere, yet it was still clearly set apart from that of man. Finally the shock waves of the Great Depression, with its conservative impact on gender ideology, seemed to set finite limits to changes in women's roles, at least for the time being. As of 1940, American womanhood stalemated somewhere beyond sex-segregated spheres but well short of parallel and equal gender roles.

S I X

A DOMESTIC INTERLUDE
IN A KALEIDOSCOPE
OF ROLES: 1940 – 1960

Whatever coherence American womanhood had acquired within the first four decades of the twentieth century seemed rapidly to disintegrate after 1940. The first shock to the gender system came with the second world war, which summarily dismissed taboos against the employment of married women. The country cheered them on as women exchanged aprons for overalls and entered weapon and munitions factories. But no sooner had the armistice been signed than this patriotic image was swept away, in turn, by the balmy climate of postwar prosperity which nurtured images of a pristinely domestic womanhood. The contradictory icons of Rosie the Riveter on the one hand, and the feminine mystique on the other, would seem to belie the notion that the years 1940 to 1960 constituted one coherent and uniform period in the history of American women.

Yet in spite of this cataclysmic sequence of national events, and beneath the surface of these contradictory images of femininity, there emerged a certain consistency, if not simplicity, in the roles and experiences of women. First of all, although Rosie the Riveter (and her real-life facsimiles) may have exited from the stage of history at the end of the war, the mass of women workers did not, at least not on a permanent basis. Between 1940 and 1960 the rate of female employment increased almost without interruption, and at twice the velocity of the previous four decades. After increasing by 23.5 percent between 1900 and 1940, the female labor force grew

by 35.8 percent in the next two decades. The war years, furthermore, broke the back of resistance to the employment of wives.
The women workers who came to the rescue of their country during
the war were drawn from the ranks of housewives, who accounted
for no less than 75 percent of the new workers in the early 1940s.
The trend was not reversed after the war: in 1950 one in three
married women was gainfully employed, up from about one in six
in 1940. Not even the 1950s, with all its effusive domesticity,
could stem the tide of married women into the labor force. By 1960
they had conquered this extra-familial space, accounting for 60
percent of the women at work outside the home.[1]

Such high rates of employment on the part of wives seemed
inconsistent with the ideology of home, family, and femininity
which had become the trademark of the 1950s. Be that as it may,
the men and women of that era were at least experienced in the art
of living with such apparent contradictions. Strains of domesticity
had serenaded even Rosie the Riveter into the labor force. The
popular song that was her namesake contained the stanza:

> Rosie got a boyfriend, Charlie;
> He's a marine
> Rosie is protecting Charlie,
> Working overtime on the riveting machine.

Tin Pan Alley, Madison Avenue, and Uncle Sam all agreed that
Rosie's consciousness was fixed on settling down with Charlie after
the War. Her wages were seen simply as a nest egg: "You will earn
more money for the needs of today as well as for the new home
furnishings, vacations and other things that will be available after
the war."[2] This was appropriate education for the affluent postwar
decades when the wages of wives would pay for much of the domestic
comfort of suburbia. Even as the income of a married woman was
justified by its domestic uses, both during and after the war, the
highest social approval still went to the homemaker, the profusely
decorated WAH (woman at home) celebrated in war-time propaganda, and the ever popular WAM (wife and mother) envied by
even college coeds during the 1950s. In sum, the contradiction
between family roles and employment was more apparent than real,
imperfectly obscuring a rampant ideology of domesticity which held
sway both in the 1940s and the 1950s.

The continuity in the organization of womanhood between 1940 and 1960 rested not on the tenacity of women's place either in the home or in the labor force, but rather on a precarious balance struck between the two roles. In 1955, the height of the baby boom and the heyday of the teenage bride, forty-six of every hundred American women were in the labor force. This feat of gender organization was engineered by a careful sequencing of women's roles. During the second world war this meant that wives entered the labor force only in middle age, when their children were old enough to be largely on their own. Through the 1950s the typical woman worker also retired into domesticity to bear and raise her children. Her stints in the labor force were placed at the temporal edges of this domestic center of her life cycle, before and after years of devoted child care.[3] Womanhood in the '40s and '50s, then, did not take the shape of a single, static role. It was experienced by individual women as more like a kaleidoscope, jarred into a sequence of different patterns as they shifted from work to family and back again. It was this changeable quality of the female gender-role which gave the womanhood of the middle decades of the twentieth century its unique, but transitory, quality.

WORLD WAR II
AND THE HOME FRONT

Prohibitions against the employment of wives seemed to be swept away amidst the wreckage at Pearl Harbor. The size and characteristics of the female labor force changed dramatically during World War II. The exigencies of mobilizing for global war warranted a clear and unambiguous invitation to women to come to work. In July 1943, when nearly all available men and single women were enrolled in the labor force, the War Manpower Commission estimated that 4 million additional workers were needed in the armed forces and munitions industries alone. Accordingly, the call for more women workers went out in clarion tones, from government, industry, and ladies' magazines alike. The War Manpower Commission actually employed Madison Avenue, namely the J. Walter Thompson advertising agency, to run its recruitment campaign for 1943. In September of that year, it spent 1.5 million dollars on radio programs alone in a concerted effort to drum up women's enthusiasm for war work. The call to the arms factory was not always clothed in feminine rhetoric. Posters announcing production jobs promised women "man-sized" jobs. War propaganda pictured women operating heavy machinery, while the *Ladies' Home Journal* placed the image of a female combat pilot on its cover. As a result of all these enticements and opportunities, no fewer than 8 million women entered the work force during World War II. The overall participation of women in the labor force jumped from 25 to 36 percent of the adult female population.[4]

Furthermore, sexual segregation within the labor force began to break down under the pressure of wartime production schedules. In heavy industry the numbers of women workers increased from 340,000 to more than 2 million. Females could now be found in such novel places as on the docks, in the steel mills and shipyards, behind the steering wheels of cabs and buses. American Airlines employed hundreds of women, not only as stewardesses, but as pilots and mechanics.[5] Some women were metamorphosed overnight from feminine stereotypes into hefty workers. One beautician, for example, became a switchwoman for 600 Long Island Railroad trains, and a onetime cosmetics salesgirl operated a 1,700-ton keel binder.[6] By the end of the war popular commentators were proclaiming the ability of women to perform all sorts of "male" tasks. Dorothy Thompson, editor of the *Ladies' Home Journal*, congratulated her sex for meeting the test of masculine strength, endurance, and agility, while sociologists attested to the fact that "there are very few jobs performed by men that women cannot do with changed conditions and methods."[7]

The entrance of women into the male preserves of the industrial labor force was not an entirely smooth and swift process. Employers resisted recruiting females as long as possible, until the supply of male workers was utterly exhausted late in 1943. Government recruitment campaigns also began in earnest only well into the war years. Trade unions at times put up staunch resistance to the employment of women. Masculine strongholds such as some shipyards voted to simply exclude women from union locals. Only when they recognized that 60 percent of their members were female did the United Auto Workers set up special programs and services for women. The war-time battle of the sexes was often fought with special virulence on the job front. As one shipyard worker described it, entering male territory could be frightening.

Maybe you don't think it took nerve for women to make the first break into the yards. I never walked a longer road in my life than that to the tool room. The battery of eyes on my jittering physique, the chorus of 'Hi Sister' and 'tsk, tsk' soon had me thinking; maybe I'm wrong. Maybe I'm just not another human being. Maybe I'm from Mars.[8]

While some women retreated into more traditional roles as a result of such fierce opposition, others relished the exhilaration of being pioneers. "It's thrilling, it's exciting," said one recruit, "and something women have never done before." Another gauged the advantages of war work against the standard of woman's conventional role: "I'd die if I had to stay home and keep house." Most women workers, however, welcomed the expansion of job opportunities for more prosaic if no less powerful reasons. Jobs in the war industries paid as much as 100 percent more than positions within the female sector of the peacetime labor force. The payoff of jobs in war industries was especially dramatic and welcome for black women, substantial numbers of whom were admitted to well-paying industrial jobs, and freed from domestic service, for the first time in American history.[9]

All the advantages of wartime industrial employment—higher pay, skilled work, union representation—were granted to women along with one qualification. Rather than a genuine alteration in the rules of gender, the admission of women to the male job sector was regarded as an emergency measure, permissible "for the duration only." As if to underscore this proviso women's war work was draped in feminine imagery. For the single woman, working on the production line was often construed as yet another post for the sexy saleslady. "Working in the war industry has made her a more self-reliant person. She has more to spend on clothes and cosmetics than ever before." The advertising campaigns of both the War Manpower Commission and Madison Avenue were also quick to enlist these workers for service among the "brides of 1942," or '43 to '46 for that matter. After the war it was even more imperative that women's prime allegiance be to the home. A female union leader announced her own retirement plans with girlish enthusiasm. "When the war is over I'll get a manicure, put on the frilliest dress I can find, pour a whole bottle of perfume over my head and then I will be glad to give up my union chair . . . to some boy who comes marching home deserving it." Even while on duty, furthermore, female industrial workers were reminded that most of their jobs were simply variations on their feminine and domestic talents—sewing parachutes was hardly different from darning socks. [10]

While labor outside the home was dressed up in domestic imagery, most women workers were also shouldering their traditional family responsibilities. By 1944 millions of American wives had responded to the call to double wartime duty. Seventy-five percent of the new workers were married, 60 percent of them were over thirty-five years of age, many of them were the mothers of school-age children. Despite recommendations from the Women's Bureau, precious little was done to ease the domestic burdens of these workers. The federal government appropriated only 1.5 million dollars to establish day-care facilities, a sum adequate to care for only about one in ten of the children of war workers. Only one in ten of the war production centers had any such facilities. [11] Similarly, the housekeeping assistance, public kitchens, and family services called for by the Women's Bureau were never forthcoming. The tacit assumption was that women could shoulder an extra burden on behalf of their country in time of crisis. [12] This was certainly the construction that advertisers placed on woman's role during the war. A lipstick manufacturer asked, "Doing Double Duty?" while another company recommended a hand cream for women "leading a double life."

Even those women who were not part of the mass movement into the labor force found their domestic duties compounded during World War II. Curtailment of the production of consumer goods, along with government rationing programs, interrupted the trend toward streamlined housekeeping. "The kitchen and the sewing room," said Uncle Sam, were "the housewife's battleground." In addition to canning and preserving foods and fashioning the family wardrobe, the patriotic wife and mother could plant victory gardens and salvage metal and newspapers. Whatever time remained could be devoted to voluntary work for the Allies' cause. Like the home and the job, the voluntary association was laced with gender stereotypes. Women served as clerical workers, not air-raid wardens, as door-to-door fundraisers, not the officers of patriotic civic organizations. [13]

Wherever and whenever women were needed—in the labor force, at home, or in voluntary service—the recruitment technique seemed the same: to trot out a string of feminine stereotypes. As a consequence, gender dichotomies assumed a larger role in American culture than in decades past. Soldiering, after all, was an archetypal expression of masculinity. The essence of femininity— reproduction and mothering—was also given special attention during World War II. In hopes of enhancing the demographic advantage of democracy, American women were enlisted in a "baby war against Hitler" and congratulated for their increased fertility during wartime.[14] At the same time the more sexual images of womanhood typical of the 1920s were toned down during the '40s, as patriots sternly condemned promiscuous "Victory girls."[15] All in all, the war brought male and female into sharper ideological relief than in decades past. The feminine side of the gender dichotomy, furthermore, was infused with especially potent images of domesticity.

THE FEMININE MYSTIQUE
AS DOMESTIC INTERLUDE

The partisans of domesticity had to surmount many obstacles before they won cultural hegemony after World War II. The early twentieth century heard cries of alarm that the home was in peril and iconoclastic assertions that "home is but a place to dine and die in." Social commentators in the 1920s took note of the rising divorce rate and wondered if monogamous marriage was a viable institution in the modern world. Sociologists cataloged a long list of social and economic functions that could now be performed outside the home: economic production, early childhood education, the recreation of family members, the inculcation of national values. Yet in the face of this skepticism, social scientists set to work to pick up the pieces of the nineteenth-century family and build a "finer, more plastic form, one which will respond more fully to the sensitive and imperative needs of the modern human being."[16]

By the 1940s their success was emblazoned across textbooks on the sociology of the family: "MARRIAGE IS A FUNDAMENTAL HUMAN NEED."[17] This need was tersely defined for high-school readers: "The family will always be necessary to give emotional stability, care and social acceptance to the child. It is the only group in which can be developed love, kindness and the enduring relations of life."[18] A young woman interviewed by the *Ladies' Home Journal* attempted to explain this growing identification between the family and all that was warm, secure, and human: "The depression or something, somehow, made human relations important again," and the war illustrated that "the only security I can count on now is emotional security."[19]

The legacy of insecurity left by the depression and World War II encouraged a turning inward toward the family for personal support and stability. One study indicated that those adolescents who experienced the most domestic disruption during the depression were also the most enthusiastic participants in the domestic revival that followed. Half of these depression daughters had become mothers by the age of twenty-four.[20] Yet the American home was also responsive to the larger sweep of social history, at a time when change had become commonplace and when public services, social needs, culture, and recreation, as well as economic relations, were increasingly installed in cold and rigid institutions. The twentieth century accelerated the privatization of the family and extended it beyond the middle class. Consequently, the psychological functions of the family, if not its social tasks, were compounded. A new definition of the home was constructed out of an absorption of all emotional satisfaction into the private sanctums, leaving the rest of society impersonal and foreboding.

The line between home and society was most tautly drawn in the social theory of Talcott Parsons.[21] According to Parsons, the family was merely a "subsystem of society" whose social strength was in its smallness and isolation. The essential function performed within the narrow, insulated sphere of the nuclear family, he maintained, was the socialization of children and the control of tension for adults. The domestic unit was an emotional refuge in a bureaucratized and routinized society. In short, the family was defined by opposition to modern societal organization, further removed from the outside world than ever before. By contrast, the nineteenth-century concept of the family allowed for the overflow of domestic values into society at large, and, in fact, many women disguised as social mothers succeeded in escaping the home via that outward-bound emotional current. Parsons, in contrast, defined the twentieth-century family as a completely privatized social unit, whose specialized functions served society only by remaining cloistered from it.

This influential theory, regardless of its accuracy as a description of actual family life in postwar America, provided the foundation for another stark dichotomy between male and female roles. It decreed that it was man's role to represent the family in society and woman's to direct the emotional and psychological functions of the home. Man's function was "instrumental"; it required the ability to earn a living, compete with other men, deal efficiently and rationally with people and things. Woman's home function was "expressive" in nature; it called forth her aptitude for divining personal needs, supplying emotional support, and monitoring interpersonal relationships. The new family system dictated that women socialize children but leave their education to schools, and soothe weary husbands but never interfere in their business affairs. The prescribed female role was more rarefied than ever, an unadulterated emotional and psychological emanation denoted by the term intimacy.

In the pages of the women's magazines these sociological postulates were transposed into a jaunty medley of feminine aphorisms. A sample of the titles and captions which Betty Friedan culled from the magazines of 1949 spells out the homely details of woman's expressive function. The division of the world by sex was put simply: "Truly a Man's World, Politics" and "Femininity Begins at Home." A model female life cycle could also be reconstructed from the catchy phrases of the magazines. It would go something like this:

"How to Snare a Man"

"Don't Be Afraid to Marry Young"

"Should I Stop Work When I Marry?"

"Have Babies While You're Young"

"Birth: The Crowning Moment of My Life"

"I Will Have Another Baby. I Must Live that Divine Experience Again."

"Give Us Back the Victorian Mothers of Seven to Ten Children."

The female who followed this prescription for womanhood would find the prime of her life absorbed in reproduction. The 1949 model even provided for the perpetuation of femininity into another generation: "Are you training your daughter to be a wife?"[22]

The ladies' magazines were hardly alone in glorifying maternity. Even before war's end women were advised to "Correct the mistakes of the 1920s and '30s" and increase the American birth rate. Television came to the aid of ladies' magazines and demographers in the fertility campaign of the 1950s. In 1953, as two-thirds of the TV audience watched from their living rooms, the drama of pregnancy unfolded on the "I Love Lucy Show." Then uncannily in the same week that the long-awaited birth flashed across the TV screen, Lucille Ball herself brought her first child into the world.[23] The rites of motherhood were performed almost everywhere in the 1940s and '50s, as women marched in and out of the labor force.

The conception of maternity which was placed at the cornerstone of the feminine mystique had a natural, atavistic, almost primitive quality about it. As Betty Friedan put it, "This femininity is mysterious and intuitive and so close to creation and the origins of life that man-made science may never be able to understand it." While true womanhood, '50s style, was construed as too exotic to conform to the rules of empirical and behavioralist science, it was not spared the supervision of experts and professionals. From the field of psychology and Freudian psychoanalysis especially, came a stream of specialists who set themselves up as the chief theorists of the new sexual dimorphism.

Freud himself had belatedly turned his attention to the psychology of women and announced his observations with a certain tentativeness. Nonetheless, he bequeathed to his disciples some notions that could be read as justifications of sexual inequality. By making the male and female genitals the center of his theory of psychic development, he divided human personality according to sex more fundamentally than ever before. Now even the unconscious was ridden with gender differences. The female psyche as depicted by the Freudians was a rather hasty creation, constructed largely by adapting the sequence of infant sexual development originally formulated for males. In her most vulgar guise, the Freudian female was a castrated male, hence fundamentally crippled and destined to a life of envy and subordination before those equipped with penises. Convinced of the inferiority of her small clitoris and therefore hopeless of possessing her mother, her first love object, the Freudian female adopted a vicarious psychic posture, choosing to live through the superior male, receiving his penis, bearing his children.

Freudian doctrine regarding the psychology of women did not become fully developed, nor widely circulated in the United States, until the 1940s. Its emergence as a theoretical bulwark of the feminine mystique was largely the work of women writers and analysts. Conducting the most sophisticated level of exigesis were Freud's own disciples, among them Helene Deutsch and Marie Bonaparte. They were joined by virtuoso popularizers such as Marynia Farnham and Marie Robinson. While there were Freudians who identified the misogynist implications of the developing female psychology (most notably Clara Thompson and Karen Horney, who challenged the biological determinism of doctrines like penis envy),[24] no one successfully transcended the entrenched gender differentiation which psychoanalysis grafted upon the theory of human personality.

One of the most immediate effects of the Freudian dogma was to create a confusing picture of female sexuality and to dispel the naive expectations of fulfillment typical of the flapper era. The genital traumas of infancy, it was contended, caused a little girl to reject the pleasure originally found in her clitoris, now judged an inferior organ by contrast with the male's penis. When in adulthood the normal female reclaimed her sexuality, according to the Freudians, sensitivity would be transferred to the vagina, now valued as the receptacle of the enviable penis. Marie Bonaparte derided those women who failed to transfer their sexuality to the vagina in a most condescending fashion: They acted "as though the clitoris were not an organ forever condemned to be inadequate, but, like the boy's would continue to grow."[25] By 1959 Marie Robinson refused to recognize the erotic nature of the clitoris: the woman who reached orgasm via the clitoris was purely and simply frigid.[26]

The Freudian psychologists refused to modify their theories to conform to the mundane realities of biology. Ordinary physicians like Robert Dickinson reported that the sexual feelings of his patients centered in the vulva and around the clitoris, and that he knew of very few cases of "exclusively vaginal orgasm."[27] Similarly, 84 percent of the women interviewed for the Kinsey report achieved orgasm through manual friction against the clitoris or labia minora. Furthermore, half of these women suffered anxiety regarding masturbation, having been informed by the Freudians that it would diminish the proper vaginal sensitivity. Kinsey set their minds at ease, explaining that "actually the vagina in most females is quite devoid of end organs of touch. It is incapable of responding to tactile stimulation, and the areas primarily involved in the female's sensory responses during coitus are exactly those which are primarily involved in masturbation, namely the clitoris and the labia."[28] It was not that the Freudians read different biological textbooks; Marie Bonaparte readily admitted that "the vaginal mucosae are almost insensitive; they barely feel heat or cold or pain. . . . Nevertheless, it is in the vagina itself, and more or less distant from the entrance, according to the individual, that for the functionally adapted and adult woman true erotic sensitivity dwells."[29]

Clearly, more than anatomical distinctions and sexual practices were at stake here. Simply physical pleasure was considered secondary to the development of the "normal" female personality— "true," "adult," and "functionally adapted." Helene Deutsch minced no words. She decreed that sexual pleasure was healthy "only under the condition that it is experienced in a feminine, dynamic way and is not transformed into an act of erotic play or sexual equality."[30] In Deutsch's multi-volume catechism of female psychology, sexuality was dissociated from the vulgar "play" and attached to the serious business of maintaining stark differences between the sexes. She wrote: "I have defined as characteristic of the feminine woman a harmonious interplay between narcissistic tenderness and masochistic readiness for painful giving and loving."[31] Marie Bonaparte described the "true woman" as "normal, vaginal, and maternal" and made frequent reference to the virtues of narcissism and masochism.[32] This new jargon refined the old-fashioned stereotype of the passive, retiring, home-bound woman, and rewarded conformity to its tenets with promises of sexual fulfillment. This crudely Freudian interpretation of the psychology of woman penetrated deeply into popular culture after World War II, when, in keeping with the "feminine mystique," it celebrated a domesticated version of female sexuality that was unadulterated by the emancipating qualities of the '20s.

First of all, the popular psychologists used Freudian sexology to reinforce the tattered cliché of feminine passivity. Deutsch contended that "the role of everything female, from the ovum to the beloved, is a waiting one. The vagina must await the advent of the penis in the same passive, latent and dormant manner that the ovum awaits the sperm."[33] Post-World War II popularizations of Deutsch, like Ferdinand Lundberg and Marynia Farnham's *Modern Woman: The Lost Sex*, gave particular attention to the passivity of woman during sexual encounters. Lundberg and Farnham employed the ludicrous but revealing metaphors typical of sex manuals to describe woman's role during intercourse. "It is not as easy as rolling off a log for her. It is easier. It is as easy as being the log itself. She cannot fail to deliver a masterly performance by doing nothing whatsoever except being duly appreciative and allowing nature to take its course."[34]

Despite this injunction to remain passive, women were held entirely responsible for their own frigidity, according to Marie Robinson, who disparaged blaming the male or resorting to new sexual techniques to reach orgasm. Frigidity resulted, she maintained, from the woman's refusal to accept "the passive attitude which nature demands of her in the male embrace." The only avenue of pleasure was the "power of sexual surrender" (a very curious mode of potency). A woman's sexual responsiveness at the same time should be instantaneous and persistent. According to Robinson's scenario of feminine perfection, "when her husband is ready to make love our lady is nearly always willing . . . and she is always willing to forego love-making if he is not ready."[35]

Such passive compliance meshed nicely with other central feminine characteristics: narcissism and masochism. If woman's satisfaction came from submitting to a man's lust, she would crave his advances primarily as testimony to her own sexual desirability, a narcissistic mode of pleasure. Accordingly, Robinson built a high degree of personal vanity into the female personality. The normal woman was "quite a show-off and likes sexual compliments from her husband dressed or undressed."[36] In Deutsch's more sophisticated paradigm, the principle of narcissism was expressed as follows: "In the sexual act her partner's elemental desire gratifies her self-love and helps her to accept masochistic pleasure without damaging her ego."[37] Having outlawed direct stimulation of the clitoris and after asking women to submit to each and every sexual request of the husband, it logically followed that Deutsch would associate female sexuality with masochism. These psychologists of sex commonly attached suggestions of violence to the penetration of the penis. Deutsch referred to the female role in intercourse as a "dangerous and painful giving."[38] Both she and Marie Bonaparte on occasion equated female sexual experience with rape. According to Bonaparte, a woman's psychic structure "impels her to welcome and to value some measure of brutality on the male's part." These apparently contradictory characteristics, narcissism and masochism, somehow transformed physical pain into psychological pleasure.

This sophistry was described by Bonaparte as follows: "Though penetration of her body will be wounding, what matter to one who is loved. The pain she feels will become yearned for pleasure and feminine masochism then reaches its heights."[39]

The ultimate expression of feminine narcissism and masochism was found not in sexual intercourse but in woman's reproductive role. According to the psychoanalysis of woman, the perfect narcissistic gratification came with the creation of another self through pregnancy; and the greatest masochistic test was the ordeal of childbirth. Bonaparte cavalierly dismissed the pain of parturition as she scoffed: "Childbirth will imply the peril of death? Who bothers about that in love's realm?"[40] Deutsch valued the pain of childbirth so highly that she suspected that the use of anesthetics was "a masterpiece of masculine efficiency designed to rob women of masochistic satisfaction."[41] Thus maternity became the ultimate fulfillment of female sexuality. In fact, Deutsch went so far as to reduce the woman's sexual desire to a maternal urge. "In the normal healthy woman coitus psychologically represents the first act of motherhood."[42] During the postwar baby boom popular writers on female sexuality delighted in propagating this interpretation of female sexuality. Farnham and Lundberg told women in 1947 that "in proportion as she inwardly rejects the idea of receiving the seed—that is of being impregnated—she fails to attain full sexual pleasure from the sex act."[43] Marie Robinson went on to say that the ideally adjusted woman unconsciously fantasized pregnancy with every act of coitus, and the hope of impregnation of itself kindled sexual desire.[44]

Thus, by the 1950s, by way of the Freudian psychology of sex, the female stereotype had completed another cycle. Women were directed right back to where they had been a century earlier—in the captivity of the cult of motherhood. All the sophisticated involutions of clinical and popular psychoanalysis only served to direct the American woman back to familiar roles, exiled her not only to the bedroom and the maternity ward, but to the kitchen, nursery, and dressing table. Deutsch dismissed working mothers as a "war evil," and in the course of psychiatric practice Marie Robinson sent doctors, lawyers, businesswomen, and academics back to the home to recapture their femininity. In addition to her domestic duties, the sex-conscious woman of the twentieth century was obliged to devote special care to physical attractiveness, to dote over her appearance and assiduously cultivate a seductive image. The psychosexual imperative only slightly updated the doctrine of separate spheres, temperaments, and roles for the sexes. The psychology of sex rendered the policy of separate and unequal as follows: "The really fundamental difference between man and woman is that he can usually give his best as a creator and she as a lover; that his nature is according to his work and hers according to her love."[45] Under the guise of achieving sexual fulfillment, women were sent to work molding their personalities into replicas of a familiar stereotype.

Few women were aware of the fine points of female psychology, and even fewer were convinced by its casuistry and willing to comply with its impossible dictates. Still, the rise of psychology had set up an important new relationship in the history of womanhood. The profession of psychotherapy, first of all, took women as its prime client class. In the suburbs of the 1950s, wives and mothers were the most frequent visitors to therapists and the most likely to be consigned to mental institutions. These women became personal captives of a profession schooled in the pernicious psychology of sex: Deutsch's two-volume opus was the bible of psychologists of women, while the doctrine of the vaginal orgasm had been written into basic gynecological texts and taught in medical schools. Second, the general tenets of this female psychology reached a mass middle-class audience through popular literary sources. They were propagated by ladies' magazines and popular paperbacks, such as Marie Robinson's *The Power of Sexual Surrender*, which sold more than a million copies. In sum, psychologists had become the high priests of womanhood in the twentieth century; their professional status granted them access to the private lives of their clients and thus permitted them to intervene even in the unconscious.

THE DEMOGRAPHIC FOUNDATION OF THE FEMININE MYSTIQUE

For a doctrine of femininity to become so elaborate and so widely touted, it had to have some grounding in the everyday realities of women's lives. The social foundation of the feminine mystique was very broad and substantial, indeed: the birth of no less than 76 million children in less than twenty years. The American birthrate began to rise sharply during the second world war, reached a peak in 1957, and did not begin its decline to prewar levels until 1964. These were the years of the great baby boom that mystified demographers and drove fertility rates upward after well over a century of steady decline. By 1960 the fertility rate stood at 3.52 children per woman, in contrast to the streamlined figure of 2.10 twenty years before. On the average the women of the '40s and '50s were bearing more children than had their mothers, sometimes even their grandmothers.[46] It had also become increasingly rare for women to remain completely childless. Whereas 180 of every 1000 white women born in 1900 would not reproduce themselves, only 6 percent of the women who came of age in the late '40s and '50s would remain childless.[47] There were more mothers and they were having more offspring, typically three rather than two children. A larger proportion of the female population had assumed the role of mother than at any other time in American history.

This demographic fact became the foundation for the social and geographical structuring of the feminine mystique. The young mothers of America claimed a turf all their own in the rapidly growing suburbs. By 1960 these residential areas on the outskirts of major cities harbored a larger portion of the nation's population than did the metropolis, the small town, or the countryside. The movement to the suburbs, which had been gaining strength since the turn of the century, reached gigantic proportions between 1950 and 1970. Suburban population doubled in those two decades and reached the sum of 72 million people. When questioned, the vast majority of migrants agreed that they left the city in order to locate in an environment better suited to child-rearing.

The postwar suburbs differed from other localities not just in the income, race, or ethnicity of their residents, but in family characteristics as well. The average suburbanite was a member of a young and growing family. The suburban woman bore more children than a city dweller and was far less likely to enroll in the labor force. In 1953, when 27 percent of all American women were employed outside the home, only 9 percent of suburban women held jobs.[48] An Ohio developer had the domestic identity of the suburb inscribed on a monument in the center of one new town: "To the wage-earners and the homemakers—the families of the American Home. They are the Americans for whom Forest Park is planned and gratefully dedicated." The initial plans for the suburban developments of the '50s were blueprints for an exclusively domestic existence. Miles and miles of single-family homes were erected before any consideration was given to shops, schools, churches, or public buildings of any sort. The suburbs were devoted to the immediate reproductive concerns of young families.[49]

Along with the baby boom, this spatial concentration of reproduction buttressed a third material foundation of the feminine mystique, a massive economic investment in domesticity. The suburban developers par excellence, Abraham Levitt and Sons, swiftly made $5 million by mass producing suburban homes. Such profits of domesticity fed vigorous economic growth as suburban homes were filled with refrigerators, washing machines, and television sets. Even before the end of the war a domesticated female consciousness was cultivated as a spur to increased sales of consumer goods. Advertisements for U.S. war bonds, for example, pictured young women dreaming of the shiny mechanized kitchen they could purchase with their savings at the close of hostilities.

By the 1950s the domestic aspirations of women had become the driving force of unprecedented expansion of the consumer sector of the economy. In 1952–53, *Fortune* magazine pinned the success of American business on the fact that more "nubile females are marrying than ever before." The market researchers at *Fortune* estimated that the young wives and mothers of the '50s could be counted on to incite $10 billion worth of home construction and expend $60 billion on food, $30 billion on family recreation, and $12 billion on home furnishings and appliances.[50] When economic growth began to slow down during the recession of 1957, market researchers relied once again on woman's domestic impulses to prime the pump. *Life* magazine crowded three dozen babies on their cover along with the caption "KIDS—Built-in Recession Cure—How four million a year make millions in business."[51]

The architects of the domestic revival were assisted by the government as well as cajoled by advertisers and the private sector. Precedents for government subsidies to domesticity were established during the New Deal when the Federal Housing Authority was established to save homeowners from foreclosure and provide low-cost, long-term mortgages. President Harry Truman promised continuing governmental support for domesticity in 1948 with a characteristically homespun pronouncement: "Children and dogs are as necessary to the welfare of the country as is Wall Street and the railroads." The housing act of 1949 was aimed explicitly at fostering domesticity. "The realization as soon as feasible of the goal of a decent home and suitable living environment for every American family." Boosted by FHA loans, and even more generous housing subsidies offered to returning veterans, American home ownership rose by 30 percent between 1940 and 1970. Government subsidies—for single-family suburban houses, for the freeways which routed men out of the domestic enclaves into urban jobs, for the GI bill which enhanced the education and earning power of males— not only sponsored domesticity but gave it a distinctive gender-cast as they constructed an isolated family space for women and children.[52]

Once the domestic and suburban stage had been set, American women went frantically to work. One young woman recounted a day in the life of the '50s wife and mother with exhausting detail.

> I get up at 6 A.M. and put on coffee and cereal for breakfast and go down to the basement to put clothes into the washing machine. When I come up I dress Teddy (1½) and put him in his chair. Then I dress Jim (3½) and serve breakfast to him and to my husband and feed Teddy.
>
> While my husband looks after the children I go down to get the clothes out of the machine and hang them on the line. Then I come up and have my own breakfast after my husband leaves. From then on the day is as follows:
>
> Breakfast dishes, clean up kitchen. Make beds, clean the apartment. Wipe up bathroom and kitchen floor. Get lunch vegetable ready and put potatoes on to bake for lunch. Do my food shopping and stay out with children till 12. Return and undress children, wash them up for lunch, prepare lunch, feed Teddy and put him to nap. Make own lunch, wash dishes, straighten up kitchen. Put Jim to rest. Between 1 and 2:30, depending on the day of the week, ironing (I do my husband's shirts home and, of course, all the children's and my own clothes), thorough cleaning of one room, weekend cooking and baking, etc.; 3 P.M., give children juice or milk, put outdoor clothes on. Out to park; 4:30, back. Give children their baths. Prepare their supper. Husband usually home to play with them a little after supper and help put them to bed. Make dinner for husband and myself. After dinner, dishes and cleaning up.

After 8 P.M. often more ironing, especially on the days when I cleaned in the afternoon. There is mending to be done; 9 P.M., fall asleep in the living room over a newspaper or listening to the sound of the radio; 10 P.M., have a snack of something with my husband and go to bed.

I read this account to my husband and he said that it sounded too peaceful, that the children seem to keep out of the way too much. I haven't conveyed to you at all the strain of being constantly with the children for twelve hours a day, day in day out.[53]

This harassed housewife was caught in the quagmire of baby-boom demographics: the short spaces between her births and her isolated domestic residence made her the lonely caretaker of two demanding toddlers.

As her children grew older the burdens of the suburban mother diminished, but hardly disappeared. The proliferation of automatic gadgets, miracle cleaning potions, and instant food products served primarily to clutter up the household and compound woman's chores. Despite the advances in domestic technology, the amount of time women spent doing housework actually increased slightly between the 1920s and 1960, from 52 to 54 hours a week on the average.[54] Some inventions actually created new jobs within the home. The washing machine, for example, brought back into the household an onerous job that often had been delegated to commercial laundries at the turn of the century. Enlarged wardrobes and higher standards of cleanliness further expanded this mode of domestic labor and this arm of the consumer economy specializing in appliances, miracle fabrics, and detergents.

In addition, as Betty Friedan discovered, the packaged foods of the '50s were advertised as a means of making cooking more elaborate and demanding rather than simplifying the homemaker's job. Just purchasing all these home products was a job in itself, consuming ten hours a week by 1960, up 100 percent from the 1920s. Cake mixes were to be used "creatively," given a "personal touch," so as to expiate the "underlying guilt" of the housewife who cut corners.[55] Cooking could, and should, be made into a complicated art, according to Lynn White, president of Mills College. White asked college women: "Why not study the theory and preparation of a Basque paella, or a well-marinated shish kebob, lamb kidney sautéed in sherry, an authoritative curry?"[56] In 1961, *The New York Times* looked forward to the development of computerized home-making, but not because it would liberate women from housework. On the contrary, "the computer would free a woman to spend her day preparing an exotic evening meal at which many foods would be tasted and consumed over a three-hour period."[57]

These soaring standards of homemaking, however, were only peripheral demands on the housewife's time. The stellar image in the kaleidoscope of woman's roles was maternal. By the 1950s, the ladies' magazines were proclaiming "motherhood is a way of life." The housewives interviewed by one sociologist ranked motherhood as their most important role; one of them confessed, "it's been my whole life." In point of fact, the amount of time housewives devoted to child care more than doubled between the 1920s and the 1960s.[58]

Motherhood, like the family, had survived the skepticism of feminists, flappers, and social theorists early in the twentieth century and rose triumphant from the tests of depression and world war. Not only were childbearing and rearing granted a position of special honor in wartime and postwar culture, but mothering became the cornerstone of proper child development.

By 1940 Dr. Arnold Gesell had revamped child-rearing theory, contradicted John Watson, and laid the groundwork for Benjamin Spock. During the throes of the depression and World War II, Gesell and his disciples became convinced that the human personality needed an atmosphere of warmth, intimacy, and trust in which to develop. The mother was called upon to provide this environment for the young child. Breastfeeding was once again in vogue, invoked in order to "strengthen the bonds between mother and child." In order to establish an infant's sense of trust, the mother was expected to be immediately responsive to her child's cry for nourishment. Feeding according to a child's demands replaced the schedule imposed by behavioralists; the infant was now the dictator of the mother's routine.[59] Helene Deutsch interpreted demand feeding so as to discourage mothers from working outside the home. She knew, she said, of working mothers who arranged somehow or other to be "ready exactly at the minute to give suck to their babies. But these modern sucklings! They do not like punctuality and at the mother's slightest gesture of impatience, her furtive glance at the clock for instance, they react as if she were as wicked as a she-wolf."[60] The mother's undivided loving attention was considered essential to emotional security in infancy, when the foundation of a healthy personality was laid.

After infancy, however, a child's development proceeded to the stages sometimes labeled autonomy or initiative. The mother's task from this point on was to gradually release her child to the world. Gesell advised an hour a day at nursery school for a child of eighteen months. The mother should take particular care to encourage her child's independence between the ages of three and five and see him or her past the crises of the Oedipal stage. Excessive maternal attention from this point on suggested overprotectiveness and a domineering mother. Still, the female parent should always be there as a reliable source of warmth and love for her growing child. The expert mother was asked to walk a fine line between coldness and excessive warmth, between negligence and possessiveness.

The mother of the postwar era, who might well be reeling with the drastic change in philosophies from the behavioralist to the developmental scheme of child care, and dizzy from trying to convey trust and encourage independence at one and the same time, found a sympathetic guide in Dr. Benjamin Spock. His tome on baby care, which was first issued in 1946 and eventually sold more than 20 million copies, opened with fatherly reassurance. "Don't be afraid to trust your own common sense. Bringing up your child won't be a complicated job if you take it easy, trust your instincts and follow the directions your doctor gives you." Spock then went on to celebrate the central feature of the postwar child-rearing ideology, mother love: "We know for a fact that the natural loving care that kindly parents give their children is a thousand times more valuable than their knowing how to pin a diaper on just right or how to make formula expertly."[61]

Spock's use of the word "parents" in his introduction is deceptive. His actual instructions on the loving care of children were addressed to mothers. Only a few paragraphs in more than 600 pages spoke to the duties of fathers. He went only so far as to say that the father might "occasionally" give the baby a bottle or change its diapers. Then he added this proviso: "Some fathers get gooseflesh at the very idea of helping to take care of a baby and there is no good to be gained by trying to force them. Most of them come around to enjoying the children later, *when they're more like real people*" (italics mine).[62] One inference to be drawn from Spock's words is that the mother's role, like her most intimate companion, was somehow juvenile and subhuman.

Arnold Gesell had set the stage for this reduction of the mother to the child's level. The ideal mother, he said, "instead of striving for executive efficiency . . . aims first of all to be perceptive of and sensitive to the child's behavior. Thus she becomes a true complement to him, alertly responsive to his needs."[63] Spock expressed this maternal duty in more homely phrases: "Don't be afraid to love him and enjoy him. Every baby needs to be smiled at, talked to, played with, fondled—gently and lovingly." The developmental approach required that a mother participate in the mental life of her child, indulge in baby talk, play childhood games, and perform the most menial tasks with childlike zest. Spock quoted one woman who seemed to have accomplished this feat. She triumphantly reported that she had toilet trained her child and "it seems to have brought us closer together. It's as if we'd found a new trust in each other."[64]

Benjamin Spock was very much aware that motherhood entailed more than a series of such edifying episodes. He told mothers to expect postnatal depression, periods of nervousness, and frequent physical exhaustion. When the strain of motherhood became overwhelming, Dr. Spock prescribed a properly feminine cure: "Go to a movie or to the beauty parlor, or to get a new hat or dress." Taking a job outside the home, on the other hand, was not advisable. Spock allowed that some mothers could not be deterred from seeking a job, but he made sure that they would leave the home with a guilty conscience: "If a mother realized clearly how vital [her love and care] is to a small child, it may make it easier to decide that the extra money she might earn, or the satisfaction she might receive from an outside job, is not so important after all." After the child reached school age, the prohibitions against a mother's working were relaxed, provided she could be at home when her offspring returned from school.[65] Thus the directives of the child-rearing theorists seemed to mesh neatly with the demands of the female labor market. They encouraged women to seek employment outside the home after the interruption of child-rearing, when they were preoccupied with family affairs and consequently well suited for and satisfied with low-paying, low-status part-time jobs.

Furthermore, the length of the interruption in the typical woman's working life was prolonged to at least a decade during the baby boom, which began in World War II and extended up to 1960. In this era, middle-class white women were typically bearing three to four children, a fertility rate that often exceeded that of their parents or even grandparents. Some commentators urged women to be even more prolific. Helene Deutsch was afraid that once the children left home a woman's narcissistic psyche would be irreparably damaged. In order to prevent this disaster she opined that "probably the path traced by nature is the most successful: having many children is the best protection against this tragic loss."[66] Farnham and Lundberg placed no maximum limit on the number of children women should bear, and in fact urged the federal government to award prizes to women for the birth of every child beyond her first. The consequences of such fecundity, a population explosion, was a problem that "would have to be solved by some future generation."[67]

Child-rearing experts like Dr. Spock were more concerned that future generations would perpetuate the appropriate sex roles. Spock's use of the pronoun *he* to designate all children was quite apt, for the chief goal of developmental child-rearing, the production of adults who were "systematic," "independent," and trained to "orderly ways of doing business," was designed for males. The girl child received special attention primarily on those occasions when Spock expounded on the importance of inculcating sex roles at an early age. He hoped that the female child would "realize that it is her destiny to be a woman" at least by age three and urged that a boy who continued to play with dolls much beyond that age should be sent to a psychiatrist.

Both mothers and fathers were admonished to present themselves as stereotypical models of masculinity and femininity for their children to imitate. In order to prepare the preschool girl "for her adult role in life," a father was told to "compliment her on her dress or hairdo or the cookies she made." The little girl's relationship with her father would determine "the way she makes friendships with boys and men later on, the kind of man she eventually falls in love with." Meanwhile, a boy's adoration of his perfectly feminine mother will lead him to "protect, please, and idolize" his wife someday. The constant and exclusive exposure of the young child to two adult models, a mother and father who represented the sharp dichotomy between male and female roles, masculine and feminine character, was conducive to the propagation of another generation of sexual stereotypes.[68]

While suburban women were absorbed with mothering, their husbands labored a world and a long commute away. A study of Westchester County, New York, in the 1930s illustrated the effect that commuter living was to have on conjugal unity. The wives of Westchester not only spent their working hours in the home, but 56 to 65 percent of their leisure time as well. The typical husband, meanwhile, with more leisure time than his wife, spent only half of it at home.[69] Sociologists who made field trips to the suburbs after World War II encountered a world of women. When a researcher succeeded in finding a husband to interview, the ensuing conversation would not be rich in domestic detail: "I'm home so little, I only see the kids for an hour in the evening, that is if I'm not going off to a meeting."[70]

The ladies' magazines of the '50s read the weak pulse of family intimacy with alarm. McCall's inaugurated a campaign for togetherness, and the Ladies' Home Journal provided a regular feature to remind its readers that "There's a Man in the House." Families were urged to devote weekends to remedial programs in family recreation and ritual enactments of fatherhood such as the backyard barbecue. Helen Lopata's investigations at the end of the decade, however, revealed that most wives had quietly discarded the goal of marital intimacy. The women she interviewed seldom spoke spontaneously of their husbands, and when asked to rank their most gratifying roles, only 8 percent attested that they found the most satisfaction in their relationship with their husbands.[71]

In point of fact then, few couples fulfilled the emotional and social stipulations of the heterosexual imperative. The suburbs remained sex-segregated social space for most of the daylight hours. In fact, whatever community activities transpired there, most of which centered around the school and the Parent Teacher Association, were likely to be an extension of woman's sphere and culture, prompting one sociologist to label the suburbs "maternal families." The twentieth-century suburb, then, created as bold a division of space by sex as could be found in the nineteenth century.[72]

There was at least one critical difference between the Victorian separation of the spheres and the gender differentiation enshrined in the feminine mystique. And that distinction contradicted the domestic conception of womanhood itself, making the mystique a kind of demographic mirage. The equation of domesticity with womanhood was undermined by the demographic causes of the baby boom itself.

The dramatic increase in the number of births between 1946 and 1964 was produced by three distinct demographic processes. The first source of the boom was births to couples who had postponed starting a family during depression and war. Added to these births were conceptions among young women who married and bore their children earlier in life than had their mothers. Finally, the birthrate was inflated by the fact that the typical woman would bear three children rather than conforming to the previous norm among the middle class of a two-child family. This was hardly profligate reproduction. Furthermore, demographic investigators have discovered that many of these third children were unplanned and unanticipated, if not entirely unwelcome. They were often caused by contraceptive failures in the days before the birth control pill and legalized abortion. The baby boom, in sum, was as much a product of unique demographic conditions as it was a mass reconversion to the notion that mothering was woman's central, all-absorbing mission in life. Still, the sheer number of births during the 1950s and 1960s was enough to sustain suburban growth, a mass market for domestic goods, and a cultural preoccupation with maternity, all at least for the time being.[73]

The demographics of the baby boom did, however, place finite time limits on the postwar domestic revival. The birthrate began to subside in 1957, and by 1965 fell below 4 million annually for the first time in a decade. Well before this time many baby-boom mothers had turned their attention away from full-time mothering. Because the women of the era tended to bear their first children at very young ages (at 21.4 on the average in 1957), spaced births closely together, and seldom bore more than three children, they ended their reproductive cycle relatively early in life. For example, of those women born in the twenties, and rearing children in the 1940s and '50s, the average age at last birth was a mere 30.5 years.[74] Before these women reached middle age, their offspring were in school and becoming more and more self-sufficient. Even Dr. Spock had granted his imprimatur to mothers who sought part-time employment as their children grew older. And as early as 1958 sociologists observed, with some concern, that the mothers of the suburbs were leaving their homes to enter the job market. The veil of domesticity was slowly falling away from the womanhood of the twentieth century.[75]

THE EXPANSION OF
THE FEMALE LABOR FORCE

Throughout the postwar period, economic conditions were quietly seducing wives and mothers out of their familial nests. The same postwar prosperity that sustained suburban domesticity also expanded the job possibilities for women workers. The tertiary sector of the labor force, which had been relying on low-cost female labor since the turn of the century, was the most rapidly growing component of the American economy. While employment in manufacturing increased 16 percent between 1948 and 1963, the service sector grew a walloping 53 percent. By 1960 the tertiary sector, which included government, trade, finance, health, transportation, recreation, research, and education, accounted for 56.6 percent of the nation's jobs. Three out of four women workers found their home-away-from-home there.[76]

The demands for female labor in the paid work force were but one element of a major shift in the organization of both production and social reproduction. First of all, the postwar period had accelerated the dispersal of many former household functions into the marketplace and the public sector. The keeping of boarders, the care of the elderly, the cultivation of backyard gardens, and domestic piecework had all but disappeared from the home after the 1930s. Second, as these social services and productive activities were transferred into the market economy or government sector, they created a demand for additional workers, a demand too large to be met by the existing supply of adult men and unmarried women. Accordingly, married women often entered the labor force to perform tasks that had once been the jurisdiction of the unpaid housewife. The fireside nurse became a hospital employee; the caretaker of an aging parent became a clerk for the social security administration; the lady bountiful became a professional social worker. In addition, the increasing portion of the economy devoted to information and communication created unprecedented demands for clerical work of all sorts, another segment of the work force which relied on female labor.

This urgent need for more women workers forced employers to override their prejudices against hiring married women. The increased demand for workers during World War II and in the postwar economy coincided with a decreasing availability of young, single workers. As a consequence of the low birthrate during the '20s and the depression, the generation of women reaching working age was an especially small one. As if to make things more difficult for employers, these women, encouraged by postwar prosperity, married and began families earlier than ever before. In the 1950s, less than 20 percent of American women fourteen years of age and over were single; their ranks were clearly insufficient to meet the demand for female labor. In addition, approximately 60 percent of the married women were mothers of children under eighteen. The businessmen of America had no alternative but to recruit wives and mothers as workers. Uncle Sam himself stood quietly behind the scenes, prompting married women to go off to work. A White House Conference on Effective Uses of Woman-Power was convened in 1955 to hear speaker after speaker express concern about the underutilization of women's capacity to work outside the home.[77]

American women welcomed this economic opportunity; between 1940 and 1960 the number of working wives doubled and the number of working mothers quadrupled. By the late 1960s the majority of female workers were married, and almost 40 percent of the mothers with children between the ages of six and seventeen held jobs. The typical workingwoman was over forty years of age, neither an aspiring young careerist nor an eager ingenue, but a woman whose youth had been spent in the nursery and the kitchen.[78]

Yet these mature women also had experience working outside the home. To put it another way, the recent entrants into the job market during the 1940s and '50s were not, by and large, newcomers to the labor force, but rather returning workers, women whose employment before marriage and motherhood had substantially dispelled most feminine shyness about taking a job. The typical woman worker during World War II was not, after all, a sprightly ingenue in the image of Rosie the Riveter, but a married woman over 35 with recollections of being a working girl in the 1920s. Joining the labor force for these women was something more than an obliging response to the prodding of the War Manpower

Commission. For one thing, it was a decision eased by prior work experience and memories of the rewards it had provided. The war-time worker was in many instances a flapper grown older. She was also a woman whose children were either in school or on their own. This transition in the female life cycle provided a second reason for entering the labor force, both during the war and thereafter. Throughout the century, as a matter of fact, these were the two best predictors of a wife's employment: previous experience on the job and the ages of her children. It was not the dictates of inter-national affairs nor supply and demand that drove women to seek employment after 1940, but their own priorities as they evolved over the life cycle.[79]

At the same time there is little doubt that family matters were very much on the mind of the woman worker. The working wife was almost always a supplementary wage-earner whose income would enhance the family standard of living, without challenging her husband's dominant position as the chief breadwinner. The sub-urban life-style, with all its domestic accoutrements, had proven costly and not always within the means of a single male wage. A wife's modest earnings, however, could bring a family comfortably above subsistence and provide what market researchers fondly called "discretionary income," the wherewithal to participate in the con-sumer enthusiasms of the '50s. In other households a working wife brought a family a taste of true affluence. Among families whose income exceeded $10,000 a year, the proportion of working wives rose as high as 60 percent by the late 1960s. For the first time, college-educated women were more likely to assist in the financial support of their families than were high-school graduates. These middle-class two-worker households spent significantly more on consumer goods than did families with a single male breadwinner. Although the working wives of the 1950s and '60s contributed, on the average, only 15 to 25 percent of the family income, they added a garnish of luxury to middle-class family life that had far-reaching consequences for "the affluent society."[80]

A woman's economic standing independent of her family in-come, however, fell far short of affluence. Her mean income relative to the male worker actually declined between 1940 and 1960, falling from a high of 63 percent of the male average to a low of 57 percent. The gains of the war years were the first to be wiped out as women were summarily fired from lucrative jobs in the skilled industrial sector, despite their expressed preference to remain on the job after the armistice. As automobile plants converted to peacetime production the proportion of female employees fell from 25 to 7.5 percent, and most of the women workers who remained were in the low-paying clerical sector.[81]

The poor showing of women's wages relative to men's was also due to the decline of female professionals and careerists. The advance of women into the professions at the turn of the century (increasing female representation by 226 percent) had subsided by 1930 and began to recede further thereafter. As of 1930, women accounted for 32 percent of the nation's college administrators and professors. The figure had plummeted to 19 percent by 1960. Despite the abolition of restrictions against women in medical and law schools by the late 1940s, women's representation in these professions remained well below 10 percent. Between 1940 and 1966, when women's rate of employment skyrocketed, the proportions of women in professions declined from 45 to 38 percent.[82] Meanwhile, these female professionals remained concentrated in their traditionally segregated job classifications, as nurses, elementary-school teachers, librarians, and social workers. All in all, it seemed the trend in woman's work was moving decisively toward the erection of a pink-collar ghetto. As the proportion of females among professionals declined by about 7 percent between 1940 and 1968, their monopoly within the clerical work force expanded from 53 to 73 percent.[83]

The lackluster quality of woman's occupational status was not unrelated to the feminine mystique, which reigned with particular virulence in the former citadels of female professionalism—American colleges and universities. Only one in four of the coeds polled during the '50s contemplated a lifelong career. Most put marriage and child-rearing first, and an appalling number (estimates run as high as 60 percent) dropped out of school, usually to marry. The overall proportion of female baccalaureates fell to a nadir of 24 percent in 1950 and women would not regain their position of academic equity until late in the 1960s. The dwindling ranks of college women were preoccupied with family matters. At Smith college, it was said that senior seminars had given way to kitchen showers, while coeds everywhere worked assiduously toward earning their MRS degrees. Yet the majority of college women, like their less educated peers, would eventually find their way back into the labor force, without the forethought or singlemindedness to overcome occupational segregation and discriminatory wages.[84]

Women whose identities were focused on their families were not prepared to challenge the sex-segregation of the labor force, which remained substantially unchanged between 1900 and 1960, despite the massive increase in the raw numbers of workingwomen.

The postwar expansion of the service and sales sector of the economy set up conditions for a more and more precise segregation of the work force by sex. By 1960 an estimated 59 percent of workingwomen were employed in industries and occupations where the majority of their co-workers were females. Perhaps as much as 48 percent of female workers found themselves in categories of employment where 80 percent of the employees were of their own sex. Women, who constituted 38 percent of the work force, accounted for 40 percent of all sales workers and two-thirds of all clerks and typists. When the levels of each occupational grouping are further refined, the sex segregation of the work force appears even more meticulous. Within the sales sector, for example, 96 percent of the clerks in American five-and-dime stores were female. The professions were similarly sex typed, as indicated by the fact that 85 percent of American elementary-school teachers were women. The single largest job category for women was clerical work, accounting for more than 30 percent of employed females in 1960. This pattern of employment demonstrated the continuation and maturation of a distinctly female labor market, a feature built into woman's dual role of the twentieth century.[85]

The routine discrimination of the postwar labor market was fully displayed in the female ghetto of clerical work. It was the lot of the occupants of this typical "woman's job" to perform monotonous, white-collar tasks, which alienated the labor of the mind as well as the body. Clerical work at times replicated the routine of a factory. In the '50s one insurance company employed more than 500 women to mechanically sort 150,000 dividend notices each week. Another firm, assisted by computers, increased the output of 85 employees (four-fifths of them women), to 850,000 transactions a month. The automation of the office resulted in the transfer of female workers from typewriters to keypunch machines. The keypunch operators in one office of the '50s were described as frozen at their places, armed with aspirins and tranquilizers. In this office the annual turnover rate for women workers was 65 percent, testifying to an assault on the woman's nervous system reminiscent of the sweatshops at the turn of the century.[86]

Not all clerical jobs reduced women to anomic captives of office machinery. The personal secretary and the receptionist, for example, were typically asked to infuse bureaucracy with the warm human qualities with which women were supposedly richly endowed. When one executive was asked if automation could replace the secretary, his answer was an emphatic "no." "Machines are poor receptionists and can't run errands and meet the public." A feminine personality was highly valued in the business office, where it served to offer the boss his coffee with a smile and pacify irate clients with soothing charm. The woman clerical worker, in short, was asked to cultivate and display an image of personal concern and to provide human warmth for public-relations purposes, all in the face of her own alienating office routine.[87]

This work regimen was perceptively analyzed by Elinor Langer, who spent several months as a participant observer among employees of the New York Telephone Company. These women workers conducted hundreds of telephone conversations a month, the object of which was to quickly and efficiently translate customer requests into bureaucratic codes, while making a convincing sales pitch for the latest models and colors in telephone apparatus. Through all this frantic activity the company representative was expected to always express interest in the caller and convey her willingness to help. The dual requirements of bureaucratic efficiency and personable public relations were enforced by the department supervisors, who periodically monitored the workers' phone conversations. By 1970 the organization of women's work at the telephone company had become a masterpiece of alienation, ensnaring the manual, mental, and emotional labor of women workers in its bureaucratic labyrinth.[88]

Yet women found ways to humanize the worst working environment. At the New York Telephone Company, for example, co-workers shared one another's duties in moments of pressure or personal strain, and supported each other during family or work-related crises. These mutual services were typical of a women's work culture that was as old as the female labor force. Waitresses and clerks in the 1920s devised collective techniques to deal with both the bosses and the customers who annoyed them. Department-store clerks found ways to undercut the competitive sales system instituted by the management—pooling their sales slips, for example, to see that every worker on the floor met her quota. Lunch hours and coffee breaks provided occasions to share compliments, form friendships, celebrate birthdays.[89] No wonder then, that the opportunity for companionship was among the major causes of job satisfaction among workingwomen.

Despite its low pay and status, women's work was also often highly skilled labor. As early as 1920, applicants for clerical jobs were expected to have a high-school education. The fact that the proportion of women who graduated from high school early in the century exceeded men by almost 20 percent accelerated female takeover of clerical work. A high-school diploma was by no means an irrelevant credential for office workers. Clerical work required the verbal skills and the level of literacy and self-discipline that a lengthy sentence in the American schoolroom instilled. Women who did not pass this educational regimen had considerable difficulty complying with the bureaucratic imperatives of an office. For example, two uneducated middle-aged women in the training program at the New York Telephone Company confessed that they "never read," and as a consequence could not comprehend the company sales manual. They admitted defeat and dejectedly returned to the ranks of manual workers in the repair department.[90] The specific skills of clerical workers—typing, stenography, filing—were acquired in the vocational programs of high schools or in specialized business courses. Entrants into the female segment of the labor force, in short, came to their jobs with considerable preparation.[91]

The skills of these women workers, unlike those of blue-collar men, were prerequisites for employment rather than the results of on-the-job training. An employer of women seldom had to invest in the training of his or her workers. In addition to this substantial saving, the employer awarded clerks and secretaries salaries far lower than those of equivalently skilled workers in the male sector of the labor force. As of 1960, 42 percent of all women workers were in jobs that required an education, but garnered wages lower than those of similarly educated men.[92] In the state of California this inequitable policy allowed a woman with a college education to make on the average only $300 more annually than a man who left school after the eighth grade.[93] The segregation of the labor force allowed employers to gauge pay scales according to the sex of their employees and to discount a woman's education and training. Because women did not compete for jobs with men, their superior qualifications were ignored; different work decreed unequal pay for women. Furthermore, the few men who entered female-dominated occupations were assigned higher positions and granted larger salaries. The income of women clerks in 1964 was only 44 percent of that of men in the same category of employment. Female sales workers earned 60 percent less than males in the sales sector of the labor force.[94]

The pattern of sexual discrimination was also a commonplace characteristic of the female professions. In 1939, for example, the salaries of women teachers and social workers amounted to approximately 70 percent of the annual income of men in these professions.[95] Much of this inequity was a function of the superior posts granted to men within each occupational category. Still, blatant sexual discrimination—unequal pay for equal work—took a heavy toll on women's wages. In a survey of 1,900 office managers conducted in 1961, one-third of the respondents admitted that they routinely paid men higher salaries than women in the same positions.[96]

The sexual segregation of the labor force also inhibited the upward mobility of women workers. Even a middle-aged wife and mother was still a "girl" in the eyes of many employers. The typical female worker was consigned to permanent occupational adolescence. Secretaries and salesgirls could not expect to rise to the posts of executives and managers. While young white-collar males embarked upon the systematic climb to higher posts in the firm, women typically performed the same functions and took home the same amount of real wages year after year. Technological advances in the woman's sector of the economy did not break this cycle of stagnation. The development of typewriters and office machines at the turn of the century created a demand for more skilled workers, but once women had secured the bulk of these positions, their prestige and pay declined. The innovations in data processing in the 1950s and '60s created higher-level positions in the field of programming, positions which in the beginning often went to women, but not at the same rate as openings in the new seats of monotony and inferiority at the keypunch machines. In sum, the quantum leap in women's participation in the work force that characterizes twentieth-century womanhood occasioned a more multifaceted and widespread pattern of sexual inequality. It welcomed females into secondary jobs outside the home, where they contributed immeasurably to the expansion of the economy and enhanced the profit margin of their employers, without adding appreciably to the economic standing of their sex.

Neither was the arrangement of women's work and home roles, typical of the 1940s and '50s, likely to disturb the traditional sexual hierarchy. The lowly position which most women obtained when they left the home for the labor force did not spark male fears about job competition or the breakdown of sex roles. Changes in male attitudes regarding woman's work did not always keep pace with the movement of wives and mothers into the labor force. A 1960 poll by the Michigan Survey Research Center revealed that only 34 percent of all the husbands questioned approved of wives working, at a point when 38 percent of the wives in the survey had earned some outside income in the last year. The vast majority of those husbands who did endorse their wives' entry into the work force justified their opinions by reference to supplementary family income earned by working wives.

An earlier poll of husbands got to the heart of the male response to working wives. The ideal was this: a wife could work and thereby increase the economic status of the family as long as she achieved only "moderate success," that is, did not challenge the superiority of the male breadwinner.[97] The frequent interruption of woman's work by pregnancy and childcare helped to bring a husband's wishes to fruition. The commonest varieties of female employment, clerical and sales work, had the additional advantage of being readily available to women whenever it became appropriate for them to reenter the work force, or wherever the family might move to enhance the husband's career. The wives' employers eagerly cooperated with American husbands in this conspiracy against women's success. As late as 1960, 68 percent of the office managers polled chafed at the idea of placing women in supervisory or management positions. Workers of either sex also resented being put under the direction of women.[98] The attitudes of employers, fellow workers, husbands, and women themselves all came together to usher the female sex into its segregated and inequitable place in the labor force.

The prescribed womanhood of twentieth-century America, like its many predecessors, was widely disseminated and neatly integrated with social and economic structure. Yet, as always, the prescriptive literature on sex roles and popular images of femininity interacted with the realities of women's life in a complex and un-predictable fashion. Women were puppets neither of Freud, Spock, General Motors, nor Madison Avenue. They shaped their kalei-doscopic personal histories, however, within the options, directives, and alternatives provided by American society.

The journals of Margaret Fowler Dunaway, dating from 1926 to 1960, give private testimony to the way at least one woman built a life within the shadow of the twentieth-century stereotypes. Mar-garet Fowler Dunaway submitted her diaries to the Radcliffe Wom-en's Archives in 1953 with "a blush of shame . . . I write painfully, acknowledging . . . to have been a Nobody all these years." In her youth three decades earlier, Margaret Dunaway was not given to such self-abnegation. She had been a charter member of the League of Women Voters and harbored strong personal ambitions. Later, she recalled "the desire for marriage and a career, coming from different directions, and about the same time, and the whirlwind of conflict can never be erased from my memory. I chose, as most, I imagine, both, but took marriage first." In the 1920s she sur-rendered her aspirations for personal achievement to dedication to the welfare of her husband and three children, but not without second thoughts. "My office as a Mother seems to take all my time but it should not. I am an individual outside of that." Occasionally she expressed her restlessness in verse: "So goes the morning / So go my days / So go the years / Why, why, do I long for achieve-ment?"[99]

Still, Mrs. Dunaway set out in search of personal satisfaction rather than public achievement. She sought fulfillment, first of all, in conjugal intimacy, "longing for the perfect marriage—the un-iting and flowing together in one large and powerful stream of life." In her case the pursuit of this goal met with more than the usual obstacles. Not only was Mr. Dunaway preoccupied with his career, in some vague business that his wife seemed to know or care little about, but the difficulties of the depression took him to jobs half a continent away from his family. For years on end Mrs. Dunaway saw her husband only on holidays and during vacations. As her elder children left home, more and more of her family relations were conducted through letters—"so necessary to keep the sense of unity alive." While her husband and older children were off achiev-ing, Mrs. Dunaway devoted herself to her youngest daughter, Joan. She devised new plans of character development, joining in her daughter's games and school projects, deliberated over her education, and speculated on her future. At the same time Mrs. Dunaway disdained maternal possessiveness: "Your children are not your children. They are the sons and daughters of life's longing for itself. . . . They come through you, but not from you. And they are with you yet they belong not to you." When her youngest child graduated from high school, Margaret Dunaway observed: "Mothering, a wonderful profession! But it leaves one always looking for someone to clutch on to, to mother. Now I shall subdue the mother instinct and perhaps be an individual for a few years." But even with her children grown and scattered around the world, Mrs. Dunaway's journals changed little, were still chiefly the repository of domestic details.[100]

Margaret Dunaway had no regrets about the course her life had taken. She took abundant satisfaction in the successes of her three children, and found contentment in the company of her spouse, especially after his retirement. Her journal of the 1950s did not echo with the malaise of her youth. She no longer lamented the fact that the prose, poetry, and religious theory of her journal were never made public. "The office of Mother and of Wife—and now of Grandmotherly joy—still bring me into the current of supreme satisfaction." Still, the life of Margaret Dunaway was hedged in by the conventions of womanhood, and abraded by the shifts of the female life cycle. One comment in her diary of 1928 obliquely suggests that Margaret Dunaway dimly recognized the subtle strictures of woman's role. "I saw today a little bride entering her bright new home on the arm of her elderly husband. Why did I think of a little bird entering a shiny new cage?"[101] Was Mrs. Dunaway merely reacting with distaste to the couple's age difference? Or did that metaphor convey her own sense of claustrophobia in woman's place?

Margaret Dunaway's account of the lives of her daughters provides a glimpse of the alterations that were made in the cage of womanhood after 1940. Her oldest daughter, Dorothy, left home in the middle '30s and found herself in a position typical of her generation, a low-paying, dead-end office job. Dorothy became "so tired of the dead, dull routine of the law office" that she retired into marriage. Her younger sister, Joan, also devoted her youth to marriage. It was only in 1959, more than twenty years after she had graduated from high school, that Joan decided to go to college and get a teaching credential. "I have debated this so long . . . I am at last really excited at the prospect of preparing to do something useful." Dorothy also reentered the work force late in life, finding a job in the admissions office of the University of Chicago. Mrs. Dunaway was able to find much of interest in the work of her daughters. Her son and son-in-law, on the other hand, had truly notable careers, one as a Standard Oil Executive, and the other with the Atomic Energy Commission, occupations whose "usefulness" was rarely open to question in the American value system. Although a woman's work often paled by comparison, the wives of these successful men shared in and contributed to the family status. Joan and Dorothy provided expressive support to their struggling husbands and later contributed their hard-won earnings as well. The wife of Don Carlos Dunaway played the classic role of the executive wife, right down to wining and dining his business contacts. In 1960 Mary Dunaway's indirect contribution to America's international oil interests entailed, among other things, entertaining thirty-two Arab business affiliates—"I cooked two entire days."[102]

Mrs. Dunaway's daughter-in-law illustrated a widespread middle- and upper-class phenomenon, the two-person career. Like the scholar's private typist, editor, and critic, the professional's undemanding and supportive mate, and the politician's ceremonial companion, a business executive's wife devoted her time and energy to promoting her husband's career. When worldly success came to such a couple, it would be acclaimed as the man's achievement, and his helpmate would be left with only the lowly title "housewife."

Mrs. Dunaway's own daughters demonstrated a more typical life pattern for women in the postwar era, a kaleidoscopic dual role. They devoted their youth and consigned much of their identity to marriage and motherhood. When they reentered the labor force, it was with rusty skills and their attention distracted by domestic responsibilities. These women were ideal recruits for the discriminatory female labor force. When a woman assisted in performing the breadwinner role, her husband did not reciprocate by taking on an equal share of home chores. At best, the male might lighten the working wife's load by drying the dishes and taking out the garbage, leaving her to fill, if not two, at least one and a half jobs. This dual role approached a double burden. Yet it had its compensations, and its expanding effect on woman's consciousness. Mrs. Dunaway's daughter Joan, for example, had taken a major step

toward a new womanhood, summoning the energy and education
to begin a new career in middle age. This was a significant twist
in the kaleidoscope of womanhood; at a certain turn in the life cycle
many woman of the 1950s began to juggle both home responsibilities and career aspirations simultaneously.

THE SHATTERED KALEIDOSCOPE:
RACE, ETHNICITY, AND GENDER IN
THE TWENTIETH CENTURY

Not all women balanced their dual roles as deftly as these middle-
class wives of the 1950s. Some women overemphasized the home
roles; others seemed to slight domesticity and devote more attention
to their jobs; both forms of deviation from the norm could provoke
public condemnation.

The first aberration, obsession with mothering, became the
object of particular scorn early in the 1940s. In a book entitled
Generation of Vipers, Philip Wylie excoriated American mothers for
smothering their sons with excessive, cloying affection and thereby
emasculating them. In the postwar period this particular twist of
the kaleidoscope became associated with an ethnic stereotype, the
image of the Jewish mother. The domineering mother was rendered
in the broadest comic tones in Philip Roth's 1965 novel, *Portnoy's
Complaint*. A caricature named Sophie Portnoy carried maternal
solicitude, love, and devotion to the grotesque extreme.[103] Other
authors of more serious intent painted stereotypes in strokes that
were nearly as broad and derogatory as was Roth's farce. Irving
Howe in a celebration of Jewish immigrant culture, *The World of
Our Fathers*, alluded to the Jewish mother as "the looming figure
who would inspire, haunt and devastate generations of sons." Al-
ternatively, she was described as "absurdly outrageously protective,"
a "brassy scourge with her grating bark," "expert at groaning,
cajoling, intimidating."[104] The object lesson of the Jewish mother
was that too much investment in a child could be dangerous, even
in the age of the feminine mystique.

Jewish women were in fact placed in special jeopardy of becoming excessively involved in the lives of their children. At a time
when nearly 40 percent of the total population of adult females

were in the labor force, only 23.7 percent of Jewish women worked outside the home. Jewish women also had the lowest fertility rate of any major religious group, and thus fewer children on whom to lavish their free time. Finally, Jewish women were more likely than either Catholics or Protestants to experience relative idleness and aimlessness in middle age, when their children left home. Only one in three Jewish women over the age of forty-five was in the labor force at a time when almost half of all other American women had found this alternative occupation.[105] In all these respects, the Jewish mother was not unique among American women. In fact, she was probably typical of the wives of comfortably upper-middle-class and professional men, women who were often without jobs or large families to distract them from maternal obsessions.

Accordingly, the stigma borne by Jewish women refracted the actual social and demographic circumstances of many women of similar background and experience. It could betoken very painful personal experience as well. The contradictions of motherhood in the twentieth century had produced a special female complaint, the empty-nest syndrome. Once their children left home, full-time mothers, Jewish or not, confronted premature retirement, which sent some back to work and others to the therapist's couch, the bottle of tranquilizers, or to mental institutions.[106] The latter had failed to maneuver that difficult and crucial turn in the twentieth-century female life cycle, the shift in middle age from home to work as the focus of their activity and identity. Among the consequences of this failure were the loneliness of the empty nest and the stigma of the Jewish mother.

More disastrous consequences than these accumulated on the racial underside of twentieth-century womanhood. The watchword of black womanhood was not momism but matriarchy. Through this latter concept, the mainstream American culture condemned the antithesis of the Jewish mother, the woman who neglected her home responsibilities to pursue work outside the home. The term matriarchy was first applied to black women by the sociologist E. Franklin Frazier in the 1930s, and referred to domestic units that lacked a strong, authoritative male head. In 1965 the concept was given new currency in a government publication entitled *The Negro Family: The Case for National Action*, which was written by Daniel Patrick Moynihan. Matriarchy now appeared as a thinly disguised indictment of black women for emasculating their mates. The specific charges against black women were actually rather innocuous: that they maintained a rate of employment and level of education, relative to the men of their race, that were significantly higher than the white norm. By so doing, the black woman overstepped the bonds of feminine propriety and presumably sapped the ego strength of her mate, thus inhibiting him from achieving middle-class status in America.[107] Black women, in Moynihan's estimation, seemed to be placing too much stock on the public and economic side of the dual role. In fact, by the late nineteenth century their rate of employment had reached the level that white women would not achieve until the 1950s.

A second minority group, Spanish-speaking Americans, chiefly recent migrants from Mexico, threw the middle-class gender system off balance in yet another way. Mexican-American culture was charged with allowing too much latitude to male bravado and sexual dominance, indicted, that is, not for matriarchy but for "machismo." This allegation, like the pejorative categorization of the black family, was first bandied about by sociologists and social psychologists during the 1930s, and gained wider circulation during the civil rights struggles of the 1960s. Machismo, as defined by social scientists from outside Chicano culture, denoted excessive concern with virility as demonstrated, not in the all-American mode of self-control and economic achievement, but in physical aggression, sexual conquest, and the domination of wives. Its correlate, sometimes called hembrismo, was a set of feminine attributes including docility, deference to males, and maternal sacrifice. These deviations from standardized gender roles of the 1950s were once again held responsible for the failure of an impoverished, socially marginal group to enter the American mainstream.[108]

Both terms, matriarchy as well as machismo, reflect in a distorted and stereotypical fashion the distinct gender systems that evolved within populations which had lived for centuries outside of the American mainstream. Both cultures came into sharp confrontation with American norms in the twentieth century, when migration from Mexico and the black South accelerated rapidly, especially after World War II, and culminated by the late 1950s and early 1960s in militant demands for inclusion in the American political and economic system. The force of this collision generated a debate about race, ethnicity, and gender which necessitates a review of women's history as seen from the perspectives of black women and Chicanas.

For both groups that history was deeply rooted in rural agricultural economies. As late as 1940 the majority of American blacks resided in the rural South, where gender roles were built up around a sharecropping economy. Most blacks worked on small plots of land, usually less than fifty acres, returning the bulk of their produce (everything beyond a meager subsistence) to the white landlord. Survival under these circumstances required the labor of the entire family, young and old, male and female. The sexual division of labor among sharecroppers can be classified as parallel but overlapping, ordaining that males specialized in field labor while females stayed closer to the home and garden plot. Yet the system was flexible enough to allow women to regularly work in the fields, and for men to lend a hand at housework. Young males, furthermore, could be found helping with domestic as well as field chores, from the age of six and upwards.[109]

This system of labor produced women who were well-informed about agricultural economics and vital to family subsistence, all-around hardy farmers. White as well as black farm women thrived on agricultural labor; one put it this way, "Gimme the field every time and tobacco growing." The farm partnership initiated women into all the instrumental functions of the household provider, a role that many would have to shoulder alone in their widowhood. The economic capabilities of the black woman were abundantly illustrated in this letter to the Department of Agriculture during the depression: "I am a widow woman with seven head of children; and I live on my place with plenty of help. All are good workers and I want to farm." She requested government relief in the form of a mule, wagon, and feed, and closed with businesslike bluntness: "Because I am a woman I wants to ask you all to please help me to make a crop this year and let me hear from you by return mail. Yours for business. Mosel Brinson."[110]

Farmer Brinson also illustrated the muted shape of domestic roles for black women in the rural South. Motherhood, first of all, was not a highly differentiated role for adult women. To white and black sharecroppers alike, children were valuable farm laborers, set to simple household chores when two years old and occupied in the fields by the age of ten. Young children themselves became surrogate mothers, caretakers for the younger siblings soon after they could walk. The consequent reduction of specifically maternal duties, like the woman's expanded work role, was an essential adjustment to tenant farming.

The conjugal relation also took a unique form in the share-croppers' home economy. The low valuation of the tenant farmer's property offered minimal economic prerogatives to the male head of the household. Title to a leased lot was hardly an awesome rod of authority. Conversely, women with land to till, farming experience, and the labor power of their children could subsist without the assistance of a husband and father. Accordingly, women were relatively free to abrogate the marriage vow. One self-reliant female reported this practice to Charles Johnson: "Everybody don't get married and if I can't get the one I want I don't want to get married." At the same time the majority of black tenant farmers did live in stable marital partnerships, indicating that the male-female bond remained strong even in the face of these alternatives.[111]

The black culture of the rural South was also tolerant of illegitimacy. When Johnson asked one black mother to plot the lineage of her children, she responded: "No sir, they ain't by the same father. Them three is but the two darkest ones ain't. Ain't seen the daddy of the first one since year fore last. He's married and don't give no help. We started going together when I was a girl and we just kept it up. I ain't seen their daddy since the last one was born. I been married to another man now for most twelve years." Despite this complex marital and childbearing history, all the children of the household were treated alike, and all shared a father figure in their mother's current husband. The father's family was almost as likely as the mother's to take in illegitimate children and provide them with respectability and a stable family life.[112]

The ease and frequency of adoption was but one component of another distinguishing feature of the southern black gender system. The personal relations of the sexes, rather than being concentrated within the nuclear family, were diffused through a large and elaborate kinship network. When asked to identify their relatives, southern blacks could commonly name one hundred persons or more. These large networks of kinfolk, related by blood, marriage, adoption, and friendship, were linked by reciprocal responsibilities as well as affection. Anthropologists have found cases, for example, where upwards of a hundred persons drew on one another's economic resources. These vast webs of kinship laced through the South and occasionally sent tentacles northward as well. Southern families sometimes had extensions in northern and western cities where they provided critical services to new migrants.[113] Needless to say, these elaborate kinship systems were sexually integrated, and therefore placed black women at the center of critical social and economic functions.

The status accruing to these hard-working farm women and vital agents of the kinship system, in some ways extended beyond the family. Black women were esteemed in their communities as teachers, practitioners of midwifery and folk medicine, and as "church mothers." If they were denied the right to vote or to assume political office, so too were their menfolk, who endured the spectre of lynching along with disenfranchisement. Because Southern blacks were denied basic access to the American political system, their communities were regulated in more informal ways, through the church and neighborhood and extended family, places to which women had access as well as men. Woman's power, nonetheless, had definite limits: husbands enjoyed superior property and legal rights; the all-important black ministry was open only to males; men were the typical perpetrators of the domestic violence which so often accompanies poverty.

In sum, the black family of the rural South cannot be categorized by reference to either a resident patriarch or matriarch. Some form of cooperative teamwork, within an extended kinship network, allowing for female power and yet a margin of male dominance, is a more plausible description of this unique gender system. This system did indeed differ from white mainstream standards, in both the nineteenth or twentieth century. And it did create some remarkable women, if not matriarchs. Such a woman was Fannie Lou Hamer, one of twenty children born to a tenant farm family, who recalled picking cotton at age six and counted about 150 people in her personal kinship system. By the 1960s after a lifetime of back-breaking labor, beatings, jailings, and bombings, Fannie Lou Hamer still stalwartly championed the rights of black men and women, even before the national elite of the Democratic party as she led a challenge to the political system which had excluded her race for centuries.[114]

The history of Chicanas in some ways resembles, in other ways sharply contrasts with, that of black women. They too were mired in rural poverty until very recently. The history of gender south of the Rio Grande, however, harked back not to African matrilocal tribes, but to fiercely patriarchal Aztecs. According to the ancient Aztec Code, a girl-child would be addressed as follows at birth:

> You should be inside the home as the heart is inside the body; you should not tread outside the home nor should you make it your habit to go anywhere. You should be like the ashes that cover the hearth of the home. You should sweat next to the ashes of the hearth. [115]

The Mexican peasants of the twentieth century were historically and socially very remote from the Aztec nobility for whom these codes were written, yet the restrictions on women's activities remained extreme. In villages like Tepoztlán near Mexico City, adolescent girls were not allowed outside the home unchaperoned and were ostracized for premarital sexual activity. Their mothers seldom dared to lift their eyes in the presence of men and risked the charge of witchcraft if they spent too much time outside the home. Both daughters and mothers were sentenced to endless work—grinding corn alone required six hours of female labor daily. [116]

Yet this sharply sex-segregated culture, as is often the case, allowed certain space for the exercise of woman's power as well. Mexican peasant women claimed a right to the income from their own production, be it cloth or garden crops. They commonly managed the entire family purse as well. Within her legitimate sphere, the kinship group, a peasant woman could exert considerable moral power, especially over her sons. Her power often extended into church groups as well. On the eve of migration to the United States, furthermore, the status of Mexican women seemed to be changing for the better. The eventual mechanization of corn grinding liberated female labor, which was then often converted into the cultivation and sale of foodstuffs. These enterprising women won access both to the market towns and to discretionary income. The Mexican peasant's gender system was, in short, hardly a simple case of macho domination of women. [117]

This gender system was also vital enough to adapt to the shifting circumstances, and to change. As Mexican men and women moved northward into the United States, the contours of womanhood were altered in subtle but consequential ways. One El Paso Chicana recalled these changes in the 1960s. Thirty years before, she said,

"There was no one else but the father who gave the word in family activities. His word was an order." But patriarchy had mellowed since until "a man and his wife may talk things out. They might try to put the things of the two minds together and solve something that bothers them." The barrier between male and female, typical of traditional Mexican culture, was clearly eroding. So too were the constrictions on the freedom of young single women, who found ways to elude chaperons and resist the arranged marriages that had been common in the past, south of the border. Such changes in the relations of the sexes clearly indicated that the social roles of family members had been transformed as well.[118]

At the most basic level the sharp dichotomy between male and female economic roles could not be sustained north of the Rio Grande. The spatial segregation, which sent males to distant fields while women worked around the home, swiftly broke down. Even in the barrios of California during the late nineteenth century, the work of male and female came to resemble each other. While the Chicano male typically worked for a pittance in unskilled jobs, increasing numbers of widowed and single women, if not wives, entered the labor force to supplement family income through domestic service or laundry work. Both male and female work was rewarded with a small wage. The sexual division of labor broke down ever further in the rich farmlands of the Southwest where the bulk of Mexican migrants found employment after 1910. Most Mexicans who entered the United States in two great waves, the first in the 1910s and '20s, and the second after 1940, were recruited as migrant agricultural laborers who worked in family teams. Male and female, young and old, commonly performed the same tasks, for the same piece-rate, in close proximity to one another.[119] The consequences of this reorganization of the labor force were demonstrated by the oral testimony of an experienced field worker named Jessie Lopez De la Cruz. When she excelled her brother-in-law and his peers in picking lettuce, the men quit work. "They said, 'I'm ashamed to have a woman even older than I am work faster than I can. This is a woman's job.' I said, 'Hey what do you mean? You mean the men's job is washing dishes and baking tortillas?' "[120] The sexual politics of the lettuce field portended major changes in the relations of Mexican-American men and women.

In this instance the course of gender change veered in the direction of minority protest politics and a kind of feminism. Cesar

Chavez recruited Jessie Lopez De la Cruz into the United Farm Workers of America where, with other women like the union's leader and co-founder, Dolores Huerta, she testified to the recognition that any improvement in the collective status of farm workers would require the participation of females as well as males. From her position within the union Jessie De la Cruz defended the position of her sex, including their right to equal work and equal pay.[121] Even as the United Farm Workers were winning the battle for the unionization of migrant agricultural workers, however, the pace of Mexican-American history was rapidly passing beyond them. As the volume of migration from Mexico mushroomed after 1960, the bulk of the Spanish-speaking population would settle in the cities, where they faced a new set of challenges to their culture and their gender system.

The Chicano migrants would find that American cities were already occupied by a poor racial minority, for the black exodus from the rural South had reached major proportions after 1940. Between 1940 and 1960 no less than 3½ million blacks made this journey north, most of them moving from farm to city in the same process. By 1960, 73 percent of the black population resided in urban areas. Urbanization clearly had its disruptive effect on the rural family patterns and multiplied the social indicators used to designate the black "matriarchy." Even during the nineteenth century, those black families located in cities had higher rates of single-parent households than did their neighbors, both the native-born and immigrants. The longer they resided in cities, furthermore, the higher were their chances of marital disruption.

As the black population moved relentlessly cityward during the twentieth century, the rates of family disruption grew almost apace. The percentage of black families containing both a husband and wife declined from 67 percent in the 1910s to 62 percent in 1940, and 58 percent in the 1960s. During the peak years of black urbanization, between 1940 and 1968, the black illegitimacy rates rose from 17 to 27 percent of all births. The proponents of the matriarchy theory add one further index of family disarray among blacks, the growth of female participation in the labor force from 38 percent in 1938 to 58 percent in 1960, twenty percentage points higher than the rate of employment for white women.[122] These statistics do not, however, add up to an indictment of black family structure as essentially and perversely matriarchal. Not only did the majority of black children live in two-parent households, but many of the remainder were securely cared for by widowed mothers and fathers. The proliferation of fatherless households among blacks cannot be understood without reference to the social conditions that breed them. When the statistical breakdown of family disruption was calculated in terms of wealth and place of residence, the differential between white and nonwhite family structure was drastically reduced. Among urban families of the 1960s whose income amounted to less than $3,000 annually, 53 percent of the nonwhite families and 62 percent of the white were fatherless. When only those urban families with incomes of more than $3,000 a year were compared, the black and white rates of female-headed households came within four percentage points of one another. Because black wage earners made considerably less than whites, even above the poverty line this narrow differential was almost meaningless. In point of fact, well over 90 percent of the black families with merely subsistence income managed to hold the two-parent family unit together.[123]

Still, the fact remains that during this century black women were most likely to experience the worst of urban poverty, which brutally overtaxed them in their roles of wife and mother as well as worker. The difficult family history of black urban women was apparent even in the nineteenth century, when they represented but a small portion of their sex and race. When historian Elizabeth Pleck traced the black women of Boston through the public records of the 1880s she found that only three in five of them remained with their spouses for the space of a decade. This domestic instability was most common when the husband was underemployed, unemployed, or low-paid. Since the dismal economic prospects of black urban males have not improved substantially over time, black marriages continue to be fragile. Ever since the rate of unemployment has been calculated by the U.S. government, black unemployment has been nearly twice that of whites, and commonly measured in double digits.[124]

Rather than bequeathing to women the role of matriarch, the impoverishment of the black male has jeopardized the very reproduction of the black population. Well less than half of the black women born between 1890 and 1934 managed to live out their lives within stable families composed of husband, wife, and their children. A sizable portion of black women never married, due largely to the scarcity and poor economic prospects of black men in the cities where they settled. Even more remained childless, often due to infertility caused by poor nutrition and rampant tuberculosis.[125] The remainder saw their marriage vows become a casualty of poverty and urban anomie. Black women bemoaned these consequences of ghetto life. Residents of one small midwestern town disdained moving to Chicago, for example, because it was harder for a woman to "hold her man" there.[126]

The relations of the sexes were most cruelly tested in urban ghettoes, where black women were so often held solely responsible for their own support and that of their children. Black women rose to this challenge by achieving the highest rates of employment in the history of American women, reaching a level of participation in the labor force in the nineteenth century that white women would not approach until a century later. Neither age, marital status, nor childbearing responsibilities placed restrictions on the employment of black women outside the home. Black women went to work in greater numbers than even those women (such as the wives of European immigrants in the nineteenth century) whose families experienced comparable conditions of urban impoverishment. Clearly, the distinctive history and culture of black Americans, as well as the force of economic circumstances, contributed to this unprecedented rate of female employment. The legacy of slavery and sharecropping had habituated black women to hard work, wherever it could be found, and also fostered a strong commitment to using women's wages to finance the education of children. As one domestic servant put it, "I don't care how hard I have to work if I can only send Sally and the boys to school looking decent."[127]

The jobs that black women found within the American occupational structure did not, however, offer many intrinsic rewards. Until relatively late in the twentieth century, the majority of black women workers were engaged in domestic service, a status many of them deemed hardly a step above enslavement. If not working in a white woman's kitchen, the black female worker at the turn of the century could most likely be found in a commercial laundry, a less servile but more dangerous and menial occupation. In the 1930s, when white women had already moved en masse into clerical work, black women still had difficulty securing employment in factories. The southern textile mills, which did admit black women, either put them to work in segregated quarters or relegated them to "scrubbing floors and cleaning lint and cotton from the machines. They had no hope of promotion to anything else, as the skilled operations were performed by white women." The few other industries that employed black women, peanut factories and stockyards, for example, provided only loathsome chores and meager wages. As of the 1930s, clerical jobs were closed to black women, and in the retail sector of the labor force, dark faces were hidden in the back rooms, packaging goods.[128]

Black women jumped at the opportunity for industrial labor offered by wartime industrial expansion. In the second world war they actually mounted militant campaigns, complete with picket lines and threats of mass marches, to try to desegregate the munitions factories. Although they did win admission to the industrial labor force during the war, it was only after employers' preferences for both white women and black men had been satisfied. Even then, the black woman worker's wartime battle was not over. In one of the ugliest episodes in the history of women, white female workers in a number of plants rioted against sharing bathroom facilities with black co-workers. After the war, black, like white, women saw their economic gains in the industrial sector quickly wiped out. But unlike white women, blacks found limited positions in the expanded white-collar sector. As of the 1960s only 34 percent of black women workers, as opposed to 63 percent of whites, were white-collar employees. As the streamlined home and then the feminine mystique shrunk the number of domestic workers, black women became cleaning women in public buildings and offices. Nearly half of all black workers were still employed as either household or service workers in 1960.[129]

Given the abysmal wages afforded by most of these jobs, and the increasing likelihood that they would be the chief support of their children as well as themselves, black women had to devise additional strategies for survival. They turned to another black tradition, the extended kinship system, for assistance. The black kinship system was transported to the northern city and elaborated into what anthropologist Carol Stack has called a domestic network. According to this social form, writes Stack, "domestic functions are carried on by urban blacks by clusters of kin who may or may not live together." Writing around 1900, a social worker spelled out how such a network might operate.

> "Meals are furnished to the hungry, funds are provided for the penniless, garments are given to the shivering poor-clad ones; remittances of money and boxes of clothing are sent to the homefolks in the South. The family of seven persons living in a basement took in and sheltered without charge for a winter a family of five individuals."

The same kind of safety net protected black women and their families in the post-war ghettoes. An individual in distress could call on a personal network, sometimes as vast as 100 relatives and friends, to provide childcare, meals, transportation, shelter, clothing, and financial assistance. Although the urban domestic network most always included males, among them a biological or social father for most illegitimate children, its nucleus was usually a mother and child, and its leader was often an elderly grandmother. In one black neighborhood the female center of this support system was identified with the simple observation: "Everyone turns to Aunt Jane when in trouble."[130]

The strong female work ethic and the woman-centered domestic network were among the chief strategies whereby black Americans survived and reproduced themselves under the most difficult of circumstances. This history is distorted by the term matriarchy and often romanticized by the expression "the strength of the black family." Black women's history also fails utterly to conform to the neat and well-balanced patterns of the kaleidoscope of roles enacted by white middle-class women between 1940 and 1960. Living beneath the poverty line, and responsible for the support of themselves and their families, black women could ill-afford to keep their economic roles neatly balanced with their purely domestic concerns. In the face of chronic unemployment of husbands and fathers it was suicidal for women to maintain an economic status modestly inferior to male standards of achievement. The exigencies of survival for the black urban poor did not make for smooth relations between the sexes. The high incidence of desertion, divorce, illegitimacy, and domestic violence was real, painful, and growing, as black men and women continued to move northward and cityward.

Yet when white feminists examine the history of black women and compare it with their own, they are sometimes tempted to underplay these bleak circumstances. Just as the women's rights advocates of the 1850s could be blinded to Sojourner Truth's scars as a slave by her vibrant strength as a woman, feminists of the 1960s sometimes let their fascination with the personal power of ghetto women obscure the viciousness of their situation. The hardships of black history had freed women from at least one malady of white womanhood, that sense of fragility and timidity in the world outside the home. Black women often projected a self-image of confidence, strength, even power. Some of them even evoked the image of matriarch themselves. Amy Jacques Garvey, arguing for better representation of women within the United Negro Improvement Association (a nationalist group founded by her husband Marcus in the 1920s), could make the following pronouncement without any apparent uneasiness. "Mr. Black man watch your step. Ethiopia's queens will reign again and her Amazons protect her shores. We will replace you and lead you on to victory and glory."[131] Mary McCleod Bethune, black educator and New Deal official, claimed a similar heritage. "My mother was of royal African blood of a tribe ruled by matriarchs. Through all the years of bitter slavery she managed to preside with her queen-like dignity."[132]

The black power movement of the 1960s too often ignored or rebuked this history. The writers who led the campaign to create a black identity in the '60s, for example, were not above sex scapegoating. Such black leaders as Claude Brown, Eldridge Cleaver, and Stokeley Carmichael sent women to the back of the movement, often escorted by crudely misogynist epithets. Black women often agreed that females should step aside into positions of support for the members of their race who had long been denied their "manhood." One black female scholar concluded that: "The tradition of the strong black woman has probably outlived her usefulness because this role has been challenged by the black man, who has demanded that white society acknowledge his manhood and deal directly with him instead of using his woman—considered the weaker sex—as a buffer."[133]

Very few black women were likely to heed this advice. Women, in fact, were long a strength of black politics itself. It was, after all, a black workingwoman named Rosa Parks who refused to move to the back of the bus, who inaugurated the Civil Rights Movement itself. Women were also the bulwark of one of the most powerful black organizations of the 1960s, the National Welfare Rights Organization. With a membership of 250,000 during its peak years, this union of black mothers forced through fundamental changes in welfare policy and grasped greater public benefits for the families they headed.[134] There was no sign, furthermore, that black women planned a retreat from the positions in the labor force that their sex and race had occupied for generations.

Such a reversal would have been particularly ironic at a time when white women were moving so rapidly in the opposite direction. As white women as well as black women moved into the labor force in the mid-twentieth century, they encountered prospects of developing self-assurance, wider knowledge, and higher aspirations. Perhaps it would be only a matter of time before they would grow discontent with the inequity of their dual roles.

In fact, it is possible to detect a kind of protofeminism beneath the surface of the "feminine mystique." The cutting edge of the kaleidoscope of roles repeatedly slashed across American movie screens, particularly in the 1940s, when it was brought to life by the brash, sometimes strident, even ruthless career women played by the likes of Joan Crawford, Katharine Hepburn, and Rosalind Russell. No one portrayed the contradictions of twentieth-century womanhood as powerfully as Vivien Leigh in the role of Scarlett O'Hara, the heroine of *Gone With the Wind*. Scarlett was probably the most familiar fictional character in the history of womanhood, read about, viewed, and reviewed (as best seller, box-office hit, and TV special) by millions of women from the 1930s through the 1960s. If women responded at all sympathetically to Scarlett O'Hara they were not choosing a sweet domesticated heroine. She mixed feminine vanities and romantic fantasies with open contempt for motherhood, and ruthless ambition in the world of work and business. She symbolized a sassy restlessness with the twentieth-century arrangement of women's roles. This discontent would not rise to the surface of American history until the mid-1960s. Yet there may be intimations of feminism, as well as hopes for a romantic happy ending, in the famous last words of Scarlett O'Hara, "I'll think about it tomorrow."

SEVEN

TOWARD GENDER SYMMETRY:
FEMINISM AND FAMILY CHANGE,
1960 – 1980

T
he signs of change in women's place piled one upon another in the 1960s and '70s, mounting to such proportions that it looked as if a whole new epoch in the history of gender was about to dawn. The quantitative indices of changes in womanhood which were visible for several generations took on a qualitative significance in the second half of the twentieth century. By 1980 the *majority* of American women were enrolled in the labor force. The *majority* of families had two breadwinners, one of whom was female. And the *majority* of school-age children had working mothers. The rate of employment for men declined during the same period until the gender differential in labor force participation had narrowed to a margin of 30 percent. As the dimensions of woman's work outside the home expanded after 1960 the extent of her domestic relationships shrank. The divorce rate doubled; the marriage rate became unexpectedly sluggish; and the birthrate reached an all-time low. The center of gravity for womanhood shifted from the family toward the labor force, and the balanced pattern of the kaleidoscope of roles shattered seemingly beyond repair. The contours of womanhood began, in fact, to resemble the male gender role.[1]

General changes in the organization of the American economy and society, underway since 1960, were substantial enough to accommodate and support such a major transformation in womanhood. Here too the transformation was more cumulative than cataclysmic. The '60s and '70s continued the long-term shift away from an industrial economy and toward one dominated by the vast array of service and white-collar jobs identified as the tertiary sector. Since 1970 for example, the tertiary sector of the economy grew 3 percent annually, while the secondary sector, composed of manufacturing and construction, was practically stationary. Social as well as economic relations have been revolutionized over the last two decades by critical innovations in the technology of communication and information: electronic data processing and mathematical models of organizing knowledge. This rapid advance of high technology has been accompanied by the proliferation of quite another breed of economic enterprise, the so-called human service industries devoted to dispensing everything from meals to health, hygiene, and psychic well-being. The expansion of both these economic domains, the information sector and the human service sector, has created a robust demand for female workers. The second has also absorbed unto itself still more of the functions once performed in the home by women.

The reorganization of American life and work over the past two decades has been so decisive that social theorists have searched about for a new name for the society they inhabit. The label which has stuck, "post-industrial society," at least has the virtue of connoting a magnitude of social and economic change capable of sustaining a transformation in the gender system.[2]

With the 1960s came one additional and unmistakable sign of fundamental alterations in American womanhood. "Woman's place" became the topic of fervid public debate and the basis of a radical and vociferous social movement. On the very heels of the feminine mystique came an all-out attack on domesticity and femininity. The new women's movement of the 1960s was bolder and more disdainful of gender distinctions than any of its predecessors. Its goal was nothing less than the "liberation" of women. The rekindling of feminism in the 1960s was only one early expression of a major upheaval in popular attitudes about both gender and the family. By 1980 a whole panoply of conventions had been reduced to the outmoded opinion of the minority. By then most Americans endorsed working wives, females in high political office, males doing housework, and sex outside of marriage for both men and women. The changes were real and their direction clear—toward more symmetrical male and female roles.[3] Just how far these changes would proceed, whether they would stop short of equality, and what new shape the gender system would finally take, all remained open questions in the 1980s.

THE REVIVAL OF
THE WOMEN'S MOVEMENT

Even during the high tide of the feminine mystique the discerning observer could identify undercurrents of gender change. Social scientists noted that many women were uncomfortable with their assigned places; sociologists talked about role conflict and psychologists worried about identity crises. The editors of the *Ladies' Home Journal* were surprised by the voluminous correspondence generated by articles on "Mothers Who Run Away," and "Why Women Feel Trapped." These quiet tremors of discontent were hardly all that lurked beneath the peaceful domestic surface of the 1950s.

Countless wives and mothers had taken their personal dilemmas into their own hands, often half-consciously and without any societal endorsement, to remodel gender roles more to their own liking. A Los Angeles housewife by the name of Rosalind Loring reported the slow but steady steps that could lead to a remodeled womanhood. "You make minor decisions at first. The first decision is yes I will take a course for credit or I will find some other mothers to start a nursery school and take turns babysitting so I can take a part-time job or work in a voting campaign."[4] In the case of Mrs. Loring these decisions mounted one upon another until she was back in the labor force full-time and embarked on a career all her own. She was not alone. The millions of women who went back to school or back to work in the 1950s may not have been self-conscious feminists, but their individual acts of confidence and courage were the makings of a major transformation in the gender system.

Not until well into the 1960s, however, were these personal decisions articulated as a conscious break with convention or organized into a political or social movement. The word "feminism" was scarcely uttered during the 1940s and 1950s, except to refer to musty relics of the past. Women's politics was confined to voluntary service in the community, feminism to a few veterans of the Woman's party who doggedly introduced the Equal Rights Amend-

308   TOWARD GENDER SYMMETRY: FEMINISM

ment before Congress year after year. Explicitly women's issues were not placed on the political agenda in any visible way until 1961, when John F. Kennedy appointed a Presidential Commission on the Status of Women. The establishment of the Commission was a kind of consolation prize to the women of the Democratic party, whose efforts in the 1960 campaign were rewarded with only a few low-level appointments. Proposed by Esther Peterson, long-time labor activist and veteran of the Women's Trade Union League, and chaired by Eleanor Roosevelt, the Commission's lineage went back to the public women of the Progressive era.

The first report of the Commission, issued in 1963, put this old-fashioned social feminism on full display. It focused on the wages and conditions of women's work, skirted the issue of the Equal Rights Amendment, and disavowed any intention of undermining women's domestic roles. Nonetheless, the Kennedy Commission marked a new beginning as well. It gave women's issues a prominent place on the political agenda for the first time in decades and, perhaps more importantly, put a group of women and men together and set them to thinking concertedly about questions of gender. By sponsoring auxiliary state organizations and providing for extended deliberations, the Commission put into operation a small but viable and visible network of women's politics. It provided an institutional base for the revival of feminism.[5] Whether the Commission on the Status of Women was dealing with industrial workers or educated professional women, its members could not escape the contradictions of the kaleidoscope of roles.

At about the same time that the Commission sat down to work on this problem, Betty Friedan was facing a critical moment in the female life cycle — returning to the labor force after years of child-rearing. From her position on the editorial staff of a women's magazine, Friedan began to overhear and then publicize murmurings of discontent among the home-bound women of suburbia. In the *Feminine Mystique*, published in 1963, Friedan became a best-selling author on the strength of her attack upon domestic womanhood. The quagmire of woman's dual role was given scholarly attention in 1964 in the spring issue of the prestigious journal, *Daedalus*. In a path-breaking article entitled "Equality of the Sexes: An Immodest Proposal," the sociologist Alice Rossi translated these inchoate grumblings into an explicitly feminist manifesto. Slowly the smoldering complaints of workingwomen and restless housewives began to cohere as a platform for reform.

All these concerns came together in Washington, D.C., in 1966 when women assembled for a meeting of the National Conference of Commissions on the Status of Women. In Betty Friedan's hotel room the National Organization of Women (NOW) was founded, the first explicit feminist organization since the suffrage era.[6] In the early years of its existence, NOW propounded a legalistic brand of feminism, demanding equality of opportunity and speaking to the concerns of the educated, relatively affluent professional women who comprised its initial constituency. This first impulse of organization in behalf of women seemed to take clues from moderate civil rights organizations such as the National Association for the Advancement of Colored People. The aim of NOW, as reputedly scribbled on a napkin in a Washington hotel, was "To take actions needed to bring women into the mainstream of American society now with full equality for women in fully equal partnership with men."

Even at the outset, however, this women's movement of the 1960s distinguished itself from the older feminism in critical ways. It had, first of all, stepped clearly outside women's sphere and set its mind on the integrationist goal of "full partnership with men." Second, NOW proclaimed its intention to critically assess and reform the private and domestic realm. "We believe," said the founding members of NOW, "that true partnership between the sexes demands a different concept of marriage, and equitable sharing of the responsibilities of home and children and the economic and social value of homemaking and child care." Clearly, an eventful span of history had intervened between the culmination of the suffrage movement and the formation of NOW in 1966. It placed on the agenda a new set of issues appropriate to the heterosocial emphasis and dual roles of twentieth-century womanhood. Still, the largely professional and middle-aged women who founded NOW could conceive of only traditional political means of working toward their novel goals. Their policy statement on domestic issues concluded rather lamely, "To these ends, we will seek to open a reexamination of laws and mores governing marriage and divorce."[7]

By the mid-1970s NOW claimed 800 chapters and 55,000 members and a much broader program of reforms. Its original focus on legal equality and labor-force discrimination had been extended to encompass such issues as legalized abortion, day care, political power, and family reform. It began to champion the rights of the poor, minorities, and lesbians. The expansion of NOW's program was inspired by the protests of an independent flank of the nascent women's movement, one associated with younger women allied with the New Left and calling itself Women's Liberation.

Feminist consciousness seemed to erupt just as suddenly on college campuses as it had among the career women who founded NOW. Yet Women's Liberation was rooted in basic structural changes in womanhood that were evolving within the life cycles of these younger women. The generation of women that unfurled the banners of Women's Liberation was composed in large part of the daughters of those middle-aged women who were returning to work in ever larger numbers. The younger women, however, should they follow in their mothers' footsteps, would advance into the labor force with greater planning, skills, and forethought. While their mothers had often dropped out of high school during the depression and rarely completed college, the women of the 1960s left secondary school with their diplomas in hand and fully one-third of them went on to college where, by 1968, they constituted 40 percent of the student body.

As education was prolonged, so was marriage delayed; the median age of brides, which had fallen to its all-time low in 1950, began slowly to rise. At college, these women drew away from the parental home and entered into a sphere of independent activity, casual association with male peers, and coequal involvement in preparing and planning for the deployment of their knowledge and talents. By the 1970s, 37 percent of the women between the ages of twenty and twenty-four were single. More women than ever before were at a point in their life cycles and a place in the social system where they could seriously contemplate a choice between marriage and a career.[8] The community of their peers, the experience of their working mothers, the example of NOW, all inspired a conscious assessment of the choices open to them as women.

The turbulent campus politics of the 1960s combined with this shifting structure of womanhood to catalyze a special breed of feminism. Women students had entered freely and fully into the enlivened political arena of the '60s. They went south to claim civil rights for black men and women; they denounced the war in Vietnam; and they participated in the ideological stirrings that defined a New Left in America. The women who lent their wholehearted support to these movements, however, confronted some particularly grating exhibitions of misogyny. In the New Left they were routinely delegated the most menial tasks, like leafleting, mimeographing, and generally serving as secretaries to the revolution. They were often expected to be sexually accommodating as well, best suited to a "prone" position, according to one leader of the Student Nonviolent Coordinating Committee (SNCC) and "saying yes to men who say no" in the antidraft movement.

It was a group of black women working in the South with SNCC who first began to protest against this kind of treatment. In 1966 a women named Ruby Dory Smith Robinson issued a formal attack on the sexual politics of the civil-rights movement, particularly the relations between black men and white women. Two white women, Casey Hayden and Mary King, responded to these stirrings of discontent with a position paper entitled "Sex and Caste: A Kind of Memo." It received national circulation in the April issue of the New-Left periodical *Liberation*. The first volley in what was to be the women's liberation movement had been fired.[9]

This rendition of the origins of women's liberation, as largely an angry reaction to the chauvinism of the male Left, is a familiar story. A recent historian of the movement, Sara Evans, has exposed some of the more intricate and intriguing permutations of women's consciousness that fomented this rebellion. Women had also reaped some positive experience within the New Left, and particularly in the community organizing projects in the South. Successful civil-rights activity in southern towns called for something more than masculine modes of political action—theorizing, debating, and orating before the public. It put a premium on cultivating personal relationships on a face-to-face neighborhood level, skills that women have always exhibited. In order to refine these essential political tools, civil-rights workers turned not to the male leaders of the movement for instruction but to the black women of the community. The ability of local black women to organize everyday social life garnered a level of self-assurance and respect within the community, which awed and inspired female students from the North. This apprenticeship in an age-old mode of woman's politics taught young white women a sense of female competency and self-respect and provided a positive impetus toward feminism.[10]

In the last half of the 1960s, in the scattered, decentralized enclaves of the student movement, this education was repeated over and over again. Women's caucuses grew up amid student protests, community organizing projects, and antiwar activities across the country. When New Leftists gathered in Chicago in 1967 to plan a national strategy of action, this scenario was enacted on a larger stage. A woman raised the issue of sex discrimination at what was called the New Politics convention, only to be patted on her head and called a "little girl." The political maturity of this woman, Shulamith Firestone, would soon be displayed in a book called *The Dialectics of Sex*. This volume articulated, in brilliant and audacious fashion, the contributions of Women's Liberation to the feminism of the late twentieth century. Firestone brought together all the issues that were absorbing the small circles of women that had grown up across the country and that had acquired the name "consciousness-raising" groups. Their discussions dwelt on themes of immediate interest to young, unmarried women: sex, love, reproduction, family relationships — the private side of the inequality of the sexes. With the slogan, "The personal is political," Women's Liberation opened the whole spectrum of human experience to feminist scrutiny. This critical perspective flushed with that of NOW to bring work and family, public and private life, mother and daughter, under the tutelage of a rising women's consciousness.[11]

It would be mistaken to place too much emphasis on strictly political history, be it the Kennedy administration, the civil rights movement, or the New Left, as the point of origin for the new feminism. In some ways the collision with conventional politics was incidental to more basic causal factors intrinsic to the gender system itself. The Women's Liberation movement grew directly out of at least three structures of womanhood which had evolved in the twentieth century.

First of all, feminism grew up within the crevices between women's multiple roles as they unfolded over the course of the female life cycle. For the cohort of middle-class women who formed NOW, the empty-nest stage was the seedtime of feminism. When maternal responsibilities subsided and women began to contemplate returning to school or to the labor force, they became acutely conscious of the restrictions of gender. Domestic roles were suspended in a more radical way for the generation which created the Women's Liberation movement. In the late 1960s more women than ever before in American history were in college, living away from their parental homes, and freed by the affluence of the era from the exigencies of earning their own living as well. Suspended between the families of their birth and the family of marriage, these women were in an ideal position to reconsider woman's place. Those women who went south to participate in the civil rights movement, and ended up in the vanguard of a new feminism, illustrate this principle in the extreme. Almost entirely college educated, three-quarters of them planned to go on to graduate or professional school. One of their number captured the possibilities of this moment in the female life cycle in just a few words: "I have no husband to consult . . . no degree to finish."[12]

Thus, two generations of women, each in their own ways enjoying a reprieve from domesticity, worked unconsciously in tandem to resurrect feminism. This generational cross-fertilization is a second structural base of the feminist revival. In some cases, for example, when founders of Women's Liberation recalled being introduced to *The Feminine Mystique* by their mothers, the matrilineage of the women's movement was direct and explicit.[13] More often the influence of the mother's generation was more diffuse, but equally powerful. As the daughters left for college, their own mothers presented models of something more than domesticity: they engaged in voluntary work, resumed their education, or reentered the labor force. The life cycles of the two generations, in other words, intersected in such a way as to reinforce the impression that womanhood was no longer a simple and single matter of homemaking.

The feminism which emerged at this juncture was deeply marked by a third circumstance of its founding. Unlike the nineteenth-century women's movement, the new feminism emerged from conditions of contact and similarity between the sexes, not out of a separate woman's sphere. For the older group associated with NOW, women's revolt was stimulated by contact with the labor force, a previously male sphere. On the job, in a breadwinning role parallel to that of their husbands, the women of the 1960s saw sexual discrimination with a new clarity, in the stark reality of unequal paychecks.

The special anger of the younger cohort of feminists was kindled by abrasive contact with their male peers—in the classroom, the political meeting, and the bedroom and kitchen as well. Intimate contacts between the sexes proved especially explosive. The college students of the 1960s were the first generation in American history to engage in premarital promiscuity and cohabitation in any appreciable numbers. When sexual contacts and shared housekeeping occurred outside the bonds of engagement or matrimony, the conventional sexual division of power and of work became suspect. Women began to complain about male roommates who enjoyed the privileges of the bed but wouldn't make it. It was contact with males or the male world, that is, participation in the heterosocial atmosphere of twentieth-century women, that sparked the anger so essential to the resuscitation of American feminism.

The conditions which enkindled feminist consciousness in the late 1960s all turned into major historical trends in the decade that followed. Women's participation in the labor force grew at an unprecedented rate in the 1970s until it accounted for the majority of women, regardless of marital status. Female college enrollment mounted at a similar pace while the marriage rate declined, and the proportion of young women living on their own more than doubled. The generational continuity was also maintained as the daughters of working mothers demonstrated greater career ambitions, and the new generation of women built securely on the work rate of their mothers to rise to even higher levels of employment.[14] Whether in the labor force or in the playgrounds of the swinging '70s, finally, the mingling of the sexes continued to mark women's experience and generate both sexual combat and gender consciousness.

Consequently, the women's movement and the ideology of women's liberation grew rapidly in the 1970s and its programs became more comprehensive, more unified, and more structured. An estimated 300,000 women enrolled in formal feminist organizations. NOW was joined by the Women's Equity Action League; working-class and black women, once highly suspicious of the women's movement had, by the middle '70s, formed their own feminist associations. The Congress of Labor Union Women, affiliated with the AFL-CIO, had more than fifty chapters. Workingwomen also formed associations outside the male union structure in New York, Boston, Chicago, and San Francisco, to name a few major cities. Black feminist groups formed in New York and San Francisco. Meanwhile, such mainstream women's organizations as the Girl Scouts of America, the League of Women Voters, and the YWCA began to support feminist crusades. Consciousness-raising groups spawned a bevy of local self-help projects: women's centers, homes for battered wives, women's health clinics, rape crisis centers. At one awkward moment in the early '70s the movement was ripped through with factions. NOW and Left feminist groups such as Red Stockings eyed one another with suspicion, while lesbians distrusted heterosexual feminists and vice-versa.

But by 1977 all these diverse factions were able to work together in relative harmony and even to luxuriate briefly in a sense of unified and triumphant feminism. The occasion was the meeting of the International Women's Year Congress in Houston, Texas. The 2,000 official delegates to the International Women's Year Congress in Houston represented an unprecedented breadth and depth of feminist consciousness. They had been selected at fifty-six state and territorial meetings attended by more than 130,000 women. The delegates were an almost perfect cross section of the female population: white, black, and Hispanic, rich and poor, the famous and the anonymous, the young and the old. Unlike the suffragists, or even the Women's Liberation movement of the late 1960s, this congress of women could not be dismissed as a white middle-class coterie.

The twenty-five resolutions drafted in Houston were equally comprehensive. They spoke to the interests of minorities and businesswomen, of workers and homemakers, of wives and of lesbians. Nor did the National Plan of Action seem to neglect a single aspect of women's lives: the inequities in the home, on the job, and in Washington were all addressed. Despite the special urgency directed to the passage of the Equal Rights Amendment (a legal reform first proposed a half century earlier), the feminists of the 1970s were not pinning all their hopes on one solitary reform as had the suffragists. They also broke with feminists of the Progressive Era by rejecting political strategies that would designate their demands as isolated women's issues and segregate them in a woman's sphere.

The only resolution defeated by the Houston delegates recommended establishing a separate women's department in the federal government. Rather, the women's movement of the 1970s claimed a position at the very center of public policy and American life. Their meeting had been funded by the United States Congress. A network of feminists had quickly swung into action all across the country, and in less than a year parlayed the relatively small appropriation of $5 million into a vast machinery of national communication, grass-roots debate, and public attention. Thus a movement that had begun scarcely a decade before, among chortles about bra-burners and man-haters, now basked in legitimacy and brandished its political savvy on the front pages and television screens of the land.[15]

There was, of course, some very vocal resistance to this emerging feminist consensus. Opponents of Women's Liberation had conspired to turn the Houston meeting into a celebration of women's contentment in the home and under the protective wing of their husbands. They had succeeded in some states; the antifeminist delegation from Mississippi, for example, included five male members of the Ku Klux Klan. Yet for all their energy and organizational support from conservative organizations, the antifeminists secured only one-quarter of the seats at Houston. The prediction of opposition spokeswoman Phyllis Schafly, that the Houston meeting would mark the ignominious defeat of Women's Liberation, proved to be a mistaken political forecast. The disgruntled minority was left to meet outside the official assembly in another Houston amphitheater, where they focused their outrage on the feminist support of legalized abortion, the rights of lesbians, and the Equal Rights Amendment. None of these antifeminist positions conformed to majority opinion in the United States in 1977.[16]

By then, feminist consciousness had also infiltrated American popular culture. During the fervid beginnings of Women's Liberation, a group of women had staged a sit-in at the offices of the *Ladies' Home Journal* and won the right to publish their feminist protests within the pages of the oldest citadel of the feminine mystique. Just a few years later the editors of the *Journal* routinely laced women's culture with feminist concerns and rhetoric. Even more conservative women's magazines, such as *Family Circle*, greeted housewives at supermarket checkout counters with explicit attacks on the "sex discrimination" to which homemakers and workingwomen were equally susceptible. The workingwoman, not the feminist per se, was given the largest and most respected treatment in these popular journals. Whole new magazines were devoted to her, *The Working Woman, The New Woman*, and *Savvy*, for the females of the executive suite. The same magazines that had courted young women with marital fantasies in the 1950s now offered career counseling and even some oblique incitement to feminist protest. *Ma-*

demoiselle, for example, broke with a long-standing taboo and reported statistics on the wage differential between male and female workers. Then the author glibly raised this rhetorical question: "What if everyone gathered together and rose one by one out of the closet. Pandemonium."[17]

Women awakened in the 1970s to discover, along with their new-found strength and confidence, that they were still in many ways the second sex. The massing of women in the labor force had made at least one species of sexual inequity patently obvious, for now a woman's secondary status could be measured by the clear and definitive standard of her paycheck, which usually amounted to several thousand dollars less than a male's annual income. The demand for equal pay for equal work became almost as all-American as apple pie and was edging out motherhood as the preoccupation of contemporary women. In fact, the majority of Americans endorsed Women's Liberation as a package. In 1971, 42 percent of the population expressed general agreement with the goals of the women's movement, and by 1975 feminism was endorsed by a solid majority, 59 percent of the American people.[18]

THE PROMISE AND THE FRUSTRATION OF THE FEMALE LABOR MARKET

Since its very inauguration, the women's movement had been standing watch over female workers and defending them against discrimination. NOW was instrumental, for example, in pressing for government enforcement of the sex provisions of the Civil Rights Act of 1964, and of the Equal Employment Opportunities Commission. A ground swell of feminist consciousness helped to explain the fact that women have so fully utilized this agency for judicial redress. By 1973 women were filing more than 30,000 complaints against their employers annually. Some women won lucrative settlements from violators of their civil right to equal pay for equal work. The most celebrated case extracted approximately $70 million in back pay from the American Telephone and Telegraph Company.[19]

In 1978, the cause of the woman worker became the concern of the majority of American women. In that year one-half of all adult women were enrolled in the labor force; by 1982 the figure had risen to 53 percent. The improvement of women's wages was also clearly in the interest of the men and the children of the United States. As of 1978, 51 percent of all families contained a working wife or mother, and one in four children relied on a woman as his or her chief support. Husbands with working wives enjoyed a family income one-third higher than those who depended on a single male wage-earner. Work and home were no longer dichotomous aspects of womanhood—either/or choices to be confined to separate portions of the life cycle. In fact, in 1979 the mothers of school-age children had a higher rate of employment than did childless women.[20]

Large numbers of the women who flocked into the labor force in the 1970s also transgressed against the conventional sex-typing of occupations. The busy traffic across gender lines led, for example, to a 144 percent increase in the number of female accountants and a 100 percent increment of women chemists. Conversely, the '70s saw a 152 percent growth in the number of male nurses and a 4,000 percent rise in the ranks of male dental hygienists. In many cases these infractions against the older gender codes enhanced women's economic and social status. In general the higher ranks of the occupational structure, especially professional-technical and managerial-administrative positions, exhibited the strongest growth rates for female employment between 1970 and 1979. This trend promises to continue, according to a recent poll of college freshmen which found that the proportions of women who contemplated professional careers rose threefold between 1969 and 1979; the comparable figure for aspirants to business careers had quadrupled.

By 1980, women had made a solid dent in the male facade of the most prestigious professions. The proportion of women among lawyers had risen from 4 percent in 1972 to 13 percent in 1980. At the same date women occupied about one in three of the seats in the nation's law schools. The gender cast of the medical profession was undergoing a similar facelifting: less than one in ten medical students were female in 1960; almost one in five were in 1980. The change seemed nothing short of revolutionary in the ranks of America's young elite. When the Princeton class of 1973 held its fifth reunion, only 2 percent of the female graduates were housewives, while 22 percent were either doctors or lawyers.[21]

Beneath and behind these dramatic examples of women's success, however, were the majority of female workers whose humbler

positions in the labor force drastically deflated the overall measure
of women's economic status. On the average, the wages of women
relative to men declined slightly over the last two decades, dropping
from about 64 percent in 1955 and 61 percent in 1960, to 59
percent in 1970, where it remained in 1979. Women workers
continued to congregate at the lowest rungs on the economic ladder
throughout the '60s and the '70s. Late in the last decade only 1.1
percent of all women workers made more than $15,000 a year; 45
percent earned less than $5,000.[22]

Much of this inequity is a function of the continuing sex segregation of the labor force. Most of the women who flocked to work
in the 1960s and '70s went directly into low-paying sex-typed jobs.
Nearly half of these new women workers, some 5 million in number,
settled for low-level office jobs. Clerical work had become the an-
alogue of domestic service a century earlier, a virtual ghetto of
women workers. More than one in three women workers could be
found in this single job pool, where 80 percent of all employees
are female. The occupants of this woman's sphere are ill-paid but
not uneducated. Forty-seven percent of all women who graduated
high school became secretaries or kindred workers; fully one in six
college graduates joined them at these jobs. Taken as a whole, the
sales sector of the occupational structure was more integrated sexually. A closer look, however, locates large pockets of sex discrimination within this segment of the labor force as well. In the large
department stores of Manhattan during the mid '70s, for example,
it was virtually impossible to find a saleswoman earning more than
$10,000 a year. Females were crowded behind counters laden with
cheaper goods, where their labor was typically rewarded by $70
weekly. Whatever the segment of the labor force, employers were
ingenious at devising job classifications that rationalized low pay
for women's work. In one electrical company, for example, 75
percent of all women and 45 percent of all men were found in the
four lowest job classifications.[23]

The female sector of the American occupational structure was
large and diversified enough by 1980 to harbor the most archaic as
well as the most futuristic job categories. On the one hand, sweatshops were still hidden away on the narrow streets of lower Manhattan or Chinatown in San Francisco, beckoning the newest female
immigrants from the Caribbean, Latin America, and the Far East.
Chicana workers labored in the garment factories of Los Angeles

ten hours a day and six days a week for well below the minimum wage.

At the other end of the spectrum, women were found wielding the most advanced machinery of the information age. In the last quarter of the twentieth century, women clerical workers took the helm of complicated new machinery for the processing of information. Large insurance companies and corporate offices were dividing their paper work into single, minute, repetitive tasks for individual employees. In "word-processing centers," for example, women would spend entire days operating one machine—a typewriter, telephone, or computer terminal. This highly specialized division of labor extracted its usual price of fatigue and alienation. Keypunch operators in one large firm, for example, resorted to a clever stratagem, synchronizing the rhythms of their office machines, in order to maintain their sanity. One worker explained: "I guess it was the only kind of entertainment you could have. Like I said, your hands were occupied, your eyes were occupied, you couldn't move your body, couldn't talk. You only had the numbers on the sheets and the sound of the other machines." Predictably, work situations like these were noted for a very high rate of turnover and in themselves offered little ground for feminist celebration of women's advance into the labor force.[24]

Although the majority of women were fully integrated into the labor force by 1980 including its most modern sectors, they still were not placed within easy reach of economic or political power. In the high technology industries, for example, women were operatives and clerical workers, not designers or managers. In fact, women were very ill-prepared to take command of the most rapidly growing job sector, technical and scientific employment. Women accounted for only 3 percent of all engineers in the '70s, and only a tiny proportion of young women had the background in mathematics to qualify them even to major in technical fields in college.

Despite the greater glamour attached to the business woman during the 1970s, females were not making great inroads into the field of management, where they accounted for only 2 percent of all top executives as of the mid 1970s. Similarly, women occupied precious few positions of political power. A study in the mid 1970s counted only 51 women in high political posts. As of 1982, they held no governorships, one cabinet-level position, only a handful of seats in Congress, and of course, one post on the Supreme Court. Perhaps the advance of women into top level positions is only a matter of time, the time it takes for the women educated since the feminist revival to work their way to the top. Between 1972 and 1975, for example, the number of women within state legislatures more than doubled, while masses of others were beginning their political apprenticeship in law school. Whether these younger educated women would continue their career climb and ultimately reshape the sexual division of power in America will not be determined for some time to come.[25]

THE DELICATE IMBALANCE: FAMILY AND WORK IN THE 1970s

The past history of their sex would suggest, however, that during the '70s and '80s the young women who grew up with the feminist movement were fast approaching a critical period in their life cycles. It remained to be seen whether marriage and motherhood would diminish their appetite for a hefty masculine portion of power and wealth. When less ambitious and privileged women returned to work after the interruptions of infant care, they might be bound all the more tightly to low-level jobs. Women of the last quarter of the twentieth century still face these formidable domestic hurdles.

First of all, although the birthrate and marriage rate have fallen precipitously, very few women have forsworn matrimony and childbearing entirely. Less than 10 percent of all women in their early thirties were single, and only 13 percent of those married were childless.[26] While work was proving more compatible with marriage, it was still difficult to ally with the responsibilities of the young mother. In fact, the majority of the mothers of children under three, approximately 60 percent, stayed home to care for their infants.[27] It is still only the childless, single, black, and professional women who routinely followed the completely uninterrupted work pattern that men took for granted. The employers of women could, and did, rely on what they called "attrition and pregnancy" to keep a good supply of cheap female laborers flowing in and out of their employment.[28] All the domestic impediments to occupational success had hardly disappeared.

TOWARD GENDER SYMMETRY: FEMINISM

Women had succeeded, however, in minimizing the duration of their maternity leaves. The baby boom had already begun to subside in the late 1950s, and soon thereafter women acted decisively to keep their families small. The availability after 1960 of highly effective oral contraceptives facilitated this diminution of maternal responsibilities. But even if this failed, women remained adamant about limiting the number of births. Already in 1961, it was estimated that from 200,000 to 1.2 million women resorted to abortion. In 1973, after the Supreme Court approved termination of pregnancy in the first trimester, American women maximized their control over reproduction. In the same year, most young women identified two children as their preferred family size. The mothers of the '70s typically bore their last child before they were twenty-five and their children were all in school soon thereafter (41 percent of children aged three to five attended nursery or preschool). With some tight planning, women could reenter the labor force after less than a ten-year interlude of full-time mothering. When she reentered the labor force, the young mother of the 1970s might have slightly tarnished skills, but they had not become hopelessly rusty.[29]

Still, the mother who returned to the labor force was not footloose and free of domestic responsibilities. Studies of family time budgets in the 1970s reveal that the typical workingwoman still devoted at least thirty hours a week to home duties, bringing her total labor time to somewhere between sixty-six and seventy-five hours, usually a good fifteen hours in excess of her husband's working time. Keen-eyed social scientists have been able to detect only tiny, if any, increases in husbands' involvement in housework when their wives entered the labor force. A man's surplus leisure undoubtedly sent him back into the labor force more rested and relaxed than his spouse. The freedom from household chores, furthermore, allowed ambitious men to devote extended hours to professional and business advancement. Working mothers, on the other hand, would have some difficulty arranging the seventy-hour workweek that was routine among up-and-coming male careerists. More often, young wives and mothers could not manage even a full forty hours of work outside the home: fewer than half of all workingwomen were employed full time through the year. The deficits associated with part-time work include diminished wages, lesser chances of promotion, and loss of fringe benefits. This pattern of female labor-force participation offered considerable savings to the employer, however, and was increasingly coveted by managers of the sales and service sector of the economy.[30]

Part-time work is only one of the compromises that makes the increasing employment of mothers possible. It is but one element in a complex rearrangement of women's time and labor whereby American families coped with the inflationary spiral of the '70s. By then, less than half of all male jobs could support a family of four in comfort. Thus, the proportion of families that lived on the income of one male worker declined sharply from the rate of fifty-six in a hundred in 1948 to thirty-one in a hundred by the mid '70s. Women's income, though typically less than one-third of the total family budget, was essential insurance against poverty or a severely lowered standard of living. Two-thirds of all working-women did yeoman service as breadwinners: either supporting themselves, their fatherless families, or households where male income was less than $7,000 annually.

The complicated and tightly scheduled allocation of women's time between the home and the labor force was the pivot of family finances in the '70s, the lynchpin of what scholars were calling the "new home economics." The efficiency of this system was worked out by the Social Security Administration in 1976. According to their estimates, the young family would actually lose money if the mother entered the labor force and paid the going market price for child care and housework. According to this mathematical model, it was only when a woman reached her late twenties and her children entered school, that her outside earnings would exceed the cost of her purchase of necessary domestic services. And even then, she would net only a paltry $1,078 for her pains.[31]

The strategy that worked so economically for the family often operated to the detriment of women as individuals. It could lock a wife into a low-paying job and grant to her husband the superior domestic authority conveyed by his larger paycheck. It kept her frantically busy. Within the American working class this compromise strained the relations of husband and wife at the same time that it undermined the conservative values of the males. One woman reported:

My husband says I don't have to work, but if I don't, we'll never get anywhere. I guess it's a matter of pride with him.

It makes him feel bad, like he's not supporting us good enough.
I understand how he feels but I also know that, no matter
what he says, if I stop working, when the taxes on the house
have to be paid there won't be any money if we didn't have
my salary.

Her husband grudgingly agreed: "I guess she's right; I don't want
her to work but even if I worked at night too I don't know how
much money I'd make."

While this working-class husband clung weakly to the ideal of
the one male breadwinner, a middle-class student made his compromise with the new family economy in a more arrogant fashion.

"I believe that it is a good thing for mothers to return to full-
time work when the children are grown, provided the work
is important and worthwhile. Otherwise, housewives get hung-
up with tranquilizers because they have no outlet for their
abilities. A woman should want her husband's success more
than he should want hers. Her work should not interfere with
or hurt his in any way."

This reaction was typical of ivy-league males in the early 1970s,
50 percent of whom wanted their prospective wives to remain sta-
tioned in the home until their children were grown. By the third
quarter of the twentieth century, the ideal household division of
labor had been pared down to this fine point: the majority of men
and women agreed that both spouses should work, but that if either
partner were to sacrifice career gains for the other, it should be the
wife.[32]

Thus, within the American home, male and female teetered on
a delicate imbalance of power, while wide margins of inequity
separated the sexes in the labor force. Yet there is no doubt that
male attitudes were shifting slowly toward greater recognition of
women's value as workers. At the same time social scientists recorded a dramatic decline of the work ethic among men. Women,
for their part, were clearly finding satisfaction in the new adjustment
of their home and work roles. Despite all the exhausting schedules
and low pay, women consistently reported basic contentment with
their jobs. "I guess I really work because I enjoy it," said one
working-class woman. "I'm good at it, and I like that feeling. It's

good to feel like you're competent." Although most women claimed that they went to work primarily to meet family expenses, they also reaped personal rewards from involvement in the outside world, interaction with their co-workers, and the intrinsic interest of their work. The greatest cause of dissatisfaction among workingwomen was still conflict about their home responsibilities. As one woman described it, "You're either at work feeling like you should be at home with your sick child or you're at home feeling like you should be at work." The contradictions of the dual roles of women had not all evaporated in the 1970s.[33]

How did the American woman manage to shoulder this double burden and even find some cause for joy in it? If the American advertisers are to be believed, a quaff of iron supplement, a stock of aspirin, and regular trips to the fast-food counter would make her busy life tolerable. Relief from the tension and fatigue of the dual role, in other words, was offered for sale in the consumer economy. The working wife increasingly delegated the chores of the family cook to restaurateurs and the manufacturers of prepared foods. In 1980, one in every two food dollars was being spent in a restaurant. The trend appeared even in domestic architecture, where plans for the dining room were erased from blueprints for model homes and apartments.

The most personalized family services could now be purchased in the marketplace. Early in the 1970s *Barrons* magazine alerted the American business community to the profits awaiting those who invested in child-care facilities. Since then, the number of children within licensed day-care centers has more than tripled. Still, a large unexploited market remains, as only one in ten of the children of working mothers is enrolled in such facilities. During the mid '70s a St. Louis businessman named Perry Mendel had set about providing this family service, much in the manner of McDonalds or Colonel Sanders. Mendel owned approximately 170 standardized day-care centers located in eighteen states. He expected in the near future to be the corporate foster parent of 50,000 children, superintending them behind the bright plastic facades of Kinder-cares located in shopping centers across the country. Kinder-care is the most lurid example of how women's domestic roles can be absorbed into the marketplace, converted from private services into private profits. Thus women's employment has necessitated alterations in the relationships between the family and private enterprise, and tips the balance of providing personal services further in the direction of the marketplace.[34]

Neither market researchers nor family sociologists would predict that the family was about to be eliminated from this uneasy partnership. In fact, the family still acted as the chief manager of personal services; husbands and wives still made the decisions necessary to supply the everyday human needs for food, shelter, clothing, education, comfort, love, and companionship. Families, and especially mothers, still made the exhausting trips to the marketplace to purchase these services.

Women also continued to invest great energy in cultivating personal intimacy and overseeing child development, aspects of human experience that have not yet been transformed into cash exchanges. Consequently, the labor of wives and mothers still required a minimum of thirty hours a week. Hence, if woman's double burden was to be reduced further, some rearrangement of roles within the home would be required. It is highly unlikely that in the 1980s a spate of domestic servants, apprentices, and extended relatives will appear and rescue the worker-homemaker in her hours of need. If the burden of domestic responsibilities was to be lifted from woman's back, it would have to be taken up, at least to some extent, by her mate. This was no longer a tabooed subject nor an outrageous proposal. In fact, it was timidly discussed even in the women's magazines, where short articles on fathering were quietly planted within the female world of the home.

Dr. Benjamin Spock himself repented his former neglect of the male role in child care: "Now I recognize," he wrote in the 1976 edition of *Baby and Child Care*, "that the father's responsibility is as great as the mother's." This proposition received considerable support among the educated population; among college students polled recently, the vast majority of both males and females endorsed the statement that fathers and mothers should spend equal amounts of time with their children. Whether up-and-coming businessmen and burly truck drivers would, in fact, put these newly acquired values into practice remains an open question. Still, this shift in attitudes cannot be overemphasized, for it challenged one of the oldest and most fundamental components of the gender system — the near monopoly of females in matters of child care. Similarly, while men were not fighting to usurp the role of the housewife, they were slowly accepting a few extra chores around the house, notably shopping and dishwashing. Still, these changes were only whispered promises of a more balanced allocation of family labor. Workingwomen themselves tended to delegate domestic tasks to their daughters rather than their spouses.[35]

Men were also reluctant to provide psychological support and personal service to working spouses. The female breadwinner, in other words, was often denied the benefits of wifely assistance traditionally supplied to workingmen. Married women continued to suffer what sociologist Jesse Bernard called a "relational deficit." Their requests for emotional sustenance and understanding from their husbands were repeatedly met with rejection, indifference, or passivity. At the same time, American wives, even among the working class, were no longer satisfied with this emotional imbalance. Not even the stridently antifeminist tract *Total Womanhood* tolerated the traditional emotional and psychological wall between the sexes. Its author, Marabel Morgan, addressed herself to an audience of wives whose mates, "like so many American males, may be like an empty cup emotionally." Of her early married life Morgan said, "if I were to have any meaningful conversations, I decided that they would have to be with my girl friends."[36]

While a generation ago working-class women complacently accepted their sex-segregated sphere, resorting to mothers and sisters for advice and companionship, now they were making emotional demands on their husbands. Some were slowly receiving a positive response. One working-class husband exhibited his troubled, painfully shifting consciousness this way: "I sometimes think I'm selfish. But when she needs support, I just don't give it to her. Maybe it's not just selfishness, it's that I don't know what she wants and I don't know how." Thus, a delicate emotional imbalance between the sexes had also become a matter of conscious struggle between men and women. Whether they expressed it in the clichéd tones of *Total Womanhood* or in the protests of women's liberation, females were beginning to question another fundamental principle of gender asymmetry, the bifurcation of temperament between the masculine and feminine poles of reason and the emotions.[37]

Men were playing a largely passive, reactive role in such revisions of the gender system. Females made the major break with the sexual division of labor by transforming themselves into nearly lifelong workers. It was women who pressured for changes within the family and in intimate relations. Not all males responded positively and pacifically to the active demands of women. The amount of domestic violence grew appreciably in the 1970s. Estimates of the number of battered wives ran as high as 1 million annually and constituted as much as 70 percent of all assault victims in some city hospitals.[38] These statistics could be interpreted in several different ways. They might be simply another sign of women's rising level of resistance, their refusal to remain silent about the crimes perpetrated against them, even by their husbands. The increase in wife beating and rape could also represent a brutal backlash against feminism and the threatened independence of the female sex. As such, violence against women could be either the futile reaction of beleaguered males, or a blunt reassertion of male authority capable of intimidating women back into quiescence. Either way, the battle of the sexes still raged on, and at this most primitive level where the male maintained his ancient form of dominance, brute strength. It added a final sense of apprehension and uncertainty to the contemporary position of women.

THE DISENGAGEMENT OF THE SEXES AND THE FEMALE-HEADED FAMILY

One possible response to the contemporary tension between the sexes is simply to retreat from the chief battleground of male and female, the family. Indeed, this possibility stalks ominously through contemporary consciousness and behavior. During the 1970s, an avalanche of self-help literature for the divorced and Madison Avenue's ardent courtship of the "single" suggested that family breakdown had assumed the dimensions of a major social phenomenon. The Carnegie Foundation, as well as the White House, sponsored studies of the family crisis, sure signs that the trouble in the American home had become a matter of major national concern.

The 1980 census established that deviation from the traditional family structure—the co-residence of two parents and their natural children—had become almost a convention in its own right. Twenty-one percent of all Americans lived in female-headed households, up from 9 percent twenty years earlier. Twenty-seven percent of all residential units were labeled "non-family" households by the census bureau since they did not contain any persons related by blood, marriage, or adoption. The rapid increase in the divorce rate projected a particularly high incidence of family discontinuity for American children: demographers predicted that two in five of them could expect, at some time in their youth, to reside with only one parent. Conversely, only 38 percent of all households contained any children under eighteen. Although the majority of Americans still lived with relatives, no one could deny that alternative domestic arrangements were now more than occasional deviations from the norm. It was a very realistic possibility that larger numbers of husbands, wives, and children—male and female—would go their separate ways into the 1980s.[39]

The 1970s witnessed not only an epidemic of uncoupling, but also an increasingly recalcitrant rate of family formation. Demographers described this phenomenon as "the rise of the primary individual," meaning that, for the first time in American history, significant numbers of men and women chose to live alone. In 1900 only 4 or 5 percent of the population resided alone or with non-relatives. The proportion had risen to 9.3 percent a half century later. By 1980 the ratio was more than one in four adults. The changing behavior of young women made a substantial contribution to this statistical trend. Already in 1970, 17 percent of all females aged eighteen to twenty-four were "primary individuals" living apart from their parents and without spouses. In other words, significant numbers of young women were no longer waiting for husbands to escort them outside their parental homes. At the same time, they were postponing marriages with greater alacrity. Over 50 percent of all women aged twenty to twenty-four were single in 1980. The percentage of women who remained unmarried in their late twenties nearly doubled between 1970 and 1980, accounting for close to 30 percent of the women in that age group.[40]

The young, independent woman was what the market researchers had in mind when they relished the consumer habits of the single. Magazines such as *Glamour*, *Mademoiselle*, and *Cosmopolitan* cultivated the tastes of the "primary individual" for personal pleasures—furnishing her single apartment, decorating her young body, eating, drinking, and traveling. These magazines courted advertisers with the boast that their readers were "college-educated, career-oriented and committed to good health, good looks, and good living." According to the business pages of *The New York Times*, advertisers were puzzling over "How Do You Talk to a Working

Woman?" If this workingwoman was single and relatively affluent, they resorted to direct appeals to hedonism. A model spendthrift proclaimed from an advertisement in *Psychology Today*, "I love myself." The species of narcissism intoned by magazine editors and advertisers was hardly self-contained. It almost always appeared in consort with two intimate partners, men and money. *Mademoiselle* magazine introduced this triumvirate with special panache in an article entitled "Money, Men and You." "Money means success. Power. Clout. It's the latest equalizer in the battle between the sexes and, quite possibly, the new erogenous zone." This latest fashion in womanhood had been stripped of the self-sacrificing aura of mothers and wives. It presumed that sexual gratification would be found outside of marriage and was, in fact, relatively oblivious to the family, the essential habitat of womanhood past.[41]

Some women, to some extent, and for at least some portion of their lifetimes, lived out the hedonistic, extrafamilial female image. The vast majority of women who came of age in the 1960s and '70s would engage in sexual intercourse before marriage. Surveys of college students actually demonstrated that some single women were more active sexually than were their male peers. Yet, by and large, males were still more likely to sustain the sybaritic and self-absorbed life-style. After all, if money was the great aphrodisiac of the 1970s, as *Mademoiselle* contended, men certainly retained greater control over this sexual resource. They were better equipped to maintain the affluent, single life-style. Single households were more prevalent among young men; and their numbers grew eightfold between 1950 and 1974. Thus, whatever carefree *joie de vivre* came with the decline of the marriage rate was more likely to accrue to bachelors than to single women.[42]

Whatever the joys of the single state, over 90 percent of all women had married by their early thirties. Yet even these not-so-young couples were recalcitrant about homemaking, as increasing numbers of women postponed or forswore childbearing. The percentage of thirty-year-old women who were childless rose from a postwar high of 14 percent in 1969 to almost 26 percent ten years later. And the rates were expected to go even higher. Surveys of young women indicated that as many as 20 percent of them expected to forego the role of mother, while demographers predicted that as much as 50 percent of the women born during the baby boom would bear one or no children. Although the '80s saw a minor baby boom for older women it was hardly large enough to recoup all the lost fertility of the barren 1970s.[43]

For many women the dramatic curtailment of fertility was a positive and a self-assured choice. For others it was a result of what appeared to be a kind of crisis of reproduction. The necessity of supporting herself, maintaining a career, or supporting a dual income household, along with the lowered marriage rate and the high prospects for divorce, all made it increasingly difficult to find the time, energy, and security necessary for parenting. By choice or circumstances, women were becoming disengaged from ties to children as well as mates.

Probably the most commonplace crisis in the social relations of gender was experienced in yet another way, through marital conflict, separation, and divorce. It was estimated that 40 percent of the marriages formed in the 1970s would end in divorce. The high incidence of divorce, that defined the family status of millions of women in the 1960s and 1970s, is subject to several different interpretations. On the one hand, it is testimony to women's greater independence. Thanks to the skills, economic power, and worldly experience acquired in the labor force, women are now better prepared to terminate unsatisfactory marriages. Yet it would be a mistake to assume that divorce simply liberated women from the family. In fact, it was far more likely to compound her domestic burdens, as she assumed responsibility for the bulk of the financial support as well as the personal care of the children.

Since the 1960s, the divorce rate has skyrocketed among families with children, the number of children affected by divorce growing by 700 percent. Most of these children continue to reside with their mothers; few of them are adequately supported by alimony or child-support payments. Since women were (and still are) bearing the brunt of the cost of family breakdown, divorce bred gross sexual inequity. Studies made in the early '70s demonstrated the price of divorce in graphic terms. The typical monthly salary of a divorced man was $800, as opposed to $300 for the divorced female. According to another sociological accounting, the income of a typical divorced man went up 16 percent over the five-year period after the termination of his marriage; that of his wife declined by 6.7 percent. Thus, divorce is hardly an unalloyed act of women's liberation, and predictably most divorcées, motivated in no small part by the difficulties of rearing children alone, soon remarried. Yet the rate of remarriage also declined in the 1970s, especially among older divorced women, many of whom faced a prolonged solitary struggle to rear America's children. Theirs would be a quadrupled burden, playing both male and female roles, both in the home and in the labor force.[44]

Consequently, family instability was a fearful prospect to many women, particularly to those who still remained full-time wives and mothers. One happily married woman could not dispel this anxious premonition, "there's this ghastly blast that homemaking is a hazardous occupation. If he keels over or takes off with some young thing where does that leave the typical homemaker?" Another housewife put it this way: "All of a sudden he is laid off his job or he has a heart attack or he tells you he wants a divorce or maybe, like me, you want it first and then you see how vulnerable a homemaker is, how dependent you have been on his goodwill and good fortune all these years. And then you start to shake."

Even the women's magazines felt obliged to grapple with this problem. *Family Circle* magazine could no longer take the domestic circumstances of its female readers for granted. It proffered advice for "displaced homemakers," "twenty million middle-aged women, victims of age and sex discrimination as well as their own rusty skills." For the divorced woman, *Family Circle* recommended the help of voluntary associations, government appropriations, and advice on "how to find a job after twenty years." In the 1970s this magazine, once the bastion of comfortable domesticity, exuded a sense of family emergency. Its pages also harbored such ominous titles as this: "If Your Husband Dies: What Every Wife Should Know." Such anxieties could feed the "pro-family" movement and preoccupy the candidates for *Total Womanhood*.[45]

No longer could the female-headed household be regarded as a deviant family form associated with racial minorities. In 1980, 21 percent of the families with children had only one parent, and in nine cases out of ten, that parent was a female. At the same time the economic position of female-headed families, relative to unbroken homes, was worsening for blacks and white alike. In 1967 the income of female-headed households amounted to 60 percent of that of two-parent families. Within five years, the figure had been reduced to 46 percent for whites and 44 percent among blacks. Female-headed households were in great risk of falling beneath the poverty level. In 1980, when 12 percent of all U.S. households were impoverished, the standard of living in one of two households headed by women was beneath the poverty level. The latter figure had risen from 37 percent only ten years earlier. Yet female household heads were more likely to be full-time workers, regardless of the age and number of their children. To put it bluntly, family disruption in the 1970s dealt its most pernicious consequences and most onerous burdens to females who were raising children alone.

Family breakdown also combined with the meager wages of women workers to create a major source of economic deprivation in America. In the 1970s, female-headed families accounted for 40 to 50 percent of all the U.S. households living in poverty. As a matter of fact, the entire increase in poverty in that decade could be accounted for by a rise in the number of families headed by women. The impoverishment of these families, furthermore, threatened to multiply economic hardship over the generations. Half the children under eighteen who live in female-headed households were poor. Three out of five of those under six years of age were growing up under conditions of material deprivation. Thus, sexual inequality combined with the disengagement of the sexes to set the lowest boundaries of the American social structure.[46]

These complications of gender in the contemporary United States also underpinned racial inequality, which was increasing rather than abating since the 1960s. The real income of black families amounted to less than 60 percent of the white average in 1978. Yet among married-couple households the ratio was much less dramatic, black-income amounting to 81 percent of the white standard. The overall increase in the dollar margin of racial inequity correlated directly with the rise in black female-headed households. While 11.6 percent of white families were maintained by women in 1979, more than four out of ten black families depended solely on female income, which averaged out to less than a third of the American median.

The cruelest blow was dealt to America's black children, more than 50 percent of whom were growing up in poverty-stricken homes without a regular male wage-earner. The dire condition of black households could no longer be dismissed by sanguine references to the "strengths of black families." In the 1980s America's ghettoes were breeding a second generation of impoverished children. With the black unemployment rate on the rise, and as high as 60 percent among urban teenagers, the prospects of fostering domestic security for ghetto women were hardly bright. Sex, class, and race came together in its complex, but familiar pattern, and appeared more devastating than ever in its consequences for black women.[47]

The history of women seemed to be boldly shifting course in the 1980s, twisting in a novel, sometimes threatening, sometimes promising direction. Woman's role in reproduction, traditionally the very bedrock of her gender status, was no longer clear and assured. On the one hand, women still shouldered a domestic burden considerably heavier than did men and were still handicapped thereby when they sought wealth, power, or simple equity in the labor force or the public sector. Yet on the other hand, the imperative that women contribute to the support of the family through employment outside the home, along with the increasing instability of the conventional two-parent family, had jeopardized women's reproductive role itself. For many black women this crisis of social reproduction meant that they were raising another generation in poverty, while countless more divorced white women struggled to rear their children on an ill-paying clerical salary. At the other end of the class structure, the crisis of reproduction took another form. Educated and affluent women determined to continue their climb up the occupational ladder faced the pressure to forego bearing children, a prospect that had seldom confronted their male counterparts in the past.

Just how this crisis will be resolved remains uncertain. Some experts regarded all these indices of volatility in family and gender forms as primarily symptoms of temporary dislocations in the social and economic system, especially the inflation and recessions of the 1970s and the related demographic maladjustments following the baby boom. Still, it's hard to say how the relations of the sexes will sort themselves out should these social and economic problems be resolved. The performance of the economy during the early 1980s, for example, has been so sluggish that the century-long increase in the female labor force has begun to subside.[48] Should this continue, will it mean a return to old gender roles or greater competition between males and females for fewer jobs? Demographers are predicting that once the large baby-boom generation passes into adulthood in the 1990s, the economic pressures on families will subside, causing the marriage and birthrates to rise again, while the divorce rate declines. They debate, however, what effect this will have on gender. Some predict that with prosperity, women will return happily to the home and baby making, while others maintain that women have become too habituated to their expanded social roles to be seduced by a refurbished feminine mystique.[49] It would seem that the force of the last half-century of women's history supports the latter prediction. But then the past history of women was not without its devious shifts and turns.

FAMILY POLICY AND
FEMINISM FOR THE 1980s

Predicting the future course of the American gender system is complicated even further by the currently volatile political climate. The election of President Ronald Reagan in 1980 brought to power a man who not only espoused some old-fashioned ideas about women and the family, but also a politician who was indebted to an avowedly and vehemently antifeminist faction dubbed the New Right. The protection of the traditional family was a recurrent theme in the popular appeals of this tightly-organized and sophisticated political machine. The array of interest groups associated with the New Right took the offensive on questions of gender and the family in the late 1970s and won some notable victories.

The National Right to Life Organization, for example, with some 1,500 local chapters, successfully lobbied in Congress to restrict the funding of abortion. They succeeded in several localities in restricting abortion, sex education, and the civil rights of homosexual men and women. They had laden the congressional agenda with legislation designed to "preserve traditional family values in America." An omnibus bill put forward by Senator Paul Laxalt, entitled "The Family Protection Act," revealed the multiple political uses of invocations of family ideology. Under the banner of protecting the family, the Laxalt bill called for everything from curtailing school busing for purposes of racial integration to support for prayer in public schools.[50]

Clearly the New Right had calculated that appeals to the family anxieties of American citizens reaped popular support and financial contributions. The spectre of rebellious children appeared again and again in New Right literature opposing abortion, prohibiting sex education, or restricting the sale of contraception to minors. But perhaps more than anyone else, the New Right based its appeal for public support on invocation of the precarious condition of older gender roles. The Family Protection Act, for example, would deny Federal funds for textbooks or school programs which "belittle the traditional role of women in society." The New Right identified the National Organization of Women, *Ms.* magazine, and the Equal Rights Amendment as the chief agents of "anti-family" liberal politics.[51]

The principle antifeminist tracts were steeped in anxiety about the insecurity of the feminine domestic role. One unpleasant reality kept popping up amid the Pollyanna prose of Marabel Morgan: the high incidence of divorce. The candidates for Total Womanhood were preoccupied with the fear or probability of family disruption. A typical testimonial for a traineeship in Total Womanhood read like this: "If I had taken a course like this seventeen years ago I am sure my husband wouldn't have left. Because of it I had to bring up my children by myself."[52] In this instance, the proponents of true womanhood did not speak to a tiny, insignificant minority, for one in three women was likely to be divorced in the last half of the twentieth century. And well might they anticipate the breakup of marriage with apprehension. That domestic apocalypse, "I had to bring up my children alone," brought millions of American women face to face with financial and personal crises. A campaign to defend the family would make good sense to the many women whose own welfare and comfort was still bound up with their marital status. From a pragmatic perspective, a "pro-family" policy seemed in the best short-term interest of many women.

Having built a small but zealous and well-organized constituency around appeals to domestic worries, the New Right became a major political force in the 1980s when its strength was magnified by its strategic relationship with the Reagan administration, its loyalists in Congress, and sympathizers on the Supreme Court. The feminist gains of the 1970s were threatened and sometimes lost. The Reagan administration effectively suspended affirmative action rules; the Congress limited funding of abortion; the Supreme Court limited the possibilities of receiving paid maternity leaves. Sundry government services of special interest to women became casualties of Reagan economics. Just as poverty in America was becoming feminized with the dramatic increase in female-headed households, government supports for the poor were being systematically withdrawn. Welfare rolls were reduced, food stamp programs curtailed, and medical benefits drastically cut. Needless to say, the immediate possibilities of enacting the expensive feminist reforms, proposed so optimistically a decade earlier, were nil. In an era of drastic cutbacks of social services, no one even dared to raise a demand like twenty-four-hour free day care. Uncle Sam, it seemed, would no longer be a party to the support or reduction of women's responsibilities for social reproduction. Then in June of 1982 came what some saw as the *coup de grâce* of the women's movement—the defeat of the Equal Rights Amendment.

Under these circumstances feminists easily became demoralized and defensive. Already in the late '70s some veterans of the women's movement had become faint-hearted, and revealed some second thoughts about earlier feminist positions on family issues. A report in *The New York Times* in 1977 cited two veteran feminists among the conservative commentators on the contemporary domestic issues. Sociologist Alice Rossi and psychologist Judith Bardwick both confessed anxiety that further changes in sex roles would seriously threaten the already precarious position of the American family.

In the same year, Rossi returned to the forum of her "immodest" feminist proposal, *Daedalus* magazine, to recommend a considerably more timorous course of action. She had been chastened, she wrote, by recent sociobiological research. From this body of knowledge, the meaning of which is subject to considerable debate among both biologists and social scientists, Rossi excerpted a hodgepodge of experimental evidence that suggested there was an instinctual basis for mother-child bonding. According to her reading of the literature, fathering had a far weaker basis in nature. She left no doubt, at the same time, that the shifts in her thinking were prompted not just by pure science, but also by her concern for the fragility of traditional family forms. Her anxiety was expressed in rather exaggerated recitations of the incidence of promiscuity, hedonism, and child neglect. Rossi gingerly proposed that the most economical and direct means of preserving the family and protecting children would be to exploit and reinforce the biological ties between mothers and children.[53]

Rossi was not alone in these conservative second thoughts of the '70s. Judith Bardwick's feminist confidence faltered in the face of the cross-cultural breadth of male dominance. She told a *New York Times* reporter, "When something is so universal—as reluctant as I am to say it—the probability is that there is some quality in the organism that leads to this condition. So women may achieve greater parity but will they achieve full parity? I don't know."[54] Once again, sexual inequality was being justified by references to the biology of reproduction and some "natural" basis in the family. And even the feminists of the 1970s began to waver.

To some this new deference to the family relations was a simple case of backlash; to Betty Friedan it was the harbinger of the "Second Stage" of the women's movement.[55] In a book of that title Friedan doubled back on her own feminist course and, in response to intimations of family crisis in the 1970s and '80s, reconsidered some aspects of the feminine mystique. Writing in the 1980s, Friedan championed not the trapped housewife but the troubled young career woman who saw her chances of raising a family being foreclosed by the demands of her job. The responsibility of feminists in these circumstances, as Friedan saw it, was to further those social changes which would allow women to find fulfillment both at home and in their work. To this end she proposed a number of commonsense reforms: flexible work schedules, job sharing, daycare facilities, supportive friendship networks, more involvement of males in the work and life of the family.

As accurate as Friedan's diagnosis of the reproductive crisis as experienced by many middle- and upper-class women, and as reasonable as the reforms she suggested, *The Second Stage* had some disquieting overtones, especially to readers of the *Feminine Mystique*. First of all, she seemed to target feminism as the ogre of the family crisis, focusing on what she read as rhetorical excesses of the women's movement rather than the structural conditions that continued to shore up sexual inequality at home and outside of it. Second, Friedan almost reduced the feminist agenda to family issues, at a time when the political and economic status of women still fell very short of equality with men. Third, by placing so much emphasis on the overloaded term "family," Friedan charted an ideological course which came perilously close to the border of the feminine mystique. She wrote that "to deny the part of one's being as woman that has, through the ages, been expressed in motherhood—nurturing, loving softness, and tiger strength—is to deny part of one's personhood as a woman."[55] These were indeed age-old characteristics associated with the female gender; but they were also associated historically with eras of extreme gender polarization and asymmetry, be they the 1850s or the 1950s.

Old-fashioned notions of femininity were also given a new lease on life in other segments of the women's movement. The radical feminists of the 1960s had evolved by the late 1970s into the celebrants of "women's culture." In their nearly self-sufficient communities of women—female friendships, lesbian couples, expressly feminine art forms, and sex-segregated institutions—these activists built a shrine to a positive gender identity. Some of the goddesses they venerated, however, resembled the same feminine stereotypes against which the feminists of the 1960s had rebelled. To be a woman, they implied, was to be endowed with special powers of nurture and affection, a sense of unity with nature, and a commingling of feeling and thought. It placed the mother-and-child bond at the center of its Utopian vision. The feminist poet, Adrienne Rich, for example, claimed that even women's "thinking must be transformed" into a more crystalline feminine shape; it must be returned from its sterile exile "outside the female body." Rich also spoke for a strong tendency among feminists when she asserted that "the mother-child relationship is the essential human relationship." Regardless of the seductiveness of an ideology that venerated things female, radical feminism could also be used to justify the institutions and stereotypes (e.g., motherhood and maternal "instincts") that have underpinned the practical inequality and relative powerlessness of women.[56]

Both feminists and historians must be careful, however, not to read too much into all these symptoms of a revival of femininity and family feeling. Neither the politics of the New Right, the timidity of some feminists, nor the symbols of women's culture, necessarily reflect the priorities of the American majority. If public opinion polls are to be believed, most Americans are not waxing nostalgic over the loss of the old family and the old femininity. Only 20 percent of those polled in 1979 agreed that they would like to return to the "good old days" when men were breadwinners and women were housekeepers. At least fifty years of women's history, furthermore, has been eroding the barriers between home and work, masculinity and femininity.

Since early in this century, men and women have been moving ever closer together in the spaces they occupy, the roles they assume, the values they expound. By the 1980s their paths were intersecting regularly at home and outside it. Although we are still far short of gender symmetry, the direction of change is clear and the base for further equalization is sound. Rather than taking cues from the forces of nostalgia, we might do well to build on the receptivity to change. In this regard it is worth pondering one last opinion poll: a survey in 1980 revealed that the majority of Americans agreed with the postulate that both sexes have the responsibility to care for small children.[57]

It is this growing detachment from gender differentiation that fed and nourished the women's movement since the 1960s and whose simple demands for sexual symmetry remain powerful in a period of crisis in social reproduction. Its lessons should not be lost in a preoccupation with family issues. It was one of the first impulses of the women's movement to transform the basic pattern of sexual differentiation, beginning at the fundamental level of the male and female personality. Children of both sexes would be socialized to perform a full range of familial roles—both as breadwinners, parents, supportive spouses, homemakers. Ideally, both the men and women who completed this reeducation would be equally capable and predisposed to earn a living and to nurture children.

In fact, a remodeling of popular notions of masculinity and femininity is already under way. Certainly, the image of woman as an able breadwinner is paraded across popular culture. Models of masculinity, however, remained more static. Even feminists emphasize the projection of models of "strong" women rather than gentle and nurturing men. At the same time, movements are under way to renovate the structural foundation of sex roles and male and female temperament. By permitting paternity as well as maternity leaves, some employers encourage greater male involvement in the traditional female role of parenting. Proposals to reorganize the male career pattern would facilitate greater male participation in the family. They would encourage men to calibrate their occupational activity according to the rhythms of family life, retiring temporarily or pursuing part-time labor when their children are young. An alteration of the male career pattern would also place wives and mothers in a better position to compete on the job.

The reform of male roles within the family tilts the balance of sex roles in a particularly important direction, toward a family structure that would surround the next generation with parallel models of male and female behavior and temperament. To replace mothers with fathers or both parents is to fundamentally restructure the process of sexual identity formation. Perhaps even the Freudian scaffold of Oedipal and Electra complexes will be toppled if mothers share or surrender their once-exclusive role in the care of infants and young children.

A second lesson to be drawn from the history of women in the twentieth century is the critical importance of women's position, not within the family, but within the labor force. The steady and voluminous flow of women into the labor market presents the greatest opportunities and challenges of the 1980s. Now that the majority of women, regardless of age, marital status, or childbearing history, are gainfully employed outside the home they are in an opportune position to overcome domestic isolation and engage in organized collective action. This consequence of entry into the labor force was already in evidence during the 1970s, when the percentage of women in labor unions grew from 23.5 percent in 1970 to 27.4 percent only eight years later.[58] The masses of women workers, especially in the white-collar sector, still remain unorganized, yet the campaign to expand their union membership is now well under way, leading some union leaders to predict that in the 1980s the cause of collective bargaining in the female sector will be as crucial to the course of labor history as was the rise of industrial unions in the 1930s.

The labor force has also become an arena in which sex segregation has come under a serious attack. The women's union movement, impatient with the slow process of infiltrating the male job sector, or fighting for better wages on a piecemeal basis, has resorted to an ingenious demand called "comparable worth." According to this principle, predominantly female job categories are matched with male positions which require similar levels of skill, training, and mental exertion. Employers are being asked to make their pay levels comparable as well. This strategy has already brought wage increases to female municipal employees in San Jose, California, has been judged a legitimate labor demand by the United States Supreme Court, and is the focus of a forceful campaign by one of the major women's unions, the American Federation of State, County, and Municipal Employees. The demand for comparable worth is just one example of the possibilities for movement toward gender equality now that women's position within the labor force is assured.

A third simple proposition of the women's movement still bears repeating in the 1980s. That now hackneyed expression, the personal is political, has a special resonance at a time when the boundary between private and public concerns has become so muted that it is almost transparent. The tension between these two abstract categories of social life generated a political and fiscal crisis beginning with the taxpayers' revolt that began in California in 1978 and reached national proportions and the federal level in the 1980s. Ostensibly, American voters have become disgruntled at the high cost of public services. Yet the sources of their discontent could be located in the private sphere as well.

The inflation generated in the private-enterprise system has extracted exorbitant cost from consumers, while the private world of the family bore the pressures of that runaway inflation. Meeting the rising cost of living sent a second adult out of most families and into the labor force. The integration of women into the labor force in turn had made families increasingly dependent on cash expenditures for the services once supplied gratis in the home— most notably child care, but also supplementary expenditures for the sewing, laundry, cooking, housework, and voluntary social services once provided by the unpaid domestic labor of wives. In sum, the abundance of women's domestic labor that once separated the private and public world, and acted as a bulwark against the cold calculations of cash and consuming, was rapidly disappearing. As American families were besieged by financial worries, many of their members lashed out at the most visible public enemy, the tax collector.

It seems on the surface that rebellious taxpayers were poised in direct opposition to feminist goals, jealous as they were of any public expenditures, including the expensive governmental bill drawn up at the International Women's Year Congress in Houston. Yet to many women, benefits such as day care do not appear as external, public, alien costs, but as necessary social expenditures which can enhance private life and even reduce pressures on the families of irate taxpayers. Feminist theory and perception can expose the ersatz barricade between family and public life. Early in the women's movement Juliet Mitchell noted that the four basic structures underpinning womanhood—the systems of socialization, reproduction, sexuality, and production—actually transcend this barrier.[59] These essential social functions, once based in women's labor in the family, are now scattered all along the slowly graded spectrum between the private individual and the official public sector. The rhetorical demand of some women's groups for wages for housework makes this point in a more graphic form. Either feminist approach underscores the fact that there are essential social tasks of both a productive and reproductive nature that must be paid for, either by public taxes, private expenditure, or unpaid labor in families. This full range of social needs and the means of financing them, not just the size of taxes, has been quietly placed on the political agenda along with the goals of the feminist movement.

Emotional as well as economic pressure was building up to crisis proportions within private families of the 1970s. As both husbands and wives spent much of their week in the labor force, the time and energy for relaxed family life diminished apace. Husbands were losing the personal psychological services formerly provided by unemployed women and incurring, at the same time, unexpected demands for support from their weary wives. Social life had become anchorless for both sexes as work and home become increasingly bifurcated. The locations of the vast majority of American homes, in large cities or suburbs, tended to distend the family ties to a wider social space. It is primarily in small, isolated towns that men and women are regularly involved in community activity outside the family. The American home itself has shrunk to almost the narrowest social space imaginable. As one social scientist describes it, household structure now approximates "invariable and perhaps uncompromising nuclearity."[60] Its average size in 1980 was only 2.75 persons. The historical trend of privatization and the narrowing of personal face-to-face relations may have reached its absolute and intolerable limits in the 1980s, overtaxing the emotional resources of couples, swelling the divorce rate, and generating the shrill demands for intimacy and sexual ecstasy that pervade popular culture.

Contemporary feminism, and women's history as well, elucidate some avenues out of this claustrophobic social space. The first is encapsulated in the feminist practice of sisterhood. During the early stirrings of the women's liberation movement the young women of the 1960s rediscovered the bonding between members of their own sex that had been the special resource and strength of many generations before them. These same-sex and extrafamilial associations can now operate as alternatives, supplements, or antidotes to the obsessive heterosexual coupling venerated in twentieth-century popular culture. From such unlikely places as Victorian parlors and black ghettoes, feminist scholars have retrieved ideas about how to pool human resources in social networks that are far wider and more flexible than the nuclear family. Women's voluntary associations, past and present, offer a second model for more satisfying social life as well as the alternative organization of public services. Whether they be nineteenth-century charities or contemporary women's centers, these female associations project a decentralized, participatory method of maintaining public services, one which circumvents the alienating, intrusive organization or large government bureaucracies and massive service agencies. These bonds and associations need not be confined to the female sex. The women's perspective on the contemporary crisis offers this final insight, a preliminary blueprint for building a web of social relations within the chill spaces that currently separate the family from the world of work and government.

□

It is the pivotal social, historical position of the female sex that affords feminists this illuminating perspective on the contemporary social malaise. Women are now located at the volatile center of the social order, where family and the labor force, private and public life, reproduction and production meet. The status of women has always been embedded in the larger social and economic structure; today the transformation of the gender system is in itself a force capable of reshaping American society.

The march of women into the labor force has been called "the single most outstanding phenomenon of this century."[61] This change has rippled through the everyday lives of the great mass of Americans. Woman's place at the center of social change is a precarious one, still situated as she is in the realm of social and economic inferiority and relative political powerlessness. The changes in women's status could proceed in any direction from this uneasy vantage point. The history of women could stalemate in the current compromise of roles, leaving females stranded in the inequality created by their double burdens as workers and homemakers. The class and racial divisions of American womanhood could grow wider in the last quarter of the twentieth century, as educated white women ride the tide of women's liberation into higher-paying jobs, while more poor black women and their children are propelled into poverty by a wave of family breakdown.

Fortunately the 1960s and '70s also produced a conscious, vocal, and incisive criticism of the gender system. An alert women's movement still scrutinizes the economic inequity, cultural stereotyping, social exclusion, and political underrepresentation of their sex. The women who grow up in the late twentieth century will be prepared by education and work experience to move into the male sphere in greater numbers than ever before. The feminism of the 1980s, furthermore, conceives the task ahead more broadly and deeply than at any time in the past. The contemporary women's movement challenges the fundamental presuppositions of American social order almost unquestioningly accepted since the days of Plymouth, when the Pilgrims discarded their Utopian ideal, divided the new land into private property, and scattered into separate households where women labored in subordination to husbands and fathers.

The feminists of the present and future may taste failure, but they cannot turn back history. The uncertain but opportune circumstances of the late twentieth century promise women a major role in reshaping both womanhood and society.

NOTES

INTRODUCTION: GENERAL REFERENCES

Philippe Ariès, *Centuries of Childhood; A Social History of Family Life* (New York, 1962).

Michèlle Barrett, *Woman's Oppression Today* (London, 1980).

Ester Boserup, *Woman's Role in Economic Development* (London, 1970).

Elizabeth Bott, *Family and Social Network: Roles, Norms and External Relationships in Ordinary Urban Families* (London, 1957).

Judith K. Brown, "Iroquois Women: An Ethnohistoric Note," in *Toward an Anthropology of Women*, Rayna R. Reiter, ed. (New York, 1975).

Nancy Chodorow, ed., "Mothers, Reproduction, and Male Supremacy," in *Capitalist Patriarchy and the Case for Socialist Feminism*, Zillah Eisenstein, ed. (New York, 1978), pp. 56–82.

Barbara Easton, "Feminism and the Contemporary Family," *Socialist Revolution*, Vol. 8, No. 3 (May–June, 1978), pp. 11–36.

Felicity Edholm, Olivia Harris, and Kate Young, "Conceptualizing Women," *Critique of Anthropology*, Vol. 3 (1977), pp. 101–130.

Zillah Eisenstein, ed., *Capitalist Patriarchy and the Case for Socialist Feminism* (New York, 1978).

William Goode, *The Family* (Englewood Cliffs, N.J., 1964).

Ann Gordon, Mary Jo Buhle, and Nancy Schrom, "Women in American Society: A Historical Contribution," *Radical America*, Vol. V, No. 4 (July–August 1971).

Tamara K. Hareven, "Modernization and Family History: Perspectives in Social Change," *Signs: A Journal of Women in Culture and Society*, Vol. 2, No. 1 (Autumn, 1976), pp. 190–207.

Mary Hartman and Lois Banner, eds., *Clio's Consciousness Raised: New Perspectives on the History of Women* (New York, 1974).

Harriet Holter, *Sex Differences and Social Structure* (Oslo, Norway, 1970).

Eleanor Macoby, ed., *The Development of Sex Differences* (Stanford, 1966).

Margaret Mead, *Sex and Temperament* (New York, 1963).

Juliet Mitchell, *Woman's Estate* (New York, 1972).

John Money and Anke A. Ehardt, *Man and Woman, Boy and Girl* (Baltimore, 1973).

Sherry B. Ortner, "Is Female to Male as Nature Is to Culture?" *Feminist Studies* (Fall 1972).

Rayna R. Reiter, ed., *Toward an Anthropology of Women* (New York, 1975), especially "Men and Women in the South of France: Public and Private Domains," pp. 252–82.

Susan Carol Rogers, "Female Forms of Power and the Myth of Male Dominance: A Model of Female/Male Interaction in Peasant Society," *American Ethnologist*, Vol. 2, No. 4 (November 1975), pp. 727–56.

————, "Woman's Place, A Critical Review of Anthropological Theory," *Comparative Studies in Society and History*, Vol. 2, No. 1 (January 1975), pp. 123–62.

Michelle Zimbalist Rosaldo, "The Use and Abuse of Anthropology: Reflections on Feminism and Cross-cultural Understanding," *Signs*, Spring 1980, pp. 389–417.

Michelle Zimbalist Rosaldo and Louise Lamphere, *Woman, Culture and Society* (Stanford, 1974).

Sheila Rowbotham, *Women, Resistance and Revolution* (New York, 1973).

Gayle Rubin, "The Traffic in Women: Notes on the Public Economy of Sex," in *Towards an Anthropology of Women*, Rayna R. Reiter, ed. (New York, 1975).

Joan W. Scott and Laurie A. Folly, "Women, Work and the Family in Nineteenth-Century Europe," *Comparative Studies in Society and History*, Vol. 17, No. 1 (January 1975), pp. 36–64.

Lawrence Stone, *The Family, Sex and Marriage in England, 1500–1800* (London, 1977).

Eli Zaretsky, "Capitalism, The Family and Personal Life," *Socialist Revolution*, Vol. 3, Nos. 1–3 (1973).

ONE: ADAM'S RIB

1. Lawrence Stone, *The Family, Sex and Marriage in England, 1500–1800* (London, 1977).

2. William Secker, *A Wedding Ring, Fit for the Finger* (Boston, 1750).

3. Keith V. Thomas, "Women and the Civil War Sects," *Past and Present*, No. 13 (1958), p. 44.

4. Peter Laslett, *The World We Have Lost* (New York, 1965), pp. 81–106.

5. Lorena S. Walsh, "Servitude and Opportunity in Charles County, Maryland, 1658–1705," in *Law, Society, and Politics in Early Maryland*, Aubrey C. Land, Lois Green Carr, and Edward C. Papenfuse, eds. (Bal-

timore, 1977), pp. 111–33; Berthold Fernow, ed., *The Records of New Amsterdam*, Vol. 1 (New York, 1897), p. 162; Robert Bremner, ed., *Children and Youth in America: A Documentary History* (Cambridge, Mass., 1970), p. 16.

6. Julia Cherry Spruill, *Women's Life and Work in the Southern Colonies* (Chapel Hill, N.C., 1938), p. 9.

7. John Demos, *A Little Commonwealth, Family Life in Plymouth Colony* (New York, 1970), p. 61.

8. Edith Abbott, *Women in Industry: A Study in American Economic History* (New York, 1919), p. 12.

9. Spruill, *op. cit.*, p. 11.

10. Sumner Chilton Powell, *Puritan Village: The Formation of a New England Town* (Middletown, Conn., 1963), Chapter VIII, pp. 116–32.

11. Josephine C. Frost, ed., *Records of the Town of Jamaica, Long Island, New York, 1656–1751* (Brooklyn, N.Y., 1919), Vol. 1, p. 1.

12. *Collections of the Massachusetts Historical Society* (Boston, 1843), Vol. VIII of the Third Series, "A Coppie of the Liberties of the Massachusetts Colonie in New England," p. 229.

13. Kenneth Lockridge, *A New England Town: The First Hundred Years* (New York, 1970), p. 144; Frost, *op. cit.*, p. 438.

14. Secker, *op. cit.*, p. 13. Laurel Thatcher Ulrich, *Good Wives: Image and Reality in the Lives of Women in Northern New England, 1650–1750* (New York, 1982), pp. 35–50.

15. James W. Dean, "Patterns of Testation: Four Tidewater Counties in Colonial Virginia," *American Journal of Legal History*, Vol. XVI, No. 2 (April 1972), pp. 154–76.

16. John J. Waters, "Patrimony, Succession and Social Stability: Guilford, Connecticut in the Eighteenth Century," *Perspectives in American History*, Vol. X (1976), pp. 129–63; Daniel Blake Smith, *Inside the Great House: Planter Family Life in Eighteenth-Century Chesapeake Society* (Ithaca, 1980), p. 245.

17. Susie Ames, ed., *County Court Records of Accomach-Northampton, Virginia* (Washington, D.C., 1954), p. 63; Ulrich, *op. cit.*, p. 46.

18. Fernow, *op. cit.*, Vol. 1, pp. 296–7; Vol. 7, p. 186.

19. *Early Records of the Town of Providence* (Providence, R.I., 1892), Vol. XIV, pp. 61–2; Vol. III, pp. 172–4; Demos, *op. cit.*, p. 86.

20. Spruill, *op. cit.*, p. 78.

21. Darrett B. Rutman, *Husbandmen of Plymouth, Farms and Villages in the Old Colony, 1620–1692* (Boston, 1967), p. 13.

22. Charles Edward Ironside, *The Family in Colonial New York: A Sociological Study* (Ph.D. Thesis, Columbia University, 1942), Chapter III.

23. Eve Merriam, *Growing Up Female in America: Ten Lives* (New York, 1971), p. 297.

24. Alice Morse Earle, *Margaret Winthrop* (New York, 1896), p. 229; Ulrich, *op. cit.*, pp. 51–67.

25. Ames, *op. cit.*, p. 15.

26. R. M. Downs, ed., *America Begins: Early American Writing* (New York, 1950), pp. 232–64.

27. *Early Records of the Town of Providence*, *op. cit.*, Vol. IX, pp. 5–6.

28. Abbott, *op. cit.*, p. 1.

29. Fernow, *op. cit.*, Vol. 7, p. 74.

30. Benjamin Wadsworth, *The Well-Ordered Family* (Boston, 1712), p. 29; Cotton Mather, *Ornaments for the Daughters of Zion* (Cambridge, Mass., 1692), p. 38; Secker, *op. cit.*, p. 22.

31. Spruill, *op. cit.*, pp. 3–7.

32. Russell Menard, "Immigrants and Their Increase: The Process of Population Growth in Early Colonial Maryland," in Land, Carr, and Papenfuse, *op. cit.*, pp. 88–110; Lois Green Carr and Lorena S. Walsh, "The Planter's Wife: The Experience of White Women in Seventeenth-Century Maryland," *William and Mary Quarterly*, Vol. XXXIV, No. 4 (October, 1977), pp. 542–71.

33. Fernow, *op. cit.*, Vol. 7, p. 74.

34. *Ibid.*, pp. 37–38.

35. Cotton Mather, *Bonifacius (Essays to Do Good)*, (Gainesville, Fla., 1967, original Boston, 1710), p. 69.

36. Franklin P. Rice, ed., *Worcester Historical Society, Collections* (Worcester, Mass., 1882), Vol. 10, p. 325.

37. Ulrich, *op. cit.*, pp. 51–67.

38. Edmund S. Morgan, *The Puritan Family* (New York, 1966), Chapter II, *passim*; D. B. Smith, *op. cit.*, pp. 165–68.

39. Ulrich, *op. cit.*, p. 7.

40. Demos, *op. cit.*, p. 83.

41. Fernow, *op. cit.*, p. 60.

42. Lyman Chalkey, ed., *Chronicles of the Scotch-Irish Settlement in Virginia, Extracted From the Original Court Records of Augusta County, 1745–1800* (Baltimore, 1965), Vol. 1, p. 162.

43. *Ibid.*, pp. 81–91.

44. Mather, *Ornaments, op. cit.*, p. 79.

45. Wadsworth, *op. cit.*, pp. 38–39.

46. Demos, *op. cit.*, p. 194.

47. Mather, *Ornaments, op. cit.*, p. 7.

48. Bremner, *op. cit.*, p. 37.

49. Mather, *Ornaments, op. cit.*, p. 9.

50. *Ibid.*, p. 74.

51. Daniel Scott Smith, "Parental Power and Marriage Patterns: An Analysis of Historical Trends in Hingham, Massachusetts," in *The American Family in Social-Historical Perspective*, Michael Gordon, ed., 2nd ed. (New York, 1978), pp. 87–100.

52. Mather, *Ornaments, op. cit.*, "The Virtuous Wife."

53. *Early Records of the Town of Providence, op. cit.*, Vol. VI, pp. 109–11.

54. William Cairns, ed., *Selections From Early American Writers, 1607–1800* (New York, 1915), p. 249.

55. Ironside, *op. cit.*, p. 44.

56. Michael Hindus and Daniel Scott Smith, "Premarital Pregnancy in America, 1640–1971: An Overview and Interpretation," *Journal of Interdisciplinary History*, Vol. V, No. 4 (Spring 1975), pp. 537–70; G. R. Quaife, "The Consenting Spinster in a Peasant Society: Aspects of Premarital Sex in 'Puritan' Somerset, 1645–1660," *Journal of Social History*, Vol. 11, No. 2 (Winter 1977), pp. 228–44.

57. Fernow, *op. cit.*, Vol. 1, pp. 238–9.

58. Ames, *op. cit.*, p. 20.

59. Edmund S. Morgan, "The Puritans and Sex," in Michael Gordon, ed., *The American Family in Social-Historical Perspective* (New York, 1973), p. 289; Lyle Koehler, *A Search for Power: The 'Weaker Sex' in Seventeenth-Century New England* (Urbana, Illinois, 1980), pp. 94–98.

60. Franklin P. Rice, ed., *Worcester Historical Society Collections* (Worcester, Mass., 1883), Vol. 5, p. 80.

61. Morgan, *op. cit.*, p. 284.

62. Russell Menard, *op. cit.*, p. 100; John Demos, *op. cit.*, p. 151; Lois Green Carr and Lorena S. Walsh, *op. cit.*, p. 551.

63. Wadsworth, *op. cit.*, p. 24.

64. Stone, *op. cit.*, p. 281; Michael Zuckerman, "Pilgrims in the Wilderness: Community, Modernity and the Maypole at Merry Mount," *New England Quarterly*, Vol. I, No. 2 (June 1977), pp. 255–77.

65. Wadsworth, *op. cit.*, pp. 24, 27.

66. Secker, *op. cit.*, p. 16.

67. Wadsworth, *op. cit.*, p. 36; Mather, *Ornaments, op. cit.*, p. 79; Secker, *op. cit.*, p. 16.

68. Mather, *Ornaments, op. cit.*, p. 79; Wadsworth, *op. cit.*, p. 26.

69. Wadsworth, *op. cit.*, pp. 28–32.

70. *Ibid.*

71. Spruill, *op. cit.*, pp. 45–46.

72. William H. Grabill, *et. al.*, *The Fertility of American Women* (New York, 1958), p. 5; Menard, *op. cit.*

73. *Early Records of the Town of Providence, op. cit.*, Vol. III, pp. 112–7.

74. Demos, *op. cit.*, p. 66.

75. Cotton Mather, *Elizabeth on Her Holy Retirement* (Boston, 1710), pp. 3, 5, 18.

76. Wadsworth, *op. cit.*, p. 45.

77. Catherine M. Scholten, "On the Importance of the Obstetrick Art: Changing Customs of Childbirth in America, 1760–1825," *William and Mary Quarterly*, Vol. XXXIV, No. 3 (July 1977), pp. 426–45; Richard W. Wertz and Dorothy C. Wertz, *Lying-In: A History of Childbirth in America* (London, 1977), p. 4.

78. Mather, *Elizabeth on Her Holy Retirement, op. cit.*, p. 31.

79. Mather, *Ornaments, op. cit.*, p. 96.

80. Isaac Ambrose, *The Well-Ordered Family* (Boston, 1762), p. 10.

81. Wadsworth, *op. cit.*, pp. 43–46.

82. Fernow, *op. cit.*, Vol. 1, p. 131.

83. *Early Records of the Town of Providence, op. cit.*, Vol. VI, p. 61.

84. Robert V. Wells, "Demographic Change and the Life Cycle of American Families," *The Journal of Interdisciplinary History*, Vol. II, No. 2 (Autumn 1971), pp. 273–82.

5. Cairns, *op. cit.*, p. 132; Earle, *op. cit.*, p. 327.

86. Stone, *op. cit.*, pp. 105, 196.

87. Mather, *Ornaments, op. cit.*, p. 3; Ulrich, *op. cit.*, p. 167.

88. Wadsworth, *op. cit.*, pp. 2–3.

89. *Ibid.*

90. Roger Thompson, *Women in Stuart England and America* (London, 1974), p. 225; Spruill, *op. cit.*, pp. 242–3.

91. Chalkey, *op. cit.*, p. 27.

92. *Early Records of the Town of Providence, op. cit.*, Vol. III, pp. 30–2.

93. *Ibid.*, Vol. III, p. 6; Vol. X, p. 23.

94. Frost, *op. cit.*, p. 186.

95. Thomas, *op. cit.*, p. 54.

96. Earle, *op. cit.*, pp. 266–7; Gerald F. Moran, "Religious Renewal, Puritan Tribalism and the Family in Seventeenth-Century Milford, Con-

necticut," *William and Mary Quarterly*, April 1979, pp. 237–54.

97. Morgan, *op. cit.*, p. 44.

98. Cairns, *op. cit.*, p. 147.

99. Nancy F. Cott, ed., *Root of Bitterness* (New York, 1972), pp. 31–46.

100. Rufus M. Jones, *The Quakers in the American Colonies* (New York, 1962), pp. 84–9.

101. Cott, *op. cit.*, pp. 47–58; Koehler, *op. cit.*, p. 190.

102. Richard P. Gildrie, *Salem, Massachusetts, 1626–1683: A Covenant Community* (University Press of Virginia, 1975), p. 83.

103. Fernow, *op. cit.*, Vol. IV, pp. 3, 32.

104. Cott, *op. cit.*, pp. 47–58.

105. Chalkey, *op. cit.*, p. 64.

106. Spruill, *op. cit.*, p. 333; Ulrich, *op. cit.*, p. 189.

107. Ames, *op. cit.*, p. 85.

108. Cott, *op. cit.*, p. 48; Chadwick Hansen, *Witchcraft at Salem* (New York, 1969), p. 35.

109. Paul Boyer and Stephen Nissenbaum, eds., *Salem Village Witchcraft: A Documentary Record of Local Conflict in Colonial New England* (Belmont, Calif., 1972), Part III, pp. 137–79, *passim*.

110. Paul Boyer and Stephen Nissenbaum, *Salem Possessed, The Social Origins of Witchcraft* (Cambridge, Mass., 1974), p. 80, *passim*.

111. John Demos, "Underlying Themes in the Witchcraft of Seventeenth-Century New England," *American Historical Review*, Vol. LXXV, No. 5 (June 1970), pp. 1311–26, *passim*.

112. Hansen, *op. cit.*, p. 55.

113. Cott, *op. cit.*, p. 67.

114. Boyer and Nissenbaum, eds., *Salem Village Witchcraft, op. cit.*, p. 202.

115. Boyer and Nissenbaum, *Salem Possessed, op. cit.*, pp. 33–35.

TWO: PATRIARCHY IN DISARRAY

1. Charles Francis Adams, *Familiar Letters of John Adams and His Wife Abigail Adams, During the Revolution. With a Memoir of Mrs. Adams* (Boston, 1875), p. 149.

2. Sidney Herbert Ditzion, *Marriage, Morals and Sex in America: A History of Ideas* (New York, 1953), p. 42.

3. Linda Kerber, *Women of the Republic: The Intellect and Ideology in Revolutionary America* (Chapel Hill, N.C., 1980).

4. R. M. Tryon, *Household Manufactures in the United States, 1640–1860* (New York, reprint 1966), p. 55.

5. Adams, *op. cit.*, pp. 8, 152.

6. Mary Beth Norton, *Liberty's Daughters: The Revolutionary Experience of American Women, 1750–1800* (Boston 1980), p. 225.

7. Nancy F. Cott, "Divorce and the Changing Status of Women in Eighteenth-Century Massachusetts," *William and Mary Quarterly*, Vol. XXXIII, No. 4 (October 1976), pp. 586–612.

8. Norton, *op. cit.*, pp. 295–99.

9. James T. Lemon, *The Best Poor Man's Country* (Baltimore, 1972); Robert D. Mitchell, *Commercialism and Frontier Perspectives in the Early Shenandoah Valley* (Virginia, 1977).

10. Philip J. Greven, *Four Generations: Population, Land, and Family in Colonial Andover, Massachusetts* (Ithaca, N.Y., 1970); Charles S. Grant, *Democracy in the Connecticut Town of Kent* (New York, 1961); Kenneth Lockridge, *A New England Town: The First Hundred Years, Dedham, Massachusetts, 1636–1736* (New York, 1970).

11. Lemon, *op. cit.*, Mitchell, *op. cit.*

12. Benjamin Bell, *The Character of the Virtuous Woman* (Windsor, N.H., 1794), p. 14.

13. John Cosens Ogden, *The Female Guide* (Concord, N.H., 1793), pp. 3–13.

14. Elizabeth Anthony Dexter, *Colonial Women of Affairs*, 2nd ed. (Boston, 1931), pp. 119–21.

15. *Worcester Society of Antiquity, Collections* (Worcester, Mass., 1898), Vol. 8, p. 56.

16. Carl Nordstrom, *Frontier Elements in a Hudson River Village* (Port Washington, N.Y., 1973), p. 51.

17. Nancy F. Cott, *The Bonds of Womanhood: "Woman's Sphere" in New England, 1780–1835* (New Haven, Conn., 1977), Chapter 1.

18. James A. Henretta, *The Evolution of American Society: An Interdisciplinary Analysis* (Lexington, Mass., 1973), p. 194.

19. Edith Abbott, *Women in Industry: A Study in American Economic History* (New York, 1919), pp. 71–2.

20. Howard P. Chudacoff, *The Evolution of American Urban Society* (Englewood Cliffs, N.J., 1975), p. 24.

21. Dexter, *op. cit.*, pp. 7, 31–2.

22. Charles Edward Ironside, *The Family in Colonial New York: A Sociological Study* (Ph.D. Thesis, Columbia University, 1942), p. 36; S. R. Stearns, *Abridged Journal*, manuscript, the Arthur and Elizabeth Schlesinger Library for the Study of Women's History, Radcliffe College, Cam-

bridge, Mass., Vol. II, 1810–1812, p. 4. (Hereafter referred to as Schlesinger Library.)

23. Dixon Wecter and Lazer Ziff, eds., *Benjamin Franklin: Autobiography and Selected Writings* (New York, 1969), p. 64.

24. Dexter, *op. cit.*, pp. 18–25.

25. *Ibid.*, pp. 73, 81, 88.

26. Carl Bridenbaugh, *Cities in the Wilderness: The First Century of Urban Life in America, 1625–1742* (New York, 1955), p. 72.

27. David H. Flaherty, "Law and the Enforcement of Morals in Early America," in *Perspectives in American History*, Vol. V (1971), p. 240.

28. Raymond A. Mohl, *Poverty in New York, 1783–1825* (New York, 1971), p. 31.

29. Wecter and Ziff, *op. cit.*, p. 179.

30. Mary Beth Norton, "Eighteenth-Century American Women in Peace and War: The Case of the Loyalists," *William and Mary Quarterly*, Vol. XXXIII, No. 3 (July 1976), pp. 386–409.

31. Joan Huff Wilson, "The Illusion of Change: Women and the American Revolution," in *The American Revolution: Explorations in the History of American Radicalism* (Dekalb, Ill., 1976), pp. 383–446.

32. Suzanne Dee Lebsock, "Women and Economics in Virginia: Petersburg, 1784–1820," (Unpublished Ph.D. dissertation, University of Virginia, 1977), Joan R. Gunderson and Gwen Victor Gampel, "Married Women's Legal Status in Eighteenth-Century New York and Virginia," *William and Mary Quarterly*, January 1982, pp. 114–135.

33. Laurel Thatcher Ulrich, *Good Wives: Image and Reality in the Lives of Women in Northern New England, 1650–1750* (New York, 1982), p. 76.

34. George F. Dow, ed., *Holyoke Diaries, 1789–1825* (Salem, Mass., 1911).

35. Martha C. Codman, ed., *The Journal of Mrs. John Amory and Letters from Her Father Rufus Greene* (Boston, 1923), p. 8.

36. *Eunice Callender Diaries, 1808–1824*, manuscript, Schlesinger Library.

37. Abbott, *op. cit.*, pp. 265–6.

38. Billy G. Smith, "The Material Lives of Laboring Philadelphians, 1750 to 1800," *William and Mary Quarterly* (April 1981), pp. 163–200.

39. *Worcester Society of Antiquity, Collections, op. cit.*, Vol. 10, p. 232.

40. Mohl, *op. cit.*, p. 25.

41. Farber, *op. cit.*, pp. 144–5, 183.

42. Abbott, *op. cit.*, p. 32.

43. Mohl, *op. cit.*, pp. 44, 85.

44. *Worcester Society of Antiquity, Collections*, Vol. 10, pp. 109–10.

45. Robert Dodeley, *The Oeconomy of Human Life* (Philadelphia, 1751), pp. 45–6.

46. Abbott, *op. cit.*, p. 22.

47. *Ibid.*, pp. 40, 50–51.

48. *Ibid.*, pp. 268–9.

49. *Ibid.*, pp. 46, 85, 275.

50. Bernard Bailyn and Lotte Bailyn, *Massachusetts Shipping 1697–1714: A Statistical Study* (Cambridge, Mass., 1959), pp. 56–73.

51. Bernard Farber, *Guardians of Virtue: Salem Families in 1800* (New York, 1972), p. 126; Daniel Blake Smith, *Inside the Great House: Planter Family Life in Eighteenth-Century Chesapeake Society* (Ithaca, N.Y., 1980).

52. Julia Cherry Spruill, *Women's Life and Work in the Southern Colonies* (Chapel Hill, N.C., 1969), p. 127.

53. Ironside, *op. cit.*, p. 36.

54. Codman, *op. cit.*, p. 8.

55. D. B. Smith, *op. cit.*, p. 77; Samuel Woodworth, ed., *Ladies Literary Cabinet*, Vol. 1, No. 1 (April 1819), p. 1.

56. William Kendrick, *The Whole Duty of Woman* (Philadelphia, 1788), p. 5; Dodeley, *op. cit.*

57. Gregory, *op. cit.*, pp. 6–7.

58. Dodeley, *op. cit.*, pp. 45–6.

59. *The Lady's Pocket Library* (Philadelphia, 1792), pp. 5–6.

60. Dodeley, *op. cit.*, p. 46.

61. Pierre Joseph Boudier de Villement, *The Ladies' Friend, Being a Treatise on the Virtues* (Philadelphia, 1771), p. 2; Amos Chase, *On Female Excellance* (Litchfield, Conn., 1792), p. 7.

62. Villement, *op. cit.*, p. 5.

63. James Bowdoin, *A Paraphrase on Part of the Economy of Human Life* (Boston, 1759), pp. 14, 15, 16.

64. Gregory, *op. cit.*, pp. 31–32.

65. Antoine Leonard, *Essays on the Character of Women* (Philadelphia, 1774).

66. Edward Ward, *Female Policy Detected, or the Arts of Designing Women* (Boston, 1786); Leonard de Vrier and Peter Fryer, eds., *Venus Unmasked or an Inquiry into the Nature and Origin of the Passion of Love* (London, 1967), p. 60.

67. Susanna Rowson, *Mentoria or the Young Ladies' Friend*, Vol. II (Philadelphia, 1794), p. 11; Charlotte Temple, *A Tale of Truth* (Philadelphia, 1794).

68. Rowson, *op. cit.*, p. 32.

69. James Fordyce, *The Character and Conduct of the Female Sex* (Boston, 1781), p. 20.

70. Bowdoin, *op. cit.*, p. 32.

71. Thomas Gisborne, *An Inquiry into the Duties of the Female Sex* (Philadelphia, 1798), p. 2.

72. George Strebeck, *A Sermon on the Character of the Virtuous Woman* (New York, 1800), p. 19.

73. Leonard, *op. cit.*, p. 7.

74. *Ibid.*

75. Farber, *op. cit.*, pp. 147–8.

76. Ethel Armes, ed., *Nancy Shippen, Her Journal Book, The International Romances of a Young Lady of Fashion of Colonial Philadelphia with Letters to Her and About Her* (Philadelphia, 1935), pp. 40–1, 101.

77. *Ibid.*, pp. 221–2.

78. Woodworth, *op. cit.*, p. 5.

79. Kendrick, *op. cit.*, p. 54.

80. *Ibid.*, p. 55.

81. Ogden, *op. cit.*, p. 34.

82. Mason Locke Weems, *The Lover's Almanac, No. 1* (Alexandria, Va., 1798).

83. Ironside, *op. cit.*, p. 58.

84. Dexter, *op. cit.*, p. 18.

85. Reverend Thomas Humphrey, *Marriage as an Honorable Estate* (Boston, 1752), p. 3.

86. Edward Ward, *New Proverbs on the Tricks of Women* (Boston, 1787), p. 7.

87. Wecter and Ziff, *op. cit.*, pp. 184–6.

88. Anonymous, *Reflections on Courtship and Marriage* (London, 1779), p. 22.

89. Michael S. Hindus and Daniel Scott Smith, "Premarital Pregnancy in America 1640–1971: An Overview and Interpretation," *Journal of Interdisciplinary History*, Vol. 5, No. 4 (June 1975), pp. 537–70; Lois Green Carr and Lorena S. Walsh, "The Planter's Wife: The Experience of White Women in Seventeenth-Century Maryland," *William and Mary Quarterly*, Vol. XXXIV, No. 4 (October 1977), pp. 542–71.

90. Cedric B. Cowing, "Sex and Preaching in the Great Awakening," *American Quarterly*, Vol. XX, No. 3 (Fall 1968), pp. 624–44.

91. Robert A. Gross, *The Minutemen and Their World* (New York, 1976), p. 122.

92. *Ibid.*, p. 78.

93. Greven, *op. cit.*, Part III.

94. Daniel S. Smith, "The Demographic History of Colonial New England," in Michael Gordon, ed., *The American Family in Social-Historical Perspective* (New York, 1973), pp. 397–411; Susan I. Norton, "Population Growth in Colonial America: A Study of Ipswich, Massachusetts," *Population Studies* (November 1971), pp. 433–52; Robert V. Wells, "Family Size and Fertility Control in Eighteenth-Century America: A Study of Quaker Families," *Population Studies* (1971), pp. 173–82.

95. Smith, *op. cit.*

96. Wells, *op. cit.*

97. Nancy Osterud and John Fulton, "Family Limitation and Age at Marriage: Fertility Decline in Sturbridge, Massachusetts, 1730–1850," *Population Studies*, Vol. 30, No. 3 (November 1976), pp. 481–94.

98. Maris A. Vinovskis, "Socioeconomic Determinants of Interstate Fertility Differentials in the United States in 1850 and 1860," *Journal of Interdisciplinary History*, Vol. 6 (Winter 1976), pp. 375–96.

99. Bridenbaugh, *op. cit.*, p. 340.

100. Ditzion, *op. cit.*, pp. 53–7.

101. Anonymous, *Reflections on Courtship and Marriage* (London, 1779), p. 22.

102. Anne K. Nelsen and Hart M. Nelsen, "Family Articles in Frontier Newspapers: An Examination of One Aspect of Turner's Frontier Thesis," *Journal of Marriage and the Family*, Vol. 32, No. 4 (November 1969), pp. 644–9.

103. Benjamin Rush, *Thoughts on Female Education* (Philadelphia, 1787), p. 5; Cott, *Bonds of Womanhood, op. cit.*, p. 112.

104. Linda Kerber, "The Republican Mother: Women and the Enlightenment—An American Perspective," *American Quarterly*, Vol. 28 (Summer 1976), pp. 187–205.

105. Strebeck, *op. cit.*, p. 20.

106. *The Maternal Physician. A Treatise on the Management of Infants, from Their Birth until Two Years Old.* By An American Matron (New York, 1972, reprint of original published at Philadelphia, 1811), p. 8.

107. Woodworth, *op. cit.*, Vol. V, No. 1, p. 5.

108. James Armstrong Neal, *An Essay on the Education and Genius of the Female Sex* (Philadelphia, 1795), pp. 9, 17, 18.

109. *Ibid.*, p. 29.

110. Richard D. Brown, *Strain of Violence: Historical Studies of American Violence and Vigilantism* (New York, 1975), Appendix.

111. Stearns. *op. cit.*

112. Keith Melder, "Ladies Bountiful: Organized Women's Benevolence in Early 19th Century America," *New York History*, Vol. XLVIII, No. 3 (July 1967), pp. 231–54.

113. Stearns, *op. cit.*

114. *Eunice Callender Diaries, 1808–1824*, *op. cit.*, Vol. II, p. 2.

115. Catharine Maria Sedgwick, *Diaries*, 28th December 1854, Mss., Massachusetts Historical Society.

116. Mrs. Juliana Frances Turner, *Harp of the Beechwoods* (Montrose, Pa., 1822), p. 51.

117. Nelsen and Nelsen, *op. cit.*, p. 647.

THREE: CREATING WOMAN'S SPHERE

1. William Forrest Sprague, *Women and the West: A Short Social History* (New York, reprint 1972, originally published in Boston, 1940), pp. 54–5; Eliza Woodson Farnham, *Life in a Prairie Land* (New York, reprint 1972, originally published 1846), p. 254.

2. Ruth E. Finley, *The Lady of Godey's, Sarah Joseph Hale* (Philadelphia, 1931), p. 124; Michael Gordon and M. Charles Bernstein, "Mate Choice and Domestic Life in the Nineteenth Century Marriage Manual," *Journal of Marriage and the Family*, Vol. 34 (November 1970), p. 670.

3. Frances Parkes, *Domestic Duties*, 3rd ed. (New York, 1931), p. 356.

4. William W. Fowler, *Women on the American Frontier* (New York, reprint 1970, originally published in Hartford, Conn., 1879), p. 171; Henry C. Wright, *The Empire of the Mother over the Character and Destiny of the Race* (Boston, 1870), p. 4; Catharine E. Beecher, *The Duty of American Women to Their Country* (New York, 1845), p. 210, *passim*; Margaret Coxe, *Claims of the Country on American Females* (Columbus, Ohio, 1842), p. 13; Roger W. Lotchin, *San Francisco 1846–1856, From Hamlet to City* (New York, 1974), pp. 256–7.

5. John Mack Faragher, *Women and Men on the Overland Trail* (New Haven, Conn., 1979).

6. Hannah Josephson, *The Golden Threads: New England's Mill Girls and Magnates* (New York, 1949), p. 202; Thomas Louis Dublin, "Women, Work, and Protest in the Early Lowell Mills: The Oppressing Hand of Avarice Would Enslave Us," *Labor History*, Vol. 6, No. 1 (Winter 1975), pp. 99–116; see also Thomas Louis Dublin, *Women at Work: The Transformation of Work and Community in Lowell, Massachusetts, 1826–1860* (New York, 1979).

7. Alan Dawley, *Class and Community: The Industrial Revolution in Lynn* (Harvard, 1976), pp. 76–7.

8. Howard P. Chudacoff, *The Evolution of American Urban Society* (Englewood Cliffs, N.J., 1975), p. 50.

9. Dublin, *Women at Work, op. cit.*; Herbert G. Gutman, "Work, Culture, and Society in Industrializing America, 1815–1919," *American Historical Review*, Vol. 78, No. 3 (June 1973), pp. 550–3.

10. See: Mary P. Ryan, *Cradle of the Middle Class: The Family in Oneida County, New York, 1790–1865* (Cambridge, 1981).

11. W. Elliot Brownlee and Mary M. Brownlee, *Women in the American Economy, a Documentary History 1675–1929* (New Haven, Conn., 1976), p. 146; Edith Abbott, *Women in Industry: A Study in American Economic History* (New York, 1919), p. 275; Dublin, *Women at Work, op. cit.*; Thomas Dublin, "Women Workers and the Study of Social Mobility," *Journal of Interdisciplinary History*, Spring 1979, 647–661.

12. Barbara Mayer Wertheimer, *We Were There: The Story of Working Women in America* (New York, 1977), p. 67; Keith E. Melder, *Beginnings of Sisterhood: The American Women's Rights Movement 1800–1850* (New York, 1977), pp. 45–46; Dawley, *op. cit.*, p. 178.

13. Dublin, "Women, Work, and Protest," *op. cit.*, pp. 105–6; Dawley, *op. cit.*, p. 82; Melder, *ibid.*, p. 82.

14. Thomas Louis Dublin, "Women, Work and the Family: Female Operatives in the Lowell Mills, 1830–1860," *Feminist Studies*, Vol. 3, No. 1/2 (Fall 1975), pp. 30–9.

15. Judith A. McGaw, "A Good Place to Work, Industrial Workers and Occupational Choice: The Case of Berkshire Women," *Journal of Interdisciplinary History*, Autumn 1979, pp. 227–48.

16. Whitney Cross, *The Burned-over District; The Social and Intellectual History of Enthusiastic Religion in Western New York, 1800–1850* (Ithaca, N.Y., 1950); Nancy F. Cott, "Young Women in the Second Great Awakening in New England," *Feminist Studies*, Vol. 3, No. 1/2 (Fall 1975), pp. 15–29.

17. Cott, *ibid.*; Barbara Easton, "The Rebellious Heart: Religious Conversion Experiences of Some New England Women 1740–1840," paper delivered at the Third Berkshire Conference of Women Historians, June 1975.

18. Mary P. Ryan, "A Woman's Awakening: Evangelical Religion and the Families of Utica, New York," *American Quarterly*, Winter, 1978.

19. Melder, *op. cit.*, pp. 52–76; Regina Morantz, "Making Women Modern: Middle Class Women and Health Reform in Nineteenth-Century America," *Journal of Social History*, Vol. 10, No. 4 (June 1977), pp. 490–508; Carroll Smith-Rosenberg, "Beauty, the Beast and the Militant

Woman: A Case Study in Sex Roles and Social Stress in Jacksonian America," *American Quarterly*, Vol. 23, No. 4 (October 1971), pp. 562–84.

20. Angelina Grimké, *Appeal to the Christian Women of the South* (New York, 1856), p. 25; Morantz, *op. cit.*, p. 492.

21. Gerda Lerner, *The Grimké Sisters from South Carolina* (New York, 1967), p. 272; Leonard Richards, *Gentlemen of Property and Standing* (New York, 1970).

22. Barbara J. Berg, *The Remembered Gate: Origins of American Feminism, The Woman and the City 1800–1860* (New York, 1978), pp. 211–12; Melder, *op. cit.*, p. 73.

23. Judith Wellman, "'Are We Aliens Because We Are Women?': Female Abolitionists and Abolitionists' Petitions in Upstate New York," Paper presented at the National Archives Conference on Women's History, April 1976; Melder, *op. cit.*, p. 59.

24. Smith-Rosenberg, *op. cit.*; Berg, *op. cit.*, pp. 186–7.

25. Berg, *ibid.*, p. 187; Nehemiah Adams, quoted in *Annual Report of Boston Female Anti-Slavery Association* (Boston, 1837), pp. 42–3; Catharine Beecher, *An Essay on Slavery and Abolitionism with References to the Duty of American Females* (Boston, 1839), pp. 98–9, 136.

26. Mrs. L. Maria Child, *The Girl's Own Book* (New York, 1833), pp. 78–79.

27. Peter Andrews, "Games People Played," *American Heritage Magazine* (June 1972), pp. 70–1.

28. Melder, *op. cit.*, Chapter 2; Thomas Woody, *A History of Women's Education in the United States* (New York, 1966, originally published 1929).

29. Laurence Glasco, "The Life Cycles and Household Structure of American Ethnic Groups; Irish, German, and Native Born Whites in Buffalo, New York, 1855," *Journal of Urban History*, Vol. 1, No. 3 (May 1975), pp. 399–465; Michael Katz, *The People of Hamilton Canada West; Family and Class in a Mid-Nineteenth-Century City* (Cambridge, Mass., 1975), pp. 271, 272; Richard Sennett, *Families Against the City: Middle Class Homes of Industrial Chicago 1872–1890* (New York, 1974), p. 103.

30. Richard Bernard and Maris Vinovskis, "The Female School Teacher in Ante-Bellum Massachusetts," *Journal of Social History*, Vol. 10, No. 3 (March 1977), pp. 332–45.

31. *Ibid.*

32. Daniel Scott Smith, "Parental Power and Marriage Patterns: An Analysis of Historical Trends in Hingham, Massachusetts," *Journal of Marriage and the Family*, Vol. 35, No. 3 (August 1973), pp. 419–28; Ryan, *op. cit.*; Peter R. Uhlenberg, "A Study of Cohort Life Cycles: Cohorts of Native Born Massachusetts Women, 1830–1920," *Population Studies*, Vol. 23, Part 3 (November 1969), pp. 407–20.

33. Margaret Graves, *Girlhood and Womanhood* (Boston, 1844), p. 152.

34. Parkes, *op. cit.*, p. 356.

35. Clyde Griffin and Sally Griffin, "Family and Business in a Small City, Poughkeepsie, New York, 1850–1880," *Journal of Urban History*, Vol. 1, No. 3 (May 1975), pp. 316–39.

36. Wilson H. Grahill, Clyde V. Kiser, and Pascal K. Whelpton, *The Fertility of American Women* (New York, 1958), pp. 14–15.

37. Daniel Scott Smith, "Population, Family and Society in Hingham, Massachusetts, 1650–1880" (unpublished Ph.D. dissertation, University of California, Berkeley, 1973).

38. James C. Mohr, *Abortion in America: The Origins and Evolution of National Policy, 1800–1900* (New York, 1978), pp. 69–86.

39. Linda Gordon, *Woman's Body, Woman's Right: A Social History of Birth Control in America* (New York, 1976), pp. 95–116.

40. G. J. Barker-Benfield, "The Spermatic Economy: A Nineteenth-Century View of Sexuality," in Michael S. Gordon, ed., *The American Family in Social-Historical Perspective* (New York, 1973), pp. 336–72; Charles E. Rosenberg, "Sexuality, Class and Role in 19th Century America," *American Quarterly*, Vol. 25 (May 1973), pp. 131–53; William D. Sanger, *The History of Prostitution* (New York, 1858); Thomas L. Nichols, *Esoteric Anthropology*, 15th ed. (London, n.d.), p. 100.

41. Dr. G. Ackerley, *On the Management of Children in Sickness and in Health*, 2nd ed. (New York, 1836), p. ii; Dr. William Dewees, *A Treatise on the Physical and Medical Treatment of Children*, 5th ed. (Philadelphia, 1833), pp. 64–5; Mrs. Lydia Sigourney, *Letters to Mothers* (New York, 1846), p. vii.

42. Finley, *op. cit.*, p. 128; Wright, *op. cit.*, p. 4.

43. Dewees, *op. cit.*, p. 54; Richard Kissan, *The Nurse's Manual and Young Mother's Guide* (Hartford, 1834), p. 90.

44. Herman Humphrey, *Domestic Education* (Amherst, Mass., 1840), p. 184; Sigourney, *op. cit.*, p. 32.

45. John Abbott, *The Child at Home* (New York, 1833), pp. 12–13, 213.

46. *The Mothers' Assistant and Young Ladies' Friend*, Vol. XIII, No. 3, p. 77.

47. Nancy F. Cott, *The Bonds of Womanhood: "Woman's Sphere" in New England, 1780–1835* (New Haven, Conn., 1977), p. 68.

48. Tamara Hareven and John Modell, "Urbanization and the Malleable Household: An Examination of Boarding and Lodging in American

Families," *Journal of Marriage and the Family*, Vol. 35, No. 3 (August 1973), pp. 467–79; Carol Groneman, "She Earns as a Child; She Pays as a Man: Women Workers in a Mid-Nineteenth Century New York City Community," in *Class, Sex, and the Woman Worker*, Milton Cantor and Bruce Laurie, eds. (Westport, Conn., 1977), pp. 89–90; Katz, *op. cit.*, p. 222.

49. Suzanne Dee Lebsock, "Women and Economics in Virginia: Petersburg, 1784–1820" (unpublished Ph.D. dissertation, University of Virginia, 1977), pp. 286–8; author's examination of the will books of Utica and Oneida counties, N.Y., 1798–1865.

50. Ike Marvel (Donald Grant Mitchell), *Dream Life: A Fable of the Seasons* (New York, 1889); Herman Melville, "I and My Chimney," *The Appletree and Other Sketches* (Princeton, 1922), pp. 109–66; Sennett, *op. cit.*, pp. 47, 50.

51. Daniel Scott Smith, "Family Limitation, Sexual Control, and Domestic Feminism in Victorian America," *Feminist Studies*, Vol. 1, No. 3/4 (September 1973), pp. 40–57.

52. Carroll Smith-Rosenberg, "The Female World of Love and Ritual: Relations Between Women in Nineteenth-Century America," *Signs*, Vol. 1, No. 1 (Autumn 1975), pp. 1–29.

53. Berg, *op. cit.*, p. 156; Melder, *op. cit.*, pp. 40–5.

54. Carroll Smith-Rosenberg, *Religion and the Rise of the American City* (Ithaca, N.Y., 1971); Berg, *op. cit.*, p. 288.

55. Katz, *op. cit.*, p. 183.

56. Berg, *op. cit.*, pp. 165–70; Susan Porter Benson, paper delivered at the Third Berkshire Conference on the History of Women, June 1976.

57. Kathleen Conzen, *Immigrant Milwaukee 1836–1860: Accommodation and Community in a Frontier City* (Cambridge, Mass., 1976), p. 48; Mary Catherine Mattis, "The Irish Family in Buffalo, New York, 1855–1875: A Socio-Historical Analysis" (unpublished Ph.D. dissertation, Washington University, 1975).

58. Oliver MacDonagh, "The Irish Famine Emigration to the United States," *Perspectives in American History*, Vol. X (Cambridge, Mass., 1976), pp. 357–488.

59. Frank L. Mott, "Portrait of an American Mill Town: Demographic Responses in Mid-Nineteenth Century Warren, Rhode Island," *Population Studies* (March 1972), p. 156; Daniel J. Walkowitz, "Working-Class Women in the Gilded Age: Factory, Community and Family Life Among Cohoes, New York, Cotton Workers," *Journal of Social History*, Vol. 5, No. 4 (Summer 1972), pp. 464–90.

60. Conzen, *op. cit.*, p. 93; Groneman, *op. cit.*, pp. 85–6; Katz,

op. cit., p. 289; Glasco, *op. cit.*, pp. 355–7; *America's Working Women*, Rosalyn Baxandall, Linda Gordon, and Susan Reverby, eds. (New York, 1976), p. 137.

61. Conzen, *op. cit.*, p. 93; Jay P. Dolan, *The Immigrant Church: New York Irish and German Catholics 1815–1865* (Baltimore, 1975), p. 119; Groneman, *op. cit.*, pp. 93–4; Katz, *op. cit.*, p. 254; Ryan, *Cradle, op. cit.*, p. 156.

62. Dolan, *op. cit.*, p. 132.

63. Herbert G. Gutman, "Work, Culture, and Society in Industrializing America, 1815–1919," *American Historical Review*, Vol. 78, No. 2 (June 1973), p. 575.

64. Adrian Cook, *Armies of the Streets* (Lexington, Ky., 1974), p. 126.

65. Theodore Hershberg, "Free Blacks in Ante-Bellum Philadelphia: A Study of Ex-Slaves, Free-Born and Socio-Economic Decline," *Journal of Social History*, Vol. 5 (1971–72), pp. 183–209; Elizabeth H. Pleck, "The Two-Parent Household: Black Family Structure in Late Nineteenth-Century Boston," *Journal of Social History*, Vol. 6 (Fall 1972), pp. 3–31.

66. Eugene D. Genovese, *Roll Jordan, Roll, The World the Slaves Made* (New York, 1974), pp. 494–8.

67. *Ibid.*

68. Reynolds Farley, *Growth of the Black Population* (Chicago, 1970), p. 2; E. Franklin Frazier, *The Negro Family in the United States* (Chicago, 1939).

69. Gutman, *The Black Family, op. cit.*, p. 167. Lawrence Levine, *Black Culture and Black Consciousness: Afro-American Folk Thought From Slavery to Freedom* (New York, 1977), p. 110.

70. Lebsock, *op. cit.*, p. 195; Gutman, *The Black Family, op. cit.*, p. 115.

71. Genovese, *op. cit.*, p. 414; Gutman, *op. cit.*, pp. 19, 60.

72. Robert H. Bremner, ed., *Children and Youth in America: A Documentary History*, Vol. 1 (Cambridge, Mass., 1970), p. 376; Mel Watkins and Jay Donald, *To Be a Black Woman: Portraits in Facts and Fiction* (New York, 1970), p. 17; Robert S. Starobin, "Privileged Bondsman and the Process of Accommodation: The Role of Houseservants and Drivers as Seen in Their Own Letters," *Journal of Social History*, Vol. 5, No. 1 (Fall 1971), p. 70; Gutman, *The Black Family, op. cit.*, pp. 199–229; Louise Lamphere, "Strategies, Cooperation, and Conflict Among Women in Domestic Groups," in *Woman, Culture, and Society*, Michelle Zimbalist Rosaldo and Louise Lamphere, eds. (Stanford, Calif., 1974).

73. Genovese, *op. cit.*, p. 477.

74. Gerda Lerner, ed., *Black Women in White America* (New York,

1972), p. 35; Loren Schweninger, "A Slave Family in the Ante-Bellum South," in *Our American Sisters, Women in American Life and Thought*, 2nd ed., Jean F. Friedman and William G. Shade, eds. (Boston, 1976), pp. 163–78.

75. Melder, *op. cit.*, p. 148.

76. Ellen Carol Dubois, *Feminism and Suffrage: The Emergence ·of an Independent Women's Movement in America, 1848–1860* (Ithaca, N.Y., 1978) pp. 27, 37; letter from Sarah M. Grimké to E. B. Loring, February 10, 1856, Lydia Maria Child, Mss., New York Public Library.

FOUR: THE BREADGIVERS

1. Allen F. Davis, *American Heroine: The Life and Legend of Jane Addams* (New York, 1973), pp. 19–20.

2. Anzia Yezierska, *Bread Givers* (New York, 1925).

3. W. Elliot and Mary Brownlee, *Women and the American Economy, A Documentary History, 1675 to 1929* (New York, 1976), p. 3.

4. Barbara Klaczynska, "Why Women Work: A Comparison of Various Groups—Philadelphia, 1910–1930," *Labor History*, Vol. 17, No. 1 (Winter 1976), pp. 73–87; Thomas Kessner, *The Golden Door: Italian and Jewish Immigrant Mobility in New York City, 1800–1915* (New York, 1977), p. 30.

5. Lucie Cheng Hirata, "Free, Indentured, Enslaved: Chinese Prostitution in Nineteenth-Century America," *Signs*, Autumn 1979, pp. 3–29; *Asian Women* (Berkeley, 1971), *passim*.

6. Elizabeth Faulkner Baker, *Technology and Women's Work* (New York, 1964); Robert W. Smuts, *Women and Work in America* (New York, 1959), p. 17; Lucy Maynard Salmon, *Domestic Service* (New York, 1927, reprint of 1897 edition), p. 75, *passim*.

7. William I. Thomas and Florian Znaniecki, *The Polish Peasant in Europe and America* (New York, 1958), Vol. 1, pp. 775–6; David Katzman, *Seven Days a Week, Women and Domestic Service in Industrializing America* (New York, 1978).

8. Baker, *op. cit.*, p. 77.

9. Caroline Manning, *The Immigrant Woman and Her Job* (New York, 1970), p. 22.

10. Elizabeth Beardsley Butler, *Woman and the Trades* (New York, 1969, reprint of 1909 edition), pp. 75–101; Manning, *op. cit.*, p. 107.

11. Butler, *op. cit.*, pp. 60–1, 210–11.

12. Edith Abbott, *Women in Industry: A Study in American Economic History* (New York, 1919), p. 252.

13. Butler, *op. cit.*, pp. 44–52, 84–92, 115–22, 212.

14. *Ibid.*, pp. 96, 212.

15. Manning, *op. cit.*, p. 98.

16. Elizabeth Hasanovitz, *One of Them, Chapters from a Passionate Autobiography* (Boston, 1918), p. 272.

17. Manning, *op. cit.*, pp. 98, 212.

18. *Ibid.*, p. 118.

19. Butler, *op. cit.*, p. 337.

20. Carroll D. Wright, *The Working Girls of Boston* (New York, 1969, reprint of 1889 edition), p. 77.

21. Hasanovitz, *op. cit.*, p. 272.

22. Manning, *op. cit.*, p. 121.

23. Wright, *op. cit.*, pp. 20–1.

24. Butler, *op. cit.*, pp. 318–20.

25. Manning, *op. cit.*, p. 36.

26. *Abstracts of the Reports of the Immigration Commission*, Senate Doc. 747, U.S. Government Printing Office, Washington, D.C., 1911, Vol. 7, pp. 414–17.

27. Smuts, *op. cit.*, p. 19.

28. Judith E. Smith, "Our Own Kind: Family and Community Networks," *Radical History Review*, Vol. 17 (Spring 1978), pp. 99–120.

29. Rose Cohen, *Out of the Shadow* (New York, 1918), p. 108.

30. Smith, *op. cit.*, p. 116.

31. Elizabeth H. Pleck, "A Mother's Wages: Income Earning Among Married Italian and Black Women, 1896–1911," in *The American Family in Social-Historical Perspective*, 2nd ed., Michael Gordon, ed. (New York, 1978), pp. 490–510.

32. Kessner, *op. cit.*, pp. 75–84.

33. Manning, *op. cit.*, p. 14.

34. *Ibid.*, pp. 52–3.

35. *Ibid.*, p. 61.

36. Helen Campbell, *Prisoners of Poverty, Women Wage Workers: Their Trades and Their Lives* (New York, 1970, reprint of 1887 edition), pp. 18–29.

37. Manning, *op. cit.*, p. 60.

38. *Ibid.*, p. 34; Leslie Woodcock Tentler, *Wage-Earning Women: Industrial Work and Family Life in the United States 1910–1930* (New York, 1979), p. 152.

39. Thomas and Znaniecki, *op. cit.*, Vol. 2, pp. 1661–7.

40. Klaczynska, *op. cit.*; Manning, *op. cit.*, p. 139.

41. Virginia Yans-MacLaughlin, *Family and Community: Italian Immigrants in Buffalo, 1880–1930* (Ithaca, N.Y., 1977), pp. 52, 53, 164.

42. Thomas and Znaniecki, *op. cit.*, Vol. 1, p. 730.

43. Cohen, *op. cit.*, p. 155, *passim*.

44. Irving Howe, *World of Our Fathers* (New York, 1975), p. 171; Charlotte Brown, Paula Hyman, and Sonya Michel, *The Jewish Woman in America* (New York, 1976), pp. 92–98.

45. Margaret Von Staden, "My Story (The History of a Prostitute's Life in San Francisco)," Mss., Schlesinger Library, p. 2.

46. The "Maimie" Papers, Schlesinger Library, April 1911, *passim*.

47. Mary (Kenney) O'Sullivan, *Autobiography*, Mss., Schlesinger Library, p. 141.

48. Roy Lubove, *The Progressives and the Slums: Tenement House Reform in New York City, 1891–1917* (Pittsburgh, 1963), Ch. 4, pp. 91–2.

49. Manning, *op. cit.*, p. 70; Margaret F. Byington, *Homestead: The Households of a Mill Town* (University of Pittsburgh, 1974, reprint of the 1910 edition), p. 145.

50. Moses Rischin, "The Lower East Side," in Leonard Dinnerstein and Kenneth T. Jackson, eds., *American Vistas*, Vol. 2 (New York, 1971), p. 44.

51. Susan J. Kleinberg, "Technology and Women's Work: The Lives of Working Class Women in Pittsburgh, 1870–1900," *Labor History*, Vol. 17, No. 1 (Winter 1976), pp. 58–72.

52. Tentler, *op. cit.*, p. 150.

53. O'Sullivan, *op. cit.*, p. 8.

54. Tamara K. Hareven and Maris A. Vinovskis, "Marital Fertility, Ethnicity and Occupation in Urban Families: An Analysis of South Boston and the South End in 1880," *Journal of Social History*, Vol. 8, No. 3 (Spring 1975), pp. 69–93; Yans-MacLaughlin, *op. cit.*, p. 105.

55. Emma Goldman, *Living My Life* (New York, 1931), pp. 185–6.

56. Yans-MacLaughlin, *op. cit.*, p. 193.

57. Campbell, *op. cit.*, pp. 133–4.

58. Jane Addams, *Twenty Years at Hull House* (New York, 1960), pp. 244–7.

59. Von Staden, *op. cit.*, p. 5.

60. *Ibid.*, pp. 102, 171.

61. Thomas and Znaniecki, *op. cit.*, Vol. 2, 1800–1821, p. 2225.

62. Smith, *op. cit.*, p. 106; Jon M. Kingsdale, "'The Poor Man's Club': Social Function of the Urban Working Class Saloon," *American Quarterly*, Vol. 25, No. 4 (October 1973), p. 473.

63. Herbert Gutman, "Work, Culture, and Society in Industrializing America, 1815–1919," *American Historical Review*, Vol. 78, No. 2 (June 1973), pp. 531–88.

64. Alice Kessler Harris, *Out to Work: A History of Wage-Earning Women in the United States* (New York, 1982), pp. 76–86.

65. Alice Kessler Harris, "Where Are the Organized Women Workers?" *Feminist Studies*, Vol. 3, Nos. 1/2 (Fall 1975), pp. 92–110.

66. Mari Jo Buhle, "Women and the Socialist Party, 1901–1914," *Radical America*, Vol. IV, No. 2 (February 1970), pp. 36–55; Mari Jo Buhle, *Women and American Socialism, 1870–1920* (Urbana, Ill., 1981).

67. Lewis (Lorwin) Levine, *The Women's Garment Workers* (New York, 1924), pp. 146–7.

68. Leon Edel, ed., *The Diary of Alice James* (New York, 1934), p. 43.

69. Charlotte Perkins Gilman, *The Living of Charlotte Perkins Gilman* (New York, 1935), pp. 89–96.

70. Addams, *op. cit.*, pp. 21, 44.

71. Mary Ashton Livermore *My Story of the War* (Hartford, Conn., 1888), pp. 135, 355.

72. Addams, *op. cit.*, p. 93.

73. Jane Cunningham Croly, *The History of the Women's Club Movement* (New York, 1898), p. 14.

74. William J. O'Neill, *Everyone Was Brave: A History of Feminism in America* (Chicago, 1971), p. 36.

75. *Diaries and Notebooks of Leonora O'Reilly*, Schlesinger Library, Vol. 18 (December 10–12, 1911).

76. Mary Jones, *The Autobiography of Mother Jones* (Chicago, 1972).

77. Frances E. Willard, *Woman and Temperance: Or the Work and Workers of the Women's Christian Temperance Union*, 6th ed. (Evanston, Ill., 1897), p. 82; Mary Earhart Dillon, *Frances Willard: From Prayers to Politics* (Chicago, 1944), p. 152.

78. Goldman, *op. cit.*, p. 61.

79. Eliza Burt Gamble, *The Sexes in Society and History* (originally published as *The Evolution of Woman*, 1894; rev. ed., 1916), p. 17.

80. William I. Thomas, *Sex and Society: Studies in the Social Psychology of Sex* (Boston, 1907); Lester Ward, *Dynamic Sociology* (New York, 1968, reprint of 1883 edition), p. 615.

81. Livermore, *op. cit.*, p. 57.

82. Addams, *op. cit.*, p. 57.

83. *Ibid.*, p. 59; William Leach, *True Love and Perfect Union: The Feminist Reform of Sex and Society* (New York, 1980), pp. 313–5.

84. Sarah H. Gordon, "Smith College Students: The First Ten Classes, 1879–1888," *History of Education Quarterly*, Vol. XV, No. 2 (Summer 1975), pp. 147–67.

85. Addams, *op. cit.*, pp. 93, 94, 98.

86. Allen Davis, *Spearheads for Reform: The Social Settlements and Progressive Movement 1890–1914* (New York, 1967), p. 12.

87. Mary Ritter Beard, *Women's Work in Municipalities* (New York, 1915), from Introduction by Clinton Rogers Woodruff, p. x.

88. Croly, *op. cit.*, p. 112.

89. Sophonisba Breckinridge, *Women in the Twentieth Century: A Study in Their Political, Social and Economic Activities* (New York, 1933), pp. 11–42; Barbara Leslie Epstein, *The Politics of Domesticity: Women, Evangelism and Temperance in Nineteenth-Century America*, pp. 126–7.

90. *Ibid.*

91. Dillon, *op. cit.*, p. 153.

92. Barbara M. Cross, *The Educated Woman in America* (New York, 1965), pp. 30–45.

93. Breckinridge, *op. cit.*, pp. 187, 305–21; Beard, *op. cit.*; Cynthia Fuchs Epstein, *Woman's Place* (Berkeley, Calif., 1971), pp. 7, 8.

94. Karl E. Tauber and James A. Sweet, "Family and Work: The Social Life Cycle of Women," in *Women and the American Economy, A Look to the 1980's* (Englewood Cliffs, N.J., 1976), p. 42; Mary Jo Bane, *Here to Stay, American Families in the Twentieth Century* (New York, 1976), p. 8.

95. Elizabeth Kemper Adams, *Women Professional Workers* (New York, 1921), p. 23.

96. Dolores Hayden, *The Grand Domestic Revolution: A History of Feminist Designs for American Homes, Neighborhoods, and Cities* (Cambridge, Mass., 1981).

97. Lillian Faderman, *Surpassing the Love of Men* (New York, 1980), pp. 190–230.

98. Blanche Wiesen Cook, "Female Support Networks and Political Activity: Lillian Wald, Crystal Eastman, Emma Goldman," *Chrysalis, a Magazine of Women's Culture*, No. 3 (1977), pp. 43–61.

99. Dillon, *op. cit.*, p. 82.

100. Richard Jensen, "Family, Career and Reform: Women Leaders of the Progressive Era," in Michael Gordon, ed., *The American Family in Social-Historical Perspective* (New York, 1973), pp. 267–80; Ruth Bordin, *Woman and Temperance: The Quest for Power and Liberty, 1873–1900* (Philadelphia, 1981), pp. 163–75; Karen J. Blair, *The Clubwoman as Feminist: True Womanhood Refined 1868–1914* (New York, 1980), p. 60, *passim*.

101. Addams, *op. cit.*, p. 76.

102. Dorothy Rose Blumberg, *Florence Kelley: The Making of a Social Pioneer* (New York, 1956); quoted in Gladys Broone, *The Women's Trade Union League in Great Britain and America* (New York, 1942), p. 99.

103. Addams, *op. cit.*, pp. 174, 438.

104. Buhle, *op. cit.*, pp. 68–69.

105. Charlotte Perkins Gilman, "The Home," in William J. O'Neill, ed., *The Woman's Movement: Feminism in Europe and America* (London, 1969), pp. 129, 131; Charlotte Perkins Gilman, *The Man-Made World or Our Androcentric Culture* (New York, 1970, reprint of 1911 edition), p. 131; Charlotte Perkins Gilman, *Women and Economics* (Boston, 1898).

106. Rosalind Rosenberg, *Beyond Separate Spheres: Intellectual Roots of Modern Feminism* (New Haven, 1982).

107. Buhle, *op. cit.*, p. 160.

108. Beard, *op. cit.*, p. 35.

109. *Ladies' Home Journal*, September 1890, p. 10; Margaret Gibbons Wilson, *The American Woman in Transition: The Urban Influence 1870–1920* (Westport, Conn., 1979), p. 8.

110. *Ladies' Home Journal*, December 1899; March 1910.

111. Buhle, *op. cit.*, pp. 36–55; Wilson, *op. cit.*, appendix.

112. Aileen S. Kraditor, *Up From the Pedestal: Selected Writings in the History of AmericanFeminism* (Chicago, 1968), p. 263; Gilman, "The Home," *op. cit.*, pp. 122–3.

113. Livermore, *op. cit.*, p. 436.

114. Beard, *op. cit.*, pp. 46–47.

115. Ellen Dubois, "The Radicalism of the Woman Suffrage Movement: Notes Toward the Reconstruction of Nineteenth-Century Feminism," *Feminist Studies*, Vol. 3, No. 1/2 (Fall 1975), pp. 63–71.

FIVE: THE EROSION OF WOMAN'S SPHERE

1. Jane Addams, *The Second Twenty Years at Hull House* (New York, 1930), pp. 110, 120.

2. William Henry Chafe, *The American Woman: Her Changing Social, Economic and Political Roles, 1920–1970* (New York, 1972), pp. 25–47; J. Stanley Lemons, *The Woman Citizen* (Urbana, Ill., 1973).

3. Chafe, *op. cit.*, Sophonisba Breckinridge, *Women in the Twentieth Century. A Study in Their Political, Social and Economic Activities* (New York, 1933).

4. Addams, *op. cit.*, pp. 192–8.

5. Richard W. Wertz and Dorothy C. Wertz, *Lying-In: A History of Childbirth in America* (New York, 1977), pp. 207–8.

6. Robert Lynd and Helen Merrell Lynd, *Middletown: A Study in Contemporary American Culture* (New York, 1956), p. 88.

7. Otis Pease, *The Responsibilities of American Advertising* (New Haven, Conn., 1958), p. 23.

8. *Ibid.*, p. 41.

9. Breckinridge, *op. cit.*, p. 55.

10. Pease, *op. cit.*, p. 35.

11. *Ladies' Home Journal*, survey of advertisements in the 1920s and '30s.

12. Mary Sidney Branch, *Women and Wealth* (Chicago, 1934), p. 107.

13. *Ibid.*

14. Warren Waite, *The Economics of Consumption* (New York, 1928), p. 196.

15. Isabel Ely Lord, *Getting Your Moneysworth* (New York, 1922), p. 3; Lynd and Lynd, *op. cit.*, p. 196.

16. Eleanor Roosevelt, *It's Up to Woman* (New York, 1933), p. 248.

17. *The Consumers' League of Connecticut*, pamphlet, Schlesinger Library.

18. Frances R. Donovan, *The Saleslady* (Chicago, 1929), p. 96.

19. Henry James Forman, *Our Movie-Made Children* (New York, 1933), pp. 151, 154, 167.

20. Paula S. Fass, *The Damned and the Beautiful: American Youth in the 1920's* (New York, 1977), pp. 278–9, 291.

21. Margaret Gibbons Wilson, *The American Woman in Transition: The Urban Influence 1870–1920* (Westport, Conn., 1979), p. 124.

22. Paula Fass, *op. cit.*, p. 124.

23. Claudia Goldin, "The Work and Wages of Single Women, 1870–1920," *Journal of Economic History*, Vol. 40 (March 1980), pp. 81–8.

24. Elizabeth Ewen, "City Lights: Immigrant Women and the Rise of the Movies," *Signs*, Spring 1980, supplement, p. 56.

25. Anzia Yezierska, *Bread Givers* (New York, 1925), p. 28.

26. Maurine Weiner Greenwald, *Women, War, and Work: The Impact of World War I on Women Workers in the United States* (Westport, Conn., 1981).

27. *Ibid.*, p. 196.

28. *Ibid.*, Chapter 5.

29. Havelock Ellis, *The Psychology of Sex: A Manual for Students* (New York, 1960).

30. Hale, *op. cit.*, p. 338.

31. Robert Latou Dickinson and Lura Beam, *A Thousand Marriages: A Medical Study of Sex Adjustment* (Baltimore, 1932), p. 129; G. Stanley Hall, *Adolescence: Its Psychology*, Vol. II (New York, 1922), p. 109. Corinne Agnes Krause, *Grandmothers, Mothers and Daughters: An Oral History Study of Ethnicity, Mental Health and Continuity of Three Generations of Jewish, Italian and Slavic American Women* (a publication of the Institute on Pluralism and Groups Identity of the American Jewish Committee); Blanche Wiesen Cook, ed. *Chrystal Eastman* (New York, 1978), p. 47.

32. Norman Himes, *Medical History of Contraception* (New York, 1963), p. 340.

33. V. F. Calverton, *The Bankruptcy of Marriage* (New York, 1928).

34. Samuel D. Schmalhauser and V. F. Calverton, eds., *Woman's Coming of Age: A Symposium* (New York, 1931), p. 484.

35. Suzanne La Follette, *Concerning Women* (New York, 1926), pp. 73–4.

36. Katherine B. Davis, *Factors in the Sex Life of Twenty-Two Hundred Women* (New York, 1929), p. 247.

37. Calverton, *op. cit.*, as quoted on p. 101.

38. Donovan, *op. cit.*, from "Introduction by Robert Park," p. viii.

39. *Ibid.*, p. 238.

40. V. F. Calverton, "Are Women Monogamous?" in Schmalhauser and Calverton, *op. cit.*, pp. 475–88.

41. Dr. G. V. Hamilton, "The Emotional Life of Modern Woman," in Schmalhauser and Calverton, *op. cit.*, pp. 207–29.

42. Alfred C. Kinsey, *et al.*, *Sexual Behavior in the Human Female* (Philadelphia, 1953), p. 349.

43. *Ibid.*, p. 467; Carl N. Degler, "What Ought to Be and What Was: Women's Sexuality in the Nineteenth Century," *American Historical Review*, Vol. 79, No. 5 (December 1974), pp. 1467–90.

44. Degler, *op. cit.*, p. 1490.

45. Havelock Ellis, *Man and Woman: A Study of Human Secondary Sexual Characteristics* (New York, 1911), pp. 25–6.

46. Hall, *op. cit.*, Vol. II, p. 391.

47. Havelock Ellis, *The Task of Social Hygiene* (New York, 1927), Introduction.

48. Hall, *op. cit.*, Vol. I, p. 512.

49. H. W. Frink, *Morbid Fears, and Compulsions* (New York, 1918), pp. 134–5, 136.

50. Dickinson and Beam, *op. cit.*, p. 443.

51. Helene Deutsch, *The Psychology of Women: A Psychoanalytic Interpretation*, Vol. II (New York, 1945), pp. 7–9.

52. Lillian Faderman, *Surpassing the Love of Men* (New York, 1980).

53. Gladys Groves, *Marriage and Family Life* (New York, 1942), p. 137.

54. Caroline Wormeley Latimer, *Girl and Woman: A Book for Mothers and Daughters* (New York, 1916), pp. 1–2.

55. *Ibid.*, p. 255.

56. Lynd and Lynd, *op. cit.*, pp. 140–2.

57. Phyllis Blanchard and Carlyn Manasses, *New Girls for Old* (New York, 1930), p. 142–3.

58. *The Ladies' Home Journal, passim.*

59. Groves, *op. cit.*, p. 145.

60. Lynd and Lynd, *op. cit.*, pp. 263–4.

61. George Lundberg, Mirra Komarovsky, and Mary Alice McInerny, *Leisure: A Suburban Study* (New York, 1934), p. 182.

62. Leo Handel, *Hollywood Looks at Its Audience* (Urbana, Ill., 1950), p. 122.

63. Blanchard and Manasses, *op. cit.*, p. 37.

64. Ben Lindsay as quoted in Wilhelm Reich, *The Sexual Revolution* (New York, 1971), p. 93.

65. Frances Donovan, *The Woman Who Waits* (Boston, 1920), p. 42; Leslie Woodcock Tentler, *Wage-Earning Women: Industrial Work and Family Life in the United States, 1900–1930* (New York, 1979), pp. 69–80; Nancy Schrom Dye, *As Equals and as Sisters: Feminism, the Labor Movement, and the Women's Trade Union League of New York* (Columbus, Missouri, 1980), p. 47.

66. Davis, *op. cit.*, p. 190.

67. Frances Donovan, *The Schoolma'am* (New York, 1938), pp. 35–6.

68. Blanchard and Manasses, *op. cit.*, p. 174.

69. Margaret Wilson, *op. cit.*, pp. 41–43; Peter Uhlenberg, "Cohort Variation in Family Life Cycle of U.S. Females," *Journal of Marriage and the Family*, May 1974, pp. 284–92; Karl E. Tauber and James A. Sweet, "Family and Work: The Social Life Cycle of Women," in Juanita Kreps, *Women and the American Economy, A Look to the 1980's* (Englewood Cliffs, N.J., 1976), pp. 31–60.

70. Ernest R. Groves and Gladys H. Groves, *The Contemporary Family* (Chicago, 1947), p. 746.

71. Fass, *op. cit.*, p. 107.

72. Elaine Tyler May, *Great Expectations: Marriage and Divorce in Post-Victorian America* (Chicago, 1980), p. 85 and *passim*.

73. Gwendolyn Wright, *Moralism and the Model Home* (Chicago, 1980), Part III.

74. Joann Vanek, "Time Spent in House Work," *Scientific American*, November 1974, pp. 116–20.

75. Peter Uhlenberg, *op. cit.*, pp. 284–292.

76. Judy Barrett Litoff, *American Midwives 1860 to the Present* (Westport, Conn., 1978); Richard W. Wertz and Dorothy C. Wertz, *Lying-In: A History of Childbirth in America* (New York, 1977).

77. John B. Watson, *Psychological Care of Infant and Child* (New York, 1928), pp. 5, 6, 44, *passim*.

78. Ruth Lindquist, *The Family in the Present Social Order* (Chapel Hill, N.C., 1931), pp. 151–3; Nancy Weiss, "Mother, the Invention of Necessity: Dr. Benjamin Spock's Baby and Child Care," *American Quarterly* (Winter, 1977), p. 544.

79. Lindquist, *op. cit.*, p. 153.

80. Rosalind Rosenberg, *Beyond Seperate Spheres* (New Haven, 1982), *passim*; Joyce Antler, "Feminism as Life Process: The Life and Career of Lucy Sprague Mitchell," *Feminist Studies*, Vol. 7, No. 1 (Spring 1981); Elizabeth Kemper Adams, *Women Professional Workers* (New York, 1921), pp. 31–32.

81. Lois Scharf, *To Work and To Wed: Female Employment, Feminism, and the Great Depression* (Westport, Conn., 1980), p. 31.

82. Mary Ross, "The New State of Women in America," in *Woman's Coming of Age*, S. D. Schmalhauser and V. F. Calverton, eds. (New York, 1931), p. 546.

83. Alice Kessler-Harris, *Out to Work* (New York, 1982), Chapter 7.

84. *Ibid.*, p. 321; Martha May, "The Historical Problem of the Family Wage: Ford Motor Company and the Five Dollar Day," *Feminist Studies*, Vol. 8, No. 2 (Summer 1982), pp. 399–424.

85. Winifred Wandersee, *Women's Work and Family Values, 1920–1940* (Cambridge, Mass., 1981), *passim*.

86. *Ibid.*, Chapters 2, 3, 4, p. 74.

87. William Henry Chafe, *op. cit.*, pp. 56–57.

88. Lois Scharf, *op. cit.*, p. 48.

89. *Ibid.*; Susan Ware, *Beyond Suffrage: Women in the New Deal* (Cambridge, 1981), pp. 129–30.

90. Valerie Kincade Oppenheimer, *The Female Labor Force in the United States; Demographic and Economic Factors Governing its Growth and Composition* (Berkeley, 1970), p. 44.

91. Mirra Komarovsky, *The Unemployed Man and His Family* (New York, 1940), p. 49.

92. Glen Elder, Jr., *Children of the Great Depression* (Chicago, 1974), Chapter 4, pp. 64–84.

93. Rosenberg, *op. cit.*, p. 209.

SIX: A DOMESTIC INTERLUDE

1. Valerie Kincade Oppenheimer, *The Female Labor Force in the United States; Demographic and Economic Factors in Governing Its Growth and Changing Composition* (Berkeley, Calif., 1970), p. 6.

2. Alice Kessler-Harris, *Out to Work: A History of Wage-Earning Women in the United States* (New York, 1982), p. 276; Eleanor Straub, "Women in the Civilian Labor Force" in *Clio Was a Woman: Studies in the History of American Women*, Mabel E. Deutrich and Virginia Purdy, eds. (Washington, 1980), p. 213.

3. Oppenheimer, *op. cit.*, pp. 6–19.

4. Straub, *op. cit.*, pp. 206–26.

5. Joan Ellen Trey, "Women in the War Economy," *The Review of Radical Political Economies* (July 1972), pp. 40–57.

6. William Henry Chafe, *The American Woman: Her Changing Social, Economic, and Political Roles* (New York, 1972), p. 137.

7. Dorothy Thompson, "Women and the Coming World," *Ladies' Home Journal* (October 1943), p. 6.

8. Karen Anderson, ed., *Wartime Women: Sex Roles, Family, Relations and the Status of Women During World War II* (Westport, 1981), p. 8.

9. *Ibid.*, pp. 28, 29.

10. *Ibid.*, p. 59.

11. *Ibid.*, Chapter IV; William Henry Chafe, *op. cit.*, pp. 144–5, 165–73.

12. Chafe, *op. cit.*

13. Anderson, *op. cit.*, pp. 88–93.

14. Landon Jones, *Great Expectations: America and the Baby Boom Generation* (New York, 1980), pp. 17–18.

15. Anderson, *op. cit.*, p. 103.

16. Lundberg and Farnham, *op. cit.*, p. 278.

17. Gladys Groves, *Marriage and Family Life* (New York, 1942), p. 338.

18. Paul Landis, *Your Marriage and Family Living* (New York, 1946), pp. 32–33.

19. *Ladies' Home Journal*, February 1943, p. 35.

20. Glen Elder, Jr., *Children of the Great Depression* (Chicago, 1974), p. 207.

21. Talcott Parsons and Robert Bales, *Family Socialization and Interaction Process* (New York, 1955).

22. Betty Friedan, *The Feminine Mystique* (New York, 1963), p. 38.

23. Eric Barnwov, *The Image Empire* (New York, 1970), p. 18.

24. Helene Deutsch, *The Psychology of Women: A Psychoanalytic Interpretation* (New York, 1945), Vol. II, p. 107; Marie Bonaparte, *Female Sexuality* (New York, 1973), p. 55; Karen Horney, *Feminine Psychology* (New York, 1973); Clara M. Thompson, *On Women* (New York, 1964), p. 177.

25. Bonaparte, *op. cit.*, p. 55.

26. Robinson, *op. cit.*, p. 69.

27. Dickinson and Beam, *op. cit.*, p. 63.

28. Kinsey, *op. cit.*, p. 171.

29. Bonaparte, *op. cit.*, p. 85.

30. Deutsch, *op. cit.*, pp. 102–3.

31. *Ibid.*, p. 17.

32. Bonaparte, *op. cit.*, p. 1.

33. *Ibid.*, p. 54.

34. Lundberg and Farnham, *op. cit.*, p. 275.

35. Robinson, *op. cit.*, p. 34.

36. *Ibid.*, p. 32.

37. Deutsch, *op. cit.*, p. 105.

38. *Ibid.*, p. 105.

39. Bonaparte, *op. cit.*, p. 129.

40. *Ibid.*, p. 129.

41. Deutsch, *op. cit.*, p. 258.

42. *Ibid.*, p. 107.

43. Lundberg and Farnham, *op. cit.*, p. 278.

44. Robinson, *op. cit.*, p. 36.

45. Havelock Ellis, *The Task of Social Hygiene* (New York, 1927), p. 65.

46. Jones, *op. cit.*, pp. 11–18.

47. Peter Uhlenberg, "Cohort Variation in Family Life Cycle," *Journal of Marriage and the Family*, May 1974, pp. 284–92.

48. John Modell, "Suburbanization and Change in the American Family," *Journal of Interdisciplinary History*, Spring 1979, pp. 621–46; William Dobriner, ed., *The Suburban Community* (New York, 1958), p. 157.

49. Zane Miller, *Suburb, Neighborhood and Community in Forest Park, Ohio, 1935–1976* (Knoxville, 1981), p. 48; Gwendolyn Wright, *Building the Dream: A Social History of Housing in America* (New York, 1981), Chapter XIII.

50. Joann Vanek, "Time Spent in Housework," *Scientific American*, November 1974, pp. 116–20.

51. Jones, *op. cit.*, p. 41.

52. Wright, *op. cit.*, p. 246.

53. Mirra Komarovsky, *Women in the Modern World* (Boston, 1953), pp. 108–9.

54. Joann Vanek, *op. cit.*, pp. 116–20.

55. Betty Friedan, *The Feminine Mystique* (New York, 1970), p. 203.

56. Komarovsky, *op. cit.*, pp. 7–8.

57. Russell Lynes, *The Domesticated Americans* (New York, 1957, 1963), p. 271.

58. Lopata, *op. cit.*, p. 207.

59. Arnold Gesell and Frances L. Illg, *Infant and Child in the Culture Today* (New York, 1943), pp. 56–57.

60. Helene Deutsch, *op. cit.*, p. 292.

61. Benjamin Spock, M.D., *The Common Sense Book of Baby and Child Care* (New York, 1970), p. 3.

62. *Ibid.*, p. 31.

63. Gesell and Illg, *op. cit.*, p. 56.

64. Spock, *op. cit.*, p. 269.

65. *Ibid.*, p. 564.

66. Deutsch, *op. cit.*, p. 331.

67. Lundberg and Farnham, *op. cit.*, p. 256.

68. Spock, *op. cit.*, pp. 321–2.

69. Lundberg, Komarovsky, and McInerny, *op. cit.*, pp. 177, 178.

70. John R. Seeley, R. Alexander Sim, and Elizabeth Loosley, *Crest-

wood Heights: A Study of the Culture of Suburban Life (New York, 1956), p. 174.

71. Lopata, *op. cit.*, p. 217.

72. Seeley, Sim, and Loosley, *op. cit.*, pp. 201–2.

73. Jones, *op. cit.*, pp. 26–27.

74. *Ibid.*, p. 222; Paul Glick, "Updating the Life Cycle of the Family," *Journal of Marriage and the Family*, Vol. 34, No. 1 (February, 1977), pp. 5–13; Mary Jo Bane, *Here to Stay: American Families in the Twentieth Century* (New York, 1976), p. 25.

75. Daniel Bell, "The Sadness of Suburbia," in Dobriner, *op. cit.*, pp. 376–408.

76. Oppenheimer, *op. cit.*, pp. 70–75; James Gilbert, *Another Chance, Postwar America, 1945–1968* (Philadelphia, 1981), p. 103.

77. Oppenheimer, *op. cit.*, pp. 20–21; Harris, *op. cit.*, p. 300.

78. Chafe, *op. cit.*, p. 218.

79. Juanita Kreps and Robert Clark, eds., *Sex, Age and Work: The Changing Composition of the Labor Force* (Baltimore, 1975), p. 11.

80. Chafe, *op. cit.*, p. 219.

81. *Ibid.*, p. 180.

82. Cynthia Fuchs Epstein, *Women's Place* (Berkeley, Calif., 1970), pp. 8, 10.

83. Jo Freeman, *The Politics of Women's Liberation* (New York, 1975), p. 31.

84. Friedan, *It Changed My Life* (New York, 1976), pp. 8–16.

85. Oppenheimer, *op. cit.*, pp. 70–75.

86. Elizabeth Faulkner Baker, *Technology and Women's Work* (New York, 1964), p. 249.

87. *Ibid.*, pp. 223–5, 235.

88. Elinor Langer, "Inside the New York Telephone Company," in *Woman at Work*, William O'Neill, ed. (Chicago, 1972), p. 315.

89. Susan Porter Benson, "The Clerking Sisterhood: Rationalization and the Work Culture of Saleswomen," *Radical America*, Vol. 12, No. 2 (March-April 1978), pp. 41–55.

90. Langer, *op. cit.*, p. 310.

91. Oppenheimer, *op. cit.*, p. 104.

92. *Ibid.*, p. 99.

93. Caroline Bird, *Born Female* (New York, 1968), p. 64.

94. *Ibid.*, pp. 63–64.

95. Chafe, *op. cit.*, p. 61.

96. Bird, *op. cit.*, pp. 61–63.

97. Oppenheimer, *op. cit.*, pp. 42–52.

98. *Ibid.*, p. 107.

99. Margaret Fowler Dunaway, *Diary*, Schlesinger Library, March 4, 1953; Feb. 7, 1958.

100. *Ibid.*, Sept. 28, 1936, Feb. 7, 1958.

101. *Ibid.*, Nov. 12, 1928.

102. *Ibid.*, August 15, 1960.

103. Philip Roth, *Portnoy's Complaint* (New York, 1969).

104. Irving Howe, *World of Our Fathers* (New York, 1976), p. 174.

105. Sidney Goldstein and Calvin Goldschneider, *Jewish Americans: Three Generations in a Jewish Community* (Englewood Cliffs, N.J., 1968), pp. 72–73.

106. Pauline Bart, "Mother Portnoy's Complaint," *Trans-Action*, Vol. 8, Nos. 1 and 2 (November/December 1970), pp. 69–75.

107. Daniel Patrick Moynihan, *The Negro Family: The Case for National Action* (Washington, D.C., 1965), pp. 30–38.

108. Alfredo Mirande, "The Chicano Family: A Reanalysis of Conflicting Views," *Journal of Marriage and the Family* (November 1977), pp. 747–56.

109. Charles S. Johnson, *Shadow of the Plantation* (Chicago, 1934), *passim*; Elizabeth Rauh Bethel, *Promiseland: A Century of Life in a Negro Community* (Philadelphia, 1981).

110. Margaret J. Hagood, *Mothers of the South: Portraiture of the White Tenant Farm Woman* (Chapel Hill, N.C., 1939), pp. 14–15; Gerda Lerner, *Black Women in White America* (New York, 1972), p. 399.

111. Johnson, *op. cit.*, p. 116.

112. *Ibid.*, p. 70.

113. Demetri B. Shimkin, Edith M. Shimkin, Dennis A. Farte, eds., *The Extended Family in Black Society* (The Hague, 1978).

114. Lerner, *op. cit.*, pp. 609–14.

115. Alfredo Mirande and Evangelina Enriquez, *La Chicana: The Mexican-American Woman* (Chicago, 1979), p. 246.

116. Oscar Lewis, *Life in a Mexican Village* (New York, 1951, 1972), pp. 98–99.

117. *Ibid.*, pp. 319–29.

118. Arthur J. Rubel, *Across the Tracks: Mexican Americans in a Texas City* (Austin, Texas, 1966), p. 62.

119. Alberto Camarillo, *Chicanos in a Changing Society* (Cambridge, Mass., 1979), pp. 91–93.

120. Ellen Cantarow, "Jessie Lopez De La Cruz," in Ellen Cantarow, Susan Gushee O'Malley, Sharon Hartman Strom, *Moving the Mountain* (Old Westbury, N.Y., 1980), p. 121.

121. *Ibid.*, pp. 134–45.

122. Reynolds Farley, *Growth of the Black Population* (Chicago, 1970), p. 50.

123. Andrew Billingsley, *Black Families—White America* (Englewood Cliffs, N.J., 1968), p. 14.

124. Elizabeth Hofkin Pleck, *Black Migration and Poverty: Boston 1865–1900* (New York, 1979), p. 164; William Julius Wilson, "The Black Community in the 1980's: Questions of Race, Class, and Public Policy," *The Annals of the American Academy of Political and Social Science*, January 1981, pp. 26–41.

125. Peter Uhlenberg, *op. cit.*, p. 289.

126. Carol Stack, *All Our Kin* (New York, 1974), p. 5.

127. Elizabeth Pleck, "A Mother's Wages: Income Earning Among Married Italian and Black Women, 1896–1911," in Michael Gordon, ed., *The American Family in Social Historical Perspective* (New York, 1978), pp. 490–510.

128. Robert B. Hill, *The Strengths of Black Families* (New York, 1971), pp. 10–17.

129. Anderson, *op. cit.*, pp. 37–42.

130. Pleck, *Black Migration and Poverty*, p. 188; James Borchert, "Urban Neighborhood and Community: Informal Group Life, 1850–1960," *Journal of Interdisciplinary History*, Vol. XI, No. 4, Spring 1981, pp. 607–33.

131. Mark D. Mathews, "Our Women and What They Think: Amy Jacques Garvey and the *Negro World*," *The Black Scholar*, May-June, 1979, pp. 2–12.

132. Lerner, *op. cit.*, p. 135.

133. Mel Watkins and Jay David, eds., *To Be a Black Woman* (New York, 1970), pp. 88–90.

134. Frances Fox Piven and Richard A. Cloward, *Poor People's Movements: Why They Succeed and Why They Fail* (New York, 1977), Chapter V.

SEVEN: TOWARD GENDER SYMMETRY

1. *Population Profile of the United States: 1980*, Current Population Reports series P-20 (Washington, 1981), p. 30; Ann C. Foster, "Wives'

Earnings as a Factor in Family Net Worth," *Monthly Labor Review*, February 1981, pp. 53–57.

2. Daniel Bell, *The Coming of Post-Industrial Society* (New York, 1973).

3. Daniel Yankelovich, "New Rules in American Life: Searching for Self-Fulfillment in a World Turned Upside Down," *Psychology Today*, April 1981, p. 60.

4. Betty Friedan, *It Changed My Life* (New York, 1976), p. 35.

5. Cynthia E. Harrison, "A New Frontier for Women: The Public Policy of the Kennedy Administration," *Journal of American History*, December 1980, pp. 630–46.

6. Jo Freeman, "The Origins of the Women's Liberation Movement," *American Journal of Sociology*, January 1973, pp. 798–99.

7. Friedan, *op. cit.*, pp. 90–91, 119.

8. Karl E. Taueber and James A. Sweet, "Family and Work: The Social Life Cycle of Women," in *Women and the American Economy: A Look to the 1980's*, Juanita Kreps, ed. (Englewood Cliffs, N.J., 1976), p. 39.

9. Freeman, *op. cit.*, p. 801; William Henry Chafe, *The American Woman: Her Changing Social, Economic, and Political Roles* (New York, 1972), pp. 109–13.

10. Sara Evans, *Personal Politics: The Roots of Women's Liberation in the Civil Rights Movement and the New Left* (New York, 1979).

11. Freeman, *op. cit.*, p. 100.

12. Mary Aickin Rothchild, "White Women Volunteers in the Freedom Summers: Their Life and Work in a Movement for Social Change," *Feminist Studies*, Vol. 5, No. 3 (Fall 1979).

13. Evans, *op. cit.*, p. 122.

14. Taueber and Sweet, *op. cit.*

15. *Ms. Magazine*, Vol. VI, No. 5, November 1977; *New York Times Magazine*, December 25, 1977.

16. Marion Lockwood Carden, *Feminism in the Mid-1970s: A Report to the Ford Foundation* (New York, 1977); *Womankind Past, Present, Future*, Vol. 1, No. 4 (1978).

17. *Family Circle; Ladies' Home Journal, Mademoiselle, Redbook*, all for June 1978.

18. Janet Zollinger Giele and Audrey Chapman Smock, eds., *Women's Roles and Status in Eight Countries* (New York, 1977), p. 316.

19. Phyllis A. Wallace, "Impact of Equal Employment Opportunity Laws," in Kreps, *op. cit.*, pp. 123–45.

20. *Perspectives on Working Women: A Data Book*, U.S. Department of Labor, Bulletin 2080, October 1980 (Washington, 1980), pp. 2, 27, 51; Foster, *op. cit.*, pp. 53–57.

21. Los Angeles *Times*, October 1981, I–B 7; Ruth M. Phillips, "Women and Medicine," in *Toward the Second Decade: The Impact of the Women's Movement*, Betty Justice and Renate Pore, eds., (Westport, Conn., 1981), pp. 50–51.

22. *Perspectives on Working Women, op. cit.*, p. 52.

23. Louise Kapp Howe, *Pink Collar Worker: Inside the World of Women's Work* (New York, 1977), pp. 62–63.

24. Harris T. Schrank, and John W. Riley, Jr., "Women in Work Organizations," in Kreps, *op. cit.*, pp. 82–3.

25. Giele and Smock, *op. cit.*, p. 327; *New York Times*, November 27, 1977.

26. Bureau of the Census, Current Population Reports Series P-20, No. 365, *Marital Status and Living Arrangements, March 1980*.

27. *Perspectives on Working Women, op. cit.*, p. 27.

28. Taueber and Sweet, in Kreps, *op. cit.*, pp. 31–60; Howe, *op. cit.*, p. 162.

29. James C. Mohr, *Abortion in America: The Origins and Evolution of National Policy, 1800–1900 (New York, 1978)*, p. 254; *New York Times*, December 5, 1972.

30. Howe, *op. cit.*, pp. 123–5, 197.

31. *Ibid.*, p. 272; Martha W. Griffiths, "Can We Still Afford Occupational Segregation? Some Remarks," in *Women and the Workplace, the Implications of Occupational Segregation*, Martha Blaxall and Barbara Reagan, eds. (Chicago, 1976), pp. 7–14; *New York Times*, January 13, 1976.

32. Lillian Breslow Rubin, *Worlds of Pain: Life in the Working Class Family* (New York, 1976), pp. 173–4; Mirra Komarovsky, "Cultural Contradictions and Sex Roles," *American Journal of Sociology*, Vol. 78, No. 4 (January 1973), p. 881.

33. Paul J. Andrisani, "Job Satisfaction Among Working Women," *Signs*, Vol. 3, No. 3 (Spring 1978), pp. 588–607; Rubin, *op. cit.*, pp. 170–2.

34. Katharine Ellis and Rosalind Petchesky, "Children of the Corporate Dream: An Analysis of Day Care as a Political Issue," *Socialist Revolution* (November-December 1972), pp. 22–3; *New York Times*, January 5, 1977, April 10, 1977; Giele and Smock, *op. cit.*, p. 327.

35. Nancy Pottishman Weiss, "Mother, the Invention of Necessity: Dr. Benjamin Spock's Baby and Child Care," *American Quarterly*, Vol. 28, No. 4 (Winter 1977), p. 544.

36. Morgan, *op. cit.*, pp. 18, 57.

37. Rubin, *op. cit.*, p. 129.

38. Dell Martin, *Battered Wives* (New York, 1977), pp. 12–13.

39. Bureau of the Census, "Household and Family Characteristics: March, 1981," Current Population Survey, P-20, Number 371 (Washington, D.C., 1981); *New York Times*, November 27, 1977; Kenneth Keniston and The Carnegie Council on Children, *All Our Children: The American Family Under Pressure* (New York, 1977), p. 4.

40. *Population Profile, op. cit.*, p. 14; Frances E. Kobrin, "The Fall in Household Size and the Rise of the Primary Individual in the United States," *Demography*, Vol. 13, No. 1 (February 1976), pp. 123–37; Juanita Kreps and Robert Clark, *Sex, Age and Work: The Changing Composition of the Labor Force* (Baltimore, 1975), p. 27.

41. *New York Times*, July 6, 1978, June 18, 1978; *Mademoiselle*, June 1978.

42. Kobrin, *op, cit.*, pp. 123–37.

43. Stephanie J. Ventura, "Trend in First Births to Older Mothers, 1970–79," *Monthly Vital Statistics Reports*, May 27, 1982.

44. Keniston and The Carnegie Council on Children, *op. cit.*, p. 4; Griffiths, *op. cit.*, p. 8; Saul Hoffman, "Marital Instability and the Economic Status of Women," *Demography*, Vol. 14, No. 1 (February 1977), pp. 67–76; Bane, *op. cit.*, p. 34.

45. Howe, *op. cit.*, pp. 220–1; *Family Circle*, June 1978.

46. Isabel Sawhill, "Discrimination and Poverty Among Women Who Head Families," in Blaxall and Reagan, *op. cit.*, pp. 201–11; Beverley L. Johnson, "Women Who Head Families, 1970–1977: Their Numbers Rose, Their Income Lagged," *Monthly Labor Review* (February 1978), pp. 32–7. *Population Profile, op. cit.*, p. 39, *passim.*

47. *Ibid.*, p. 39; *Perspectives on Working Women, op. cit.*, Part VI, pp. 62–83.

48. *Perspectives on Working Women, op. cit.*, p. 100.

49. Richard Easterlin, *Birth and Fortune: The Impact of Numbers on Personal Welfare* (New York, 1980); Landon Y. Jones, *Great Expectations: America and the Baby Boom Generation* (New York, 1980), pp. 294–97.

50. *Newsweek*, June 5, 1978, p. 39; Richard A. Viguerie, *The New Right: We're Ready to Lead* (Falls Church, Va., 1981), pp. 151–62.

51. Viguerie, *op. cit.*, p. 155.

52. Morgan, *op. cit.*, pp. 22, 60, 187.

53. *New York Times*, November 30, 1977; Alice Rossi, "A Biosocial Perspective on Parenting," *Daedalus*, Vol. 106, No. 2 (Spring 1977), pp. 1–32.

54. *New York Times*, November 30, 1977.

55. Betty Friedan, *The Second Stage* (New York, 1981).

56. Adrienne Rich, *Of Woman Born: Motherhood as Experience and*

Institution (New York, 1976); Mary Daly, *Gyn/ecology: The Metaethics of Radical Feminism* (Boston, 1978); Gayle Kimball, ed., *Women's Culture: the Renaissance of the Seventies* (Metuchen, N.J., 1976).

57. Yankelovich, *op. cit.*, p. 60.
58. K. S. Kozcara and D. A. Pierson, "The Task of Female Union Leaders," *Monthly Labor Review*, May 1981, pp. 30–32.
59. Juliet Mitchell, *Woman's Estate* (New York, 1971).
60. Kobrin, *op. cit.*, pp. 123–37.
61. Eli Ginsberg, *New York Times*, November 28, 1977.

INDEX